1966
The Supreme Court Review

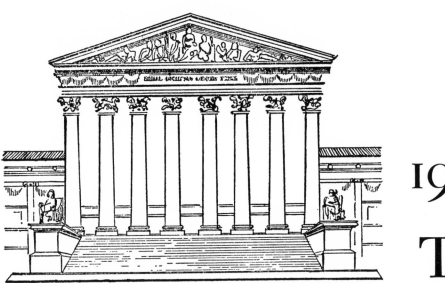

1966
The

"Judges as persons, or courts as institutions, are entitled to
no greater immunity from criticism than other persons
or institutions . . . [J]udges must be kept mindful of their limitations and
of their ultimate public responsibility by a vigorous
stream of criticism expressed with candor however blunt."
—*Felix Frankfurter*

". . . while it is proper that people should find fault when
their judges fail, it is only reasonable that they should recognize the
difficulties. . . . Let them be severely brought to book,
when they go wrong, but by those who will take the trouble
to understand them."
—*Learned Hand*

THE LAW SCHOOL

THE UNIVERSITY OF CHICAGO

Supreme Court Review

EDITED BY

PHILIP B. KURLAND

 THE UNIVERSITY OF CHICAGO PRESS

CHICAGO AND LONDON

LIBRARY OF CONGRESS CATALOG CARD NUMBER: 60-14353

THE UNIVERSITY OF CHICAGO PRESS, CHICAGO & LONDON
THE UNIVERSITY OF TORONTO PRESS, TORONTO 5, CANADA

TO ELLEN

"Beautiful as sweet!
And young as beautiful! and soft as young!
And gay as soft! and innocent as gay!"

CONTENTS

ARCHIBALD MacLEISH

FELIX FRANKFURTER:

A LESSON OF FAITH

The wisest of the Greeks is said to have warned his fellow mortals to "call no man happy till he dies." Justice Frankfurter, whose impetuous Viennese parents ignored that famous injunction, was known to innumerable friends throughout a long life as Felix. And yet his history, if one considers rightly what old Solon meant, makes no exception to the rule. It was not until Felix Frankfurter died—not 'til his life could be judged as a completed thing, safe from its own vicissitudes—that any of us understood how truly happy it had been.

I do not mean, of course, that it was only happy, or always happy, or happy in all its accidents and chances. The Justice had his disappointments like other men and, like other men, his failures. His death was difficult and its sufferings—the long inhibition of movement and of speech—were precisely the sufferings he was least prepared by nature to endure . . . though he endured them. I mean simply that the distinction of his life, the quality above all others which distinguished it, was its happiness: not its extraordinary success, not its good fortune, its offices, its honors, but its happiness.

It is not, I know, a quality much considered in this generation. We regard ourselves as sadder, wiser men (in the modern world increasing wisdom is always increasing sadness) who have learned at last that life is tragic and that those in other ages who accounted

---

Archibald MacLeish is the poet and playwright, lawyer and librarian, professor and diplomat, friend and admirer of Felix Frankfurter.

happiness its crown were immature or ignorant or both. Even our own American ancestors, with their eloquent talk of the pursuit of happiness as the ultimate end and aim of man's existence, leave us uncomfortable and cold. We have seen too much of the world's realities, have looked too deeply into science and men's minds. Happiness, we tell ourselves, happiness in an age like ours, is an incongruity to be left to children—or not, perhaps, to children even: to that innocuous, fairy-tale universe of television and of advertisement where all the words are wishes and only photographs come true.

But the fact is, notwithstanding, that it was precisely in an age like ours, because it *was* our age, that Felix Frankfurter's life was lived. And the fact is, further, that his life was happy in that age in the old, high, noble, classic sense. Which means, in the deliberate sense, in the conscious sense: a happiness well aware of the risks of happiness. Yeats described it: the happiness of

> such men as come
> Proud, open-eyed and laughing to the tomb.

When an insensitive man, a thoughtless man, an unthinking man, lives contentedly through brutal and blundering wars, through the destruction of civilizations, through a world-wide psychological collapse which opens cisterns of human depravity long sealed up, long forgotten, his happiness is an affront, a deformity which condemns himself and the society which produced him. But when an intelligent man, a man of more than ordinary intelligence, more than ordinary sensitivity and perception, lives through such a time knowing what it is he lives through, facing its dreadful revelations not in his mind alone but on his physical nerves, himself an intended victim of its most horrifying inhumanity—when such a man can live through such a time believing in life, believing in human kind, delighting still in his work, his world, his friends, his country, that man's happiness is not ignorance or immaturity. It is not deformity or defect. It is not complacency. It is greatness.

Felix Frankfurter's greatness—and we have not yet perceived how truly great it was—was of this kind. He was one of the few—one of the very few—who kept the belief in life alive in a generation which had more reason than any other in three hundred years to lose it. No one, I think, will ever know how many of his contemporaries in positions of high and difficult responsibility thought of him as Landor thought of that fire at which he warmed his hands.

And as for the young—as for the intellectual leaders and articulators of the generation which followed his own, the generation which grew older from one world war to another through those years of social and psychological disintegration which were once regarded as nothing worse than economic depression—as for the young of those years, not even the most intelligent of them knew what they owed to Felix Frankfurter. The greatest gifts, the gifts of courage and belief and hope, are no more perceived than the sunlight: they are taken as they come.

But if his influence on his time, certainly one of the most remarkable influences in the history of any country, cannot be measured or defined, it can be talked of. Most men who profoundly influence the minds of others reach them as writers or as speakers: as political orators or as university lecturers or as judges of high courts with a gift like that of Mr. Justice Holmes for making the interpretation of a nation's laws interpret its nature or as novelists or even poets—a Herman Melville who can show us the white whale itself or a Robert Frost who can put words into our mouths (and into our minds) whether we like them or not. Felix Frankfurter was none of these. Or rather he was all of them—all, that is, but novelist and poet, and yet his influence was something else.

That he was an articulate speaker numerous members of the bar recall. That he was a famous dialectician in the classrooms of the Harvard Law School where Socrates was once the local divinity is a matter of academic record. That he was a brilliant journalist is notorious: his editorials for the Republican *Boston Herald* were only surpassed by his editorials for the liberal *New Republic* and his *Atlantic* piece on the trial of Sacco and Vanzetti is as unanswerable today as it was when it stung the conscience of the Boston bar. That he was a distinguished justice of the Supreme Court is, I believe, conceded even by his friends who were, of course, and over many years, his severest critics. But though all this is obvious— though he was an influential judge, an effective journalist, an exciting teacher and even, on occasion, the tongue, though not the voice, of political authority—it is equally obvious that it was in neither one capacity nor the other that his extraordinary impress on his time was made.

How then was it? That question can only be answered by looking closely at the man himself, and there Professor Isaiah Berlin of

All Souls is perhaps as good a guide as we can hope for. Speaking of Mr. Frankfurter's year as visiting professor at Oxford in 1934, Sir Isaiah describes the unsuccessful attempts of the great and the near great to lionize him "as a man of influence in Washington" and "an intimate friend and adviser of the President of the United States" and then goes on to record the impressions of the younger dons—his generation. "So far as I and my friends were concerned his genius resided in the golden shower of intellectual and emotional generosity that was poured forth before his friends. . . . Whenever I met him . . . he was the center, the life and soul, of a circle of eager and delighted human beings, exuberant, endlessly appreciative, delighting in every manifestation of intelligence, imagination and life."

It is so, of course, that we all remember him. And it is so that he touched our lives and the life of our country. It is an unusual thing, I realize, to speak on an occasion such as this, not of the works of a man, of his deeds, of his achievements, but of the man himself and more particularly of those qualities of the man himself which must necessarily vanish with him or, at the latest, with the memories of his friends. But Felix Frankfurter leaves no alternative. Great as were his achievements as judge and teacher of law his achievements as a man were greater. To rise from immigrant boy with no word of English to the most exalted court in the Republic is a remarkable accomplishment never perhaps equaled in our history. But there are greater accomplishments even than this: there is the accomplishment of a full and overflowing life.

And it is that life we remember. What Justice Frankfurter gave his time was something more than intelligence, though his intelligence was vigorous and effective; something more than courage, though his courage was unquestioned; something more than affection though affection flowed from him and love was the motive and the motion of his heart. What he gave his time was an enlargement of its human life. As long as he was in his chambers, or his house on Dumbarton Avenue, or off at Heath in the Massachusetts hills in the summers, the world had an extra dimension for us all. Whatever we did or wrote or said was somehow more significant because he knew of it or might have known, approving or disapproving—a phone call late at night or an all but illegible note scribbled on one of those little squares of memorandum paper or just a message through a friend. What mattered was not the word sent, the reproof or the commendation. What mattered was the fact that there was someone listening—someone who cared not only about you but about the world, about the country—above all about the country.

For this extraordinary web of relationships which touched so many lives was not a web spun in a private corner for friendship's sake. It was a web spun in the world for the world's sake. However much he may have given to individual human beings—and no man ever left him smaller than he came—Felix Frankfurter's gift to the Republic was greater still. His constant thought, his constant preoccupation, was not merely the well-being of his friends: it was the well-being of his friends *in* that world of possibilities, that world of promise, which the American adventure had opened to mankind. And his first and last and continuing concern was the renewal of that world, the renewal and revivifying of the terms of discourse in which its hope was first conceived.

Faith, even faith in the future of one's country, is not taught by arguments. It is taught by lives. And it was Felix Frankfurter's life which was the secret of his profound and pervasive influence on his country and his time: It was the man himself, the indescribable, inexhaustible, various, vehement, creative, understanding man who had the courage to be whole and happy in a tragic age.

C. PETER MAGRATH

THE OBSCENITY CASES:

GRAPES OF ROTH

> *What is pornography to one man is the laughter of genius to another.*
>
> D. H. LAWRENCE

In the first volume of this *Review* Professor Harry Kalven, Jr., concluded a sophisticated and witty excursion through "the metaphysics of the law of obscenity" with a hopeful prediction. The United States Supreme Court, he suggested, was gradually, if implicitly, developing a workable legal standard that would "restrict obscenity to the worthless and hence to something akin to hard-core pornography."[1] Professor Kalven also expressed his sympathy to the Court for "the extraordinary difficulty of its task," remarking that "the most impressive aspect of their task is that any decision must treat so many variables."[2]

Six years later it is painfully evident that Professor Kalven's optimism was, at best, premature, and that even his sympathy may have been misplaced. For on March 21, 1966, the Supreme Court released fourteen opinions, in effect, *seriatim*, in deciding three ob-

C. Peter Magrath is Associate Professor of Political Science, Brown University.

[1] Kalven, *The Metaphysics of the Law of Obscenity*, [1960] SUPREME COURT REVIEW, 1, 43.

[2] *Id.* at 45.

scenity cases.[3] Moreover, close examination of the decisions reveals that the present Court is propounding at least five separate tests for the "guidance" of bench and bar in obscenity cases. Although the Court deserves a sympathetic appreciation for its many and complex problems, it is not unfair to point out that many of these problems are of its own making. The Warren Court, after all, is very probably the most activist tribunal in our constitutional history,[4] and this activism is largely responsible for its confrontation with a seemingly endless crop of hard cases.[5] Moreover, in the area of the law of obscenity the Justices have needlessly confounded a confusing set of questions and have displayed a penchant for individual dogmatism and murky opinions that document some of the sharp professional criticisms directed at the Warren Court's workmanship.[6] The root problem, of course, is the Supreme Court's continuing inability to provide an intelligible definition of obscenity. In this respect the Court's performance is reminiscent of the 1923 Geneva Conference on the Suppression of the Circulation and Traffic in Obscene Publications. Unable to define obscenity at the opening of their conference, the delegates nonetheless bravely proceeded to discuss how to cope with it.[7] Unfortunately, the United States Supreme Court not only discusses what it so far has failed to define clearly but makes decisions based on its amorphous discussion.

---

[3] Ginzburg v. United States, 383 U.S. 463 (1966); Mishkin v. New York, 383 U.S. 502 (1966); Memoirs v. Massachusetts, 383 U.S. 413 (1966).

[4] See Kurland, Foreword: "Equal in Origin and Equal in Title to the Legislative and Executive Branches of the Government," 78 HARV. L. REV. 143 (1964); McCloskey, Reflections on the Warren Court, 51 VA. L. REV. 1229 (1965).

[5] As, for example, the cases on reapportionment, on the scope of religious practices in public institutions, and on the rights of the criminally accused.

[6] See, e.g., Bickel & Wellington, Legislative Purpose and the Judicial Process: The Lincoln Mills Case, 71 HARV. L. REV. 1 (1957); Brown, Quis Custodiet Ipsos Custodes?—The School-Prayer Cases, [1963] SUPREME COURT REVIEW 1; Hart, Foreword: The Time Chart of the Justices, 73 HARV. L. REV. 84 (1959); Kurland, supra note 4; Wechsler, Toward Neutral Principles of Constitutional Law, 73 HARV. L. REV. 1 (1959). There are also many defenses of the Court. See, e.g., Arnold, Professor Hart's Theology, 73 HARV. L. REV. 1298 (1960); Henkin, Some Reflections on Current Constitutional Controversy, 109 U. PA. L. REV. 1 (1959); Miller & Howell, The Myth of Neutrality in Constitutional Adjudication, 27 U. CHI. L. REV. 661 (1960).

[7] See Lockhart & McClure, Censorship of Obscenity: The Developing Constitutional Standards, 45 MINN. L. REV. 5, 58 (1960).

I. The Roth Tests, 1957–65

The Court's failures in the obscenity cases are all the more deplorable because a workable resolution of the major constitutional and definitional problems is at hand—in its own recent decisions. Although a detailed review of the Warren Court's obscenity decisions is unnecessary here, it is essential to recall the salient developments between 1957 and 1965. They show, I think, that the Justices, for all their travail with "the exquisite vagueness"[8] of obscenity, have already established many of the components for a law of obscenity that is consistent with the First Amendment, responsive to public and political needs, and sufficiently precise to guide those for whom the boundary line between licit and illicit expression is a very practical matter.

Not until 1957, when it decided *Butler v. Michigan*,[9] did the Supreme Court significantly intervene in the obscenity area.[10] That year a unanimous Court invalidated a Michigan statute prohibiting the publication of materials "tending" to incite minors to violent or depraved acts and "tending" to corrupt youthful morals. Such a ban, Mr. Justice Frankfurter wrote, was too sweeping: "The incidence of this enactment is to reduce the adult population of Michigan to reading only what is fit for children."[11] The Michigan law, therefore, violated the First Amendment. *Butler* established the principle that obscenity laws that seek to prohibit the general circulation and exhibition of questionable materials are constitutional only if they may properly be kept from the eyes of adults—not because they may be prohibited to impressionable children.

In 1957 the Supreme Court also decided the combined cases of *Alberts v. California*, testing a California statute making it a crime to distribute obscene materials, and *Roth v. United States*, testing a federal statute making it a crime to send obscene materials through the mails.[12] These cases are justly celebrated for at least three rea-

---

[8] United States v. Roth, 237 F.2d 796, 826 (2d Cir. 1956) (Frank, J., concurring).

[9] 352 U.S. 380 (1957).

[10] Prior to 1957 interpretations of the nation's obscenity law had been essentially the province of state and lower federal courts. For two surveys, see Alpert, *Judicial Censorship of Obscene Literature*, 52 Harv. L. Rev. 40 (1937); Lockhart & McClure, *Literature, the Law of Obscenity, and the Constitution*, 38 Minn. L. Rev. 295 (1954).

[11] 352 U.S. at 383.   [12] 354 U.S. 476 (1957).

sons: they mark the Court's first confrontation with the constitutionality of obscenity laws; they propound the Court's first definition of obscenity; and they represent the first, and so far the last, time that the Court has demonstrated a semblance of unity in deciding a major obscenity case.

The *Roth* decision and opinions have already been carefully dissected.[13] On the basic constitutional question Mr. Justice Brennan's opinion for a five-man majority declared that antiobscenity laws were compatible with the free speech and press guarantees of the First Amendment because, in effect, obscenity is in a class of "utterances" that are not really "speech." Obscenity, he argued, is beyond constitutional protection for the reason that it is "utterly without redeeming social importance"[14] and plays "no essential part of any exposition of ideas."[15] As a consequence, Mr. Justice Brennan neatly sidestepped the strong contention of counsel for Alberts and Roth that obscene material could not be suppressed without a showing that its dissemination created a clear and present danger of antisocial conduct: since it was inherently worthless, that is, non-speech, obscene material had no claim to being measured against any clear-and-present-danger test. Yet, paradoxically, the Brennan opinion recognized that obscenity cases are, nevertheless, First Amendment cases. For one thing, sex is a legitimate subject of artistic and literary concern, and non-obscene treatment of this "mysterious" and "absorbing" topic deserves First Amendment protection.[16] For another and related reason, there is a constant need for "ceaseless vigilance" to prevent the constitutionally justifiable regulation of obscenity from serving as a pretext to suppress legitimate communication.[17]

Roth, too, was the occasion for Mr. Justice Brennan's famous definition of obscenity: ". . . whether to the average person, applying contemporary community standards, the dominant theme of

---

[13] See especially Kalven, *supra* note 1, at 7–28; Lockhart & McClure, *supra* note 7, at 19–29.

[14] 354 U.S. at 484.

[15] *Id.* at 485, quoting Chaplinsky v. New Hampshire, 315 U.S. 568, 571–72 (1942).

[16] 354 U.S. at 487.

[17] *Id.* at 488.

the material taken as a whole appeals to prurient interest."[18] Unfortunately, this constitutional test suffers the fatal defect of being circular. It makes "prurient interest" the pivotal part of the definition, yet fails to define pruriency meaningfully.[19] Despite its ultimate indefiniteness, the *Roth* definition, building on the holding in *Butler v. Michigan*, answered some important questions, or at least helped to refine them. It made the reaction of the "average person" in the "contemporary community" the norm for evaluating obscenity, and it insisted that challenged materials be judged, not partially and selectively, but in their entirety. The consequence, naturally, was to bury that part of the weather-beaten formula in *Regina v. Hicklin*[20] that made the test of obscenity its "tendency . . . to deprave and corrupt those whose minds are open to such immoral influences."[21]

Finally, the *Roth* decision is noteworthy as one of the few instances in which the Warren Court has demonstrated a measure of unity in the obscenity area. Only Justices Black and Douglas dissented from the Court's judgment. Rejecting the assumption that there exists a category of bad expression called obscenity and unworthy of First Amendment protection, they insisted that no expression could be restricted unless "so closely brigaded with illegal

---

[18] *Id.* at 489. The Court also ruled that the California and federal statutes were sufficiently precise and gave adequate notice of the prohibited offenses; they did not, therefore, violate the due process clauses of the Fifth and Fourteenth Amendments. *Id.* at 491–94.

[19] In a footnote Mr. Justice Brennan attempted to define prurient materials as "material having a tendency to excite lustful thoughts." He cited the definition of "prurient" in *Webster's New International Dictionary* (2d ed. 1949): ". . . itching; longing, uneasy with desire or longing; of persons, having itching, morbid, or lascivious longings, or desire, curiosity, of propensity, lewd. . . ." 354 U.S. at 487 n. 20. This battery of words emphasizes the extreme subjectivity of the *Roth* definition: it tells us what obscenity-pruriency allegedly *does* to the viewer of obscene material; it does not inform us what obscenity *is*.

[20] L.R. 3 Q.B. 360 (1868).

[21] *Id.* at 371. Lord Cockburn's statement deserves full quotation: "I think the test of obscenity is this, whether the tendency of the matter charged as obscenity is to deprave and corrupt those whose minds are open to such immoral influences, and into whose hands a publication of this sort may fall. Now, with regard to this work, it is quite certain that it would suggest to the minds of the young of either sex, or even to persons of more advanced years, thoughts of a most impure and libidinous character." *Ibid.*

action as to be an inseparable part of it."[22] The other Justices concurred with Mr. Justice Brennan's view that obscenity is beyond constitutional protection, a conclusion made easier by the fact that the *Alberts* and *Roth* cases were decided within an abstract framework. In neither case did the Court confront the materials actually distributed by Alberts and Roth; instead its review was limited solely to the constitutionality of two antiobscenity statutes on their face.[23] As an antidote to the rarefied atmosphere in which the cases reached the Court, the brief of the Solicitor General of the United States in the *Roth* case explained that 90 per cent of the federal obscenity prosecutions were directed against hard-core pornography. And to drive the point home the Solicitor General shipped a carton to the Court that contained numerous samples of films, photographs, and printed matter depicting normal and abnormal sexual activity.[24] A picture, even an obscene picture, apparently is still worth a thousand words.

Despite their relative unanimity, the *Roth-Alberts* decisions also revealed profound tensions among the Court majority. Mr. Justice Harlan dissented in *Roth* on the ground that the federal obscenity statute could be constitutionally applied to reach only hard-core pornography. This limitation, he believed, had been overstepped by the trial judge's charge that the law properly applied to books that "tend to stir sexual impulses and lead to impure thoughts."[25] More important, he subjected the Brennan majority opinion to a searching critical analysis that vigorously contested the adequacy of its definition of obscenity. Prophetically, he insisted that obscenity cases turned on mixed questions of fact and law that would require appellate courts to conduct independent examinations of the allegedly offensive materials.[26] Chief Justice Warren, in a short and somewhat vague concurring opinion, con-

---

22 354 U.S. at 514 (Douglas, J., dissenting).

23 The conditional nature of the Court's review is fully explained by Lockhart & McClure, *supra* note 7, at 21–25.

24 *Id.* at 26.

25 354 U.S. at 507. Mr. Justice Harlan's differing positions in the *Roth* and *Alberts* cases is rooted in his belief that the First Amendment prescribes stricter standards in the federal sphere than it does in the state jurisdictions. See text *infra*, at notes 64–65.

26 See the commentary by Kalven, *supra* note 1, at 19–25.

tended that there were two crucial considerations in obscenity cases.
The first was that an object might "vary" in being obscene or non-
obscene "according to the part of the community it reached."[27]
The second followed from the first: "It is not the book that is on
trial; it is a person. The conduct of the defendant is the central
issue, not the obscenity of a book or a picture."[28] Alberts and Roth,
the Chief Justice concluded, were constitutionally punishable for
being in the business of "commercial exploitation of the morbid
and shameful craving for materials with prurient effect."[29]

The immediate sequel to *Roth v. United States* was cryptic. In
the 1957 Term the Supreme Court reversed, *per curiam* and without
opinion, three federal obscenity convictions that had been affirmed
by courts of appeals.[30] In each instance the Supreme Court's
order merely cited *Roth v. United States*, implying that perhaps
the Justices could agree pragmatically, if not verbally, on a constitutional formula for resolving obscenity problems.[31] In any event
the very next obscenity case, *Kingsley International Pictures Corp.
v. Regents,*[32] demonstrated that, verbally at least, they were badly
divided. It took the Court six opinions to decide that New York
could not ban the movie version of *Lady Chatterley's Lover* under
a section of the state's obscenity laws forbidding the exhibition of
"immoral" films that portrayed acts of sexual immorality "as desirable, acceptable or proper patterns of behavior."[33] Mr. Justice
Stewart's majority opinion voided the statute as a violation of the
First Amendment because it restricted, not obscenity or pornography, but the advocacy of ideas—the idea that adultery may sometimes be proper behavior. Thematic, or ideological, obscenity is
constitutionally protected. Justices Black and Douglas, while con-

---

[27] 354 U.S. at 495.   [28] *Ibid.*   [29] *Id.* at 496.

[30] Times Film Corp. v. Chicago, 355 U.S. 35 (1957), reversing 244 F.2d 432 (7th
Cir. 1957); One, Inc. v. Olesen, 355 U.S. 371 (1958), reversing 241 F.2d 772 (9th
Cir. 1957); Sunshine Book Co. v. Summerfield, 355 U.S. 372 (1958), reversing 249
F.2d 114 (D.C. Cir. 1957). See also Mounce v. United States, 355 U.S. 180 (1957),
vacating and remanding 247 F.2d 148 (9th Cir. 1957) (Customs' seizure of nudist
magazines), for reconsideration in light of *Roth.*

[31] It was the Court's disposition of these cases—involving a sexy movie, a magazine designed for homosexuals, and a nudist magazine—that led to Professor Kalven's
prediction that the *Roth* definition of obscenity would be narrowed to hard-core
pornography. *Supra* note 1, at 43.

[32] 360 U.S. 684 (1959).   [33] *Id.* at 685.

curring in the Stewart opinion, each wrote separate opinions additionally condemning New York's scheme of movie regulation as an
unconstitutional prior restraint on the right of expression.[34] Mr.
Justice Clark concurred separately on the ground that the statute
was too vague and therefore violated due process.[35] Two concurring
opinions by Justices Frankfurter and Harlan interpreted the statute
as constitutional, while contending that it had been misapplied to
Lady Chatterley's Lover.[36]

During the 1960 and 1961 Terms the Justices avoided further
pronouncements on obscenity,[37] but in 1962 the problem of obscenity appeared again. The case was *Manual Enterprises v. Day*,[38]
and it tested a federal ban under § 1461 of the Criminal Code, the
same statute that was upheld in the *Roth* case. According to the
Post Office Department, three homosexual magazines—*MANual*,
Trim, and *Grecian Guild Pictorial*—were non-mailable because obscene.[39] With only seven Justices participating,[40] a splintered Court
reversed the ban.

Mr. Justice Harlan, joined by Mr. Justice Stewart, wrote a prevailing opinion that closely examined the challenged magazines and
purported to apply the *Roth* test. The Harlan opinion began by
noting that the record of the case was largely undisputed on three
points: (1) the magazines were primarily designed for homosexuals
and lacked literary or scientific merit; (2) their appeal was to the
"prurient interest" of homosexuals; sexually normal people would
find them uninteresting; and (3) the magazines were read almost
exclusively by homosexuals. As a consequence of these findings,
counsel and the courts below had focused their attention on
whether, in a case such as this, homosexuals were the relevant "audience" for judging the magazines' "prurient interest" appeal. (The
Court of Appeals had ruled that the magazines could be evaluated
in terms of their appeal to the "average homosexual" rather than to

---

[34] *Id.* at 690, 697.   [35] *Id.* at 699.   [36] *Id.* at 691, 702.

[37] The 1959 Term decision in Smith v. California, 361 U.S. 147 (1959), was decided on procedural grounds.

[38] 370 U.S. 478 (1962).

[39] The Post Office Department also claimed that the magazines carried unlawful
advertisements for obscene materials.

[40] Justices Frankfurter and White took no part in the case.

the "average person.")[41] Here, of course, was one of the many legal land mines left lying about by the *Roth* decision: who were the "average" persons, and whose prurient interest was at issue?

Rather than try his hand at demolition work, Mr. Justice Harlan found an alternative way to resolve the case. *Roth v. United States*, he insisted, did not establish a single test of obscenity, that is, "whether to the average person, applying contemporary community standards, the dominant theme of the material taken as a whole appeals to prurient interest." After all, he argued, the words of § 1461 refer to "obscene, lewd, lascivious, indecent, filthy or vile" materials, and these "connote something that is portrayed in a manner so offensive as to make it unacceptable under current community mores."[42] To be obscene under the federal statute, material had to be patently offensive on its face, and it had to have "prurient interest" appeal[43] for some undefined adult audience.

In thus restating the *Roth* test explicitly to include patent offensiveness, Mr. Justice Harlan also developed the intriguing subthesis that the obscenity originally forbidden at common law and by the federal statutes referred to "debasing portrayals of sex," regardless of its effect on the beholder.[44] The element of effect (or of prurient interest appeal) was, in fact, grafted onto federal obscenity law from *Regina v. Hicklin*, with its concern for the "tendency" of the challenged material to corrupt the "minds" exposed to it.[45] Mr. Justice Harlan contended that a failure to give patent offensiveness its due, as it were, would be inconsistent "with *Roth*'s evident purpose to tighten obscenity standards."[46] Any other

---

[41] 289 F.2d 455 (D.C. Cir. 1961).

[42] 370 U.S. at 482.

[43] As Mr. Justice Harlan pointed out, this twofold definition parallels the definition of "obscene" currently proposed in the American Law Institute's Model Penal Code: "Material is obscene if, considered as a whole, its predominant appeal is to prurient interest, that is, a shameful or morbid interest, in nudity, sex or excretion, and if in addition it goes substantially beyond customary limits of candor in describing or representing such matters." A.L.I. MODEL PENAL CODE, Proposed Official Draft (May 4, 1962), § 251.4(1). A few questioning souls—as yet untutored in the strange world of obscenity law—may legitimately wonder how "offensive" material can have "appeal." The operative assumption is that some things simultaneously attract and repel, that revulsion and wickedness may fascinate us and play on human curiosities even as they prove disturbing.

[44] 370 U.S. at 483.

[45] *Id.* at 483–84. See note 21 *supra*.   [46] *Id.* at 487.

view, he implied, would unduly reflect *Hicklin*'s Victorian flavor and pose constitutional difficulties:[47]

> To consider that the "obscenity" exception in "the area of constitutionally protected speech or press," *Roth*, at 485, does not require any determination as to the patent offensiveness *vel non* of the material itself might well put the American public in jeopardy of being denied access to many worthwhile works in literature, science, or art. For one would not have to travel far even among the acknowledged masterpieces in any of these fields to find works whose "dominant theme" might, not beyond reason, be claimed to appeal to the "prurient interest" of the reader or observer. We decline to attribute to Congress any such quixotic and deadening purpose as would bar from the mails all material, not patently offensive, which stimulates impure desires relating to sex. Indeed such a construction of § 1461 would doubtless encounter constitutional barriers. . . .

Before turning to the magazines themselves, Mr. Justice Harlan's opinion disposed of one more subsidiary question, that of the relevant "community" for measuring patent offensiveness. This, he thought, could be no less than "a national standard of decency,"[48] especially since the federal statute covered a wide and diversified nation with many ethnic and cultural backgrounds. Examined against this cosmopolitan standard he concluded that *MANual*, *Trim*, and *Grecian Guild Pictorial* were not obscene. Although the Government made much of the fact that they contained little textual material and gave most of their space to pictures of nude and seminude males in suggestive poses, the Harlan opinion characterized them as no more than "dismally unpleasant, uncouth, and tawdry."[49] Since society tolerates portrayals of the female nude, it would be inconsistent to forbid similar portrayals of male nudity.

None of the other Justices discussed the obscenity issues in *Manual Enterprises v. Day*. Mr. Justice Black concurred without opinion. Mr. Justice Brennan, joined by Chief Justice Warren and Mr. Justice Douglas, wrote an opinion that would reverse the Post Office ban on the ground that § 1461 did not authorize the Postmaster General to exclude material from the mails based on his own administrative determination that it was obscene.[50] Mr. Justice Clark, who read the statute differently, dissented. Although he did

---

[47] *Ibid.*

[48] *Id.* at 488.

[49] *Id.* at 490.

[50] *Id.* at 495.

not reach the constitutional issues, Mr. Justice Clark revealed his feelings in a rather uncharitable blast at his colleagues for "requiring" the United States Post Office "to be the world's largest disseminator of smut and Grand Informer of the names and places where obscene material may be obtained."[51]

No "Opinion of the Court" was forthcoming when the Justices again tilted with obscenity in *Jacobellis v. Ohio*,[52] a movie censorship case involving the criminal conviction of a Cleveland Heights theater owner who exhibited a French film, *Les Amants* ("The Lovers"). *Les Amants* is the story of an unhappy marriage and a bored woman who abandons her husband and family for a young archeologist with whom she has suddenly fallen in love. The state particularly objected to an explicit love scene in the last reel, which advertisements for the movie touted as being "as close to authentic amour as is possible on the screen" and as "one of the longest and most sensuous love scenes to be seen in this country."[53]

A prevailing opinion for himself and Mr. Justice Goldberg announced the judgment of reversal of the conviction and provided Mr. Justice Brennan with the opportunity to reconsider his definition of obscenity in *Roth*. "Recognizing that the [prurient interest appeal] test for obscenity enunciated there," he wrote, "is not perfect, we think any substitute would raise equally difficult problems, and we therefore adhere to that standard."[54] But then Mr. Justice Brennan went on to "reiterate" the meaning of *Roth*, and the doctrinal complexities multiplied. Obscenity was a form of unprotected expression only because it was "utterly without redeeming social importance," and "material dealing with sex in a manner that advocates ideas, or that has literary or scientific or artistic value or any other form of social importance, may not be branded as obscenity and denied the constitutional protection."[55] Moreover, he cited approvingly, and seemed to endorse unequivocally, Mr. Justice Harlan's point in *Manual Enterprises* that patent offensiveness was a threshold requirement to any finding of obscenity:[56]

---

[51] *Id*. at 519.   [52] 378 U.S. 184 (1964).

[53] *Id*. at 201 n. 2 (Warren, C.J., dissenting).

[54] *Id*. at 191.   [55] *Ibid*.

[56] *Id*. (Emphasis added.) The opinion cited the A.L.I. Code, see *supra* note 43. Mr. Justice Harlan, of course, because of his view that the First Amendment is

"It should also be recognized that the *Roth* standard requires *in the first instance* a finding that the material 'goes substantially beyond customary limits of candor in description or representation of such matters.' "

The Brennan opinion touched on two other significant questions. First, it declared that the "contemporary community standards" of the *Roth* test, in both federal and state cases, referred to a national standard.[57] Anything less, such as a "local" definition of "community," would inadequately safeguard the First Amendment interests that are so often involved in obscenity cases. Despite the diversity of the nation's local communities and their legitimate right to combat obscenity, the status of individual expression under the Constitution could not be determined by local tolerances. For, in an echo of John Marshall's famous —if ambiguous—phrase, "It is, after all, a national Constitution we are expounding."[58] Second, the Brennan opinion confirmed Mr. Justice Harlan's insistence that since obscenity cases may involve expression protected under the First Amendment, the Court could not avoid "an independent constitutional judgment on the facts of the case as to whether the material involved is constitutionally protected."[59]

Applying this newly elaborated *Roth* test—consideration of a work's patent offensiveness, its social importance, and its prurient interest appeal measured against national standards—Mr. Justice Brennan found *Les Amants* to be non-obscene. He gave little explanation of why this was so, except to note that the film had been reviewed both favorably and unfavorably, had run in nearly one hundred of the nation's largest cities, had been challenged by the state essentially because of "an explicit love scene in the last reel,"[60] and had been viewed in the light of the trial record. Although he left the precise reason for reversal unclear, a brief opinion by

---

less demanding of the state jurisdictions, considered patent offensiveness to be only a federal requirement.

[57] In *Manual Enterprises v. Day*, Mr. Justice Harlan limited his application of a national standard of decency to the requirement of the federal statute involved in that case. 370 U.S. at 488.

[58] 378 U.S. at 195.

[59] *Id.* at 190. Mr. Justice Harlan's insistence on this point may be found, for example, in *Roth*, 354 U.S. at 497–98, and in *Manual Enterprises*, 370 U.S. at 488.

[60] 378 U.S. at 196.

Mr. Justice Goldberg (who concurred in the Brennan opinion) implied that for him the film, taken as a whole, was inoffensive.[61]

Four other Justices voted to reverse the conviction. Mr. Justice White concurred without opinion, and Justices Black and Douglas reaffirmed their position that the Constitution forbids all kinds of censorship. The sixth vote for reversal came from Mr. Justice Stewart, whose one-paragraph statement undoubtedly represents the apogee of the case-by-case approach. The *Roth* opinion, he announced, could be read "in a variety of ways," because the Court there was "trying to define what may be indefinable."[62] But, he felt, the "negative implication" of the Court's decisions since 1957 amounted to the proposition that only hard-core pornography could be constitutionally suppressed. What, then, is hard-core pornography? Mr. Justice Stewart's answer had, at least, the virtue of candor:[63]

> I shall not today attempt further to define the kinds of material I understand to be embraced within that short-hand definition; and perhaps I could never succeed in intelligibly doing so. But I know it when I see it, and the motion picture involved in this case is not that.

Unfortunately, this ultrapragmatic "approach" cannot assist book publishers and distributors, theater managers, and trial judges who do not "know it" when they "see it"—or who "see it" differently.

The three dissenters, emulating their colleagues in the "majority," also divided among themselves. To Mr. Justice Harlan, because *Jacobellis v. Ohio* was a state prosecution, the restraints of the First Amendment should be applied less stringently than in federal obscenity cases where close judicial surveillance properly limited the government's discretion. He envisioned the looser state requirement as "one of rationality" that would permit states, acting through judicial proceedings and rationally established criteria, to ban material which, taken as a whole, "treated sex in a fundamentally offensive manner."[64] Ohio's action against *Les Amants* did not exceed these limitations. This double standard, Mr. Justice Harlan contended, sensibly accommodated the over-all national interest in free

---

[61] ". . . the love scene deemed objectionable is so fragmentary and fleeting that only a censor's alert would make an audience conscious that something 'questionable' is being portrayed." 378 U.S. at 197–98.

[62] *Id.* at 197.   [63] *Ibid.*   [64] *Id.* at 204.

expression with the public interest in obscenity laws. Yet even his tests could only take on meaning on a case-by-case basis, and he confessed, "I experience no greater ease than do other members of the Court in attempting to verbalize generally the respective constitutional tests, for in truth the matter in the last analysis depends on how particular challenged material happens to strike the minds of jurors or judges and ultimately those of a majority of the members of this Court."[65]

The other dissenting opinion was by Chief Justice Warren joined by Mr. Justice Clark. The Chief Justice felt impelled to write, he explained, because most of the post-*Roth* obscenity decisions, given without opinion, failed to provide principled guidance for legislatures and lower courts. Nor, for that matter, had the *Jacobellis* decision "shed any greater light on the problem."[66] The difficulty, however, was not with the *Roth* test. It has not, he wrote, "proved unsound, and I believe we should try to live with it—at least until a more satisfactory definition is evolved."[67] So far so good, but then the Chief Justice began to explain the *Roth* opinion. Contrary to the interpretation of its author—Mr. Justice Brennan—he believed that the test's reference to "community standards" meant local community standards. There is, he argued, "no provable 'national standard,' " and the Court's task was to reconcile the conflicting rights of the nation's diverse communities with the rights of individuals.[68]

Leaving this subject dangling, Chief Justice Warren made three additional observations. First, he rejected the notion that the term "hard-core pornography" could be defined any more clearly than obscenity. Second, he repeated the suggestion of his concurring opinion in *Roth* that "the use to which various materials are put —not just the words and pictures themselves—must be considered in determining whether or not the materials are obscene." Thus, a technical or legal treatise on pornography could be generally inoffensive but could become extremely obscene if sold to children.[69]

---

[65] *Ibid.*   [66] *Id.* at 200.   [67] *Ibid.*

[68] *Id.* at 200–01.

[69] *Id.* at 201. At this point Chief Justice Warren cited the advertisements for *Les Amants*, which, he commented, "provide some evidence of the film's dominant theme." *Id.* at n. 2. The relationship of the film's theme to the variable offensiveness of a treatise on pornography is not immediately clear.

Third, he noted that obscenity judgments, both civil and criminal, had to conform strictly to constitutional procedures, and he chided law enforcement agencies for too often spoiling their cases through procedural blunders. Then, in a mysterious *non sequitur*, the Chief Justice asserted that "the foregoing" led him to "reiterate" his acceptance of the *Roth* prurient interest test.[70] Its enforcement, he continued, ought to be committed to the lower state and federal courts, with the Supreme Court limiting its supervisory role solely to a consideration of whether or not there exists "sufficient evidence" in the record to support a finding of obscenity, as there was in the case of *Les Amants*. Chief Justice Warren's *Jacobellis* dissent was presumably intended to "shed light" on the meaning of the *Roth* rule; instead, it opened up new vistas of darkness.

In two other cases decided *per curiam* during the 1963 Term, *Tralins v. Gerstein*[71] and *Grove Press, Inc. v. Gerstein*,[72] the Supreme Court again re-emphasized its confusion in the obscenity area. The cases involved Florida civil judgments that two books were obscene under the *Roth* rule, and in both instances five Justices —Brennan, Goldberg, Black, Douglas, and Stewart—voted to reverse summarily on the basis of their positions in *Jacobellis v. Ohio*. In the first case, *Tralins*, the Court's action overturned a ban against *Pleasure Was My Business*, described as a book "containing numerous descriptions of abnormal sex acts and indecent conversations supposed to have taken place in a Florida brothel."[73] In the second, it overturned a finding of obscenity against Henry Miller's controversial autobiographical journal, *Tropic of Cancer*, which is filled with four-letter words and uninhibited descriptions of sexual and excremental episodes. This latter decision was the more significant, for ever since the publication of an American edition by Grove Press in 1961, Miller's scabrous book had become the object of a massive censorship campaign.[74] Although none of the Justices voting to reverse wrote opinions, their evaluation of the *Tropic* case seems clear: to Justices Black and Douglas the censorship was inherently

---

[70] *Id.* at 202.

[71] 378 U.S. 576 (1964), reversing 151 So.2d 19 (Fla. Dist. Ct. App. 3d Dist. 1963).

[72] 378 U.S. 577 (1964), reversing 156 So.2d 537 (Fla. Dist. Ct. App. 3d Dist. 1963).

[73] 32 U.S. Law Week 3048 (1963).

[74] See Magrath, *Tropic of Cancer: The Biography of a Book*, in Tresolini & Frost, Cases in American National Government and Politics 174–82 (1966).

unconstitutional; to Justices Brennan and Goldberg the book had redeeming social importance;[75] and to Mr. Justice Stewart it was obvious that it was not hard-core pornography. Chief Justice Warren and Justices Clark, Harlan, and White refused to express any opinion in either case, simply voting to deny certiorari.[76]

Between 1957 and 1965 the Supreme Court also decided a large number of state obscenity cases on procedural grounds. The Court's disposition of these cases is nevertheless relevant. For these actions have quite consistently fulfilled the implicit promise of *Roth* that although obscenity is not "speech," all obscenity cases are First Amendment cases. They must, therefore, be tried in strict conformity to commands of the First and Fourteenth Amendments and the Constitution's fair trial guarantees. As the Court explained in 1961:[77] "It follows that, under the Fourteenth Amendment, a State is not free to adopt whatever procedures it pleases for dealing with obscenity as here involved without regard to the possible consequences for constitutionally protected speech." Thus, a narrow majority of the Court has sustained the constitutionality of injunctions against the sale of allegedly obscene materials (a form of very limited prior restraint) where there is provision for an immediate joinder of issues and an opportunity for speedy trial and judgment.[78] Indiscriminate seizures of challenged works[79] and injunctive procedures that fail to provide for a preliminary adversary hearing have been condemned.[80] Similarly, the Court has struck down a state's scheme for protecting children from obscene books and magazines through what amounted to uncontrolled adminis-

---

[75] In his *Jacobellis* discussion of the requirement that books must be "utterly" without social importance, 378 U.S. at 191, Mr. Justice Brennan approvingly cited the California Supreme Court's decision in *Zeitlin v. Arnebergh*, 59 Cal.2d 901 (1963), which overturned a ban on *Tropic of Cancer* on the ground that it possessed social importance. Or, as Ezra Pound once put it, *Tropic* is "a dirty book worth reading." Magrath, *supra* note 74, at 174.

[76] Mr. Justice White's vote to deny certiorari was enigmatic (he had concurred in *Jacobellis* without opinion), but it is probably safe to infer that the other three Justices felt that sufficient evidence justified the Florida rulings.

[77] Marcus v. Search Warrant, 367 U.S. 717, 731 (1961) (Brennan, J.).

[78] Kingsley Books, Inc. v. Brown, 354 U.S. 436 (1957).

[79] *Supra* note 77.

[80] A Quantity of Books v. Kansas, 378 U.S. 205 (1964).

trative prior restraint.[81] And it has required at least some scienter as a prerequisite to the criminal conviction of those who sell allegedly obscene books.[82] Much the same developments have occurred in the movie censorship field. Despite its narrow refusal in 1961 to declare *all* prior restraint schemes per se unconstitutional,[83] a strong majority of the Court in 1965 agreed that such censorship must be rigorously limited by procedural safeguards.[84]

As a consequence of these procedural cases, as well as those dealing with the substantive law of obscenity, three significant propositions seem no longer to be in question:

1. Obscenity—however defined—is not constitutionally protected, even though obscenity cases may well raise significant First and Fourteenth Amendment issues.

2. Obscenity judgments, whether in civil or criminal proceedings, can be imposed by government units only when their procedures are scrupulously fair.

3. Material may not be generally banned as obscene merely because of its alleged impact on children.

There is some temptation to add other propositions to the list, such as that obscenity depends on the work as a whole and on its appeal to average persons. But both of these propositions are elements of the *Roth* test, and that test, as we have seen, has meant rather different, and sometimes unclear, things to the different Justices. Not only do the cases between 1957 and 1965 demonstrate the difficulty of defining obscenity as the appeal to prurient interest, but they reveal that *Roth v. United States* spawned a menagerie of vital subsidiary questions. How much "social importance" redeems a work, qualifying it for First Amendment salvation? How is this importance to be determined? Must obscene material be "patently offensive" in terms of contemporary community standards? What is

[81] Bantam Books, Inc. v. Sullivan, 372 U.S. 58 (1963).

[82] Smith v. California, 361 U.S. 147 (1959). The difficult question how much scienter is required was left unresolved. It may be decided during the 1966 Term. See note 264, *infra*.

[83] Times Film Corp. v. Chicago, 365 U.S. 43 (1961).

[84] Freedman v. Maryland, 380 U.S. 51 (1965); Trans Lux Distributing Corp. v. Board of Regents, 380 U.S. 259 (1965), *reversing per curiam*, 14 N.Y.2d 88 (1964). Justices Black and Douglas refused to join the majority opinion in *Freedman* because of their opposition to any kind of censorship scheme.

the "community"? Is it local or is it the entire nation? How are the standards to be determined?[85] If the "average person" provides the mean for measuring prurient interest, does this average person shift as the audience that is the primary target of the material shifts? Is the distributor's conduct important? How important? And what, exactly, is the Supreme Court's responsibility? Must it conduct its own independent examination of the challenged material, or is it enough that the trial court applied the *Roth* test to sufficient evidence? The questions seem endless and many seem unanswerable.

And yet if one looks only at what the Court *did* and not at what its many tongues *said*, the decisions through 1965 seem to confirm Professor Kalven's prediction that the Court would eventually restrict obscenity to something akin to hard-core pornography. To be sure, no one could define it, but all intelligent men could instantly recognize it.[86] In no decision after 1957 did the Court uphold a finding of obscenity. In twelve cases it overturned judgments against nearly two hundred items ranging from such serious works as Henry Miller's *Tropic of Cancer* to such potboilers as *Trailer Trollop* and *The Wife-Swappers*.[87] Lower courts followed suit.[88]

---

[85] In *Smith v. California*, Mr. Justice Frankfurter argued in favor of a constitutional requirement that expert testimony be introduced on this question. 361 U.S. at 165–67 (concurring opinion).

[86] Kalven, *supra* note 1, at 43–45. See also, Lockhart & McClure, *supra* note 7, at 58–60.

[87] Times Film Corp. v. Chicago, 355 U.S. 35 (1958); Mounce v. United States, 355 U.S. 180 (1957); One, Inc. v. Olesen, 355 U.S. 371 (1958); Sunshine Book Co. v. Summerfield, 355 U.S. 372 (1958); Kingsley International Pictures Corp. v. Board of Regents, 360 U.S. 684 (1959); Smith v. California, 361 U.S. 147 (1959); Marcus v. Search Warrant, 367 U.S. 717 (1961); Manual Enterprises v. Day, 370 U.S. 478 (1962); Jacobellis v. Ohio, 378 U.S. 184 (1964); Tralins v. Gerstein, 378 U.S. 576 (1964); Grove Press, Inc. v. Gerstein, 378 U.S. 577 (1964); A Quantity of Books v. Kansas, 378 U.S. 205 (1964); Trans Lux Distributing Corp. v. Board of Regents, 380 U.S. 259 (1965). (Unlike the *Freedman* case, where the movie itself was not in dispute, *Trans Lux* involved the controversial Danish film, *A Stranger Knocks*, which included a scene depicting—clearly but discreetly—sexual intercourse.)

[88] D. H. Lawrence's novel, *Lady Chatterley's Lover*, was judicially cleared for the United States mails by a federal district court in *Grove Press, Inc. v. Christenberry*, 175 F. Supp. 488 (S.D. N.Y. 1959), a decision affirmed at 276 F. 2d 433 (2d Cir. 1960). One of the circuit judges, who deplored the new sexual and literary permissiveness, speculated that "if the trend continues unabated, by the time some author writes of 'Lady Chatterley's Granddaughter,' Lady Chatterley herself will

Time magazine, in a survey of "The New Pornography," announced that "just about anything is printable in the U.S. today."[89] Eliot Fremont-Smith, a literary critic for the *New York Times*, reviewed the sadistic French novel, *Story of O*, with the observation that its free publication in the United States "marks the end of any coherent restrictive application of the concept of pornography to books."[90]

One who agreed with these assessments was a New York editor-publisher, Ralph Ginzburg. In 1961, with the mailing of five million pieces of advertising, he announced the publication of *Eros*, *"the magazine of sexual candor,"* which has been made possible as a "result of recent court decisions that have realistically interpreted America's obscenity laws and that have given to this country a new breadth of freedom of expression."[91]

II. GINZBURG v. UNITED STATES

In 1963 a federal grand jury in Philadelphia indicted Ralph Ginzburg and three corporations controlled by him on twenty-eight counts of violating the postal obscenity law, 18 U.S.C. § 1461, by transmitting through the mails three obscene publications and advertisements providing information on how they could be obtained. Ginzburg waived a jury trial and was tried before Judge Ralph C. Body, who found Ginzburg and his corporations guilty and imposed a five-year prison sentence and fines totaling $42,000. The Court of Appeals for the Third Circuit affirmed. The Supreme Court granted certiorari and affirmed Ginzburg's conviction, ruling for the first time that the material involved in an obscenity case was obscene.[92]

----

seem like a prim and puritanical housewife." *Id.* at 433. (Moore, J., concurring.) New York's prestigious Court of Appeals declared in 1964 that *Fanny Hill*, the elegant eighteenth-century pornographic novel, did not violate its hard-core pornography test. Larkin v. G. P. Putnam's Sons, 14 N.Y.2d 399 (1964). That same year the Illinois Supreme Court reluctantly overturned a conviction of the entertainer Lenny Bruce, whose nightclub act had been attacked as obscene. People v. Bruce, 31 Ill.2d 459 (1964).

[89] 85 TIME 28 (April 16, 1965).

[90] Fremont-Smith, *The Uses of Pornography*, N.Y. Times, p. 39, col. 2 (March 2, 1966).

[91] *Eros* advertising brochure.

[92] Ginzburg v. United States, 383 U.S. 463 (1966).

In order to assess the Court's ruling in *Ginzburg v. United States,* it is essential to understand the nature of the materials involved. Of the three challenged publications the least significant was the first issue of *Liaison,* a bimonthly newsletter devoted to sex. It consisted of six pages of smutty jokes of the *Playboy* variety and short "news" stories reporting on what may be described as the world of sex. Principal attention during the trial focused on three items: "Slaying the Sex Dragon," an interview with a psychotherapist, Dr. Albert Ellis, advocating uninhibited sexual freedom; "Semen in the Diet," an article drawing on quotations from the *Journal of the American Medical Association* extolling the nutritive qualities of human semen, which was to be ingested by women practicing fellatio; and "Sing a Song of Sex Life" exemplified by such immortal lines as: "The professors have crawled out of the dust and discovered lust." During the trial and subsequent appeals no one seemed too disposed to challenge the assessment of Dwight Macdonald, an expert literary critic testifying for the defense, that the *Liaison* issue "was an extremely tasteless, vulgar and repulsive issue."[93]

Far more controversial was *Eros,* a hardcover $25-a-year quarterly magazine modeled, stylistically, after the highly successful *American Heritage* magazine. (One favorably disposed reviewer in fact dubbed *Eros* "the *American Heritage* of the bedroom.")[94] Ginzburg unsuccessfully sought mailing privileges for *Eros* first at Blue Ball and then at Intercourse, Pennsylvania; he finally obtained them at Middlesex, New Jersey. The indicted issue contained fifteen articles and photographic essays on love and sex, including such titles as "Was Shakespeare a Homosexual?" "President Harding's Second Lady," and "The Sexual Side of Anti-Semitism." Although much of *Eros'* content was admittedly non-obscene, the Government argued that four articles were obscene and that the presence of the non-obscene articles could not immunize the offensive matter since the magazine as a whole was exclusively built around a sexual theme.[95] The four offending pieces were an excerpt from Frank

---

93 Record, p. 237. Mr. Macdonald, however, claimed that it did not exceed contemporary American standards of sexual candor.

94 Quoted in *Eros* advertising brochure.

95 Brief for the United States, pp. 31–32. Judge Body had singled out four of the *Eros* articles as obscene. 224 F. Supp. at 135.

Harris' autobiography, *My Life and Loves*, containing some explicit descriptions of Harris' sexual conquests, real or imagined;[96] an article by Drs. Eberhard and Phyllis Kronhausen on "The Natural Superiority of Women as Eroticists," largely drawing on some extremely well-written excerpts from an unpublished erotic novel that gives the intimate and physical details of a woman's reactions to acts of sexual intercourse;[97] a collection of bawdy limericks described as "the folklore of the intellectual";[98] and, most disputed of all, "Black and White in Color," which the editor called "a photographic tone poem on the subject of interracial love." The "poem" consists of a series of lavish color photos depicting a very dark Negro man and a white woman, both nude, embracing each other in various poses. Dwight Macdonald described it as "very good" from an artistic point of view and "done with great taste."[99] Another defense witness, Professor Horst W. Janson, a New York University art historian, called the photographs "outstandingly beautiful and artistic."[100] But Judge Body's opinion described them as "a detailed portrayal of the act of sexual intercourse . . . leaving nothing to the imagination."[101] More cautiously, the Government's brief before the Supreme Court labeled the pictures as "amorous poses."[102]

The third Ginzburg publication, a book entitled *The Housewife's Handbook on Selective Promiscuity*, was perhaps the most controversial of all. Authored by Mrs. Lillian Maxine Serett under the pseudonymous name, Rey Anthony, it purports to be a woman's candid sexual autobiography from the age of three to thirty-six. Originally published by Mrs. Serett in 1960, it had sold approximately 1,700 copies to physicians and psychiatrists through the

---

[96] In 1963 Grove Press published an unexpurgated hardcover edition of *My Life and Loves* and, subsequently, a complete $1.65 paper edition. So far as I know, both editions are circulating freely through the federal mails.

[97] The Kronhausens are authors of an important study on law and obscenity. See PORNOGRAPHY AND THE LAW (1964).

[98] Dwight Macdonald characterized the limericks as "quite vulgar," but not "obscene or pornographic." He agreed that "some people might consider them funny." Record, p. 240.

[99] *Ibid.*   [100] *Id.* at 221.   [101] 224 F. Supp. at 135.

[102] Brief for the United States, p. 32. This less specific phrase is safer. Although depicting a man and woman in a most intimate situation, the pictures do leave a good deal to the imagination.

mails.[103] In 1962 she arranged to have the book published by Ginzburg and distributed through his mail-order business. A quotation
from an introduction to the book by Albert Ellis (who rejoiced
in its unique revelation that "sex can actually be fun") is the best
way to give a fair summary of its contents:[104]

> . . . she has given us descriptions of a highly sexed woman's
> thoughts, feelings, and reactions—descriptions that are (as yet,
> alas) pricelessly rare. How she felt before engaging in sex ac-
> tivities; what her husbands or lovers said to her before, during,
> and after these sex acts; how she thought and felt in the midst
> of and subsequent to copulative engagements—these are the
> questions that Mrs. Anthony has chosen to consider and an-
> swer.

> . . . Mrs. Anthony, on the basis of her own extensive and inten-
> sive sex experiences, manages to be duly skeptical of the al-
> legedly superlative value of simultaneous climax; to deflate the
> myth of "vaginal" orgasm; to be highly dubious of the neces-
> sity of totally unplanned "spontaneous" coital activity; and
> unprudishly to indicate the advantages of anal stimulation and
> sexual varietism.

Besides its major autobiographical section, the *Handbook* contains
a chapter with the author's observations on such sexual topics as
abortion, sex education for children, the nation's sexual laws, and—
mirabile dictu—on obscenity. (Obscenity is "where *you* find it,"
for "if you can accept a thing *for what it is*, it ceases to be obscenity.")[105]

I am compelled to add here my own observation that despite its
detailed accounts of sexual acts, including cunnilingus and fellatio
(all of which are described with medical and not "dirty" words),
the book falls short of hard-core pornography, as that concept is
being defined by scholars and specialists.[106] Some passages are highly
suggestive, but from the point of view of erotic writings the sexy
parts of the narrative are repeatedly brought down to earth by Mrs.
Serett's depressing and revolting descriptions of her venereal disease,
her organs during pregnancy, her abortions, her doubts as to the
father of her children, and her severe financial difficulties. "The

---

103 Record, p. 370.

104 THE HOUSEWIFE'S HANDBOOK ON SELECTIVE PROMISCUITY 8 (1962).

105 *Id.* at 221–22.   106 See text at notes 273–88, *infra.*

Handbook's true revelation," as an astute critic has written, "is that sex can often be a pain and a mess."[107]

Ralph Ginzburg's trial was marked by skirmishing between defense and prosecution expert witnesses, especially over the alleged value of the *Handbook* in counseling persons with psychosexual problems and by the Government's successful introduction of testimony relating to *Eros'* quest for an appropriate postal imprint.[108] The trial judge applied his understanding of the *Roth* test to the three publications. He ruled each one obscene after a fairly detailed description. His own opinion contained an interesting description of *Roth's* average person and contemporary community standards components:[109]

> We have been regaled with the theory that the susceptibility of no single segment of the community is to be the paramount consideration in deciding whether a work is obscene. This is the law and we do not argue with it. It is also the law that the community as a whole is the proper consideration. In this community, our society, we have children of all ages, psychotics, feeble-minded and other susceptible elements. Just as they cannot set the pace for the average adult reader's taste, they cannot be overlooked as part of the community. The community as a whole is not an ideal man who wouldn't seek and read obscenity in the first place. Otherwise no restraint at all would be required. Some is proper. Therefore, an ideal person without any failings or susceptibility is not the man to protect. Society as a whole, replete of course with many imperfections, must be protected.

Affirming unanimously, the Court of Appeals added little to the trial judge's opinion, except to take a judicial swipe at this "sui generis operation on the part of experts in the shoddy business of pandering to and exploiting for money one of the great weaknesses of human beings."[110]

If the Court of Appeals opinion was routine, the Supreme Court opinion was not. Under any view, Mr. Justice Brennan's opinion in *Ginzburg v. United States*, which was joined by Chief Justice Warren and Justices Clark, Fortas, and White, represents a major reinterpretation of *Roth v. United States*. Although never repudi-

---

[107] Hyman, *In Defense of Pornography*, 46 THE NEW LEADER 14 (Sept. 2, 1963).

[108] Record, pp. 152–65, 186–241, 256–348.

[109] 224 F. Supp. at 137.   [110] 338 F.2d 12, 15 (3d Cir. 1964).

ating the *Roth* test, it endorses, in "close" cases, Chief Justice Warren's suggestion that "the conduct of the defendant is the central
issue, not the obscenity of a book or picture."[111] According to Mr.
Justice Brennan, Ginzburg was engaged in "the sordid business of
pandering," which he defined with a quotation from the Chief
Justice's concurring opinion in *Roth*: ". . . the business of purveying
textual or graphic matter openly advertised to appeal to the erotic
interest of their customers."[112] In support of this charge he cited
two features of Ginzburg's behavior, his taste for unusual mailing
addresses and his advertising methods. Both reveal "the leer of the
sensualist"; the *Eros* and *Liaison* circulars openly stressed "the sexual
candor" of the publications.[113] The *Handbook*'s advertising consisted almost entirely of Dr. Ellis' introduction, in which the "remarks are preoccupied with the book's sexual imagery," and the
"indiscriminate" solicitation was not limited to such persons as
physicians or psychiatrists who might perceive its value.[114] He further noted that the advertisements for *Eros*, *Liaison*, and the *Handbook* guaranteed a refund of the purchase price in case they failed
to reach their purchasers "because of U.S. Post Office censorship
interference." Each of these actions, he concluded, "highlighted the
gloss petitioners put on the publications eliminating any doubt what
the purchaser was being asked to buy."[115]

Such evidence of the circumstances in which material is advertised and marketed, Mr. Justice Brennan argued, was a relevant
aid in determining whether or not challenged material is obscene.
In the context of Ginzburg's case it was decisive. For here the publications were deliberately portrayed as erotic, and this "stimulated
the reader to accept them as prurient; he looks for titillation, not
for saving intellectual content."[116] This analysis, he was at pains to
stress, does not change the basic *Roth* test and its concern with the
obscenity of the material itself; it simply "elaborates" that test. Nor

---

111 383 U.S. 474, 475. Chief Justice Warren's comment may be found in 354 U.S.
at 495 (concurring opinion).

112 383 U.S. at 467; 354 U.S. at 495–96.

113 383 U.S. at 467–68. Mr. Justice Brennan also quoted from passages in two
Eros brochures claiming that its publication "has been enabled by recent court
decisions." *Id.* at n. 9. The Court apparently takes a jaundiced view of the new
emphasis on predicting Supreme Court decisions—whether done by political scientists or by publishers of erotica.

114 *Id.* at 469–70.   115 *Id.* at 470.   116 *Ibid.*

is there any threat to First Amendment guarantees in the holding that "in close cases evidence of pandering may be probative with respect to the nature of the material in question and thus satisfy the *Roth* test": [117]

> A conviction for mailing obscene publications, but explained in part by the presence of this element, does not necessarily suppress the materials in question, nor chill their proper distribution for a proper use. Nor should it inhibit the enterprise of others seeking through serious endeavor to advance human knowledge or understanding in science, literature, or art. All that will have been determined is that questionable publications are obscene in a context which brands them as obscene as that term is defined in *Roth*—a use inconsistent with any claim to the shelter of the First Amendment.

Two subsidiary points in the Brennan opinion should be noted. First, it explicitly disassociates itself from the trial judge's commentary on the meaning of community standards.[118] This is fortunate, since Judge Body's version of the *Roth* test, with its emphasis on children and psychotics, smuggles the Victorian rule of *Regina v. Hicklin* in through the back door of the community.[119] Second, and more important, the Brennan opinion treats the precedential and statutory authority for its conclusion that commercial exploitation, or "pandering," is a relevant consideration in, to put it most charitably, a rather casual manner. *United States v. Rebhuhn*,[120] a 1940 Court of Appeals decision, Mr. Justice Brennan wrote, is "persuasive authority for our conclusion."[121] Aside from

---

[117] *Id.* at 475.

[118] *Id.* at 466 n. 5. This might have been reversible error, but Ginzburg's attorneys apparently failed to charge that the trial judge misconceived the *Roth* test. See Mr. Justice Brennan's comment, *id.* at 465.

[119] *Cf.* Commonwealth v. Isenstadt, 318 Mass. 543, 552 (1945), where the test given, which resulted in an obscenity judgment against Lillian Smith's well-acclaimed novel, *Strange Fruit*, is strikingly similar to Judge Body's view of *Roth*. And see Lockhart & McClure, *supra* note 7, at 72.

[120] 109 F.2d 512 (2d Cir. 1940).

[121] 383 U.S. at 472. The disposition of *Rebhuhn*, a prosecution for sending obscene material through the mails, is in fact very similar to Mr. Justice Brennan's disposition of *Ginzburg*. The Court of Appeals ruled that the indiscriminate mailing of advertising circulars for books, which had a limited place in anthropology and psychotherapy, were appeals "merely to catch the prurient." ". . . the books were not obscene per se; they had a proper use, but the defendants woefully mis-

a brief description of the *Rebhuhn* decision, which has added status because its opinion was by Judge Learned Hand, there is only this footnote remark:[122] "Our conclusion is consistent with the statutory scheme. Although § 1461, in referring to 'obscene . . . matter' may appear to deal with the qualities of material in the abstract, it is *settled* that the mode of distribution may be a significant part in the determination of the obscenity of the material involved. *United States v. Rebhuhn, supra.*"

Since neither the *Rebhuhn* decision nor the concept of pandering as a significant element of obscenity in cases arising under § 1461 were seriously discussed in the opinions below,[123] in the briefs,[124] or in the oral argument,[125] what the Court understands by "settled" appears to be unsettled.[126] One admittedly fanciful possibility is that the majority assumed that *Rebhuhn* authoritatively added the pan-

---

used them, and it was that misuse which constituted the gravamen of the crime." 109 F.2d at 514, 515.

[122] 383 U.S. at 474 n. 15. (Emphasis added.)

[123] The reference to "pandering" in the Court of Appeals opinion, text at note 110 *supra*, is no more than a general condemnation of Ginzburg's activities. The *Rebhuhn* decision was not cited.

[124] As a matter of fact, the Solicitor General's brief opposing certiorari in the *Ginzburg* case comments: "Moreover there is no basis in the trial court's findings for a contention that commercial exploitation was considered an element of the obscenity of any of the challenged works." Brief for the United States in Opposition, p. 11. This was in response to a contention by Ginzburg's attorneys that the trial court, in passing on the obscenity issue, erroneously took account of Ginzburg's exploitation of literary works for a profit. Petition for a Writ of Certiorari, p. 3.

[125] The published accounts of the oral argument do not indicate any discussion of the pandering question. N.Y. Times, p. 31, col. 1 (Dec. 8, 1965); p. 28, col. 1 (Dec. 9, 1965); 188 PUBLISHER'S WEEKLY 61 (Dec. 27, 1965).

[126] Mr. Justice Brennan also claimed that the Model Penal Code "recognizes the question of pandering as relevant to the obscenity issue." 383 U.S. at 472 n. 14. On the ground that it was too indefinite and too difficult to enforce, the A.L.I. in 1957 rejected a proposal that would have made "pandering to an interest in obscenity" a criminal offense. See Lockhart & McClure, *supra* note 7, at 69. While its actual position seems to me somewhat unclear, the obvious intent of the A.L.I. draft on obscenity is to forbid its commercial exploitation. Commercial exploitation is *the target*, not the offense, but the A.L.I. draft permits the introduction of evidence showing prurient interest appeal in the advertising and promotion of challenged material. See generally, A.L.I. draft, *supra* note 43, at 237–40; Schwartz, *Morals Offenses and the Model Penal Code*, 63 COLUM. L. REV. 677–81 (1963).

In any event, we know that the Model Penal Code is not part of the Constitution. During oral arguments last Term in the criminal confession cases there occurred this exchange between the Court and William I. Siegel, Assistant District Attor-

dering gloss to § 1461 precisely because the briefs and opinions ignored it—in other words, that *Rebhuhn* was so authoritative a precedent that all parties implicitly and *sub silentio* bowed before it. The difficulty increases when one remembers that *Roth v. United States,* which cited thirteen cases as examples of the approved obscenity formula,[127] did not mention *Rebhuhn* and that Ginzburg was not indicted or tried for commercial exploitation and pandering. We may, therefore, I think, legitimately wonder what "settled" means in the context of the *Ginzburg* case.

There are other disturbing questions prompted by the majority's disposition of *Ginzburg v. United States,* most of which were raised in the four dissenting opinions. Mr. Justice Harlan, finding that the challenged material was not hard-core pornography and therefore mailable, roundly criticized the majority for an "obscure" holding that (without benefit of the exact definitions and standards necessary in the First Amendment area) wrote a new statute, "an astonishing piece of judicial improvisation" on a straightforward century-old law.[128] He strongly, and I think correctly, argued that the Court was uneasy in justifying the convictions, since it explicitly refused to accept the trial judge's "characterizations" of the *Handbook* and similarly implied that *Eros* and *Liaison* might be non-obscene were it not for the evidence of pandering.[129] Thus, "the Court in the last analysis sustains the convictions on the express assumption that the items held to be obscene are not, viewing them strictly, obscene at all."[130] Mr. Justice Harlan was further distressed by the Court's reliance on a theory entirely different from the one on which the case was tried and decided by the district court and affirmed by the court of appeals.[131] At the very least, he con-

---

ney of Kings County (New York), who was arguing in favor of arrests for investigation:
    The Chief Justice: "Has this Court ever sanctioned this without probable cause?
    Mr. Siegel: "It's relative. The Model Code says—
    Mr. Justice Black: "Is the Model Code in the Constitution?"
34 U.S. LAW WEEK 3299 (1966). The Court's disposition of *Miranda v. Arizona,* 384 U.S. 436 (1966), confirms that the Model Code is indeed not in the Constitution.

[127] 354 U.S. at 489 n. 26.   [128] 383 U.S. at 494, 495.

[129] *Id.* at 495. Mr. Justice Harlan also noted the majority's explicit refusal to approve Judge Body's "exegesis of *Roth.*" *Id.* at 493.

[130] *Id.* at 493–94.

[131] Mr. Justice Brennan attempted to rebut Mr. Justice Harlan by arguing that the Government several times during the trial announced its theory that the mode

tended, Ginzburg was entitled to a retrial on "this new pandering
dimension to the mailing statute," which would, for example, compel the government to prove that his motives were to pander to the
human weakness for pornographic titillation and that would analyze
the types of individuals purchasing the publications (and *their*
motives).[132]

Mr. Justice Stewart's dissenting opinion echoed the Harlan dissent in arguing that Ginzburg was denied due process, since neither
§ 1461 "nor any other federal statute I know of makes 'commercial
exploitation' or 'pandering' or 'titillation' a criminal offense."[133] In
language reminiscent of his Brother Black, he excoriated censorship as "a hallmark of an authoritative regime" and praised the
framers of the First Amendment for having "charted a different
course" that kept expression "free from the interference of a policeman's intrusive thumb or a judge's heavy hand."[134] Ginzburg's
publications were "vulgar and unedifying," but they were not hard-
core pornography and therefore were not suppressible. And, perhaps to counter criticism of his *Jacobellis* dissent, Mr. Justice Stew-

---

of distribution was relevant to the obscenity question, and that the Blue Ball–
Intercourse–Middlesex mailing incidents were specifically admitted in evidence to
support the pandering element. 383 U.S. at 466–67 and nn. 5–7. In my view, a close
reading of the trial record, the opinions below, and the briefs overwhelmingly
supports Mr. Justice Harlan's contention. The closest approximation to the Government's so-called "theory" of the case are a few remarks *at the sentencing
proceeding* by the United States Attorney, who, in countering Ginzburg's claim
that (unlike a black-market pornographer) he was not publishing furtively out
of a backroom, blasted the operation as "a commercial venture" that was "a gigantic
widescale pandering to the public in an attempt to distribute and disseminate this
material." Record, pp. 369, 370. The mailing incidents, I believe, were introduced
not, as Mr. Justice Harlan thought, 383 U.S. at 497 n. 3, to establish scienter (this
was covered in a stipulation by the parties), but to establish Ginzburg's general
obscene intent for the purpose of rebutting his claim that the concededly non-
obscene portions of *Eros* and *Liaison*, evaluated as a whole, constitutionally shel-
tered the allegedly obscene pieces. If some such showing of obscene intent were
not allowed, then, as Judge Body suggested, the Bible itself could be rendered
obscene and freely distributed "merely through the expediency of illustrating
sexual references with grossest pornographic photographs and by giving the participants biblical names." 224 F. Supp. at 135.

132 383 U.S. at 495–96.

133 *Id.* at 500. And, he added, any federal law that defined these terms as "elu-
sively" as the Court did would be unconstitutionally vague. *Ibid.*

134 *Id.* at 498.

art this time provided a description.[135] Although he did not define hard-core pornography, he cited a leading scholarly article that presents a concept of it.[136]

Mr. Justice Douglas' dissent, while reaffirming his long-held conviction that the First Amendment protects all expression, the "bad" as well as the "good," also discussed the disputed material. Even under the Court's own tests of patent offensiveness and social importance he found the publications acceptable. As for the pandering test, he dismissed it with a trenchant comment: [137]

> This new exception [to the First Amendment] condemns an advertising technique as old as history. The advertisements of our best magazines are chock-full of thighs, calves, bosoms, eyes, and hair, to draw the potential buyers' attention to lotions, tires, food, liquor, clothing, autos, and even insurance policies. The sexy advertisement neither adds to nor detracts from the quality of the merchandise being offered for sale. And I do not see how it adds to or detracts one whit from the legality of the book being distributed. A book should stand on its own, irrespective of the reasons why it was written or the wiles used in selling it. I cannot imagine any promotional effort that would make chapters 7 and 8 of the Song of Solomon any the less or any more worthy of First Amendment protection than does its unostentatious inclusion in the average edition of the Bible.

---

[135] *Id.* at 495, 499. He quoted this passage from the Solicitor General's brief, which agreed with the defendant on the existence of a class of obscene materials having these characteristics:

"Such materials include photographs, both still and motion picture, with no pretense of artistic value, graphically depicting acts of sexual intercourse, including various acts of sodomy and sadism, and sometimes involving several participants in scenes of orgy-like character. They also include strips of drawings in comic-book format grossly depicting similar activities in an exaggerated fashion. There are, in addition pamphlets and booklets, sometimes with photographic illustrations, verbally describing such activities in a bizarre manner with no attempt whatsoever to afford portrayals of character or situation and with no pretense to literary value. All of this material . . . cannot conceivably be characterized as embodying communication of ideas or artistic values inviolate under the First Amendment. . . ." *Id.* at 499 n. 3. This was the type of material sent to the Court by the Solicitor General during its consideration of *Roth.* The Government brief, however, argued that obscenity was not limited to such material but also encompassed "vulgar and filthy, rather than purely erotic—and perhaps . . . filthy scatological material as well—used solely to arouse and offend and with no other purpose or context." Brief for the United States, pp. 14–15.

[136] Lockhart & McClure, *supra* note 7, at 63–64.

[137] 383 U.S. at 482–83. Mr. Justice Douglas' dissenting opinion applied also to *Mishkin v. New York,* 383 U.S. 502 (1966), discussed *infra.*

The dissent of Mr. Justice Black also covered familiar ground. He reiterated that "the First Amendment forbids any kind or type or nature of governmental censorship over views as distinguished from conduct,"[138] and he agreed with Justices Harlan and Stewart that the majority had rewritten the federal obscenity statute. In addition, he surveyed the Court's prurient interest appeal, patent offensiveness, and social importance tests and concluded with the biting comment that "not even the most learned judge, much less a layman, is capable of knowing in advance of an ultimate decision in his particular case by this Court whether certain material comes within the area of 'obscenity' as that term is confused by the Court today."[139] And he added a Cassandra-like observation:[140] "It is obvious that the effect of the Court's decisions in the three obscenity cases handed down today is to make it exceedingly dangerous for people to discuss either orally or in writing anything about sex."

For better or for worse (and probably for both) Americans will continue to celebrate in speech and in press the mysteries of sex, and we can safely disregard Mr. Justice Black's pessimistic diagnosis. But no one, I think, not even those who are very convinced that Ginzburg's publications were obscene, can be happy with the decision in *Ginzburg v. United States*.[141] For there was absolutely no showing that *Eros, Liaison*, and the *Handbook* were, in the words of the controlling *Roth* decision, "utterly without redeeming social importance" and had prurient interest appeal in terms of the "average person" and "contemporary community standards."[142] Nor was there any showing of patent offensiveness, which Mr. Justice Brennan, in a companion case to *Ginzburg*,[143] said must coalesce with a lack of social value and prurient appeal before obscenity can be found. Even if the pandering aid is valid, it would seem applicable only after a showing that the challenged material made a "close

---

138 383 U.S. at 481.

139 *Id.* at 480–81. Mr. Justice Black was referring also to the Court's decision in *Memoirs v. Massachusetts*, 383 U.S. 502 (1966), discussed *infra*, which considered the various obscenity tests.

140 383 U.S. at 481.

141 For the sake of descriptive accuracy I should amend this statement to include only those persons who, regardless of their preferences on the obscenity issue, and perhaps naïvely, still believe that one of the Court's strengths—and obligations—is opinions that are reasonably principled and at least mildly persuasive.

142 354 U.S. at 484, 489.   143 Memoirs v. Massachusetts, 383 U.S. at 418.

case."[144] The Court, of course, may have assumed that the lower court proceedings conclusively settled the material's obscenity. But this is disturbing in view of the trial judge's misconception of the *Roth* test, and his evident concern during the trial over the *Handbook*'s immoral messages and its impact on impressionable adolescents.[145] Finally, the new pandering criteria—which made Ginzburg's publications "obscene" but not, evidently, obscene[146]—were inserted *ex post facto* by the Court majority. Or, as one surprised Justice Department lawyer put it after the decision in *Ginzburg v. United States* was announced: "Perhaps it would be sensible now for Congress to draft a new mailing law referring to the way material is distributed."[147]

III. Mishkin v. New York

Mishkin v. New York,[148] decided along with *Ginzburg*, was in part a replay of its companion case. Edward Mishkin, a New York publisher of predominantly sadistic pulp novels, was convicted of violating a section of New York's obscenity law by hiring people to write obscene books, publishing them, and possessing them with intent to sell. He was given a three-year prison sentence and fined $12,000. Fifty titles, including such gems as *Dance with the Dominant Whip*, *Bound in Rubber*, and *Sorority Girls Stringent Initiation*, were involved in the appeal. Mr. Justice Brennan, who spoke for himself, Chief Justice Warren, and Justices Clark, Fortas, and White in sustaining the conviction, went uncontradicted in his description of the books:[149]

> They portray sexuality in many guises. Some depict relatively normal heterosexual relations, but more depict such deviations as sado-masochism, fetishism, and homosexuality. Many have covers with drawings of scantily clad women being whipped, beaten, tortured, or abused.

---

[144] ". . . in close cases evidence of pandering may be probative *with respect to the nature of the material in question.* . . ." 383 U.S. at 474. (Emphasis added.)

[145] Record, pp. 270–72, 296–312.

[146] "This [pandering] evidence . . . was relevant in determining the ultimate question of 'obscenity' and, in the context of this record, serves to resolve all ambiguity and doubt." 383 U.S. at 470.

[147] Christian Science Monitor, p. 11, col. 1 (March 23, 1966).

[148] 383 U.S. 502 (1966).   [149] *Id.* at 505.

Mishkin thoughtfully provided his authors with Caprio's *Variations in Sexual Behavior* and Krafft-Ebing's *Psychopathia sexualis* and gave them detailed instructions. One contract author testified that the books had to be "full of sex scenes and lesbian scenes. . . . [T]he sex had to be very strong, it had to be clearly spelled out. . . . [T]he sex scenes had to be unusual sex scenes between men and women, and women and women, and men and men. . . ." Another testified that he had been instructed "to deal very graphically with . . . the darkening of the flesh under flagellation. . . ."[150]

Mishkin's attorneys challenged the conviction on a number of grounds, but the central issue turned on the nature of his books.[151] Since much of their content dealt with deviant sexual practices, Mishkin was able to argue that they did not satisfy the prurient interest requirement of the *Roth* test. "Average" or "normal" persons, he contended, are not sexually aroused by stories that emphasize flagellation, homosexuality, and lesbianism. Thus, the Court was face to face with the question it had bypassed in *Manual Enterprises v. Day:* Is material that has a prurient appeal to sexual deviates obscene? Mr. Justice Brennan answered in the affirmative, saying that the Court was "adjusting" the *Roth* test "to social realities by permitting the appeal of this type of material to be assessed in terms of the sexual interests of its intended and probable recipient group."[152] He hastened to make it clear that since the recipient group could not be identified merely as sexually immature persons, the adjusted *Roth* test "avoids the inadequacy of the most-susceptible-person facet of the *Hicklin* test."[153] Aside from the semantic quibble that "average" or "normal" in the *Roth* definition now also means "abnormal," the *Mishkin* opinion, in conjunction with the pandering test of *Ginzburg*, suggests that the Court is moving closer to the variable obscenity approach favored by Professors

---

[150] *Id.*

[151] They asserted, for instance, that the state law was unconstitutional on its face because it suppressed "sadistic" and "masochistic" as well as "obscene" publications. The Court rejected this argument on the ground that the New York courts, whose definition of obscenity it approved, had interpreted the three words as synonymous. The Court also turned aside, with little discussion, contentions that there was insufficient proof of scienter and that the books were improperly seized and admitted into evidence. *Id.* at 506–07, 510–14.

[152] *Id.* at 509.

[153] *Ibid.*

Lockhart and McClure.[154] Without discussing the possible difficulties of that approach for the moment, one substantial question comes immediately to mind. Assuming it can be shown that "normal" persons also buy such books as Mr. Mishkin provided, are these books to be labeled as non-prurient (and hence marketable) for such audiences?[155] It is at least theoretically possible that many normal people have, in their world of private fantasy, an interest and fascination for the strange and repulsive.[156] After all, many persons who are not potential thieves and murderers are addicted to crime fiction.

In addition to readjusting the *Roth* definition to encompass books with sexually bizarre descriptions and themes, Mr. Justice Brennan's *Mishkin* opinion added that their prurient appeal was fully confirmed by the pandering criteria formulated in the *Ginzburg* case. The books, he wrote, were specifically conceived and marketed for deviant groups. Mishkin's "own evaluation of his material" confirms the finding of prurient appeal.[157] Mr. Justice Brennan's opinion, however, essentially confined itself to an abstract discussion of prurient appeal in a context of masochistic and sadistic books. And it did not attempt to measure Mishkin's books against any such criteria as their social importance (which would be hard to show, unless mere entertainment qualifies) or patent offensiveness (which would appear to be a much more open question).

In part, the reluctance of the Court opinion to examine closely Mishkin's undelectable books—all fifty of them—is understandable.[158] There is force, after all, in the exaggerated contention of

---

[154] Lockhart & McClure, *supra* note 7, at 77–88. See text at notes 238–63, *infra*.

[155] According to a recent newspaper survey, most purchasers of Mishkin-type books—an $18 million a year business—are male. The editor of one leading line believes that "frustrated men" are the primary purchasers: "The books, he says, allow such men to 'transfer their guilt feelings about their inadequacies from themselves to the women in the book.' Lesbianism is the most popular theme at present, he believes, because the reader 'gets two immoral women for the price of one.'" Montgomery, *Paperback Smut Thrives as Outlets Continue To Grow*, N.Y. Times p. 1, col. 3 (Sept. 5, 1965).

[156] Apparently the *Mishkin* case did not include any evidence that the challenged books were actually sold to groups of sexual deviates.

[157] 383 U.S. at 510.

[158] During oral argument Chief Justice Warren expressed his concern on this very point: "Do we have to read all of them [the books] to determine if they have social importance? I'm sure this Court doesn't want to be the final censor to read all the prurient material in the country to determine if it has social value. If the final

Justices Black and Douglas that in its present approach to obscenity the Court is implicitly committing itself to the impossible task of reading every challenged book and viewing every challenged movie in the United States. In part, too, the Court's desire to avoid filling the United States Reports with descriptions of Mishkin's wares was apparently made easier by its confidence in the understanding of *Roth v. United States* held by the New York Court of Appeals. For when he turned to a consideration of the material involved in the *Mishkin* case, Mr. Justice Brennan noted that the New York courts have restricted their interpretation of obscenity to hard-core pornography.[159] "Since that definition of 'obscenity' is more stringent than the *Roth* definition, the judgment that the constitutional criteria are satisfied is implicit in the application of § 1141 [the New York law] below."[160] The symmetry of this assertion, however, would be more impressive if one could be sure that the New York definition was indeed stricter than the federal one. In fact, in 1963 the New York Court of Appeals ruled that *Tropic of Cancer* could be banned as hard-core pornography;[161] in 1964 the Supreme Court cleared the book of obscenity charges.[162]

The remainder of the *Mishkin* opinions are routine. Mr. Justice Harlan, following the logic of his double standard for federal and state obscenity cases, concurred.[163] New York had applied rational criteria. Three Justices dissented. The opinions of Justices Black and Douglas echo their opinions in *Ginzburg*.[164] Mr. Justice Stewart dissented because Mishkin's "tawdry" books were not hard-core pornography.[165] *Ginzburg* and *Mishkin*, however, were only two of the three cases decided on March 21, 1966. The final one gave the Justices even greater difficulty, and since seven different positions were asserted, it most vividly reveals the Court's present fragmentation on the obscenity issue.

---

burden depends on this Court, it looks to me as though we're in trouble" N.Y. Times, p. 31, col. 2 (Dec. 8, 1965).

[159] People v. Richmond County News, Inc., 9 N.Y.2d 578, 586–87 (1961).

[160] 383 U.S. at 508.   [161] People v. Fritch, 1 N.Y.2d 119 (1963).

[162] Grove Press, Inc. v. Gerstein, 378 U.S. 577 (1964).

[163] 383 U.S. at 515.

[164] *Id*. at 515 (Black, J., dissenting); at 482 (Douglas, J., dissenting).

[165] *Id*. at 518.

IV. Memoirs v. Massachusetts

Some 217 years following its first publication, John Cleland's peripatetic novel, *Memoirs of a Woman of Pleasure*, commonly known after its heroine as *Fanny Hill*, finally engaged the attention of the United States Supreme Court. As in the novel, Fanny's presence must have been distracting, for the Justices could not agree on what to do with her and how. The case, *Memoirs v. Massachusetts*,[166] tested a 4-to-3 judgment of the Massachusetts Supreme Judicial Court that *Fanny Hill* was obscene. The Massachusetts judgment was rendered in an *in rem* proceeding, brought against the book itself and not its distributor or its publisher, G. P. Putnam's Sons. By a vote of 6-to-3, but without a majority opinion, the Court reversed the Massachusetts high court.

Before turning to the opinions, *Fanny Hill* must be introduced. Despite his distaste for the book, the summary from the dissenting opinion of Mr. Justice Clark provides a useful starting point. It illustrates, too, why the suppression of *Fanny Hill* is favored in some quarters. After noting that it takes the book but ten pages to locate the fifteen-year-old Miss Hill in a brothel, Mr. Justice Clark continued:[167]

> The remaining 200 pages of the book detail her initiation into various sexual experiences, from a lesbian encounter with a sister prostitute to all sorts and types of sexual debauchery in bawdy houses and as the mistress of a variety of men. This is presented to the reader through an uninterrupted succession of descriptions by Fanny, either as an observer or participant, of sexual adventures so vile that one of the male expert witnesses in the case was hesitant to repeat any one of them in the courtroom. These scenes run the gamut of possible sexual experi-

---

[166] 383 U.S. 413 (1966).

[167] *Id.* at 445–46. Sex is an ambiguous subject. Mr. Justice Clark's synopsis of *Fanny Hill*, which, swallowing his "embarrassment," he wrote to avoid "debasing" the United States Reports with quotations from the book, *id.* at 441, is not without its own unintentional double entendre. I cannot resist citing this passage by Charles Poore of the *New York Times*. Mr. Poore is discussing the ups and downs of literary fashions: "No truly outstanding effort is forever lost. Think of 'Fanny Hill,' for example. It's due for what I can only call a re-revival, spurred by Mr. Justice Tom Clark's disapproving but remarkably vivid condensation of the story, published in the papers on March 22. Many a reader of that Supreme Court document, so rich in detail, must have decided it was time to look Fanny up again. A publisher never knows from what quarter the winds of fortune will blow. Or a writer." N.Y. Times, p. 41, col. 2 (April 28, 1966).

ences such as lesbianism, female masturbation, homosexuality between young boys, the destruction of a maidenhead with consequent gory descriptions, the seduction of a young virgin boy, the flagellation of male by female, and vice versa, followed by fervid sexual engagement, and other abhorrent acts, including over two dozen separate bizarre descriptions of different sexual intercourses between male and female characters. In one sequence four girls in a bawdy house are required in the presence of one another to relate the lurid details of their loss of virginity and their glorification in it. This is followed the same evening by "publick trials" in which each of the four girls engages in sexual intercourse with a different man while the others witness, with Fanny giving a detailed description of the movement and reaction of each couple.

In each of the sexual scenes the exposed bodies of the participants are described in minute and individual detail. The pubic hair is often used for a background to the most vivid and precise descriptions of the response, condition, size, and color of the sexual organs before, during and after orgasms. There are some short transitory passages between the various sexual episodes, but for the most part they only set the scene and identify the participants for the next orgy, or make smutty reference and comparison to past episodes.

No one could seriously deny the substance of Mr. Justice Clark's description. In fact, a writer as tolerant as John Ciardi unhesitatingly declared that *Memoirs of a Woman of Pleasure* was written as "an overt piece of pornography," and "such it is today and will be to the dark end of time's last bookshelf."[168] Geoffrey Gorer, the anthropologist, has called it "one of the few masterpieces of English pornography."[169] Stanley Edgar Hyman, who opposes its suppression, described *Fanny Hill* as "a good example of pornography."[170] And even the ultratolerant Kronhausens concede that it is a "borderline" book.[171]

There are, on the other hand, persons who will step forward to testify that though Fanny may be without virtue, the book in which she appears has distinct literary merit. (A few people are willing to go much further. Mr. Justice Douglas, in an appendix to his concurring opinion in *Memoirs*, reproduced a sermon by a Universalist

---

168 Ciardi, *What Is Pornography?* 46 SATURDAY REV. 20 (July 13, 1963).

169 ROLPH (ed.), DOES PORNOGRAPHY MATTER? 29 (1961).

170 Hyman, *supra* note 107, at 13.

171 KRONHAUSEN, *op. cit. supra* note 97, at 210, and generally, 303–24.

minister who insisted that *Fanny Hill* is a profoundly "moral" allegory which is concerned with "healthy" people and which "beautifully describes meaningful relationships between a man and a woman.")[172] A number of qualified literary critics have argued that *Fanny Hill* is non-obscene, because it avoids four-letter words,[173] and because its ultimate conclusion is moral. For in the end Fanny settles down to live in marriage with a true lover and avers that sex with love is preferable to sex without love. "Lust sanctified by the power of love" supposedly is the final message of Cleland's novel.[174] Critics have, in addition, claimed that the book has a number of significant features. It is written, they say, in an elegant mid-eighteenth-century baroque style. Its theme, in the genre of Fielding's *Tom Jones,* is a conscious rebuttal to Richardson's prudish *Pamela.* And it contains some interesting and insightful descriptions of the clothes, manners, and sexual attitudes of Georgian England.[175] Such testimony made an impact in another *Fanny Hill* case when the New York Court of Appeals reversed a ban against the book saying, "It has a slight literary value and it affords some insight into the life and manners of mid-18th Century London."[176]

Mr. Justice Brennan's prevailing opinion, which commanded the assent of Chief Justice Warren and Mr. Justice Fortas, again managed to avoid an evaluation of the challenged material. The escape hatch this time was the Massachusetts court's "misinterpretation" of the social value criterion of the *Roth* test.[177] According to the Brennan opinion, *Roth v. United States* and its subsequent elaborations require the coalescence of three separate elements before material can constitutionally be labeled "obscene": the material

---

[172] 383 U.S. at 436, 438.

[173] The absence of four-letter words per se may well be irrelevant to obscene intent and effect. Consider this observation from a survey of the writing and distribution of sexy books: "Four-letter words, which are common in serious fiction, are carefully avoided because they are considered to have an anti-erotic effect on readers. One sex book writer who was asked if he used obscenity in his stories replied 'Good God, no—that's dirty.'" Montgomery, *supra* note 155.

[174] Quennell, *Introduction,* MEMOIRS OF A WOMAN OF PLEASURE, xi (Putnam ed. 1963).

[175] Such testimony, though disbelieved by the Massachusetts courts, was introduced by experts at the trial. 383 U.S. at 415–16 and n.2, 426 n.3, 447–50.

[176] Larkin v. G. P. Putnam's Sons, 14 N.Y.2d 399, 403 (1964).

[177] 383 U.S. at 419.

must (*a*) have a dominant theme in the work as a whole that appeals to prurient interest; (*b*) be patently offensive because it goes beyond contemporary community standards; and (*c*) be utterly without redeeming social value. The trial court had found *Fanny Hill* to be without artistic, literary, or scientific value; the Supreme Judicial Court agreed, commenting that the expert testimony for the defense indicating "some minimal literary value" was not equivalent to a showing of social importance. It added, "We do not interpret the 'social importance' test as requiring that a book which appeals to prurient interest and is patently offensive must be unqualifiedly worthless before it can be deemed obscene."[178] This, Mr. Justice Brennan declared, was reversible error, since a book cannot be banned "unless it is found to be *utterly* without redeeming social value."[179]

But we know from Mr. Justice Brennan's opinion in *Ginzburg v. United States* that in close cases evidence of pandering to prurient interests can taint otherwise passable material with the curse of "obscenity," and *Memoirs* would appear to be a close case. Since it is difficult to believe that G. P. Putnam's Sons published *Fanny Hill*, "after 214 years of suppression" as it emblazoned on the dust jacket, primarily to introduce American readers to John Cleland's observations on the clothing styles of eighteenth-century Londoners, was there a pandering dimension to *Memoirs?* Mr. Justice Brennan said there was not, noting that neither side had availed itself of a provision of the Massachusetts obscenity law permitting the introduction of evidence on the manner and form of publication, advertisement, and distribution. He went on to add, however, that *if* Cleland's book had prurient appeal and was patently offensive and had only a "minimum" of social value, then it *might* be obscene in settings where it was exploited for its prurient interest appeal. In such settings the book would lose its marginal social value. To quote his phrasing, ". . . where the purveyor's sole emphasis is on the sexually provocative aspects of his publications a court could accept his evaluation at its face value."[180] *Memoirs*, however, which involved the book only "in the abstract,"[181] was not such a case.

Two Justices, Black and Stewart, citing their positions in *Ginzburg* and *Mishkin*, concurred without opinion. Mr. Justice Douglas, also voting to reverse, wrote a concurring opinion that relied on

---

178 *Ibid.*   179 *Ibid.*   180 *Id.* at 420.   181 *Ibid.*

broad First Amendment grounds. He described the reason assigned in the Brennan opinion—the Massachusetts court's recognition that *Fanny Hill* might have some minimal social value—as "disingenuous," and he criticized as "inexplicable" the suggestion that advertising and promotional methods might yet make the book obscene.[182] Mr. Justice Douglas, in addition, made some comments on the behavioral consequences of reading obscenity; these will be considered later in conjunction with Mr. Justice Clark's important dissenting opinion.

The dissent of Mr. Justice Clark is important because it illustrates that the five-man majority (Mr. Justice Brennan, Chief Justice Warren, and Justices Clark, Fortas, and White) formed in the *Ginzburg* and *Mishkin* cases is an illusory majority; that the pandering "aid" brought forward in *Ginzburg* is no more likely to guide the Justices in future cases than the original *Roth* definition; and that "the truth" as to the behavioral consequences of obscenity, which we are often told may eventually be forthcoming and should settle the obscenity issue, is equally unlikely to determine the responses of legislators and judges. Each point deserves consideration in turn.

As did Mr. Justice Douglas, Mr. Justice Clark attacked the Brennan opinion for reversing the Massachusetts judgment against *Fanny Hill* because of the "casual" appellate statement that the book might have some minimal literary value.[183] But more significantly, he vigorously charged the Brennan opinion with wrongly adding a "new test"—social importance or value—to *Roth v. United States*. According to Mr. Justice Clark, the first reference to any such test was the Brennan opinion in *Jacobellis v. Ohio*, which was supported only by Mr. Justice Goldberg, since resigned. In Clark's view the *Roth* test has but two requirements: books must be judged as a whole, and they must be judged by their appeal to the prurient interest of the average person in terms of contemporary community standards. Since such material, by definition, lacks social value, the

---

[182] *Id*. at 426, 427.

[183] *Id*. at 445. He argued that the Supreme Court's action completely ignored the trial court's specific finding: "Why if the [appellate] statement is erroneous, Brother BRENNAN does not affirm the holding of the trial court which beyond question is correct, one cannot tell. This course has often been followed in other cases." *Ibid*.

social value test is a meaningless tautology.[184] A book's social importance, he agreed, is "relevant" to the ultimate question of obscenity but is by no means "a separate and distinct constitutional test."[185] On the book's merits, Mr. Justice Clark's detailed analysis of *Fanny Hill* convinced him that the experts who testified to its merits were gravely mistaken;[186] the book was obscene.

The failure of the Brennan opinions in *Ginzburg* and *Mishkin* to discuss meaningfully such seemingly crucial post-*Roth* issues as prurient appeal, patent offensiveness, and social importance now becomes clearer. They were not discussed because they could not be discussed; and they could not be discussed because the five-man "majority" was in fundamental disagreement over the meaning of *Roth v. United States*. Chief Justice Warren and Justices Brennan and Fortas believe that, among other things, the *Roth* definition of obscenity requires the coalescence of three separate tests: prurient appeal, patent offensiveness, and social value. Justices Clark and White[187] believe that prurient appeal alone suffices. There is, moreover, the strong suspicion that the disagreements of the *Ginzburg-Mishkin* "majority" go even further. For example, two years earlier in *Jacobellis* Chief Justice Warren and Mr. Justice Brennan, who united in the *Memoirs* prevailing opinion, clashed pointedly over the meaning of "community" in the *Roth* test and over whether the Court could sustain lower court obscenity judgments on "sufficient evidence."[188] Not surprisingly, the community standards and

---

184 *Id.* at 442–43. He noted that in *Roth* obscenity was described as having "such slight social value as a step to truth that any benefit that may be derived . . . is clearly outweighed by the social interest in order and morality. . . ." 354 U.S. at 485, quoting Chaplinsky v. New Hampshire, 315 U.S. 568, 571–72 (1942).

185 383 U.S. at 442. Mr. Justice White, in his separate dissenting opinion in *Memoirs*, agreed that *Roth* does not include a social value test. *Id.* at 461–62.

186 In tilting with *Fanny Hill* Mr. Justice Clark emerges as a pungent literary critic in his own right:

"Another expert described the book as having 'delectable literary merit' since it reflects 'an effort to interpret a rather complex character . . . going through a number of very different adventures.' To illustrate, his assertion that 'the writing is very skillfully done' this expert pointed to the description of a whore, 'Phoebe, who is "red faced, fat and in her early 50's, who waddles into a room." She doesn't walk in, she waddles in.' Given this standard for 'skillful writing,' it is not surprising that he found the book to have merit." *Id.* at 449.

187 See Mr. Justice White's dissenting opinion in *Memoirs*, 383 U.S. at 460.

188 378 U.S. 187–90, 192–95 (Brennan, J.); *cf.*, at 200–01, 202–03 (Warren, C. J.).

sufficient evidence questions are ignored in Mr. Justice Brennan's 1966 obscenity opinions; nor, for that matter, are they discussed in the dissenting opinions of Justices Clark and White.

The second, and related, illustration provided by Mr. Justice Clark's dissent in *Memoirs* is that the pandering trail charted in *Ginzburg* is quite likely to take its five proponents down two or three different byways. Since in *Mishkin* Mr. Justice Brennan's brief references to pandering were not dispositive,[189] *Memoirs* provides in a sense the first occasion after *Ginzburg* for assessing the potential utility of the new test. It will be recalled that in his *Memoirs* opinion Mr. Justice Brennan declared that evidence of pandering, which might well make *Fanny Hill* obscene, was not in the record and could not therefore assist in resolving the obscenity issue. But his assertion that the *Ginzburg* and *Mishkin* records were "significantly different"[190] is certainly debatable, and Mr. Justice Clark in any event did not see it that way. He argued that *Fanny Hill* was also obscene under the pandering test because of extrinsic evidence in the record "tending to show that the publisher was fully aware that the book attracted readers desirous of vicarious sexual pleasure, and sought to profit solely from its prurient appeal."[191] As examples he cited the publisher's introduction, which makes many references to the book's illicit history and "repeatedly informs the reader that he may expect graphic descriptions of genitals and sexual exploits,"[192] and the dust jacket, which announced its publication after 214 years of suppression and reproduced a suggestive excerpt from the introduction. Citing *Fanny Hill*'s well-known reputation as sensational erotica, he concluded, "I daresay that this fact alone explains why G. P. Putnam's Sons published this obscenity—preying upon prurient and carnal proclivities for its own pecuniary advantage."[193] Despite the fact that *Memoirs* does not provide a direct conflict on the pandering criterion between Justices Brennan and Clark, the early fallout of these

---

[189] As I read it, the majority opinion essentially confined itself to affirming that the definition of *Roth* used by the New York courts was correct.

[190] 383 U.S. at 417 n.3.   [191] *Id.* at 454.   [192] *Ibid.*

[193] *Id.* at 455. Mr. Justice Clark's own position is not free of ambiguity. It is not clear, for instance, whether in his view *Fanny Hill* is per se obscene because it is erotica with prurient appeal, or, whether it might be non-obscene in some "neutral" setting.

two *Ginzburg* confreres may be a telltale sign that the door to relative stability in obscenity cases is not labeled "pandering."

The third notable feature of Mr. Justice Clark's dissent in *Memoirs* is that it raised one of the "sleeper" issues in obscenity cases. Ever since *Roth v. United States* the Justices, with the exception of Justices Black and Douglas,[194] have avoided considering the alleged behavioral consequences of viewing obscenity.[195] The subject is at least indirectly relevant, since one of the primary justifications for obscenity laws is that obscenity incites sexually deviant behavior and is, in particular, a significant factor in stimulating adolescents toward premature sexual activity and juvenile delinquency.[196] From the other direction, the opponents of obscenity laws argue that illegal behavior only may constitutionally be punished. Until and unless, they claim, some causative link connecting alleged obscenity with social misbehavior is demonstrated, restrictions on reading or viewing sexual materials are not permissible. Thus, in his *Roth* dissent Mr. Justice Douglas took the position that there was an absence of "dependable information" on the impact of obscenity on human conduct, and that this should put the Court on the side

---

[194] In the dissenting *Roth* opinion by Mr. Justice Douglas. 354 U.S. at 509–11.

[195] Lower court discussions are equally rare. One of the few exceptions is Judge Jerome Frank's appendix to his concurring opinion in *Roth*. 237 F.2d at 806–27.

[196] There are a number of common justifications for antiobscenity legislation. A useful critical survey may be found in PAUL & SCHWARTZ, FEDERAL CENSORSHIP: OBSCENITY IN THE MAIL 191–202 (1961). Professor Louis Henkin, in a provocative though tentative statement, *Morals and the Constitution: The Sin of Obscenity*, 63 COLUM. L. REV. 391 (1963), has argued that obscenity laws are not primarily based on the utilitarian conviction that obscenity inspires sexual crimes. In his view these laws, whose justification he challenges, are rooted in a "nonutilitarian" religious morality: "Obscenity, at bottom, is not crime. Obscenity is sin." *Id.* at 395. Although a concern with morality is clearly one significant underpinning of the obscenity laws, I am not persuaded by Professor Henkin's summary dismissal of the "utilitarian" justifications. It seems to me far more accurate to assert that obscenity is both sin and crime. His article, moreover, overlooks the fact that much of the disputed material—and I am not referring to such sophisticated books as *Lady Chatterley's Lover* or even *Eros*—is aimed at children, and that, rightly or wrongly, a majority of our citizens perceive obscenity as a contributory cause of sex crimes and juvenile misbehavior. Finally, I think it relevant to note, in a day when the Supreme Court and most libertarians are so enamored of the freedom-loving legacy of the framers, that the founders of the Republic did not regard morality as "nonutilitarian." See generally, ROSSITER, SEEDTIME OF THE REPUBLIC (1953), and especially at 429–37.

of protecting literature, "except and unless it can be said that the particular publication has an impact on action that the government can control."[197] The rest of the Court, however, has managed largely to ignore this issue as judicially irrelevant because of its assumption that obscenity is in a class of intrinsically worthless utterances or non-speech. But in *Memoirs v. Massachusetts* Mr. Justice Clark, one of the Justices favorable to obscenity laws, felt compelled to debate the issue with Mr. Justice Douglas. On neither side were the results impressive, and this, I think, is a poor omen for those who recommend a healthy dose of empiricism as a solution to the obscenity issue.

The magnet that lured Mr. Justice Clark into discussing the effects of obscenity was two-pronged. In part, it was Mr. Justice Douglas' concurring opinion, which argued the absence of any proof linking obscenity to antisocial conduct, and in part, it was "the new requirement engrafted upon *Roth*"[198] by Mr. Justice Brennan's opinion. Because of the social value test, Mr. Justice Clark believed that the question of antisocial effect had suddenly become relevant to the question of social value. "To say," he wrote, "that social value may 'redeem' implies that courts must balance alleged esthetic merit against the harmful consequences that may flow from pornography."[199] On this point, he argued that behavioral scientists are divided on the relationship between obscenity and socially harmful behavior. Mr. Justice Clark cited a major survey of psychological and physiological studies on the effect that obscene books and pictures have on people.[200] It clearly indicates, he contended, that such material is sexually arousing.[201] Although conceding that such erotic stimulation does not necessarily lead to social misbehavior, he cited "medical experts" and "a number of sociologists" who "believe" and "think" that it does. His experts were

---

[197] 354 U.S. at 511.   [198] 383 U.S. at 451.   [199] *Ibid.*

[200] Cairns, Paul, & Wishner, *Sex Censorship: The Assumptions of Anti-Obscenity Laws and the Empirical Evidence*, 46 MINN. L. REV. 1009 (1962). The authors, two psychologists and a law professor, canvassed scientific reports between 1925 and 1961 and searched the files of the Institute for Sex Research.

[201] Mr. Justice Clark's summary, as far as it goes, is accurate. The authors concluded that the studies demonstrate that many Americans are mentally and physically aroused "to some extent" by sexual stimuli in pictures and "probably" also in books. These propositions refer to immediate, and not long-range, effects. *Id.* at 1032, 1034.

Dr. Frederic Wertham,[202] Dr. George W. Henry,[203] and Professor
Pitrim A. Sorokin.[204] Mr. Justice Clark in addition found "persuasive evidence" linking obscene material to sex crimes in the
testimony of police officials[205] and also in the "belief" of "the

[202] WERTHAM, SEDUCTION OF THE INNOCENT 164 (1954), where Dr. Wertham
asserts: "Our researches have proved that there is a significant correlation between
crime-comics reading and the more serious forms of juvenile delinquency." A correlation, however, does not prove cause and effect. More important, Dr. Wertham's
undocumented study of comic books, based on his clinical practice as a psychiatrist,
is filled with similar assertions. It does not rely on any statistically adequate samples,
nor on any controlled experiments. For a critique, see Denney, *The Dark Fantastic*,
130 NEW REPUBLIC 18 (May 3, 1954). Those who are concerned with the current
Batman craze induced by the television series may be further concerned by Dr.
Wertham's conclusion that "the Batman stories are psychologically homosexual":
"Only someone ignorant of the fundamentals of psychiatry and of the psycho-
pathology of sex can fail to realize a subtle atmosphere of homoeroticism which
pervades the adventures of the mature 'Batman' and his young friend 'Robin.' "
Op. cit. supra, at 189–90.

[203] Testimony before the Subcommittee of the Judiciary Committee To Investigate Juvenile Delinquency, S. Rep. No. 2381, 84th Cong., 2d Sess., 8–12 (1956).
Dr. Henry, a professor of clinical psychiatry at the Cornell University College of
Medicine, testified that in his opinion books and photographs on sexual perversions
are at least partly responsible for sex crimes. This excerpt is typical: "There is . . .
quite a large proportion of the population who are susceptible to training, training
such as may be obtained from these publications, and whether or not they arrive
at a point of violence is perhaps an academic matter in view of the other problem
that no one can tell ahead of time who is going to arrive at the goal once they have
been exposed to these publications." *Id*. at 11. No empirical data were offered.

[204] SOROKIN, THE AMERICAN SEX REVOLUTION (1956). The choice of this undocumented book to represent "a number of sociologists" is curious. While Sorokin's
thesis that every aspect of American culture "is packed with sex obsession" is
certainly arguable, he nowhere discusses the problem of obscenity and behavior
except in the most general way. Thus, the assertion about American sex obsession
is followed by a horrendous cataloging of the "rising tide" of sexually stimulated
crimes: ". . . acts of rape, of sadism and masochism; the poisoning of parents by
children anxious to obtain life insurance monies for the maintenance of their 'flames';
the crimes of husbands killing their wives, or of wives murdering their husbands
in order to gain freedom for the satisfaction of their drives; the activities of play
boys and play girls engaged in the business of seducers, procurers, and panderers;
the expanding trade of selling and buying sex services. . . ." *Id*. at 54–55. At times
Professor Sorokin's book takes on truly Spenglerian overtones as it links the "new
sex freedom" to America's drift "toward social revolution and political disorder,
toward international conflict, toward a general decline of creativity and irremediable decay of our culture." *Id*. at 133.

[205] His police officials were a Detroit police inspector who in 1952 contended
that sex murder cases were "invariably" tied to obscene writings, 383 U.S. at 452, and
J. Edgar Hoover. Although again conceding the absence of conclusive evidence,
Mr. Justice Clark contended that the files of law enforcement agencies "contain

clergy."[206] Finally, he observed that Congress and every state legislature has passed antiobscenity laws, which, in part, are justified by reference to evidence linking obscenity to socially deviant behavior.[207] And this evidence, no less than evidence showing that challenged material has "social value," may be introduced by the parties to obscenity cases.

With the single exception of the Cairns, Paul, and Wishner survey, which can be cited both ways,[208] Mr. Justice Douglas' con-

---

many reports of persons who patterned their criminal conduct after behavior depicted in obscene material." *Id.* at 453. The authorities are two pieces by the FBI Director: Hoover, *Combating Merchants of Filth: The Role of the FBI,* 25 U. PITT. L. REV. 469 (1964), and, *The Fight against Filth,* 70 AM. LEG. MAG. 17 (May, 1961). The following excerpt is typical of Mr. Hoover's argument: "On the West Coast, a young hitchhiker was picked up by two men and driven to an apartment where he was subjected to horrifying indecencies. When police, acting on information supplied by the victim, located the two men involved, a virtual storehouse of obscene photographs, literature and other pornographic material was seized." 25 U. PITT. L. REV. at 469.

[206] His clergy were Cardinal Spellman, who in a 1964 speech "stressed the direct influence obscenity has on immature persons," 383 U.S. at 453, and the Reverend Donald Soper, a Methodist minister at the West London Mission for delinquent women. At the cited pages in ROLPH, op. cit. *supra* note 169, at 47–48, Reverend Soper asserts that pornography is a primary cause of prostitution among the girls cared for at his mission; it promises the potential prostitute "excitement" and "kicks" through sensual experiences and helps to overthrow a girl's scruples. The Reverend Soper does not offer evidence that the girls were exposed to pornography (and what kind and for how long) and does not consider any other factors which might conceivably lead girls to prostitution. Elsewhere, however, and with a similar lack of documentation, he writes, "there is an unmistakable relationship between pornography and the drinking habit. . . . drinking, and social drinking in particular, are prime stimulants of pornography." *Id.* at 46. For a contrary clerical view, see Moody, *Toward a New Definition of Obscenity,* 24 CHRISTIANITY AND CRISIS 284 (Jan. 25, 1965).

[207] A typical illustration of the sources of these legislative justifications, which Mr. Justice Clark cited, is the Report of the New York State Joint Legislative Committee Studying the Publication and Dissemination of Offensive and Obscene Material (1958). This and similar reports for other years in the late 1950's and early 1960's include surveys of the kinds of material available and the opinions of the committee and the testimony of selected state law enforcement officials that "filth for profit" incites or stimulates youngsters to commit delinquent acts; the concern is almost entirely with the impact of obscenity on juveniles. Mr. Justice Clark also cited T. J. MURPHY, CENSORSHIP: GOVERNMENT AND OBSCENITY 131–51 (1963), which contains an excellent and thoughtful summary of such evidence as exists on the socially harmful consequences of obscenity. Father Murphy's book, however, is flawed by its apparent assumption that the First Amendment mainly covers political speech and not artistic and literary expression.

[208] Since it is a judicious appraisal, this study, *supra* note 200, can furnish ammunition to both friends and foes of obscenity legislation.

curring opinion in *Memoirs* cited a different set of experts to challenge the justification that obscenity laws help in the fight against social misbehavior. His primary citations were intended to demonstrate that the relationship between obscenity and antisocial sexual conduct "has yet to be proven."[209] In his view, there must be more than "a horrible example or two of the perpetrator of a crime of sexual violence, in whose pocket is found a pornographic book" before "a regime of censorship" can be imposed on the nation in violation of the First Amendment.[210]

Although Mr. Justice Douglas is correct in asserting that there is as yet no empirical proof that obscenity contributes to sexual crimes, his use of the studies is partisan and profoundly misleading. For one thing, while these studies all agree that a causal link has not been demonstrated, they are equally agreed that a causal link has not been disproved either.[211] For another, it is not clear why, in a situation of divided experts and conflicting opinions, the burden of rigorous empirical proof must be met by those who favor obscenity

---

[209] 383 U.S. at 431, citing Cairns, Paul, & Wishner, *supra* note 200, at 1035; Lockhart & McClure, *supra* note 10, at 383–87; and United States v. Roth, 237 F.2d 796, 815–16 (Frank, J., concurring), which contains a summary of a study prepared by Dr. Marie Jahoda.

[210] 383 U.S. at 432. In a footnote he comments, "It would be a futile effort even for a censor to attempt to remove all that might possibly stimulate antisocial sexual conduct." *Id.* at n. 11. He thereupon cites E. F. Murphy, *The Value of Pornography,* 10 WAYNE L. REV. 655, 668 (1964), for the proposition that obscenity is absolutely subjective—it all depends on the eyes and personality of the beholder. This is illustrated by the fact that a German rapist claimed that he was prompted to his crimes by Cecil B. De Mille's *The Ten Commandments,* and that an English vampire murderer (who sucked his victims' blood through soda straws) claimed that he was inspired to his deeds by an Anglican High Church Service. Aside from the fact that Professor Murphy fails to prove conclusively the cause and effect relationship in these two incidents, one can agree that even Mickey Mouse cartoons may stimulate some sick people into crime. But merely because we cannot remove "all" that might stimulate antisocial conduct scarcely proves that society is unjustified in trying to strike at "some," *i.e.,* obscenity.

[211] Cairns, Paul, & Wishner, *supra* note 200, at 1035; Lockhart & McClure, *supra* note 10, at 384–85. Dr. Jahoda, in her summary for Judge Frank, declared, "There exists no research evidence either to prove or to disprove this assumption definitively." 237 F.2d at 815. In fact, the legal member of the Cairns, Paul, & Wishner team (Professor J. C. N. Paul) took the position that obscenity is qualitatively different from other speech; that it may exert strong and socially undesirable influences on some sexually immature people; and that such people, while relatively small in numbers, might be numerically significant. *Supra* note 200, at 1040.

laws.[212] Of course, it may be said with Mr. Justice Douglas that obscenity is "speech" and that we are in the area of an absolute First Amendment, where not even the slightest abridgment is permissible until speech mixes with illegal action. Those who reason thus are unlikely to be persuaded, but the short answer to such contentions is that to those who framed it the First Amendment was not so absolute,[213] and that at other times in our constitutional history other, currently less favored, rights were similarly defended as intentionally and inherently absolute.[214]

Mr. Justice Douglas went beyond his challenge to the asserted behavioral consequences of obscenity to "speculate" that "one might guess that literature of the most pornographic sort would, in many cases, provide a substitute—not a stimulus—for antisocial sexual conduct."[215] This is best described as the "safety valve" thesis: the acquisition and the reading and viewing of obscene writings and pictures (probably accompanied by masturbatory fantasies) provides sexually immature persons with a harmless outlet for their potentially antisocial impulses. Or, as the angry proprietor of a store in New York's Times Square specializing in sex books and pictures put it after a police raid, "By selling this stuff we prevent sex crimes."[216] Two things seem evident with regard to the safety valve thesis. First, it is no more susceptible to conclusive empirical proof (or disproof) than the assumption that obscenity plays some role in sexual crimes. Second, it would, if ever widely accepted, provide, under the premises of the Brennan opinion in *Memoirs*, enough social value to redeem constitutionally every piece of pornography ever produced.

The most that can be said for the exchange in the *Memoirs* case between Justices Clark and Douglas on the subject of empirical

---

[212] The most sophisticated justifications for such laws do not in fact claim that obscenity is the sole or even the primary cause of sexual crime: "The fallacy is in concluding that because it is not the primary cause of the disorder it is no cause at all." T. J. MURPHY, *op. cit. supra* note 207, at 146.

[213] See LEVY, LEGACY OF SUPPRESSION (1960).

[214] McCLOSKEY, AMERICAN CONSERVATISM IN THE AGE OF ENTERPRISE, 1865–1910 (1951); MAGRATH, YAZOO: LAW AND POLITICS IN THE NEW REPUBLIC (1966).

[215] 383 U.S. at 432, citing E. F. Murphy, *supra* note 210, at 661 n. 19. For additional speculation along this line see Cairns, Paul, & Wishner, *supra* note 200, at 1036; Hyman, *supra* note 107; Kronhausen, *supra* note 97, at 337–38.

[216] N.Y. Times, p. 39, col. 6 (Feb. 26, 1964).

justifications for obscenity laws is that it is instructive. It teaches us not to expect too much help for the judiciary from social scientists and other experts in solving obscenity issues. It is surely no coincidence that both Justices drew almost all of their expert ammunition from different armories. In the one instance where Justices Clark and Douglas drew from the same source, they drew very selectively to bolster predetermined interpretations.[217] Naturally, it is possible, though I strongly doubt it, that in future cases the Court might engage in a dispassionate canvassing of social science evidence that could provide useful guidance. My doubt is based not on any assumption that the Justices' attitudes are frozen (though this cannot be entirely discounted), but on the assumption that at least for the foreseeable future social science cannot conclusively settle the question of obscenity and its social effects. Certainly at present the social science data are still inconclusive.[218] My long-range pessimism is based on the fact that the most sophisticated empirically based studies find their ultimate explanations of social and psychological events in multiple causes; and the most sophisti-

---

[217] This may be somewhat unfair to Mr. Justice Clark, who chose the easier task of merely showing that the experts were divided. As I read his opinion, however, he is in agreement with the views he cited.

[218] The most recent major study to come to my attention is GEBHARD, GAGNON, POMEROY, & CHRISTENSON, SEX OFFENDERS: AN ANALYSIS OF TYPES (1965), the latest publication of the Institute for Sex Research. After a careful survey of numerous types of sexual offenders, who were measured against samples of prisoners convicted of non-sexual crimes and an outside "normal" control group, the authors concluded that "it would appear that the possession of pornography does not differentiate sex offenders from nonsex offenders." Id. at 678. On the other hand, the study develops data which could be used by defenders of obscenity laws. Thus, it found that among those most aroused by pornography were homosexual offenders (against adults) and heterosexual offenders (against minors). Id. at 671. And with regard to the arousal of heterosexual aggressors from sadomasochistic materials it concluded: "While it is probable that in a few cases such stimuli triggered an offense, it seems reasonable to believe that they do not play an important role in the precipitation of sex offenses in general, and at most only a minor role in sex offenses involving violence." Id. at 669. One could argue that even a few cases justify the suppression of worthless sadomasochistic material. A significant, and perhaps unavoidable limitation of the study, is that its examination of psychosexual arousal was not empirically tested but depended on interviewees' statements that certain materials had in the past aroused or failed to arouse them. Nor, of course, do the authors present any actual proof of the immediate and long-range impact of pornographic materials on the sex offenders.

cated defenses of obscenity laws equally stress the multiplicity of causes affecting personal and social behavior.[219]

And if multiple causation is king, will it not be exceedingly difficult ever to prove or to disprove conclusively that obscenity is either partly responsible or wholly blameless for antisocial behavior? While it would be foolish to deny the possibility that some day social scientists may successfully factor out the relative impact (or non-impact) of allegedly obscene materials on human conduct, setting up the kind of controlled and empirically valid experiments required in this most delicate area of human personality and sexual and social conduct will be unusually challenging. The studies, for example, would have to explore the actual behavioral impact of obscenity on persons over a long period of time while holding constant such variables as education and social and economic status. Equally important, since so much of the concern is over the impact of obscenity on youngsters, some of the most crucial studies would have to obtain samples of children and adolescents who could be exposed to various forms of obscenity and whose behavior would have to be followed over a long time span. Despite the vivid demonstration provided by Masters and Johnson's recent study, *Human Sexual Response*, that some adults can be induced to serve as sexual guinea pigs,[220] few adults, I suspect, are yet willing to volunteer their children to social science. Geoffrey Gorer's comment still seems apt: "I do not think any responsible person would countenance putting the two forms of literature [pornographic and non-pornographic] in the hands of a properly selected sample of youngsters to test their reactions. This is however the only way in which the issue could be scientifically decided."[221] There are, of course, other problems too. Not only are there justifications for obscenity laws that do not turn on the alleged impact of obscenity on behavior,[222] but it is most doubtful that the defenders of these laws, who enjoy strong public support, are pre-

---

[219] Cairns, Paul, & Wishner, *supra* note 200, at 1035–36; St. John-Stevas, Obscenity and the Law 195–202 (1956); *cf.*, T. J. Murphy, *op. cit. supra* note 207, at 131–51.

[220] Masters & Johnson, Human Sexual Response (1966).

[221] Rolph, *op. cit. supra* note 169, at 40.

[222] As, for example, the government's right (in response to popular desires) to protect the psychic integrity of its citizens. Schwartz, *supra* note 126, at 671, and generally, 672–73.

pared to concede their fate solely to the findings of social science experts. There are, after all, as Mr. Justice Clark's opinion pointed out, other "experts"—clergymen, legislators, and police officials—who wish to be heard and who can claim that obscenity is much too important to be left only to the social scientists.

The other dissenting opinions in *Memoirs v. Massachusetts* can be disposed of in a few words. Mr. Justice White indicated that for him the *Roth* test properly focused on a book's predominant theme and not on some small and incidental social value that it might have.[223] Mr. Justice Harlan dissented, even though he asserted that *Fanny Hill* was not hard-core pornography and could not be banned by the federal government. The book, while it has "some quantum of social value," is offensive and salacious and could therefore be proscribed by the state without violating constitutional limits.[224] Mr. Justice Harlan's dissenting opinion also included what undoubtedly stands as the greatest understatement of the 1965 Term. It makes an appropriate conclusion to this part of the analysis: "The central development that emerges from the aftermath of *Roth v. United States* is that no stable approach to the obscenity problem has yet been devised by this Court."[225]

V. The Law of Obscenity: A Constitutional Disaster Area

Another way to describe the fruits of the Supreme Court's labors in the vineyard of obscenity law is that it has produced five separate and contradictory tests: one anti-*Roth* test and four *Roth* tests. Without considering the refinements and special nuances, the five tests and their judicial sponsors can be summarized this way:

1. All material is constitutionally protected, except where it can be shown to be so brigaded with illegal action that it constitutes a clear and present danger to significant social interests. Justices Black and Douglas.

2. All material is constitutionally protected at both the federal and state level except hard-core pornography. Mr. Justice Stewart.

3. All material is constitutionally protected at the federal level except hard-core pornography; material may be suppressed at the

---

[223] 383 U.S. at 461–62.   [224] *Id.* at 459.   [225] *Id.* at 455.

state level if reasonable evidence supports a finding that it is salacious and prurient. Mr. Justice Harlan.

4. Material may be suppressed both by the federal and state governments when prurient appeal, patent offensiveness, and an utter lack of social value coalesce; in addition, in close cases evidence that the producer or distributor commercially exploited the material so as to emphasize its pruriency withdraws constitutional protection from otherwise protected material. Chief Justice Warren and Justices Brennan and Fortas.

5. Material may be suppressed if its dominant appeal taken as a whole is to prurient interest. Justices Clark and White.

Of these five tests the "hardest" and most certain, which, strictly speaking, is a position and not a test, is that of Justices Black and Douglas. Except for the fact that the anticensorship party in every obscenity case heard by the Supreme Court can count on two automatic votes,[226] the Black-Douglas position is legally insignificant. In the ten years since *Butler v. Michigan* not a single other vote has been attracted to their position in spite of the fact that thirteen other Justices have served on the Court. Although lower court judges are naturally bound in First Amendment cases to the Supreme Court's determination that obscenity may be censored, it is my impression that little sympathy for the Black-Douglas stand exists among the lower federal and state judiciary.[227]

More important, there is in the United States a governmental and popular consensus in favor of antiobscenity control. Not only the federal government but every state and many municipalities have legislated against obscenity. The most recent polling survey appears to confirm that public opinion strongly favors these laws and, indeed, would like them to be even stricter.[228] Such laws

---

[226] The inevitable consequence of applying the clear-and-present-danger concept, which was formulated in the context of political expression, to artistic and literary expression is to rule automatically in favor of the challenged utterance. For a general discussion see BERNS, FREEDOM, VIRTUE AND THE FIRST AMENDMENT 48–72 (1957); see also FREUND, THE SUPREME COURT OF THE UNITED STATES 42–44 (1961).

[227] The only exceptions that come readily to mind are Judge Frank's concurring opinion in *Roth*, 237 F.2d at 801, and Judge Bok's opinion in *Commonwealth v. Gordon*, 66 Pa. D. & C. 101 (1949). State courts are free to construe the guarantees of their state constitutions more strictly than the federal guarantee; this has been done, for example, with respect to religion clauses.

[228] A Gallup poll on October 15, 1965, reported that 58 per cent of the respondents in a national sample felt that their state laws are "not strict enough" in regulat-

represent a firm national decision that obscenity is socially dangerous and morally repugnant. Although it is possible to object to
the constitutionality of governmental policies that promote moral
objectives, it must be recognized that many public policies—
whether civil rights laws, social welfare laws, or obscenity laws—
are an inextricable mixture of moral and pragmatic considerations.[229] Moreover, purely from a political point of view the national consensus in favor of obscenity controls cannot be lightly
disregarded. There are, presumably, political limitations on how
far even the Warren Court can go in challenging established policies and institutional arrangements. A decision constitutionally
voiding all federal and state obscenity laws might well provoke
Congress and President to join with the state governments in
severe resistance to the Court's decree—a resistance in which the
real loser could be currently protected artistic and literary expression.

To say that national sentiment must be regarded is not to say
that it must be slavishly followed, that Aristophanes' *Lysistrata* or
Goya's *Naked Maja* must be censored because a thoughtless Post
Office Department deems them to be immoral.[230] But it is to say
that in an area such as obscenity, where not all of the material is
even remotely comparable to Aristophanes' *Lysistrata* or Goya's
Naked Maja, and where the constitutional commands are not
demonstrably against a very limited form of censorship, the Court
may properly give some deference to the social welfare considerations that an overwhelming national majority believes justify antiobscenity legislation.

If the Black-Douglas position, then, is legally insignificant and
politically unrealistic, a relative solution to the obscenity problem
must be sought within the general framework of the Court major-

---

ing the sale of "dirty books"; 15 per cent felt the laws were "about right"; 23 per
cent had "no opinion"; and only 4 per cent felt the laws were "too strict." Even
college-educated persons in the sample, who tend to be the most tolerant in such
matters, favored stricter censorship by a 4-to-1 margin. American Institute of Public Opinion, "Public Dissatisfied with Laws Regulating Sale of 'Dirty Books,'"
Oct. 15, 1965.

[229] For a discussion, see ROSTOW, THE SOVEREIGN PREROGATIVE: THE SUPREME
COURT AND THE QUEST FOR LAW 45–80 (1962); Schwartz, *supra* note 126; *cf.* Henkin,
supra note 196.

[230] PAUL & SCHWARTZ, *op. cit. supra* note 196, at 104, 182–83.

ity's conclusion that some obscenity is beyond constitutional protection. The difficulty, however, as we have repeatedly seen, is that the solutions offered by the presently dominant procensorship majority—Chief Justice Warren and Justices Brennan, Clark, Fortas, and White, joined by Mr. Justice Harlan in state cases—are unusually subjective. For reasons discussed in my concluding section, I believe that the hard-core pornography test predicted by Professor Kalven and proposed by Mr. Justice Stewart (and by Mr. Justice Harlan in federal cases) offers a sensible and workable definition of obscenity.

But before examining this possible answer, it is necessary to insist, respectfully but firmly, that the Court has turned the law of obscenity into a constitutional disaster area. This judgment, I submit, involves more than a compulsive yearning for neat doctrines wrapped in tidy judicial packages. It is, rather, a matter of assuming, perhaps naïvely, that the Supreme Court of the United States has some responsibility to provide some guidelines to the nation's bar and bench in a significant legal area that concerns the authors, publishers, and distributors of books, magazines, and motion pictures.[231] At least until 1966, although the Court's disposition of obscenity cases revealed severe internal divisions and doctrinal confusion, the decisional results indicated an unarticulated pragmatic consensus—"a reasonable measure of reckonability"[232]—that hard-core pornography alone was censorable obscenity.

---

[231] "From a comparative study of the decisions the Bar must be able to form an intelligent professional judgment to predict, as well as it can, future judicial action in obscenity cases and advise those who would print books accordingly. And in this field, as in others, it is an essential judicial function to provide a reasonable measure of reckonability." Larkin v. G. P. Putnam's Sons, 14 N.Y.2d 399, 403 (1964). The state of Rhode Island, for example, which has conscientiously sought to pattern its obscenity laws on federal constitutional requirements, has found little assistance in the Supreme Court's decisions. In 1965 the legislature asked the State Legislative Council to study the Court's decisions and to prepare new legislation. The Council's study and proposals were based on all of the Court's decisions, including those of the 1965 Term which, in the words of its director, failed to provide "good guidelines." Providence Evening Bulletin, p. 8, col. 1 (May 3, 1966). And see generally, Kaul, *The State Tries Again on Obscenity*, Providence Sunday Journal, p. N-36, col. 1 (May 8, 1966). Arkansas has experienced the identical difficulty. Arkansas Legislative Council, Obscenity Laws of the Various States—A Brief Summary (1966).

[232] 14 N.Y.2d at 403.

As a consequence of the obscenity decisions of 1966, even this measure of unarticulated result-oriented guidance has evaporated. Particularly is this true now that an uneasy five-man majority, perhaps gathered together for only a fleeting moment, has announced what, with some looseness of expression, may be called the *Ginzburg* pandering doctrine: material that is not obscene may become "obscene" when its prurient appeal is commercially exploited. For in sum and in substance the net result of *Ginzburg v. United States* is to add yet another layer of subjectivity (the motives of the producer and the distributor as reflected in their advertising and promotion) onto the subjective and shifting definitions of obscenity that have been the legacy of *Roth v. United States*.

If the Court pursues the *Ginzburg* doctrine in future obscenity cases, and sooner or later lower court pressures will compel it to expand or contract the new test, many of the hard questions avoided in the 1966 cases will have to be answered. How, for instance, will the Court assess the motives of sellers? Does a venerable firm such as G. P. Putnam's Sons (established in 1838) publish *Fanny Hill* solely to make money, or does it publish the book at least in part because of its historical interest and marginal literary value and because many publishers like to develop large and varied offerings? Ralph Ginzburg presumably did not publish *Eros* solely out of a commitment to beauty and truth; yet are his motives, which might well also include a fierce ideological conviction that sex ought to be discussed more openly, any more disreputable than those of the prestigious G. P. Putnam's Sons?[233] If, as many people

---

[233] Ralph Ginzburg, in fact, is able to justify himself with eloquence and force: "I *am* a vigorous, energetic promoter and hustler, but that doesn't preclude my being a serious publisher. Under all the razzle-dazzle, flash, noise and promotion I come up with, there is a very real, beautiful, important and worthwhile philosophy. It is a philosophy that will endure, and I express it in my publications. . . . It boils down to two words: *simple honesty* . . . about all the fields that are hypocritically dealt with by the bulk of American journalism." *Playboy Interview: Ralph Ginzburg*, 13 PLAYBOY 124 (July, 1966). Are, one wonders, Ginzburg's motives and philosophy legally more censurable than those of the Bernard Geis Associates and the Doubleday Book Shops, which have published and promoted Jacqueline Susann's best-selling novel, *Valley of the Dolls*, with an ad containing this "conversation" between two of America's literati:

"What a movie it's going to make!"

"But how will they handle the nude swimming pool scene on page 260?" Advertisement, N.Y. Times, p. 40, cols. 5, 6 (April 6, 1966).

believe, human motives are mixed and complex, the Court may well need to hire a resident psychiatrist to assist it in future obscenity cases.

Mr. Justice Brennan in his *Ginzburg* opinion, of course, called primary attention to the actual advertising and promotion. In that case, given his premises, the sexy emphasis in the *Eros* brochures and the use of a mailing address with a suggestive name made his decision relatively easy. Future cases will be more difficult. Advertising in America has both its admirers and detractors; but few will deny that in sophistication, ingenuity, and technical skill it is unsurpassed in the modern world. If the hard sell, which potentially brands a sexy book or picture as impermissibly prurient, is out, why not the soft sell? The public, one attorney specializing in obscenity law has commented, "will soon know that the more circumspect the ad the rougher the material. They'll just make the same stuff look like a religious book."[234] Admittedly, it will be hard to advertise *Fanny Hill* without some reference to Fanny's occupation and the book's underground history; yet I do not for a moment doubt that it can be done. (As a matter of fact, *Fanny Hill*'s distributors need make reference only to its confrontation with the Justices, noting that it has been "approved by the United States Supreme Court.")[235] Subsequent to the *Ginzburg* ruling, for instance, Grove Press ran full-page ads for its *Story of O* that simply reproduced a *New York Times* review of the book. The review, entitled "The Uses of Pornography," points out that the book, in order to achieve its artistic purposes, uses "erotic fantasies of the most perverted 'hard-core' sort to elicit erotic reactions in the reader" and that it reeks with "the whips and chains and other paraphernalia of sadism."[236] Are the motives of Grove Press good or bad? Does its advertising for *Story of O* deliberately emphasize the book's pruriency and sadism?

The new subjectivity does not end here, for in order to apply the pandering test conscientiously, the Court will need to determine the primary audiences of challenged material and then deter-

---

[234] Mr. Ephraim London, quoted in N.Y. Times, p. 31, col. 5 (March 24, 1966).

[235] See, *e.g.*, *supra* note 167.

[236] *Supra* note 90. Grove Press has published the book at a $6.00 price, packaged it in a plain white dust jacket with an unobtrusive "limited to adults" notation, and larded the book with respectable introductory material.

mine its effect (or that of its advertising) on the intended recipients. There is, finally, another kind of problem that the *Ginzburg* doctrine may produce. Assume that a publisher (or a local distributor) treats a non-obscene but sexy book as "obscene" in his advertising and promotion and that the book is then censored as obscene by a governmental unit. In such a case has the First Amendment right of the author (who customarily has no control over the advertising and marketing of his book) to disseminate his written work been abridged? If so, who is the culprit, the prurient-minded publisher or distributor? Under such circumstances could an author bring an action against the publisher or distributor for defaming his work as "obscene" and destroying its constitutional protection? Even if one assumes that an author, in consenting to the publication of his book, consents also to the publisher's promotion, it seems farfetched to argue that he has consented to the vagaries of a bookseller's or a distributor's promotional techniques.[237]

Before departing from the *Ginzburg* pandering doctrine, we must note its partial resemblance to the "variable obscenity approach" (as distinguished from the "constant obscenity approach" of *Roth*), first fully developed by Professors Lockhart and McClure and strongly recommended as a solution to the obscenity issue.[238] In fact, *Rebhuhn v. United States*, on which Mr. Justice Brennan relied so heavily in *Ginzburg*, despite its absence from the legal briefs, may well have been suggested to him by one of

---

[237] A leading trade journal of the publishing industry has expressed an analogous fear with respect to the interests of publishers: ". . . it [the *Ginzburg* decision] suggests the prospect that any 'risque' bookseller could include any 'risque' ad—without prior knowledge of the publisher resulting in the book's being forced off sale in the jurisdiction where the ad appeared." 189 PUBLISHER'S WEEKLY 41 (April 4, 1966). People are often judged by the company they voluntarily keep. Should books also be judged by the company they involuntarily keep?

[238] See their two articles, *supra* note 7, at 77–88, 96–97, and *supra* note 10, at 340–42, 394–95. CRAIG, SUPPRESSED BOOKS 195–206 (1963), contains a good summary of the variable approach and was cited by Mr. Justice Brennan in his *Ginzburg* discussion of pandering. 383 U.S. at 472 n. 14. The revised concept of "average person" in *Mishkin* is a feature of the Lockhart & McClure test and was cited by Mr. Justice Brennan's opinion, 383 U.S. at 509 n. 7. Without much explanation, Chief Justice Warren endorsed the variable approach in *Kingsley Books*, 354 U.S. at 446; in *Roth*, 354 U.S. at 495–96; and, with Mr. Justice Clark, in *Jacobellis*, 378 U.S. at 201. Another leading recommendation in favor of the variable approach may be found in PAUL & SCHWARTZ, *op. cit. supra* note 196, at 205–19.

the Lockhart and McClure articles.[239] Since the *Ginzburg* decision
may mean that the Justices are becoming attracted to the concept
of variable obscenity, I think it important to call attention to the
pitfalls lurking within what is outwardly a very appealing proposal.

First, however, consider its basic proposition:[240]

> Variable obscenity provides solutions to most of the prob-
> lems that constant obscenity leaves unresolved. Under variable
> obscenity, material is judged by its appeal to and effect upon
> the audience to which the material is primarily directed. In this
> view, material is never inherently obscene; instead its obscenity
> varies with the circumstances of its dissemination. Material
> may be obscene when directed to one class of persons but not
> when directed to another. . . . Variable obscenity also makes it
> possible to reach, under obscenity statutes, the panderer who
> advertises and pushes non-pornographic material as if it were
> hard-core pornography, seeking out an audience of the sexu-
> ally immature who bring their "pornographic intent to some-
> thing which is not itself pornographic."

It is equally important to note carefully Professors Lockhart and
McClure's awareness that variable obscenity is not free of its own
difficulties. "To be," they write, "a reasonably satisfactory tool for
discriminating between obscene and non-obscene material in circumstances that vary in many different ways, variable obscenity
requires, in each case, careful delineation of the audience to which
material is primarily directed and evaluation of the nature of the
material's appeal to or impact upon persons making up the particular audience."[241] (Of course, nothing remotely resembling

---

[239] In the 1960 Lockhart & McClure article we find this notation: "For an illustration of how the variable obscenity concept reaches the panderer of non-pornographic material, see United States v. Rebhuhn, 109 F.2d 512 (2d Cir. 1940)." *Supra*
note 7, at 77 n. 426.

[240] *Id.* at 77, quoting Margaret Mead and citing *United States v. Rebhuhn.*

[241] *Id.* at 78, and generally, 78–80. They recommend, moreover, that "the intrinsic
nature of the material" determine where the burden of proof lies in determining
its primary audience and its appeal. If the material is hard-core pornography, the
burden of disproving inferences about its intended audience and appeal ought to
rest with the seller; if, however, the material is not intrinsically hard-core pornography, the burden of proving an intent to pander should lie with the prosecution.
The authors provide an example which shows that the Court, had it fully followed their variable approach, ought to have reversed Ginzburg's conviction.
Id. at 81–82.

careful "delineations" and "evaluations" occurred in the Court's *Ginzburg* and *Mishkin* decisions.)[242] Moreover, since Professors Lockhart and McClure recognize the enormous subjectivism inherent in the *Roth* definition of obscenity, they recommend the application of their variable concept solely to material *treated* as hard-core pornography.[243]

The Lockhart-McClure proposal, it must be conceded, seems attractive, and the reasons, I think, are obvious. Not only are its authors distinguished scholars who have written with balance, thoroughness, and tolerance on a vexing subject, but their proposal seeks to place obscenity in *context*. It seeks to take account of all the facts, all the factors, and all the diversities of human motive and personality. At a time when a tolerant relativism and not a dogmatic absolutism seems most often appropriate to the "proximate solution" of the "insoluble problems"[244] that confront the American democracy, the concept of variable obscenity has understandable appeal for judges and scholars who, at their best, think in terms of contextual settings and precise distinctions.

Yet, in spite of the qualifications carefully drawn by Professors Lockhart and McClure, the concept is likely to read much better in legal journals than it does in the United States Reports. To be sure, the mutilated versions of variable obscenity in the *Ginzburg* and *Mishkin* decisions are not a complete and a fair test. They do, however, demonstrate some of the serious difficulties in seeking to prove the intent of those who sell books, magazines, and pictures and in trying to assess the message conveyed by their advertising.[245] Even if these difficulties can be overcome, the variable obscenity approach is rooted, I believe, in the fundamental misconception that hard-core pornography does not appeal to "sexually mature" persons.[246] And it leads in consequence to an unjustifiable public policy that mature and sophisticated persons (assuming they can be easily identified) may have access to material

---

[242] See text at notes 92–147, 148–65, *supra.*

[243] Lockhart & McClure, *supra* note 7, at 80.

[244] The phrase belongs to Reinhold Niebuhr. THE CHILDREN OF LIGHT AND THE CHILDREN OF DARKNESS 118 (1944).

[245] See text *supra* at notes 233–37.

[246] Professor Schwartz, *supra* note 126, at 679, has also remarked that variable obscenity rests on a "mistaken view." And see note 250 *infra.*

that can be denied to the "sexually immature" when, in relation
to this latter audience, the distributor has treated the material as
hard-core pornography.[247]

The basic assumption of the Lockhart-McClure approach is
that hard-core pornography is "repulsive" to the "normal, sexually
mature person" and that it "appeals" to the "sexually immature
who use it to stimulate and feed their autoerotic reveries."[248] Accordingly, while their proposal would generally deny any legal
protection to hard-core pornography, it would be available to
normal persons who would presumably acquire it in socially approved ways for scholarly or scientific reasons.[249] Although we are
again in an area where empirical proof is elusive, there is good
authority for the proposition that at least some forms of hard-core
pornography do attract persons who, one hopes, are sexually mature and normal.[250] Indeed, the (Kinsey) Institute for Sex Research
has developed data showing that, generally, better educated persons are more responsive to pornography because they are more
imaginative and better able to conceptualize than persons of low

---

[247] Lockhart & McClure, *supra* note 7, at 60–84, and *passim*.

[248] *Id*. at 67. (Emphasis removed.)

[249] This occurred, for example, in "the Kinsey case," where the federal district
court applied a variable approach and permitted the Institute for Sex Research to
import concededly pornographic materials despite the customs law forbidding
importation of obscene items. United States v. 31 Photographs, 156 F. Supp. 350
(S.D. N.Y. 1957). I agree with Professor Louis Schwartz, *supra* note 126, at 679,
who would prefer that our laws provide explicit exemptions for persons with a
legitimate interest in acquiring obscenity.

[250] Lockhart & McClure, *supra* note 7, at 68, concede that normal persons might
be "curious" about hard-core pornography but not "addicted" to it. Compare:
"It is well known that policemen, lawyers, and judges involved in obscenity cases
not infrequently regale their fellows with viewings of the criminal material. Moreover, a poll conducted by this author among his fellow law professors—'mature'
and, for the present purposes, 'ordinary' adults—evoked uniformly affirmative answers to the following question: 'would you look inside a book that you had been
certainly informed had grossly obscene hard-core pornography if you were absolutely sure that no one else would ever learn that you had looked?' It is not an
answer to this bit of amateur sociological research to say that people would look
out of 'curiosity.' It is precisely such shameful curiosity to which 'appeal' is made
by the obscene. . . ." Schwartz, *supra* note 126, at 679. See also, E. F. Murphy,
supra note 210, at 663–64; KRONHAUSEN, *op. cit. supra* note 97, at 237. Despite over-
exposure to allegedly obscene materials, neither of the Kronhausens was able to
report personal 100 per cent "immunity" from its intended aphrodisiacal effects.
Id. Neither can I.

social and educational status; the latter are less likely to get excited about a picture with which they can "do nothing."[251] This attraction, of course, can take a number of directions: curiosity (and titillation) pure and simple, sexual arousal, or even sophisticated amusement.

Under the assumptions of Professors Lockhart and McClure, however, the "sexually mature," who are likely to be respectable and established persons of high socioeconomic status, could, in special cases, obtain hard-core pornography. And, more typically, they would have access to non-pornographic erotica and to such raw books as Henry Miller's *Quiet Days in Clichy* or *Tropic of Cancer*—a "privileged prurience"[252] denied to the sexually immature.[253] For the Lockhart-McClure variable obscenity approach would prohibit sales to the "sexually immature" of concededly non-obscene material in those circumstances where the conditions of sale and promotion treated the material as if it were hard-core pornography. It could not, for instance, be sold in seedy stores.[254] But the material would still be available to immature persons in more reputable environments:[255] "Though denied to an audience of the sexually immature when primarily directed to such an audience, the material is preserved for all others; and even some of the sexually immature may peruse the material if they are willing to procure it from sources that do not channel it to a primary audience of the sexually immature." How long, one wonders, would the audience of the "legitimate channels"[256] remain legitimate?

In summary, and aside from the enforcement problems, which could be monumental,[257] the variable approach requires an imposing number of determinations, some of them exceedingly subjective: (1) whether the seller is pandering by promoting material that is in fact hard-core pornography;[258] (2) whether the

---

251 GEBHARD, GAGNON, POMEROY, & CHRISTENSON, *op. cit. supra* note 218, at 671.

252 The phrase belongs to Eliot Fremont-Smith, *supra* note 90.

253 Lockhart & McClure, *supra* note 7, at 83 and n. 450.

254 *Id*. at 83.   255 *Id*. at 84.   256 *Id*. at n. 452.

257 Lockhart & McClure, however, feel that they are no more impractical than those involved in the constant obscenity approach. *Id*. at 83.

258 *Id*. at 77.

seller is pandering by representing non-obscene material as hard-core pornography;[259] (3) who is the primary intended audience;[260] (4) who is a "hypothetical person typical of that audience";[261] (5) what characteristics differentiate the "normal" and "sexually mature" from the "sexually immature";[262] (6) whether in terms of the hypothetical person of the primary audience "the material's sole or predominant appeal is to a sexually immature craving for erotic fantasy."[263] There are, one could say, too many variables in the variable obscenity approach.

Whether or not Mr. Justice Brennan's opinion in *Ginzburg v. United States* foreshadows an eventual adoption by the Supreme Court of the substance of the Lockhart-McClure proposal—a step that surely deserves the most thoughtful and searching examination —the obscenity cases of 1966 will clearly stimulate more cases and harder questions that sooner or later will demand the Justices' attention.[264] Procensorship forces in the United States are vocal and well organized. They can be extremely effective in local jurisdictions where the informal pressures on booksellers—a remark by the policeman on the beat, a visitation from an antivice committee

---

[259] *Ibid.* [260] *Id.* at 77–78. [261] *Id.* at 79.

[262] *Id.* at 79–80. [263] *Id.* at 80.

[264] During the 1966 Term the Supreme Court is unlikely to address itself to the ultimate question of what constitutes obscenity. On May 23, 1966, it denied certiorari in a case testing a federal conviction for sending through the mails two obscene recordings and circulars advertising them. Davis v. United States, 353 F.2d 614 (2d Cir. 1965), *cert. den.*, 384 U.S. 953 (1966). Justices Black, Douglas, and Stewart dissented from the denial, noting that they would have reversed the conviction. That same day the Court granted certiorari and, on the motion of the Solicitor General, vacated and remanded a § 1461 prosecution against a couple for sending nude photographs of themselves through the mail. The Solicitor General stated that the case had been erroneously initiated in spite of a general Justice Department policy against prosecuting non-commercial transmittals of obscenity through the mail. Justices Black, Douglas, and Stewart would have reversed the conviction "because it violates the Constitution." Redmond v. United States, 384 U.S. 264 (1966).

The Court, however, will be confronted with three obscenity cases testing procedural issues. Two of them, Redrup v. New York, *prob. jur. noted*, 384 U.S. 916 (1966); and Austin v. Kentucky, *prob. jur. noted*, 384 U.S. 916 (1966), test some of the scienter questions left unanswered in Smith v. California. A third case, Gent v. Arkansas, *prob. jur. noted*, 384 U.S. 937 (1966), asks whether a state obscenity law *on its face* operates as forbidden prior restraint or is unconstitutionally vague and uncertain. The Court declared that other questions, going to the material itself, were non-appealable. Justices Black, Douglas, and Stewart would have noted probable jurisdiction without limitations. *Ibid.*

—will often accomplish outside the courtroom what could not be legally accomplished inside.[265]

Within days of the decisions in *Ginzburg* and *Mishkin*, the rulings were being hailed as a shot in the arm to those enlisted in the war against obscenity. *Time* commented that "the Supreme Court seems to be catching up with the moral election returns."[266] Thirteen nationally prominent clergymen united in a statement composed by Operation Yorkville, a New York City antiobscenity organization, welcoming the decisions as a notice that "panderers of filth for profit will no longer be given a free hand in contaminating our society." The "resounding cry of the great majority of the American people," they added, "has been heard."[267] Mr. Charles H. Keating, Jr., the legal counsel and founder of the Citizens for Decent Literature, which has three hundred local chapters,[268] promised that the CDL would no longer be on the defensive as it had for ten years:[269]

> With the new Supreme Court decision things have changed. Now we are on the offensive. We intend the attack to be as brutal and unremitting as was the attack on society by pornographers in pushing their stuff. We will have no regard as to whom, what or where. We have the weapon—the law.

Many district attorneys are likely, either on their own or in response to such pressures, to initiate a new series of prosecutions against booksellers and motion picture theaters.[270] Unless these preliminary indications prove mistaken, and past experience proves

---

[265] Lockhart & McClure, *supra* note 7, at 6–13 and notes, provides an excellent summary of how the acceptance of the legitimacy of censorship can generate a vast and undiscriminating official and unofficial censorship. For a recent case study involving *Tropic of Cancer*, see Magrath, *supra* note 74.

[266] 87 TIME 56 (April 1, 1966).

[267] N.Y. Times, p. 30, col. 6 (May 3, 1966). They expressed disappointment with the ruling in *Memoirs v. Massachusetts*, but hoped that the Court would reconsider the social value rule. Among the thirteen signers were Roman Catholic Cardinals Cushing, Shehan, and Spellman; the Most Rev. Iakovos, Greek Orthodox Archbishop of North and South America; the Rev. Lloyd C. Wicke, Bishop of the Methodist Church in the New York area; the Right Rev. Richard S. M. Emrich, Episcopal Bishop of Michigan; David O. McKay, president of the Church of Latter-Day Saints; Rabbi Abraham B. Hecht, president of the Rabbinical Alliance of America; and the Rev. Dr. Norman Vincent Peale.

[268] 85 TIME 28 (April 16, 1965).   [269] N.Y. Times (May 3, 1966).

[270] Zion, *The Ginzburg Decision*, N.Y. Times, p. 31, col. 5 (March 24, 1966).

to be an inaccurate guide,[271] the prognosis is for a reinvigoration of censorship activities and a large new wave of troublesome obscenity cases for the nation's courts and ultimately for the Supreme Court of the United States.

VI. Hard-Core Pornography and the Laughter of Genius

An essay as critical as this one properly imposes on the critic the responsibility of concluding in a constructive vein. Although I fully realize that free advice is often worth no more than its price tag, it is appropriate to make a brief attempt at proposing a possible resolution to the demonstrated impasse in which the Supreme Court presently finds itself. My suggestion turns on three assumptions that should be stated explicitly. The first, a threshold assumption, has already been discussed and need only be recalled here. Our society is so deeply and firmly committed to at least *some* antiobscenity controls that any attempt judicially to proscribe them in their entirety would be constitutionally incorrect and politically suicidal.[272] The other two of my three assumptions require more discussion. The second is that the basic vice, if I may phrase it so, of the *Roth* test and its many elaborations is its permeation by the "appeals" or "effect" formula of *Regina v. Hicklin.* The third assumption is that there exists a definable, reasonably precise, concept of hard-core pornography which, at least theoretically, could unite a strong majority of the Court.

A careful reading of Lord Cockburn's famous definition in the 1867 *Hicklin* case indicates that it defines obscenity by separating the material from its appeal and then defines obscenity in terms of the appeal of the material, not the material itself, upon the reader or viewer.[273] Whatever Lord Cockburn's precise intentions may

---

[271] *Supra* note 265. The suggestion made earlier that the promoters and distributors of books, magazines, and movies may use a soft sell to hawk their messages does not lead, I think, to the conclusion that the *Ginzburg* ruling can be easily evaded without new legal action developing. It suggests, rather, that the legal questions will be subtle and difficult.

[272] See text at notes 228 *et seq., supra.*

[273] The *Hicklin* definition is set out in note 21, *supra,* and see Mr. Justice Harlan's thoughtful discussion in *Manual Enterprises,* 370 U.S. at 482–87. Lord Cockburn's opinion appears to be primarily premised on a distinction between material obscene per se and the effects such material might have. It should be noted that *Hicklin* involved an anti-Catholic tract, *The Confessional Unmasked,* that had (1) a con-

have been, the important point is that after 1867 the appeals formula of *Hicklin* swept into common usage in both English and American courts.[274] It is true that American courts have largely discarded *Hicklin*'s emphasis on appeal to the most susceptible, but they have not escaped from its basic emphasis on evaluating material, in the words of *Roth v. United States*, in terms of its "appeal to prurient interest." And this, as the Supreme Court's erratic course from *Roth* through *Ginzburg* so vividly illustrates, has turned the American law of obscenity into an impossible quagmire of subjectivity. Perhaps in a Victorian England, when the outward public consensus stood for a rather sharply defined acceptance of what was proper or improper in matters of sex and of sexual discussion, a *Hicklin*-type formula could achieve a measure of stability and non-arbitrariness. In a post-Freudian America during the second half of the twentieth century, when we know how subtle and how varied sexual appeals may be and when public attitudes and discussions reveal serious conflicts over precisely what constitutes sexually moral behavior and what is sexually appealing,[275] the appeals formula of 1867 seems singularly inappro-

---

cededly serious purpose, political-religious discourse, and (2) a concededly obscene part which focused on the supposedly indecent questions put to women by "Romish" priests. Accordingly, the only real issue was whether or not the tract's non-obscene purpose immunized its obscene part. The Queen's Bench ruled that it did not, pointing out that the obscene part would still have the deleterious effects which justified antiobscenity laws. Although Lord Cockburn's opinion is ambiguous, it may well be that his famous (or infamous) statement was *obiter dicta*, more an *explanation* than a test. This statement by his concurring colleague, Mr. Justice Blackburn, may sharpen the point:

"But I think it never can be said that in order to enforce your views, you may do something contrary to public morality; that you are at liberty to publish obscene publications, and distribute them amongst every one—schoolboys and every one else—when the inevitable effect must be to injure public morality, on the ground that you have an innocent object in view. . . . It seems to me that never could be made a defence to *an act of this sort, which is in fact a public nuisance*." L.R. 3 Q.B. at 377. (Emphasis added.)

[274] St. John-Stevas, *op. cit. supra* note 219, at 69–70, 126–27, for commentary on English law; Lockhart & McClure, *supra* note 10, at 325–29, for commentary on American law.

[275] I also reject the related concept that obscenity be evaluated in terms of its potential behavioral effect on the beholders for the reason that empirical studies are unlikely to prove satisfactorily what these effects might be. See text at notes 215–20, *supra*.

priate and unduly subjective.[276] After a century the time has perhaps come for the Supreme Court to throw out not only the bathwater of *Hicklin*—the appeal to the youngest and most susceptible —but the baby—the basic appeal formula—as well.

Can, then, the concept of hard-core pornography provide a more satisfactory and less subjective definition? Can it help us to distinguish more intelligently and more intelligibly between the material to be censored and the material that may have for some persons, if not D. H. Lawrence's "laughter of genius,"[277] at least some marginal social utility?[278] I think it can. Without attempting a comprehensive definition, I would say that there exists a reasonably identifiable category of printed and pictorial materials which primarily, and usually solely, depict sexual activities and do so in a manner "patently offensive" in terms of national standards and conventions concerning how certain sexual matters may be publicly depicted.[279] Such material, moreover, is intended primarily, and usually solely, to arouse its readers or viewers sexually, regardless of whether the intended appeal works on individual

---

[276] The previous assertion that a political and public consensus exists in favor of legally controlling obscenity is not contradicted by the fact that American sexual attitudes and practices are today more openly discussed, MASTERS & JOHNSON, *op. cit. supra* note 220, or that those who address themselves to the problem, such as the Justices of the Court, are divided over their definition of obscenity.

[277] LAWRENCE, PORNOGRAPHY AND OBSCENITY 5 (1929). Lawrence, as do many commentators and writers, used the word "pornography" synonymously with "obscenity," but he distinguished these from "genuine pornography": "underworld" material which "you can recognize by the insult it offers, invariably, to sex, and to the human spirit." Such material he would have "rigorously" censored. *Id.* at 12–13.

[278] There is, I think, wisdom in the recognition of Judge J. Irwin Shapiro of the New York Supreme Court that even the trashy pulp "dirty books" have a limited place in our society. In a 1963 ruling in a state obscenity prosecution he held that such titles as *Bedroom at the Top, Sexodus,* and *Swing Low Sweet Sinner,* though "poor writings, bad in taste, profane, offensive and disgusting," were not hard-core pornography and not therefore obscene. And he commented: "There are those who, because of lack of education, the meanness of their social existence or mental insufficiency, cannot cope with anything better. Slick paper confessions, pulp adventure and 'comic book' type of magazines provide them with an escape from reality." People v. Birch, 40 N.Y. Misc. 2d 626, 629–30; reversed by, as yet, unreported decision of the Appellate Division.

[279] I would follow Geoffrey Gorer for a description of "sexual activities": ". . . the depiction of single figures ready for sexual activity or of pairs or groups of figures engaged in sexual activity"; ". . . the description of the activities of various sets of genitals." *Supra* note 169, at 30.

readers or viewers. These two elements of the definition, it must be immediately conceded, are not wholly free of subjectivity—no definition using human language and requiring a determination of alleged facts can be. The first, the "hard-core" element, is essentially the concept of patent offensiveness relative to a "national standard of decency" developed by Mr. Justice Harlan in *Manual Enterprises v. Day* and by the American Law Institute in its Model Penal Code.[280] Needless to say, since national standards may gradually shift, the hard-core element of the test may over a period gradually shift too. This is not, I think, a reason for objecting to the hard-core component; national values and standards shift in many areas of the law, and the courts gradually take account of these shifts in opinion and value.[281]

The second element of the definition, "pornography," refers to material which is in effect self-defining. As a number of scholars and writers have agreed, pornography is clearly distinguished by its pervasive hallucinatory quality. For instance:[282]

> The object of pornography is hallucination. The reader is meant to identify either with the narrator (the "I" character) or with the general situation to a sufficient extent to produce at least the physical concomitants of sexual excitement; if the work is successful, it should produce orgasm. The reader should have the emotional and physical sensations, at least in a diminished form, that he would have were he taking part in the activities described.

(Interestingly, the etymological origin of the word "pornography" is Greek: "the writing of harlots.")[283] The Kronhausens, after a careful and detailed survey of numerous erotic writings, define hard-core pornography as writings designed to act as psychological aphrodisiacs or stimulants which keep before the reader a succession of increasingly erotic scenes.[284] Such writings (or,

---

[280] 370 U.S. at 482–87; A.L.I. *op. cit. supra* note 43, at 237.

[281] See CARDOZO, THE NATURE OF THE JUDICIAL PROCESS (1921). This, naturally, is a complicated matter, since the courts and particularly the Supreme Court may also positively contribute to changes in values and standards.

[282] Gorer, *supra* note 169, at 32. For similar statements see Lockhart & McClure, *supra* note 7, at 62–66; KRONHAUSEN, *op. cit. supra* note 97, at 285–86, 328–29. These qualities are, I believe, as true of pictorial as they are of written pornography.

[283] ST. JOHN-STEVAS, *op. cit. supra* note 219, at 2.

[284] KRONHAUSEN, *op. cit. supra* note 97, at 217–86. The Kronhausens identify and discuss twelve criteria of plot and technique which characterize hard-core pornographic writings.

for that matter, still or motion pictures) do not burden their readers or viewers with superfluous non-erotic descriptions of scenery, character portrayals, or philosophical exposition. They have, in Margaret Mead's apt expression, "the character of the daydream," the product of sheer fantasy.[285] But "life," as the Kronhausens note, "seldom presents us with a succession of erotic experiences, one more stimulating and exciting than the other."[286]

No matter how rapidly we utter the phrase "hard-core pornography" or how closely we hyphenate the words,[287] its adoption would not magically resolve all of the Supreme Court's problems. In the first place, the concept of hard-core pornography inescapably retains a degree of subjectivity.[288] In addition, the Court would still confront the task of giving content to the somewhat ambiguous idea of "national standards of decency." Nor could it avoid such subsidiary problems as that posed by cases where magazines or collections of printed and pictorial matter mix licit and illicit materials. This, of course, is the difficult question which *Eros* theoretically raised in the *Ginzburg* case. In such cases it might

---

[285] Mead, *Sex and Censorship in Contemporary Society*, in NEW WORLD WRITING 19 (1953).

[286] KRONHAUSEN, *op. cit. supra* note 97, at 328.

[287] FREUND, *op. cit. supra* note 226, at 44: "No matter how rapidly we utter the phrase 'clear and present danger' or how closely we hyphenate the words, they are not a substitute for the weighing of values."

[288] Thus, although the New York Court of Appeals verbally restricts its definition of obscenity to hard-core pornography, Mr. Justice Stewart was convinced that its categorization of the materials in *Mishkin v. New York* was erroneous. 383 U.S. at 518. Under a hard-core pornography test the most difficult problems of categorization would probably involve quality erotica, for example, *Fanny Hill* or Rembrandt's self-portrait of himself and his wife in intercourse. There is, frankly, no absolutely satisfactory answer to these borderline problems, but I think they are relatively soluble if two conditions are accepted: (1) a strict interpretation of the hard-core or patent offensiveness element; (2) a restriction of antiobscenity actions to commercial transactions. *Fanny Hill*, for instance, while almost certainly pornographic in intent, can, I think, be located on the safe side of the hard-core line. Its depictions, though shocking to many, are not patently cruder or more explicit than much already acceptable under our increasingly tolerant national standards (such as the depictions in *Lady Chatterley's Lover*). Moreover, to the modern reader, *Fanny Hill*'s archaic language mutes the offensiveness of the sexual depictions and tends to substitute humor for suggestiveness. In a sense, quality erotica such as *Fanny Hill* is *sui generis* and is perhaps far less significant than the sort of comic-strip and photographic materials which primarily occupy the attention of federal prosecutors.

be best to permit censorship of the material as a consequence of its hard-core pornography, after a determination that the illicit material was not honestly and integrally related to the licit material. Ideally, the determinations in such instances would be obtainable through civil proceedings in advance of publication or distribution.

Despite these difficulties, it is nevertheless significant that a number of qualified scholars and writers, including those who oppose restricting the definition of obscenity to hard-core pornography, recognize its existence in terms that explicitly or implicitly indicate its similarity to the concept defined and described in the preceding paragraphs.[289] Their recognition that a category of identifiable hard-core pornography exists is confirmed by at least two of the Justices[290] and by the federal government.[291] The Solicitor General, in fact, has noted that 90 per cent of its prosecutions involve this kind of material and not the kind involved in the *Ginzburg* case. These cases, apparently, are rarely contested beyond the trial level, since the material is so obviously unprotected hard-core pornography.[292] Finally, even if the difficulties of judicially applying the hard-core pornography test are greater than anticipated here, there are two compelling reasons for its adoption. First, it directs attention solely to the material per se, discarding the antiquated and ultrasubjective appeals formula of the *Hicklin* case. The Court, in other words, without worrying about whether

289 For examples of scholars see, GEBHARD, GAGNON, POMEROY, & CHRISTENSON, *op. cit. supra* note 218, at 669; Kalven, *supra* note 1, at 43–45; Lockhart & McClure, *supra* note 7, at 60–66; PAUL & SCHWARTZ, *op. cit. supra* note 196, at 209 (who feel that the hard-core pornography test "probably . . . goes too far in permitting open circulation of materials society simply will not tolerate today"); T. J. MURPHY, *op. cit. supra* note 207, at 236 (who opposes restricting obscenity to hard-core pornography). For examples of writers, see CRAIG, *op. cit. supra* note 238, at 207–15, and the citations in Lockhart & McClure, *supra* note 7, at 61–63, nn. 341–44. See also the distinction drawn by J. Edgar Hoover between the "twilight zone" and "hard-core pornography" or "the unquestionably obscene." *The Fight against Filth, supra* note 205, at 48.

290 Justices Harlan and Stewart in their opinions and positions in a number of cases: *Roth, Jacobellis, A Quantity of Books v. Kansas, Grove Press, Inc. v. Gerstein, Tralins v. Gerstein, Ginzburg, Mishkin,* and *Memoirs.*

291 Brief for the United States, Ginzburg v. United States, pp. 13–15.

292 See text *supra*, at note 24. In *Ginzburg*, the Government again pointed out during oral argument that most prosecutions under § 1461 involve hard-core pornography and, as a consequence of guilty pleas, never come before the Court. 383 U.S. at 500 n. 4 (Stewart, J., dissenting).

particularly challenged material is obscene because it has prurient interest appeal to some hypothetical average person, makes a determination on the material alone. It simply accepts as a matter of law the national assumption that a certain category of material must be banned because it violates minimum national standards by being too foul or revolting or too sexually arousing.[293] Second, the hardcore pornography test commends itself to the Court's attention for the simple reason that one hard-core pornography test is infinitely preferable to the four *Roth* tests that have so confused the American law of obscenity.

The hope that the Supreme Court will bring relative stability to the law of obscenity by adopting the concept of hard-core pornography may not be entirely utopian. The materials for such a constitutional compromise are present, including the Justices' keen awareness that the years since the *Roth* decision have led them down divergent back alleys.[294] All the Justices, always excepting Justices Black and Douglas, have reached a basic consensual agreement that some thing called "obscenity" does not enjoy First Amendment protection, and they agree that, at the very least, obscenity encompasses hard-core pornography. All the Justices, moreover, are agreed that, potentially, all obscenity cases raise First Amendment questions. And despite their partial disagreements on procedural issues, they have agreed that censorship cases must be tried according to high standards of procedural fairness. All the Justices, too, seem agreed that although adults cannot be deprived of materials that might be harmful to children or adolescents and that enforcement of statutes aimed at protecting young people must also conform to strict procedural requirements, it is constitutionally permissible for states to pass legislation intended to isolate youngsters from erotic materials and what might be termed soft-core pornography.[295]

---

[293] This assumption concerning national standards, as I have already conceded, requires a partly subjective evaluation that may shift over time. I describe the material as too foul or too arousing because the nation's obscenity laws are premised on such assumptions; some people, of course, will react to hard-core pornography with indifference and others will be revolted or aroused and sometimes both.

[294] See, *e.g.*, text at note 225, *supra*.

[295] Laws of this type are explicitly based on a limited concept of variable obscenity, with the audience clearly and consistently defined as young persons under a certain age. The Court's dispositions in *Butler v. Michigan* and *Bantam Books v.*

A Supreme Court decision redefining obscenity as hard-core pornography would, naturally, be a most controversial one. It would frankly permit the more open distribution of a great quantity of material, such as that in the *Ginzburg* and *Mishkin* cases, repellent to many Americans. It would be attacked by many clergymen, policemen, politicians, and antivice crusaders, a reaction that has been the prominent fate of a number of Warren Court decisions. Although it is exceedingly difficult to speculate on such matters, my belief is that the Court could "survive" and win the implementation of such a decision.[296] But a decision restricting obscenity to hard-core pornography would have to be tightly written. It would have to emphasize that it was not a way station toward a total abolition of obscenity control.[297] It would have to insist that adults are largely voluntary masters of what they read and view. It would have to note that carefully drawn obscenity statutes can restrict the commercial circulation of materials less offensive than hard-core pornography among young people. And, most important, it would have to command a strong majority of the Court united in a single opinion.

It might be appropriate, finally, to observe that for the Justices

---

Sullivan, which voided state practices designed to protect children from obscenity, were based on the objection that the law swept too broadly (*Butler*) and that the censorship procedures were too vague and arbitrary (*Bantam Books*). There was no implication that carefully designed laws restricting the sale of materials to children are unconstitutional, and the unanimous *Butler* decision clearly indicates the opposite. 352 U.S. at 383–84. In his opinion in *Jacobellis v. Ohio*, 378 U.S. at 195, Mr. Justice Brennan declared: "State and local authorities might well consider whether their objectives in this area [the protection of children] would be better served by laws aimed specifically at preventing distribution of objectionable material to children, rather than at totally prohibiting its dissemination." As an example he cited a decision by the Rhode Island Supreme Court upholding such a precisely drawn state statute. State v. Settle, 90 R.I. 195 (1959). But there are enforcement and other problems with these laws too. Lockhart & McClure, *supra* note 7, at 85–86. See also People v. The Bookcase, Inc., 14 N.Y.2d 409 (1964), voiding such a law for vagueness.

296 It may be of some significance that in the nearly ten years between *Roth* and *Ginzburg*, when it was regularly reversing censorship rulings and when many legal experts were announcing that it had de facto embraced the hard-core pornography definition, the Court was not severely threatened because of its obscenity decisions. For a sophisticated commentary on the elusive subject of the Court and political power, see McCloskey, *supra* note 4, at 1267–70.

297 Thus, the Kronhausens support a ban on hard-core pornography only "as an intermediary stop gap on the road to complete abolition of censorship." *Op. cit. supra* note 97, at 210; *cf.* T. J. MURPHY, *op. cit. supra* note 207, at 236, who claims that this is the ultimate objective of those who favor the test.

of the Supreme Court there is perhaps a time to be doctrinaire—
to champion a thesis and to explore tenaciously a cherished approach—and a time to be flexible in order better to serve the national interest in a reasonably stable and precise system of law.
Certainly there is nothing degrading in the idea of an intelligent
compromise in the interpretation of a Constitution whose meaning,
fortunately, is often imprecise and changeable as conditions change.
More than a century ago the Justices of the Taney Court brought
a measure of practical stability to the troublesome question of the
respective roles of the federal and state governments under the
Commerce Clause by striking a compromise in *Cooley v. Board
of Wardens*,[298] a decision that has stood the test of time as a great
and wise constitutional compromise. The *Cooley* decision, it is
fitting to recall, settled another wracking definitional dispute over
the nature of the commerce power, and it came only two years
after the *Passenger Cases*[299] of 1849 produced eight opinions revealing "a seemingly hopeless inability to agree on a general interpretation of the commerce power."[300] Much more recently, and
in the very area of censorship, involving the question of prior
restraint over motion pictures, there appears to have been a significant and intelligent compromising of positions among the Justices of the Warren Court.[301] Perhaps some day a similar constitutional compromise, whether it adopts hard-core pornography or
some other solution, will emerge in the law of obscenity.

Until such a day arrives the American law of obscenity will
remain badly confused. For on the issue of obscenity and the law
the Supreme Court of the United States, contrary to the suggestion
of Mr. Justice Black, is not acting as a Supreme Board of Censors.
A Board of Censors, after all, customarily agrees on what it is
censoring (or not censoring) and why. Such an agreement is nota-
bly lacking in the three decisions and fourteen opinions announced
on March 21, 1966. On the question of obscenity and the law a
more appropriate imagery would liken the Court to the Tower
of Babel.

---

[298] 12 How. 299 (1851). See FRANKFURTER, THE COMMERCE CLAUSE UNDER MAR-
SHALL, TANEY AND WAITE 50–58 (1937).

[299] 7 How. 283 (1849).

[300] SWISHER, ROGER B. TANEY 404 (1935).

[301] Times Film Corp. v. Chicago, 365 U.S. 43 (1961); *cf.* Freedman v. Maryland,
380 U.S. 51 (1965).

ALEXANDER M. BICKEL

THE VOTING RIGHTS CASES

Very few statutes can ever have been drafted with a warier eye
to the prospect of litigation, or a keener intention to ward it off
as long as possible, than the Voting Rights Act of 1965.[1] It was enacted, indeed, as a substitute for litigation, which had proved a sadly
inadequate engine of reform. Care was taken, therefore, to ensure
that the enterprise launched by the statute would be going before
litigation could test it in the local federal courts,[2] and § 14(b) hope-
fully designated the District Court for the District of Columbia as
the only forum in which suit attacking the statute on a broad front
could be brought.[3] Yet Congress, in trying to escape the clutches
of hostile courts, did not avoid the precipitate embrace of a sympathetic one: the Supreme Court of the United States. The Voting
Rights Act of 1965 came to judgment there with extraordinary
rapidity and under extraordinary conditions.

Alexander M. Bickel is Chancellor Kent Professor of Law and Legal History, Yale
University.

[1] The Voting Rights Act of 1965 is Public Law 89–110, 89th Cong., 1st Sess. (1965);
79 Stat. 437 (1965); 42 U.S.C. §§ 1973 *et seq.* (1965 Suppl.). It is also reproduced as
an appendix to the Court's opinion in South Carolina v. Katzenbach, 383 U.S. 301,
337–55 (1965), and, for convenience, references to the statute hereafter made will
be to the Court's appendix.

[2] See §§ 4(b), 9(a), and 14(b), 383 U.S. at 341, 346, 353.

[3] "No court other than the District Court for the District of Columbia or a court
of appeals in any proceeding under section 9 shall have jurisdiction to issue any
declaratory judgment pursuant to section 4 or section 5 or any restraining order
or temporary or permanent injunction against the execution or enforcement of
any provision of this Act or any action of any Federal officer or employee pursuant thereto." 383 U.S. at 353.

I. South Carolina v. Katzenbach

The train of events that led to the decision of *South Carolina v. Katzenbach*[4] on March 7, 1966, in the Supreme Court was apparently first set in motion some three weeks after the Voting Rights Act was approved. On August 31, 1965, Leander H. Perez, Jr., District Attorney of Plaquemines Parish, Louisiana, filed suit in the Twenty-fifth Judicial District Court of Louisiana against Bruce Rhiddlehoover and Billy Travis, federal voting examiners appointed pursuant to § 6 of the Act to serve in that parish.[5] District Attorney Perez, represented by his father, Leander the Elder, Baron of Plaquemines, asked that the defendants be forbidden to register as voters persons who, in the District Attorney's view, failed to meet valid requirements of state law. The complaint did not put in issue the constitutionality of the Voting Rights Act. It accepted *arguendo* the Act's suspension of "tests or devices" previously administered in Louisiana, and contended only that the Attorney General and the Civil Service Commission, in discharging their statutory duty of instructing examiners to abide by those other qualifications prescribed by state law which are not inconsistent with the federal Constitution and laws[6] had misinterpreted the state law; chiefly, it seems, by being in error on the question whether qualifications relating to age and residence needed to be met by the date of registration or by the date of the next election. The Fifth Judicial District Court of Louisiana issued an *ex parte* temporary restraining order, whereupon the defendant examiners removed to the United States District Court for the Eastern District of Louisiana. There the temporary restraining order was promptly dissolved on September 3. The following month, District Judge Ellis also denied plaintiff's motion to remand. Thus, except during a hurricane, registration proceeded in Plaquemines Parish, although Judge Ellis—erroneously, as one may well think—denied defendants' motion to dismiss.[7]

Other direct attacks on the administration of the Act foundered on § 14(b) with even greater promptness.[8] But a series of suits be-

---

[4] 383 U.S. 301 (1966).   [5] *Id.* at 343–44.   [6] §§ 7(b) and 9(b), *id.* at 344–45, 347.

[7] Perez v. Rhiddlehoover, 247 F. Supp. 65 (E.D. La. 1965).

[8] O'Keefe v. New York City Board of Elections, 246 F. Supp. 978 (S.D. N.Y. 1965); McCann v. Paris, 244 F. Supp. 870 (W.D. Va. 1965).

gun in September in Alabama, Mississippi, and Louisiana proved more troublesome. Injunctions were issued by state courts in a number of counties in those states against the appropriate local officials, forbidding them to place on the voting rolls the names of voters registered by federal examiners.[9] These injunctions did not interfere with registration, but they challenged the constitutionality of the Act and, if obeyed, would have rendered registration futile. If obeyed, they could also have subjected the state officials to whom they were addressed, and possibly the state officials and judges who obtained and issued them, to criminal prosecution under § 12 of the Act.[10]

Whatever their political and personal preferences, the state election officials were thus offered a Hobson's choice. It is difficult to imagine, however, that the Attorney General could not have solved their dilemma by instituting actions under § 12(d) of the Act for preventive relief against them. Actually he believed, as he later made clear, that he had ample authority to bring such suits, not only pursuant to § 12(d), but also, reasonably enough, in the exercise of the inherent power of the United States "to vindicate its rights in its own courts," as well as under 42 U.S.C. § 1971(c).[11] Yet the Attorney General made no move. His attention turned instead to the original jurisdiction of the Supreme Court.

An argument can be made, proceeding from the bare text of § 14(b),[12] that a federal district court would be free to adjudicate the constitutionality of the Voting Rights Act in a case in which the Attorney General was seeking an injunction against a state official— an injunction that, arguably, should not issue unless the Act was constitutional. In such a case, the result of a holding that the Act was unconstitutional would not be the sort of decree, forbidding execution of the Act, which § 14(b) allows only the District Court for the District of Columbia to issue. This is not much of an argument, but in voting cases tried before federal district judges in the Deep South,

---

[9] See U.S. Commission on Civil Rights, The Voting Rights Act . . . The First Months App. E, 74–78 (1965).

[10] 383 U.S. at 350–52.

[11] Brief in Support of Motions for Leave To File Original Complaints and Motions for Expedited Consideration, Nos. 23, 24, 25, Orig., at pp. 9–10, United States v. Alabama, 382 U.S. 897 (1965).

[12] See note 3 *supra.*

the Attorney General has been known to lose cases, for the time being, on arguments that were not much.[13] With spring primaries impending, time was then of the essence, and to go before some of the federal district judges in Alabama, Mississippi, and Louisiana was to take a chance. Once having taken his chances even in one district court, the Attorney General would very likely find that he had made an irrevocable election. He would be foreclosed from bringing suits against the states themselves in the original jurisdiction of the Supreme Court. For in these circumstances he would be coming into the original jurisdiction with nothing but a form of direct appeal, and possibly an interlocutory one, at that. Moreover, the outlook for the success of the Act in general was good. The Act was being widely administered and obeyed. It was, in truth, having its period of maximum effectiveness in placing large numbers of Negroes on voting rolls—more and faster than it has done since.[14] Any decree holding it unconstitutional, no matter how obviously vulnerable and temporary, would have had its adverse effect on officials elsewhere who had been complying—reluctantly and not universally, but widely and voluntarily. And so the Attorney General took no chances.

The potentially ugly situation in the several counties in Alabama, Mississippi, and Louisiana solved itself well before winter. The Alabama election officials who were under state injunction, not having been sued by the Attorney General, sued him. They obtained a decree from a three-judge federal court[15] dissolving all the Alabama injunctions.[16] In deference to the plain command of § 14(b), the court did not pass on the constitutionality of the Act but went about its business by assuming it. The efforts to thwart execution of the Act in Mississippi and Louisiana evidently then collapsed of

---

13 See, for one of many examples, the litigation history recited by the Court of Appeals in United States v. Ramsey, 353 F.2d 650 (5th Cir. 1965). And Judge Ellis, in the Plaquemines Parish case mentioned above, see note 7 *supra*, although he granted relief, failed to dismiss the case, as he should have done pursuant to § 14(b).

14 See U.S. COMMISSION ON CIVIL RIGHTS, *op. cit. supra* note 9: N.Y. Times, April 11, 1966, p. 38, col. 7 (City Ed.) ("Negro Vote Lists Rise 50% in South").

15 A three-judge court was presumably available to them, since they were formally suing to enjoin enforcement of the Act, but would not have been available to the Attorney General. *Compare* 28 U.S.C. § 2282, *with* § 101(d) of the Civil Rights Act of 1964, 78 Stat. 241, 242 (1964), 42 U.S.C. § 1971(h) (1964).

16 Reynolds v. Katzenbach, 248 F. Supp. 593 (S.D. Ala. 1965).

their own weight. But by then it was late November, and the Attorney General had long since committed himself to litigating in
the original jurisdiction.

On September 29, 1965, South Carolina moved for leave to file
a complaint against the Attorney General in the original jurisdiction
of the Supreme Court. The complaint challenged the constitutionality of the Act as a whole, except for § 3 (authorizing appointment of examiners, not by the Attorney General acting on his own,
but as part of a judicial decree),[17] § 14(c) (nullifying the New York
requirement of literacy in English as applied to Puerto Ricans educated in American-flag schools),[18] § 10 (authorizing the Attorney
General to institute suits challenging the poll tax),[19] and one or two
miscellaneous sections. The response of the Attorney General was
to move for leave to file complaints of his own, in the name of the
United States, against Alabama, Louisiana, and Mississippi. Each
of these complaints alleged that local election officials were obeying
state court injunctions that forbade them to comply with the Voting Rights Act. The Attorney General asked for judgments declaring the constitutionality of §§ 4, 6, and 7 of the Act, insofar
as these sections suspended literacy and other tests, authorized the
appointment of federal examiners, and required the listing as voters
of persons registered by examiners. He asked also that the injunctions issued against the local election officials be declared null and
void, and that these officials be ordered to do their federal duty.[20]

On the same day on which he moved for leave to file these complaints, the Attorney General responded to the South Carolina suit
in a memorandum signed by Solicitor General Marshall. The Government, said the Solicitor General, did not oppose South Carolina's
motion for leave to file a complaint. "For the reasons stated in the
brief of the United States in support of its motions for leave to file
original complaints [against Alabama, Mississippi, and Louisiana]
. . . filed with the Court this day . . . we believe that the Court has

---

[17] 383 U.S. at 338–39.

[18] *Id*. at 341–42.

[19] *Id*. at 347–49.

[20] Motions for Leave To File Complaints, Complaints, and Motions for Expedited
Consideration, Nos. 23, 24, 25, Orig., United States v. Alabama, United States v.
Mississippi, United States v. Louisiana, 382 U.S. 897 (1965).

jurisdiction to entertain this original action and may appropriately exercise its jurisdiction here."[21]

But the jurisdictional issues in the two cases, South Carolina's against the Attorney General and that of the United States against Alabama, Mississippi, and Louisiana were very different.[22] In its own suit, the United States was doing precisely what it could have done in the lower federal courts. It was seeking, by the exercise of inherent authority and of statutory authority, particularly under § 12(d) of the Voting Rights Act, to vindicate the supremacy of national law, which was being flouted by officials of the named states. The suit was against the states, rather than individual officers of the states, because these officers were acting under state law, and because suits against the states would reach them all most economically. There is nothing extraordinary about framing an action of this sort with a state as defendant. Section 601(d) of the Civil Rights of 1960 explicitly permits it, for example.[23] All that is required to make out a case against a state in such circumstances is that there be a real controversy—that officers of the state, acting under state law, be engaged in obstructing the execution of national law.[24] A controversy there was, in this instance, at the time of the filing of the motions. Whether a case was made out in the original jurisdiction thus became only a question of ripeness and *forum non conveniens*. It was along these lines that the brief for the United States constructed its argument.

Quite another sort of jurisdictional question was raised by South Carolina's complaint. South Carolina sought an injunction forbidding the Attorney General to execute the Voting Rights Act, which suspended provisions of South Carolina's voter qualification law, as well as the operation of parts of her election machinery, and substituted federal law and machinery. The constitutionality of the

---

[21] Memorandum for the Defendant, No. 22, Orig., at pp. 1–2, South Carolina v. Katzenbach, 383 U.S. 301 (1966).

[22] They had in common only the difficulty presented by § 14(b) of the Voting Rights Act, *supra* note 3, which, the Solicitor General argued, should not be read as depriving the Supreme Court of jurisdiction of appropriate original actions, "in view of the constitutional basis of this Court's original jurisdiction." Memorandum for the Defendant, *supra* note 20, at p. 2, n. 1.

[23] 74 Stat. 92 (1960), 42 U.S.C. § 1971(c) (1964); United States v. Mississippi, 380 U.S. 128 (1965); Louisiana v. United States, 380 U.S. 145 (1965).

[24] *Cf.* United States v. West Virginia, 295 U.S. 463 (1936).

Act was attacked under the Fifteenth Amendment, and also under the Due Process and Bill of Attainder Clauses. Jurisdiction was rested on Article III, because South Carolina was suing a citizen of New Jersey—not at the moment, one might think, the most relevant fact about Nicholas deB. Katzenbach, but apparently a jurisdictional fact nonetheless. The decisive issue, however, was whether South Carolina had standing. The only interests, if any, that could give South Carolina standing were her functional interest as a sovereign, her interest, that is, in the continued execution of her own laws without hindrance from national authority, and her interest as protector of those of her citizens entitled to vote under her present laws, whose vote would be diluted by the addition of new voters to the rolls. In no fashion did the brief in support of the motions of the United States to file complaints against Alabama, Mississippi, and Louisiana discuss the question of South Carolina's standing, or otherwise attempt to justify acceptance of jurisdiction in *South Carolina v. Katzenbach*, and this despite Solicitor General Marshall's assertion that for "reasons stated in the brief of the United States in support of its motions for leave to file . . . we believe that the court has jurisdiction to entertain" *South Carolina v. Katzenbach*. This was simply a way of shuffling the jurisdictional issue in *South Carolina v. Katzenbach* from one set of papers to another, faster than the eye could follow. In neither did the Government discuss it. And in the shuffle, the issue got lost altogether, for an implied promise by the Government to return to it at the argument on the merits was never carried out.[25]

---

[25] "At all events," the Solicitor General said in his memorandum in *South Carolina v. Katzenbach*, "the Court may grant the State's motion for leave to file a complaint without now resolving the question of jurisdiction, which can properly be postponed to the time when the case is considered on the merits." Memorandum for the Defendant, No. 22, Orig., at p. 2, n. 1, South Carolina v. Katzenbach, 383 U.S. 301 (1966). But in the brief for the Attorney General on the merits, jurisdictional problems were dismissed in a footnote in this fashion: "In view of the Court's decision to grant plaintiff's motion for leave to file the complaint herein, we proceed to the merits in this brief." For the rest, there was merely the suggestion, later accepted by the Court, 383 U.S. at 316–17, that §§ 11 and 12(a), (b), and (c), imposing criminal sanctions and authorizing injunctive relief, which South Carolina was attacking along with most of the rest of the Act, were not ripe for adjudication since they had not yet been invoked. Brief for the Defendant, No. 22, Orig., at pp. 2, 3, nn. 3, 4, South Carolina v. Katzenbach, 383 U.S. 301 (1966).

But see United States v. Harvey, 250 F. Supp. 219 (E.D. La. 1966), which invoked

Having decided—not unreasonably, for only hindsight tells us that the situation was going to solve itself without such drastic action—that he had no safe alternative but himself to seek redress in the original jurisdiction, the Attorney General presumably feared that it would somehow damage his position if at the same time he tried to block South Carolina's access. He wound up in the end, not with his own case, but with South Carolina's. The motions of the United States for leave to file bills of complaint against Alabama, Mississippi, and Louisiana were denied.[26] On the same day, South Carolina's motion was summarily granted, Black, Harlan, and Stewart, JJ., dissenting.[27] The Court, unaided by counsel, chose what was jurisdictionally by far the weaker of the two cases offered.

"Original jurisdiction," said Chief Justice Warren's opinion for the Court, without dissent on this issue, "is founded on the presence of a controversy between a State and a citizen of another State under Art. III, § 2 of the Constitution. See *Georgia v. Pennsylvania R. Co.*, 324 U.S. 439 [1945]."[28] But in that case Georgia had a proprietary claim, and to the extent that she was also suing as protector of her people, she was not, as Mr. Justice Douglas pointed out for the Court, suing the United States or a federal officer, and she was not seeking "to protect her citizens from the operation of Federal statutes."[29] Nor, in the instant case, was South Carolina or one of her political subdivisions suing pursuant to congressional direction, as under § 4(a) of the Voting Rights Act,[30] to establish facts on which application of federal law, or an exemption from it, is made to depend. These distinctions are crucial. It has heretofore been established that a state is not, as the phrase goes, the *parens patriae* of her citizens as against the federal government. It is no part of a state's "duty or power," said the Court in *Massachusetts v. Mellon*,[31] "to enforce their [her citizens'] rights in respect to their relations with the Federal Government. In that field, it is

---

§ 11(b). This suit was filed on December 17, 1965. The District Court (West, J.) held the section unconstitutional as applied, although it shored up its dismissal of the suit with an alternate factual finding, as well.

26 382 U.S. 897 (1965).

27 *Id.* at 898.   29 324 U.S. at 446–47.

28 383 U.S. at 307.   30 383 U.S. at 339–40.

31 262 U.S. 447, 486 (1923); and see Florida v. Mellon, 273 U.S. 12 (1927); Jones *ex rel.* Louisiana v. Bowles, 322 U.S. 707 (1944).

the United States and not the State which represents them as *parens patriae* when such representation becomes appropriate; and to the former, and not to the latter, they must look for such protection measures as flow from that status." The Court in *South Carolina v. Katzenbach* itself dismissed South Carolina's argument that she had been adjudged guilty of discrimination by the Voting Rights Act, without trial, in violation of the Fifth Amendment's Due Process Clause and of the Bill of Attainder Clause of Article I. Certainly, as the Court briefly indicated, this argument is weird enough on its merits. But the Court went on to say: "Nor does a State have standing as the parent of its citizens to invoke these constitutional provisions against the Federal government, the ultimate *parens patriae* of every American citizen. *Massachusetts v. Mellon*, 262 U.S. 447, 485–86; *Florida v. Mellon*, 273 U.S. 12, 18."[32] If this is so, it is precisely as true with respect to the argument, which the Court then proceeded to discuss at length on the merits, that Congress exceeded its powers under the Fifteenth Amendment. It is no less true that South Carolina lacked standing as the parent of her citizens to urge their claim that Congress violated the Fifteenth Amendment to their detriment, than that South Carolina lacked standing to urge her citizens' claim that Congress inflicted harm on them by an Act violating the Due Process Clause of the Fifth Amendment and the Bill of Attainder Clause of Article I.

Of course the original jurisdiction should provide a forum for the adjudication of issues that could arise, absent a federal union, between sovereigns, and that, absent such a union, would be dealt with by international arbitration, or would result in international conflict of one sort or another.[33] The original jurisdiction serves also for the adjudication of claims by the states against citizens and entities not within their control—claims that the states, if they were fully sovereign, might also prosecute in an international forum or by unilateral means. Such claims may be founded on a state's duty or desire, as *parens patriae*, to protect the interests of her own citi-

---

[32] 383 U.S. at 324.

[33] See HART & WECHSLER, THE FEDERAL COURTS AND THE FEDERAL SYSTEM 258 (1953); Arizona v. California, 373 U.S. 546 (1963); United States v. Florida, 363 U.S. 121 (1960); United States v. Louisiana, 363 U.S. 1 (1960); United States v. Texas, 339 U.S. 707 (1950); United States v. Louisiana, 339 U.S. 691 (1950); United States v. California, 332 U.S. 19 (1947).

zens, and perhaps this explains *Georgia v. Pennsylvania R. Co.* Finally, it may be that proprietary claims of the states, no matter how attenuated, may be defended in the original jurisdiction against infringement by federal law, simply and more than somewhat arbitrarily because they are proprietary rather than functional or protective.[34] But it is altogether different for a state to be raising, as did South Carolina, nothing more than her interest in the execution of her own laws rather than those of Congress, and her interest in having Congress enact only constitutional laws for application to her citizens. A state is said to have no standing in such circumstances, not because the interests asserted are unreal or inadequately particular to the state, but because by hypothesis they should not, in such circumstances, suffice to invoke judicial action. For purposes of litigation with the United States (through the officers charged with execution of federal laws), a state should have no recognizable interest in ensuring the fidelity of Congress to constitutional restraints. Only citizens and other persons have a litigable interest of this sort, and then only if they can show injury, being affected either in their pocketbooks or by a disadvantageous change in their position in the legal order. This has heretofore been the settled view, and for good reason.

One may explain away *Georgia v. Stanton*[35] as *sui generis*—a political question case.[36] There is some support also for reading *Massachusetts v. Mellon* as a holding that courts can find no criteria to define the occasions when Congress may or may not tax and spend for the general welfare—that, in other words, the General Welfare Clause raises a political question of sorts.[37] But there remains a simple proposition, which perhaps the Court has seldom had occasion to affirm unambiguously, but which it has equally seldom denied, even tacitly, before now.[38] This proposition is that the nature

---

[34] Missouri v. Holland, 252 U.S. 416 (1920).

[35] 6 Wall. 50 (1867).

[36] *Cf.* Mississippi v. Johnson, 4 Wall. 475 (1867); but *cf.* Texas v. White, 7 Wall. 700 (1869).

[37] *Cf.* Steward Machine Co. v. Davis, 301 U.S. 548 (1937); but *cf.* United States v. Butler, 297 U.S. 1 (1936).

[38] Some subterranean implications that may be read into the brief order in Alabama v. United States, 373 U.S. 545 (1963), need to be noted. The case is the subject of a curious and totally ambiguous citation in the Memorandum for the

of the federal union, the power and function of Congress and the President, and the power and function of the judiciary all would be radically altered if states could come into the original jurisdiction at will to litigate the constitutional validity of national law applicable within their territories. To allow the states to litigate in this fashion—which is precisely what South Carolina was allowed to do—would be a fundamental denial of perhaps the most innovating principle of the Constitution: the principle that the federal government is a sovereign coexisting in the same territory with the states and acting, not through them, like some international organization, but directly upon the citizenry, which is its own as well as theirs. The states are built into the political structure of the federation, and play their part in the formation of its institutions. But they are not to contest, as if between one sovereign and another in some quasi-international forum, the actions of the national institutions. For the national government is fully in privity with the people it governs, and needs, and should brook, no intermediaries.

It would make a mockery, moreover, of the constitutional requirement of case or controversy, which is at the heart of Marshall's argument in *Marbury v. Madison*[39] and forms an essential limitation on the reach of the power of judicial review, to countenance automatic litigation—and automatic it would surely become—by

---

Defendant filed in answer to South Carolina's motion for leave to file in *South Carolina v. Katzenbach*. The passage in question is as follows: "Federal jurisdiction is premised upon the portion of Clause 1 of the same Section [Art. 3, § 2] that extends the judicial power of the United States to 'Controversies . . . between a State and Citizens of another State.' Attorney General Katzenbach is a citizen of New Jersey. See Alabama v. United States, 373 U.S. 545." Memorandum for the Defendant, No. 22, Orig., at p. 2, n. 1, South Carolina v. Katzenbach, 383 U.S. 301 (1966). *Alabama v. United States* was Governor George C. Wallace's motion for leave to file a complaint in the spring of 1963 to prevent the President from using troops in Birmingham, during the marching there. In a brief order, instead of dismissing for lack of jurisdiction with a citation to *Massachusetts v. Mellon*, the Supreme Court said that all the President was shown to have done was to alert troops for possible use in Birmingham. Such merely preparatory measures and their possible effects in Alabama could afford no basis for relief, the Court said, and so denied leave to file. One can hardly credit the implication of this brief order that Alabama might otherwise have had standing, any more than one could credit its implication that, everything else being equal, the Supreme Court would undertake to review the exercise of presidential discretion in the use of troops under 10 U.S.C. § 333.

[39] 1 Cranch 137 (1803).

states situated no differently than was South Carolina in this instance. The distinction between a Supreme Court, generally limited in the timing and circumstances of its interventions to "cases" in which public authority has touched private interests or the supremacy of national law needs to be brought home to persons private or public, on the one hand, and the sort of council of revision rejected by the framers,[40] on the other, would then be almost wholly obliterated. There would then be no need to worry about who could sue if Congress or the President created a duke, or supported an ambassador at the Vatican, or established a church,[41] or conducted atomic tests, or this or that disagreeable war.[42] South Carolina could sue, and one or another South Carolina undoubtedly always would, and promptly too. The consequent aggrandizement of the judicial function is something to contemplate. Nor would there be any call, and scarcely the possibility, as there was not in *South Carolina v. Katzenbach,* for a record exemplifying the actual operation of a statute, bringing to the Court for constitutional judgment not Congress' prophecy of the consequences of its action but the actual flesh and blood of those consequences in the life of the society. Time and again, precisely like a council of revision, the Court would be pronouncing the abstraction that some law generally like the one before it would or would not generally be constitutional in the generality of its applications. Such an abstraction was what the Court was reduced to pronouncing on the merits of *South Carolina v. Katzenbach.*

The Court did no more than skim the surface of the Act. Application of the Act is triggered by a formula having to do with the use by a state or county of tests (such as literacy) as a prerequisite to voting, and with the incidence of a low voting rate. The Court held the formula rational, emphasizing that it only amounted, after all, to a presumption, since § 4(a) also provides for termination of coverage in any state or county which can prove to the satis-

---

40 See Griswold v. Connecticut, 381 U.S. 479, 507, 513–14, n. 6 (1965) (Black, J., dissenting).

41 *Compare* Brown, *Quis Custodiet Ipsos Custodes?—The School Prayer Cases,* [1963] SUPREME COURT REVIEW 1, 15–33, *with* Black, *Religion, Standing and the Supreme Court's Role,* 13 J. PUB. LAW 459 (1964).

42 See Pauling v. McNamara, 331 F. 2d 796 (D.C. Cir., 1963), *cert. denied,* 377 U.S. 933 (1964). Cf. Luftig v. McNamara, 252 F. Supp. 819 (D. D.C. 1966).

faction of the District Court for the District of Columbia that for
five years past it has used no test or device "for the purpose or
with the effect of denying or abridging the right to vote on account
of race or color." South Carolina contended that these supposed
termination proceedings were a snare and could not come to anything, because the burden of proof was impossible. Hence the presumption should be treated as conclusive. Not so, said the Court.
The burden of proof would turn out to be "quite bearable."[43] But
this could only be the rankest speculation, one way or the other.
It is almost farcical that such an issue should have been decided
otherwise than on the full record of an appeal from an actual termination proceeding. The Court could not possibly know when it
decided *South Carolina v. Katzenbach* what a termination proceeding would look like.

The formula that triggers the Act is in turn triggered when the
Attorney General determines that a state or political subdivision
maintained as of November 1, 1964, "any test or device," and the
Director of the Census certifies that fewer than 50 per cent of persons of voting age residing there were registered on November 1,
1964, or voted in the presidential election of that year. Section 4
goes on to say that a determination or certification of this sort by the
Attorney General or the Director of the Census, as well as a determination that the conditions for appointing examiners have been
met (§ 6), or that examiners should be withdrawn (§ 13), "shall
not be reviewable in any court." The Supreme Court read this provision as denying judicial review (although what is meant by the
word "reviewable" would be open to question, depending on the
procedures used to invoke judicial action)[44] and held it constitutional as such, citing *United States v. California Eastern Line*[45] and
Switchmen's Union v. National Mediation Board.[46] But the *California Eastern Line* case itself indicates that the issue of a right to
judicial review has not usually been dealt with by the Court in these
absolute terms. The kind of action sought to be reviewed (whether
within administrative discretion or arguably *ultra vires*), and other
statutory and procedural variables have often been decisive. And

---

[43] 383 U.S. at 332.

[44] *Cf.* Leedom v. Kyne, 358 U.S. 184, 188 (1958).

[45] 348 U.S. 351 (1955).   [46] 320 U.S. 297 (1943).

the authority of the *Switchmen's Union* case, beyond its own narrow circumstances, is more than highly dubious.[47] It is no daring guess to assert that if the Court had been faced with an actual case, rather than with the bare bones of the statute, it would not have been content with the advisory abstraction that it handed down on the issue of a right to judicial review. The result it would have reached would have depended on circumstances now unknown.

Finally, there was the issue which drew a pained dissent from Mr. Justice Black. Section 5 of the Act provides that whenever any state or county which is covered by the Act under the automatic trigger provisions "shall enact or seek to administer any voting qualification or prerequisite to voting, or standard, practice, or procedure with respect to voting different from that in force or effect on November 1, 1964," it must either submit it for approval to the Attorney General, or else bring an action for a declaratory judgment in the District Court for the District of Columbia, and show that the new qualifications, prerequisite, etc., "does not have the purpose and will not have the effect of denying or abridging the right to vote on account of race or color."[48] Unless the Attorney General approves, or a declaratory judgment is obtained, the new qualification, prerequisite, etc., cannot be effective. Mr. Justice Black thought that this provision was unconstitutional, because the declaratory judgment action in the District of Columbia could not be a case or controversy.[49] To this the Court's reply, in something less than a paragraph, was that the controversy would be real and concrete enough,[50] which is probably right, since in the manner characteristic of declaratory judgment actions, all that the section effects is to reverse the parties; and as under § 4(a), the point of *Massachusetts v. Mellon*, discussed earlier, would not be encountered. An additional answer is that even if one suspects that such a controversy might not be sufficiently concrete, it was surely premature to hold the section unconstitutional on this basis.

Mr. Justice Black also thought, however—and he laid much more stress on this point—that it was, in any event, unconstitutional for Congress to put such a suspensive veto on state laws.[51] As to this,

---

[47] See JAFFE, JUDICIAL CONTROL OF ADMINISTRATIVE ACTION 339–53 (1965).

[48] 383 U.S. at 342–43.   [49] *Id.* at 357–58.   [50] *Id.* at 335.

[51] *Id.* at 358 *et seq.*

the Court answered even more briefly that Congress had had experience with legislative stratagems continually invented by the states to frustrate decrees and statutes in implementing the Fifteenth Amendment and that under "the compulsion of these unique circumstances, Congress responded in a permissibly decisive manner."[52] The constitutional holding, and the reasoning supporting it, are all contained in the word "permissibly." But the issue surely has complexities, and surely depends on variables that could not conceivably form the basis for either the Court's or Mr. Justice Black's conclusion at this time, on this record. At one extreme, there should not be much question that Congress could, under the Fifteenth Amendment, prospectively suspend not only the literacy and understanding tests which have been in use in some states but also any future variations of them.[53] At the other extreme, if a state changed its minimum age for voting and refused to submit this change either to the Attorney General or to the District Court for the District of Columbia, it would have a strong constitutional case. And there is a whole spectrum of problems between these extremes, which might have become evident and to which solutions might have varied, if the Court had allowed real cases to arise.

II. Harper v. Virginia Board of Elections

The Court was not quite finished with the Voting Rights Act of 1965. Two weeks after the abstractions of *South Carolina v. Katzenbach*, came *Harper v. Virginia Board of Elections*,[54] holding the poll tax unconstitutional.

The poll tax provision of the Act, § 10, is the result of much travail in Congress. Section 10 "finds" that the poll tax inhibits voting by the poor, is not reasonably related to "any legitimate State interest in the conduct of elections," and in some areas has the effect of discriminating by race. "Upon the basis of these findings, Congress declares that the constitutional right of citizens to vote is denied or abridged in some areas by the requirement of the pay-

---

[52] *Id.* at 335.

[53] Compare the way in which the Court dealt, in Louisiana v. United States, 380 U.S. 145 (1965), with a new "citizenship" test adopted after suit in that case had been filed.

[54] 383 U.S. 663 (1966).

ment of a poll tax as a pre-condition to voting."[55] But § 10 does
not outlaw the poll tax. Rather it authorizes and directs the Attorney General to implement the declaration just recited by bringing suit in the name of the United States for declaratory judgment
or injunctive relief against enforcement of the poll tax. Although
the point does not appear to have bothered the lower courts that
have acted under it,[56] § 10 raises all that has not yet been interred
of the difficulty in *Muskrat v. United States*.[57] Since *Harper v.
Virginia Board of Elections* arose independently of § 10, however,
the Supreme Court did not need to concern itself with the *Muskrat*
issue. Nor, in an opinion by Mr. Justice Douglas, did the Court
concern itself with very much else.

The opinion, resting exclusively on the Fourteenth Amendment,[58]
takes comfort in contemporary constitutional history—everything
from *Edwards v. California*,[59] *Skinner v. Oklahoma*,[60] *Brown v.
Board of Education*,[61] and *Malloy v. Hogan*,[62] to *Reynolds v.
Sims*;[63] everything, that is, save the relevant precedents of *Lassiter v.
Northhampton Education Board*,[64] which is dealt with lightly, and
Breedlove v. Suttles,[65] which is overruled. "Voter qualifications,"
the Court said, "have no relation to wealth nor to paying or not
paying this or any other tax. . . . To introduce wealth or payment
of a fee as a measure of a voter's qualifications is to introduce a
capricious or irrelevant factor."[66] There was nothing in the Court's

---

[55] 383 U.S. at 348.

[56] See United States v. Texas, 252 F. Supp. 234 (W.D. Tex. 1966), *aff'd*, 384 U.S.
155 (1966); United States v. Alabama, 252 F. Supp. 95 (M.D. Ala. 1966).

[57] 219 U.S. 346 (1911).

[58] Under the Fifteenth Amendment, the question, would, of course, have taken
on a different aspect. It would not have been easy to make out a case against the
poll tax as a vehicle for depriving Negroes of the vote. The tax has disfranchised
people, at least in combination with other factors, but it does not appear to have
been aimed solely at Negroes, or to have operated so as to disfranchise them alone.
See KEY, SOUTHERN POLITICS 534–35, 537–39, 542 *et seq.*, 579, 585, 597–98, 600–08
(1950). Perhaps in Alabama, recent facts would have made it possible to build a
fairly strong Fifteenth Amendment case. See United States v. Alabama, *supra*
note 56.

[59] 314 U.S. 160 (1941).

[60] 316 U.S. 535 (1942).

[61] 347 U.S. 483 (1954).

[62] 378 U.S. 1 (1964).

[63] 377 U.S. 533 (1964).

[64] 360 U.S. 45 (1959).

[65] 302 U.S. 277 (1937).

[66] 383 U.S. at 666, 668.

opinion, Mr. Justice Black complained in dissent, "which advances even a plausible argument as to why the alleged discriminations which might be effected by Virginia's poll tax law are 'irrational,' 'unreasonable,' 'arbitrary,' or 'invidious' or have no relevance to a single policy which the State wishes to adopt. The Court gives no reason. . . ."[67] Mr. Justice Black, if one may say so, was quite right. The Court gave no reason. It did not even notice the obvious argument, mentioned by Mr. Justice Harlan (in another dissent, joined by Mr. Justice Stewart), that payment of a minimal poll tax might rationally be thought to promote "civic responsibility, weeding out those who do not care enough about public affairs to pay $1.50 or thereabouts a year for the exercise of the franchise."[68] This may be thought a pretty argument and a worthy one, or it may be thought ugly and mean. But irrational?

Mr. Justice Douglas flirted with, but did not adopt, a quite different position. He quoted Judge Thornberry, of the three-judge court that struck down the Texas poll tax in a case arising under § 10, as remarking that if Texas were to place a tax, no matter how small, on the right to speak, no court would hesitate to declare it unconstitutional, for such a tax would be in blatant violation of the First and Fourteenth Amendments.[69] Obviously, however, as Mr. Justice Black suggested, the right to speak could also not be freely abridged on the basis of age, illiteracy, conviction of a felony, or residence; and yet the right to vote is commonly qualified on these grounds.

III. Katzenbach v. Morgan

The third case of the term to pass on the Voting Rights Act of 1965, *Katzenbach v. Morgan*,[70] upheld § 4(e), giving the right to vote to Spanish-speaking Puerto Ricans in New York. It was decided together with a companion case, *Cardona v. Power*,[71] which had arisen and been disposed of in the New York courts before the enactment of the Voting Rights Act of 1965. The Supreme Court vacated and remanded the *Cardona* case, without deciding the constitutionality under the Fourteenth Amendment of the requirement

---

[67] *Id*. at 676–77.   [68] *Id*. at 685.

[69] *Id*. at 665, n. 2, quoting from 252 F. Supp. at 254.

[70] 384 U.S. 641 (1966).   [71] 384 U.S. 672 (1966).

of the New York law that voters be literate in English. (Justices Douglas and Fortas, dissenting, would have held it unconstitutional.)[72] So § 4(e) of the Voting Rights Act, which forbids a state to condition the vote of a person educated in an American-flag school on his ability to read and understand the English language, came to judgment on the assumption that the constitutionality of literacy in English as a condition on the right to vote is an open question under the Fourteenth Amendment.

The Court, Mr. Justice Brennan writing, began by restating a point made in *South Carolina v. Katzenbach*, namely, that Congress is empowered by § 2 of the Fifteenth Amendment and § 5 of the Fourteenth to enact legislation appropriate to those constitutional provisions. Such legislation may reach into the affairs of the states further and differently than the Amendments themselves, applied by the courts without the aid of implementing legislation, would necessarily do.[73] This much is obvious enough. But in enacting appropriate legislation, is it up to Congress to define the substance of what the legislation must be appropriate to? If something is not an action of a state denying or abridging the right of citizens of the United States to vote, on account of race, color, or previous condition of servitude, may Congress say that it is, and thus reach it by legislation? If something is not an irrational classification by a state, may Congress say that it is and that it violates the Equal Protection Clause, and thus reach it by legislation? Of course, Congress may amass evidence and add the weight of its views, and thus affect, and affect powerfully, the Court's judgment of the applicability of the Fifteenth and Fourteenth Amendments. But may Congress under those Amendments, any more than under, for example, the Commerce Clause, determine the allocation of functions between federal and state governments, and the extent of its own powers? May it determine, not what means are appropriate to the enforcement of the Fourteenth and Fifteenth Amendments, or to the discharge of the function conferred by the Commerce Clause, but the content of those Amendments and of that clause?

These questions did not arise in *South Carolina v. Katzenbach*, where only the appropriateness of the means chosen by Congress was at issue. But in *Katzenbach v. Morgan* the Court did answer

---

[72] *Id.* at 675.   [73] See 383 U.S. at 325–27.

these questions. For it rested its conclusion that § 4(e) is constitutional at least in part on a holding that § 5 of the Fourteenth Amendment empowered Congress to act, whether or not, in the judgment of the Court, the requirement of literacy in English may be regarded as a discrimination forbidden by the Equal Protection Clause. It was urged, said the Court, "that § 4(e) cannot be sustained as appropriate legislation to enforce the Equal Protection Clause unless the judiciary decides—even with the guidance of a congressional judgment—that the application of the English literacy requirement prohibited by § 4(e) is forbidden by the Equal Protection Clause itself. We disagree."[74] To the extent that the Court, in this branch of its decision, purported to rely on evidence of the intent of the framers of the Fourteenth Amendment, the sufficient reply that can be made is James A. Garfield's to John A. Bingham in the House, nearly a century ago. My colleague, said Garfield, "can make but he cannot unmake history."[75] Nothing is clearer about the history of the Fourteenth Amendment than that its framers rejected the option of an open-ended grant of power to Congress to meddle with conditions within the states so as to render them equal in accordance with its own notions. Rather the framers chose to write an amendment empowering Congress only to rectify inequalities put into effect by the states. Hence the power of Congress comes into play only when the precondition of a denial of equal protection of the laws by a state has been met. Congress' view that the precondition has been met should be persuasive, but it cannot be decisive. That is the history of the matter.[76] But perhaps the Court meant to override history in order to bring § 5 of the Fourteenth Amendment into harmony with some general premise of our constitutional system.

Yet, while Congress must be allowed the widest choice of means in the discharge of its function, the general premise of *Marbury v. Madison*,[77] and of *M'Culloch v. Maryland*[78] also, is that Congress

---

[74] 384 U.S. at 648.

[75] Quoted in Bickel, *The Original Understanding and the Segregation Decision*, 69 HARV. L. REV. 1, 60, n. 115 (1955).

[76] See *id*. at 32–40; HARRIS, THE QUEST FOR EQUALITY 34–50 (1960). The argument in Frantz, *Congressional Power To Enforce the Fourteenth Amendment against Private Acts*, 73 YALE L.J. 1353 (1964), is not really to the contrary. See 73 YALE L.J. at 1358–59.

[77] 1 Cranch 137 (1803).   [78] 4 Wheat. 316 (1819).

does not define the limits of its own powers. It belongs, rather, to the Court, exercising the function of judicial review, to do so. When it applies the dormant Commerce Clause to the states, or when it protects federal instrumentalities from taxation by the states, the Court acts as a surrogate of Congress, and Congress, therefore, has the last word.[79] In a few other areas—taxation and spending for the general welfare is one; exclusion of aliens has been thought to be another—the Court, finding no standards to guide the exercise of judicial review, has abandoned the function. But the function has not yet been abandoned across the board. Whatever, then, could be the reasons for abdicating judicial review in this area of the Fourteenth Amendment, where it has been traditionally dominant? Certainly no general presumption of our constitutional system counsels any such abdication.

There is a second branch to the Court's decision in *Katzenbach v. Morgan*, which is subtler and more interesting. Congress, said the Court, may not have considered the New York requirement of literacy in English as itself a violation of the Fourteenth Amendment. Rather Congress may have been concerned with evidence of discriminatory treatment of the Puerto Rican community at the hands of New York public agencies. The Court was able to adduce no evidence of such discrimination, either out of the materials that were before Congress or independently of those mate-

---

[79] See Brown, *The Open Economy: Justice Frankfurter and the Position of the Judiciary*, 67 YALE L.J. 219, 221 (1957); FREUND, THE SUPREME COURT OF THE UNITED STATES, 92, 93 (1961). But in a letter to Senator Robert F. Kennedy, dated May 17, 1965, which the Senator relied on in the course of debate on § 4(e), Professor Freund wrote: "It would be agreed, for example, that if a State were to deny the franchise to Catholics or to a group of Protestants, the classification could be struck down by Congress or the courts under the 14th amendment's guarantee of equal protection of the laws. The courts do not have sole responsibility in this area. Just as Congress may give a lead to the courts under the Commerce Clause in prohibiting certain kinds of state regulation or taxation, and just as Congress may expressly prohibit certain forms of taxation of Federal instrumentalities, whether or not the courts have done so of their own accord, so in implementing the 14th and 15th amendments Congress may legislate through a declaration that certain forms of classification are unreasonable for purposes of the voting franchise." 111 CONG. REC. 11062, 89th Cong., 1st Sess. (May 20, 1965). But surely the analogy between the respective functions of the Court and the Congress in the areas of state taxation and regulation of interstate commerce and of state taxation of federal instrumentalities, on the one hand, and the area of the Fourteenth Amendment, on the other, is too readily drawn by Professor Freund in this letter.

rials.[80] But perhaps, with some stretching, the presumption of constitutionality should make up for this lack of evidence.[81] The argument then proceeds in this fashion. Instead of directly attacking the discrimination practiced against the Puerto Ricans, as it

---

[80] The only item of relevant evidence cited (but not quoted, or even paraphrased) by the Court is the following letter received in 1962 by the Subcommittee on Constitutional Rights of the Senate Committee on the Judiciary, and incorporated in the record of hearings the subcommittee held in the course of that year on literacy tests and other voter qualifications. The letter, dated at New York, April 16, 1962, is signed, Gene Crescenzi. It is short, and the gist of it needs to be quoted in full:

"The fact of disfranchisement of these citizens [Puerto Ricans in New York] operates to make them subject to all kinds of abuses and denials of the equal protection of the law. More serious than this, a fifth column type of activity has arisen in our governmental agencies and among elected public officials in respect to the disfranchised Puerto Ricans.

"In the week of January 2 to 9, 1962, the employees of Flower Hospital went on strike, they are mostly Puerto Ricans earning $35 to $40 per week, approximately 35 of these people were beaten and arrested. In this same week, the mayor of New York raised his wages $10,000. On January 17th the General Sessions Court announced that it would require probationers who don't speak English to learn English, as the lack of English was the cause of their problems. I could write volumes on the cruelty, brutality, murder, mayhem and general abuse delivered upon the disfranchised Spanish-speaking citizens in New York by the various agencies of our Government, all of which is directly due to their disfranchisement. Having no vote, they have no representation and no means of redress.

"The English literacy requirement is an instrument of racist policies of the State of New York, and it is used to circumvent the U.S. Constitution. It is more vicious in its application in the State of New York because it has driven its racist politicians underground, than in Southern States where segregation has long been a way of life and may be fought in the open in the American way." Literacy Tests and Voter Requirements in Federal and State Elections, Hearings before the Subcommittee on Constitutional Rights of the Committee on the Judiciary on S. 480, S. 2750, and S. 2979, 87th Cong., 2d Sess. 507–08 (1962).

A statement in 1965 to a subcommittee of the House Committee on the Judiciary by Herman Badillo, a leading Puerto Rican politician and now Borough President of The Bronx, pleaded for passage of what was to become § 4(e), but nowhere charged discrimination in public services or by any public agencies in New York against Puerto Ricans. See Voting Rights, Hearings before Subcommittee No. 5 of the Committee on the Judiciary on H.R. 6400, House of Representatives, 89th Cong., 1st Sess. 508–17 (1965).

[81] The stretching, however, would be considerable. It would amount, to change the figure somewhat, to a leap from a presumption buttressed by data, even if data "offered not for the truth of the facts asserted but only to establish that responsible persons have made the assertion and hold the opinions which are disclosed," FREUND, ON UNDERSTANDING THE SUPREME COURT 88, and see also 87–89 (1951), to a presumption that makes up for the lack of any data at all—a presumption that, in a case such as the present one, puts the party attacking constitutionality to the task of proving a negative.

could plainly have done under the Fourteenth Amendment, Congress decided to reach it indirectly. It secured the vote for the Puerto Rican community, in the belief that its political power would then enable that community to ensure non-discriminatory treatment for itself. The vote is thus seen as a means of enforcing the Fourteenth Amendment, not as itself the end of the congressional action, and Congress is not in the position of having undertaken to determine the substance of Fourteenth Amendment rights. Congress is merely presumed to have established facts showing that those rights, as judicially defined, have been or may be denied, and of choosing a suitable remedy:[82]

> It was for Congress, as the branch that made this judgment, to assess and weigh the various conflicting considerations—the risk or pervasiveness of the discrimination in governmental services, the effectiveness of eliminating the state restriction on the right to vote as a means of dealing with the evil, the adequacy or availability of alternative remedies, and the nature and significance of the state interests that would be affected by the nullification of the English literacy requirement as applied to residents who have successfully completed the sixth grade in a Puerto Rican school. It is not for us to review the congressional resolution of these factors. It is enough that we be able to perceive a basis upon which the Congress might resolve the conflict as it did.

The argument is superficially attractive. But suppose Congress decided that aliens or eighteen-year-olds or residents of New Jersey are being discriminated against in New York. The decision would be as plausible as the one concerning Spanish-speaking Puerto Ricans. Could Congress give these groups the vote? If Congress may freely bestow the vote as a means of curing other discriminations, which it fears may be practiced against groups deprived of the vote, essentially because of this deprivation and on the basis of no other evidence, then there is nothing left of state autonomy in setting qualifications for voting. The argument proves too much. The Court relied on Marshall's famous pronouncement: "Let the end be legitimate, let it be within the scope of the constitution, and all means which are appropriate, which are plainly adapted to that end, which are not prohibited, but consist with the letter and spirit of the constitution, are constitutional."[83] The

---

[82] 384 U.S. at 653.   [83] 4 Wheat. at 421.

Court duly emphasized appropriateness, and adaptation to a given end, but it de-emphasized altogether too much Marshall's caveat that the means chosen must also not be prohibited, and must "consist with the letter and spirit of the constitution."[84]

IV. Conclusion

The impatience exhibited in *South Carolina v. Katzenbach* with jurisdictional problems of first importance reflects sadly both on the Court and on that very special officer of the Court, the Solicitor General. The Court, to be sure, has been known to swallow jurisdictional scruples before now, with no permanent ill effect. But while no ominous view need be taken of this or other isolated instances, only the most ominous of views can be taken of the practice.

The Court's other two encounters with the Voting Rights Act of 1965 are not a little ironic. No Justices have been more jealous

---

[84] A dissent by Judge McGowan from the decision below, Morgan v. Katzenbach, 247 F. Supp. 196, 204 (D. D.C. 1965), and the opinion of a three-judge court in New York in another case, in which an appeal was aborted by the intermediate decision of *Swift & Co. v. Wickham* (382 U.S. 111 [1965]), United States v. County Board of Elections of Monroe County, 248 F. Supp. 316 (W.D. N.Y. 1965), *appeal dismissed for want of jurisdiction*, 383 U.S. 575 (1966), attempt to rest the constitutionality of § 4(e) on a narrower and more persuasive ground, though one that is also not free from difficulties. Being empowered to make rules and regulations for the governance of territories, Congress bestowed citizenship on natives of Puerto Rico, while at the same time permitting them to be educated in schools in which the language of instruction is Spanish. It also permitted them freely to migrate to the mainland. If Congress now thought that, having migrated to the mainland, Puerto Ricans should not be deprived of a voice in the government of whatever state they settled in because of a lack of literacy in English, which is itself owing to the kind of education Congress provided them with, Congress could, the argument runs, in pursuance of its power to govern the territories, decree that Puerto Ricans must be allowed to vote whether or not literate in English. From this point on, of course, the Supremacy Clause goes the rest of the way to overcome the law of New York. But suppose Congress wanted Puerto Ricans who were altogether illiterate to vote in New York. Or suppose it wanted natives of Guam, whom it had not chosen to make citizens, to vote in New York. Or suppose it wanted Puerto Rico, in its present status, not as a state, to be represented in the Senate and to vote in presidential elections. Congress, moreover, also has power to admit or exclude aliens, and to naturalize them or not. Suppose Congress thought it well that aliens, or aliens of a given nationality, should vote in state elections from the moment they arrived in a state, regardless of the length of their residence, and regardless of their age, or of their previous criminal record. Neither the power to govern territories nor the power to conduct foreign relations has hitherto been thought necessarily to carry everything before it.

guardians of the judicial prerogative, or more energetic wielders of judicial power, than the governing majority of the present Court. And yet *Katzenbach v. Morgan* constitutes restraint, if not abdication, beyond the wildest dreams of the majority's usual *bête noire*, James Bradley Thayer, and in fact beyond anything he intended to recommend. And *Harper v. Virginia Board of Elections* harks attentively to even a timid hint from Congress. One doubts, nevertheless, that a new trend has really been inaugurated.

JOHN H. MANSFIELD

THE ALBERTSON CASE: CON-
FLICT BETWEEN THE PRIVILEGE
AGAINST SELF-INCRIMINATION
AND THE GOVERNMENT'S NEED
FOR INFORMATION

I. ALBERTSON V. SUBVERSIVE ACTIVITIES CONTROL BOARD

In *Albertson v. Subversive Activities Control Board*,[1] the Supreme Court decided questions of self-incrimination that four years earlier, in *Communist Party of the United States v. Subversive Activities Control Board*,[2] it had held not ripe for adjudication. In the *Communist Party* case the Court sustained the obligation of the Party to register as a "Communist-action organization" in compliance with an order of the Subversive Activities Control Board. It did not, however, pass upon the question whether individual officers of the Party or other persons were entitled to refuse to register the Party, or to register for the Party, on grounds of self-incrimination. Nor did it pass upon the question whether members of the Party could refuse to register in compliance with a Board order directed to them as individuals.

Following the decision in the *Communist Party* case, the Party

John H. Mansfield is Professor of Law, Harvard University.

[1] 382 U.S. 70 (1965).   [2] 367 U.S. 1 (1961).

failed to register within the period provided by the statute,[3] and as a result was prosecuted and convicted of the offense of failing to register. This conviction was reversed by the Court of Appeals for the District of Columbia[4] on the ground that the officers of the Party who had refused to register the Party were entitled to refuse to register it on the ground that to do so might tend to incriminate them. The case was remanded to the district court to give the government an opportunity to show that someone was available to register the Party who would not thereby incriminate himself or who was willing to register the Party notwithstanding a danger of incrimination.

When the Party failed to register, the provisions of § 8 of the Subversive Activities Control Act became applicable.[5] Under that section, when an organization fails to register in compliance with an order of the Board, individual members of the organization must register. Pursuant to § 13 of the Act,[6] the Attorney General initiated a proceeding before the Board for the purpose of obtaining an order directing the petitioners in *Albertson* to register as members of the Communist Party. The Board determined that petitioners were members of the Party and ordered them to register. This order was affirmed by the Court of Appeals. The Supreme Court reversed the judgment of the Court of Appeals and set aside the order of the Board.

The Court held that the order directing petitioners to register as members of a Communist-action organization and to file an accompanying registration statement violated their privilege against self-incrimination. The Court found that the privilege question was ripe for adjudication and on this point contrasted *Albertson* with the situation in the *Communist Party* case:[7]

> Here, in contrast, the contingencies upon which the members' duty to register arises have already matured; the Party did not register within 30 days after the order to register became final and the requisite 60 days since the order became final have elapsed. As to the officers obliged to register the Party, *Com-*

---

[3] 50 U.S.C. § 793(b) (1964).

[4] Communist Party of the United States v. United States, 331 F.2d 807 (D.C. Cir. 1963).

[5] 50 U.S.C. § 787 (1964).

[6] 50 U.S.C. § 792 (1964).   [7] 382 U.S. at 74–75.

munist Party held that the self-incrimination claim asserted on their behalf was not ripe for adjudication because it was not known whether they would ever claim the privilege or whether the claim, if asserted, would be honored by the Attorney General. But with respect to the orders in this case, addressed to named individuals, both these contingencies are foreclosed. Petitioners asserted the privilege. . . . In each instance the Attorney General rejected their claims. . . .

The Court pointed out that petitioners risked very heavy penalties for failing to register:[8]

Petitioners must either register without a decision on the merits of their privilege claims, or fail to register and risk onerous and rapidly mounting penalties while awaiting the Government's pleasure whether to initiate a prosecution against them. To ask, in these circumstances, that petitioners await such a prosecution for an adjudication of their self-incrimination claims is, in effect, to contend that they should be denied the protection of the Fifth Amendment privilege intended to relieve claimants of the necessity of making a choice between incriminating themselves and risking serious punishment for refusing to do so.

Although one cannot quarrel with the Court's determination that petitioners' claim of privilege was ripe for adjudication, the last reason given in the quoted passage is somewhat confusing. Ordinarily the statement that "the privilege is intended to relieve . . . of the necessity of making a choice between incriminating . . . and risking serious punishments for refusing to do so" is used simply to describe the purpose and effect of the privilege when it is applicable, and is not addressed to the problem of when a claim of privilege is ripe for adjudication. If a case falls within the privilege, the claimant is relieved of the necessity of choosing between incriminating himself and being punished for refusing to do so. But if a case does not fall within the privilege, then, of course, the claimant is not relieved of this choice. What concerns the Court, evidently, is that one who is in fact entitled to the protection of the privilege may not benefit from it because he is unwilling to run the risk of prosecution involved in finding out whether or not he is privileged. A means of obtaining judicial enforcement of the privilege that does not involve a risk of criminal prosecution is essential to the enjoyment of the privilege by

---

[8] *Id.* at 75–76.

those entitled to its protection. For this reason it can be said that the answer to the ripeness question is dictated by the policy of the privilege itself. As for persons who are not privileged to refuse to answer, they perhaps are entitled, simply on grounds of fairness, to learn that this is the case without running the risk of criminal prosecution.

The Government argued against the availability of the privilege in *Albertson* that, since the Board had already determined that petitioners were members of the Communist Party, their compliance with the Board's order to register would not further incriminate them.[9] This argument was an effort to assimilate the situation in *Albertson* to the case where, because a person has already been convicted of a crime, he is not privileged to refuse to testify about it. The Court properly refused to consider the cases to be the same or to accept the argument that the privilege was inapplicable because petitioners' registration would provide no information that the Government did not already possess. The Board's finding that petitioners were members of the Party and the order to register would not protect petitioners from prosecution for crimes of which membership is an element or to which it is relevant. The registration order would not provide a basis for a plea of *autre fois convict*. And petitioners' registration and the information in the registration statement might be found by the trier of fact in a subsequent criminal proceeding to have incriminating evidentiary value. The Court found that the immunity provision included in the statute was insufficiently broad to protect against such a disadvantageous consequence.[10]

Had the immunity provision been broader, or were the decision of the Board in fact the equivalent of a conviction, the privilege would not have been available. So far as immunity is concerned, this conclusion must be taken as firmly established by *Counselman v. Hitchcock*[11] and *Brown v. Walker*,[12] and recently reaffirmed

---

[9] Brief for Respondent, p. 21.

[10] The immunity provision, § 4(f) of the act, 50 U.S.C. § 783(f) (1964), not only failed to protect petitioners from prosecution, it even failed to prohibit the use of their registration as an investigatory lead, or the use of the information called for in the registration statement either as an investigatory lead or as evidence in a possible criminal prosecution. See 382 U.S. at 80.

[11] 142 U.S. 547 (1892).   [12] 161 U.S. 591 (1896).

in *Ullman v. United States.*[13] This result has been adhered to notwithstanding serious misgivings about the consequences other than criminal punishment that may be visited upon a person who is forced to disclose incriminating information about himself. From non-governmental sources there may come loss of employment and social ostracism, and the government itself may withdraw a variety of benefits. Even if the purpose of the privilege is only to protect from the danger of criminal prosecution, it is nevertheless true that when the privilege is available, because there has been no grant of immunity, there is in fact protection from these other consequences as well, whether or not such protection is within the purpose of the privilege. The decision in *Murphy v. Waterfront Commission,*[14] which makes the danger of prosecution under federal law a basis for invoking the privilege in a state investigation and thus overrules the line of cases that includes *United States v. Murdock,*[15] indicates a continuing unease about the range of consequences to which a person can be exposed without destroying the substance of the privilege.

That prior conviction of the very crime inquired about should render the privilege unavailable is perhaps more obvious than that it should be unavailable when there has been a grant of immunity. If a person has been convicted, the likelihood is that he has already suffered all the non-penal disadvantages that can be visited upon him. His confession of the crime and testimony as to its details will probably not result in any significant further disadvantage, even though for some persons there may be a special humiliation in confessing guilt and in effect ratifying the jury's verdict. Of course, if a convicted person is called before an investigatory body and asked questions that may expose him to a danger of prosecution for crimes other than the one for which he has already been convicted, the privilege remains in force. Whether there is such a danger will be affected by whether prosecution for these other crimes should have been joined with prosecution for the crime of which he has been convicted, and whether he is protected by principles of double jeopardy and procedural fairness. Also, even though a person has been convicted, he neverthe-

---

[13] 350 U.S. 422 (1956).

[14] 378 U.S. 52 (1964).   [15] 290 U.S. 389 (1933).

less may be in danger of prosecution under the laws of another jurisdiction.[16]

Reina v. United States[17] shows that even when a person has been convicted it is frequently necessary to grant immunity before testimony can be compelled because of the danger of prosecution for other crimes or under the laws of another jurisdiction. Nevertheless, the Court's opinion in that case restates the general proposition that conviction renders the privilege unavailable in respect to questions relating to the crime covered by the conviction, and even though a compelled admission of guilt may cause humiliation.

In *Piemonte v. United States*,[18] a convicted person refused to testify before a grand jury partly out of fear of retaliation by other criminals against himself and his family. Mr. Justice Frankfurter stated the principle that conviction destroys the privilege in this way:[19]

> If two persons witness an offense—one being an innocent bystander and the other an accomplice who is thereafter imprisoned for his participation—the latter has no more right to keep silent than the former. The Government of course has an obligation to protect its citizens from harm. But fear of reprisal offers an immunized prisoner no more dispensation from testifying than it does any innocent bystander without a record.

Of course, if the accomplice is neither convicted nor immunized, he is excused from testifying when the innocent person is not. The privilege may then have the incidental effect of saving him from reprisal. Because of the privilege the guilty are sometimes better off than the innocent. Unhappiness with this fact can be the source of pressure to erode and cut down the privilege. The refusal to permit a person engaged in an illegal business to use the privilege to escape punishment for failure to file a tax return, a situation that will be discussed later, is one example of resistance to the privilege when it seems to give criminals an advantage over the law-abiding.

United States v. Castaldi[20] presented the more troubling case of an acquittal and its effect on the availability of the privilege.

---

16 See Murphy v. Waterfront Commission, *supra* note 14.

17 364 U.S. 507 (1960).   18 367 U.S. 556 (1961).   19 *Id.* at 559 n. 2.

20 338 F.2d 883 (2d Cir. 1964), *judgment vacated and case remanded for reconsideration of a different point*, 384 U.S. 886 (1966).

The defendant in that case was called before a grand jury and asked questions relating to a crime of which he had been acquitted. When he refused to answer, he was convicted of contempt and this conviction was affirmed on appeal. The significance of the decision is somewhat blurred by the fact that the defendant was also granted immunity from prosecution.

If the purpose of the privilege is solely to protect from the danger of criminal prosecution and punishment, the case of acquittal is no different from that of conviction. In either case there is no further danger of prosecution. On the other hand, the practical consequences of confessing guilt are likely to be very different. As noted above, a convicted person will probably not suffer any significant additional disadvantage as a result of his confession. This is not true when a person has been acquitted. An acquittal may save a man's reputation, may prevent him from losing his job, may preserve to him a variety of other benefits. It may undo to a considerable extent the evil consequences that frequently flow from the mere fact of being charged with a crime. But if after acquittal the defendant confesses that, after all, he is guilty, many of the disadvantages held off by the acquittal will be visited upon him. The case of a grant of immunity lies somewhere between conviction and acquittal. There has been no authoritative finding, before the witness is forced to incriminate himself, either of innocence or of guilt.

An argument can be made that the policy underlying the acquittal of a criminal charge should preclude compelling a person to confess his guilt and expose himself to a range of serious consequences. This is so, it can be said, because of the distinct policy underlying acquittal and not because of the privilege against self-incrimination. The privilege may be conceded to take into account only the danger of criminal prosecution, but the policy of acquittal has a different aim. Is it not possible that in this manner those who dissent from *Brown v. Walker*[21] and *Ullman v. United States*[22] may still rescue something from what they considered the calamity of those cases in withdrawing protection against self-disgrace, social ostracism, and economic ruin?

In the case of conviction, even if one accepts the view that the privilege is unavailable, there may in certain circumstances be

[21] 161 U.S. 591 (1896).   [22] 350 U.S. 422 (1956).

other objections to compelling a person to confess his own crime. There may be objections under the free speech provision of the First Amendment or the Due Process Clause of the Fifth. An imaginative argument for the applicability of these other constitutional provisions was made by petitioners in *Albertson*,[23] but the ground of decision that the Court took made it unnecessary to pass upon the questions presented. The arguments made by petitioners assumed that registration would not expose them to the danger of criminal prosecution, but that nevertheless they should not be compelled to register.

The first question that might be asked is what purpose does it serve to compel a convicted person to admit his guilt? What purpose did it serve to compel petitioners to register themselves as members of the Communist Party when the Board had already made a determination that they were members? If no purpose is served that the government is entitled to pursue, there is a denial of due process. The effort of an investigating agency such as a grand jury to obtain from a witness not only a simple confession of guilt but also information regarding the commission of the crime and the circumstances surrounding it, information that may be useful in the detection and prosecution of other criminals, would seem a permissible governmental purpose. So far as a simple confession of guilt or confirmation of facts already found is concerned, can it be said that the government is entitled to compel such incriminating testimony from a convicted person for the sake of giving the authorities a firmer assurance of the truth of the matters involved? Given such assurance, they may have stronger reason to take certain further steps in law-enforcement. This argument seems feeble, and perhaps can be outweighed by some significant interest of the convicted defendant in not confessing.

The purpose of extracting an admission of guilt or confirmation of facts may be simply to allay fears that the verdict was wrong. Or it may be to humiliate the defendant and cause him to suffer.[24]

---

23 Brief for Petitioners, pp. 33–41.

24 In Piemonte v. United States, 367 U.S. 556 (1961), Chief Justice Warren, in dissent, spoke of the contempt conviction of a person who refuses to answer questions relating to a crime of which he has been convicted as "unjustified harassment" that "violates the spirit of the Double Jeopardy Clause of the Fifth Amendment." He also spoke of the "fundamental unfairness" of the proceeding. "I do not mean to imply that a person who is incarcerated may, for that reason alone be

If the purpose is to humiliate, the proceeding may run afoul of the prohibition against cruel and unusual punishments. This prohibition might serve to give partial recognition to the sentiments that found a place in earlier, broader notions of the privilege against self-incrimination which shielded against self-disgrace even when there was no danger of conviction. An argument can also be made that when the purpose is to humiliate and the means used are words compelled from a man's mouth and thoughts from his mind, there is a violation of the free speech guarantee of the First Amendment.

Some might argue that compelling a convicted person to confess his crime is important to rehabilitation. Sentencing courts and parole boards may occasionally allow their determinations to be affected by whether or not the defendant admits his guilt and shows contrition.[24a] There is a disturbing possibility here involving penetration into the mind and personality and suggesting notorious practices in other political systems.

It has been assumed so far in this discussion that all that is sought from the person interrogated is that he tell the truth, that he admit committing the crime if he did in fact commit it. Suppose, however, that he is required to make certain statements whether or not he believes them to be true. And suppose further that a third person hearing or reading these statements thinks they expressed the defendant's actual belief. In *Albertson*, petitioners argued that they were being ordered to state that they were members of the Communist Party even though they did not necessarily believe this to be true.

This is essentially the situation involved in a series of Labor Board cases some twenty-five years ago. The courts refused to

excused from testifying before a grand jury. However, I do believe that he cannot be compelled to testify concerning the alleged activity for which he has been incarcerated." *Id*. at 564 and n. 4.

[24a] In the recent extraordinary hearing in the Supreme Court of Canada to review the 1959 conviction of Steven Truscott for murder, there was introduced into evidence Truscott's application for parole in 1964. In this application Truscott asked to be given a chance "to prove one dreadful mistake does not mean that I will ever make another one." Before the Supreme Court, Truscott testified that he wrote these words not as an admission of guilt, but because the parole board believed him guilty, and "if I kept stating my innocence, it would hurt my chances of getting out." BOSTON GLOBE, Oct. 10, 1966, morning ed., p. 2.

sustain Board orders issued to employers who had been found guilty of unfair labor practices to post notices that they would cease and desist from such practices.[25] Although a case raising this question went to the Supreme Court, the Court found it unnecessary to decide the issue, since the Board had modified its practice in regard to such orders.[26] The decisions of the lower courts rested on the ground that the Board had no statutory authority to issue such orders, but the opinions are heavy with constitutional implications. In one case Judge Learned Hand stated:[27]

> But we think that to compel him to say that he will "cease and desist," necessarily imports that in the past he has been doing the things forbidden; indeed we find it hard to see how the contrary can be rationally argued. Forcibly to compel anyone to declare that the utterances of any official, whoever he may be, are true, when he protests that he does not believe them, has implications which we should hesitate to believe Congress could ever have intended. At any rate, until the Supreme Court speaks, we will not so construe the statute; nor are we disposed nicely to examine the scruples alleged; too long a history, and too dearly bought privileges, are behind such refusals.

The particular evil here is compulsory propagation of erroneous views about what a person believes. Either the free speech guarantee or the Due Process Clauses may serve as a barrier to compelled statements of this sort. Where the compelled statement is incriminating, as in *Albertson*, perhaps the privilege against self-incrimination itself can be invoked. Even if the privilege does not protect from compulsory self-disgrace that is truthful, might it not perhaps give protection against compulsory self-disgrace that in the eyes of the person forced to speak is false?

If no one hearing or reading the compelled utterance would believe that it expressed the speaker's state of mind, precisely because someone compelled him to make the statement, it is more

---

25 Art Metals Constr. Co. v. N.L.R.B., 110 F.2d 148 (2d Cir. 1940); Hartsell Mills Co. v. N.L.R.B., 111 F.2d 291 (4th Cir. 1940); N.L.R.B. v. Louisville Refining Co., 102 F.2d 678 (6th Cir.), *cert. denied*, 308 U.S. 568 (1939).

26 N.L.R.B. v. Express Publishing Co., 312 U.S. 426, 438–39 (1941).

27 Art Metals Constr. Co. v. N.L.R.B., 110 F.2d 148, 151 (2d Cir. 1940). In Hartsell Mills Co. v. N.L.R.B., 111 F.2d 291, 293 (4th Cir. 1940), it was said: "We cannot imagine a court sending an employer to jail for not publishing a confession that he has been guilty of violating the law, for not even a convicted felon can be required to confess his guilt."

difficult to articulate a constitutional objection. Suppose in *Albertson*, for example, it was perfectly clear that registration was an involuntary act done solely to comply with the order of the Board and to avoid criminal punishment. No one learning of the registration would suppose that it was an indication of what petitioners actually believed. Still, is there not humiliation and degradation in being compelled to recite a lesson that is set for you by an official and that imputes criminality to you? Being compelled to recite words determined by another seems potentially more degrading than being compelled to perform many other sorts of acts. This may be because when a person is compelled to speak, power is assumed over a function intimately connected with the personality. But if there is humiliation and degradation, is it sufficiently serious to constitute a cruel and unusual punishment, or, because words are compelled, a violation of free speech, that is, of the right not to speak? An argument in favor of compelling such utterances for the sake of rehabilitation seems here even closer to a defense of brainwashing. The idea would be to bring a person to believe that he committed a crime by having him say that he did. If no purpose that the government is entitled to pursue can be served by such compelled repetition of an official order— in *Albertson* the order of the Subversive Activities Control Board —there is a denial of due process.

II. ALBERTSON CASTS ITS SHADOW

In *Albertson*, as already noted, the Court found it possible to avoid these difficult questions and to rest its decision on a seemingly straightforward application of the privilege against self-incrimination. The Board's order to register was not the equivalent of a conviction. The immunity provision in the statute was inadequate. Petitioners were exposed to prosecution for a variety of crimes. The Court particularly cited the possibility of prosecution under the membership clause of the Smith Act,[28] and under § 4(a) of the Subversive Activities Control Act.[29] Evidentiary use of petitioners' registration or information called for in the registration statement could be made either directly by introduction in a subsequent prosecution or indirectly as investigatory

---

[28] 18 U.S.C. § 2385.   [29] 50 U.S.C. § 783 (a) (1964).

leads. Having taken note of this, the Court went on to conclude, without any significant further discussion, that therefore the privilege against self-incrimination was available and petitioners were constitutionally entitled not to register or file a registration statement.

Not discussed by the Court was the relation between its decision in *Albertson* and decisions in a number of earlier cases involving situations not entirely dissimilar to *Albertson*. In some of these cases the Court had held that the privilege was not available in spite of the fact that disclosure would incriminate and no immunity was granted. Conspicuous by its absence is any reference in *Albertson* to *Shapiro v. United States*.[30] In that case the Court sustained a conviction for violation of price regulations based in part upon evidence derived from the defendant's business records. These records had been surrendered in compliance with a subpoena, and under protest, in the course of an investigation by the Office of Price Administration. The Court held that the defendant was not privileged to withhold the records because:[31]

> The record involved in the case at bar was a sales record required to be maintained under an appropriate regulation, its relevance to the lawful purpose of the Administrator is unquestioned, and the transaction which it recorded was one in which the petitioner could lawfully engage solely by virtue of the license granted to him under the statute.

In *Albertson* petitioners' registration as members of a Communist-action organization was evidently thought by Congress to be necessary to effecting a regulatory program of great public importance.

Also omitted from the opinion in *Albertson* was any reference to *United States v. Kahriger*[32] and *Lewis v. United States*.[33] The statute involved in these cases, like that in *Albertson*, required registration as part of a governmental program that on its face at least was not aimed at criminal detection and punishment. *Kahriger* and *Lewis* upheld a statute that made it a crime to accept wagers without first registering with the Internal Revenue Service and paying a wagering tax.[34] That these wagering tax cases are

---

[30] 335 U.S. 1 (1948).   [32] 345 U.S. 22 (1953).

[31] *Id.* at 35.   [33] 348 U.S. 419 (1955).

[34] For the statutory provisions relating to the wagering tax, see 26 U.S.C. §§ 4411, 4412, 4422, 7202, 7203, 7272.

somehow relevant to the problem presented by *Albertson*, and
have perhaps been called into question by that decision, is indicated
by the fact that following *Albertson* certiorari was granted in a
case essentially indistinguishable from *Kahriger* and *Lewis*.[35]

The Court did seek to distinguish *United States v. Sullivan*,[36]
a case involving a conviction for failure to file an income tax return. The taxpayer sought to justify his failure to file on the
ground that a correct return would reveal that he was engaged in
a business that violated the National Prohibition Act. Mr. Justice
Holmes, for the Court, rejected this argument:[37]

> If the form of return provided called for answers that the de-
> fendant was privileged from making he could have raised the
> objection in the return, but could not on that account refuse
> to make any return at all. We are not called on to decide what,
> if anything, he might have withheld. Most of the items war-
> ranted no complaint. It would be an extreme if not an extrava-
> gant application of the Fifth Amendment to say that it author-
> ized a man to refuse to state the amount of his income because
> it had been made in crime. But if the defendant desired to test
> that or any other point he should have tested it in the return
> so that it could be passed upon. He could not draw a conjurer's
> circle around the whole matter by his own declaration that to
> write any word upon the government blank would bring him
> into danger of the law. . . .

In *Albertson* the Court compared the situation in the case before
it with *Sullivan*:[38]

> A tribunal, the Board, had an opportunity to pass upon the pe-
> titioners' self-incrimination claims; and since, unlike a tax re-
> turn, the pervasive effect of the information called for by
> Form IS-52 is incriminatory, their claims are substantial and
> far from frivolous. In *Sullivan* the questions in the income tax
> return were neutral on their face and directed at the public at
> large, but here they are directed at a highly selective group in-
> herently suspect of criminal activities. Petitioners' claims are
> not asserted in an essentially noncriminal and regulatory area

---

[35] Costello v. United States, 352 F.2d 848 (2d Cir. 1965), *cert. granted*, 383 U.S.
942 (1966). The petition for certiorari was granted limited to the question: "Do
not the Federal wagering tax statutes here involved violate the petitioner's privilege
against self-incrimination guaranteed by the Fifth Amendment? Should not this
court, especially in view of its recent decision in *Albertson* v. *Subversive Activities
Control Board* . . . overrule *United States* v. *Kahriger* . . . and *Lewis* v. *United
States* . . .?"

[36] 274 U.S. 259 (1927).   [37] *Id.* at 263–64.   [38] 382 U.S. at 79.

of inquiry, but against an inquiry in an area permeated with criminal statutes, where response to any of the form's questions in context might involve the petitioners in the admission of a crucial element of a crime.

It seems clear that *Albertson* stands at the threshold of an effort by the Court to re-examine this whole group of cases, perhaps in the hope of rationalizing them more successfully, perhaps with the thought that changed notions of the privilege that have emerged in various contexts[39] must now be brought to bear on the problems raised by these older cases. The result may be that relatively more weight will be given to the policy of the privilege as against the government's need for information. If one considers the whole line of cases from the early case involving the compelled production of incriminating corporate documents[40] to the wagering tax cases, the whole subject has resisted with remarkable success efforts to discover and apply simplifying general principles capable of both respecting the policy of the privilege and taking due account of important governmental interests. The limitations on the privilege that have been developed seem for the most part arbitrary and easily capable of being extended so as entirely to destroy the privilege. The *Shapiro* case is an example. Although on its face the privilege may seem more absolute and fixed than certain other constitutional provisions, less likely to yield to competing interests, in actual application it has been as capable of narrow or generous interpretation as more obviously elastic constitutional provisions. It is the advent of a renewed effort to understand what principles should limit the privilege and how they are to be applied both to preserve the policy of the privilege and to give adequate recognition to strong competing interests that is signaled by the *Albertson* case and the decision to reconsider the wagering tax cases. To this effort the following reflections may perhaps contribute.[41]

At the start it may be well to mention and put to one side two principles that are sometimes said to provide an explanation for

[39] See, *e.g.*, Malloy v. Hogan, 378 U.S. 1 (1964); Murphy v. Waterfront Commission, 378 U.S. 52 (1964); Griffin v. California, 380 U.S. 609 (1965).

[40] Wilson v. United States, 221 U.S. 361 (1911).

[41] Of course, any discussion of these problems is inescapably indebted to Meltzer, *Required Records, the McCarran Act, and the Privilege against Self-Incrimination*, 18 U. Chi. L. Rev. 687 (1951), and Maguire, Evidence of Guilt §§ 209(2)–(3) (1959).

the kind of case with which we are concerned. In fact, these principles usually do not provide a satisfactory explanation and serve only to conceal the real difficulties. They provide a way of avoiding the necessity of discerning and reconciling seriously competing interests. These explanations are that the compelled disclosure is not in fact incriminating; and that even if it is incriminating, it is not testimonially incriminating, and so not within the privilege.

In the *Sullivan* case, which has already been mentioned, one of the grounds for decision suggested by Mr. Justice Holmes was that the mere filing of a tax return could not incriminate and that much of the information called for by the government form would be entirely neutral and innocent. Whether the defendant would have been entitled not to report certain items of income or not to reveal the source of certain items, were questions that the Court did not find it necessary to decide, for it was clear that the defendant was at least under an obligation to file a return of some sort. And yet it seems inescapable that filing any sort of a return, at least a truthful return, would have tended to incriminate the defendant. It would have incriminated him in the sense that it would have increased the likelihood of prosecution and conviction under the National Prohibition Act. The filing of a return stating that the defendant had received income of an undisclosed amount from an unnamed source and that the missing information was withheld because it would tend to incriminate would certainly give rise to an inference that the defendant was engaged in an illegal enterprise. Under ordinary tests of relevancy and cogency, and in the absence of an exclusionary rule based on the fact that the defendant had filed the return in compliance with law, the fact that he had filed such a return would be admissible in evidence in a prosecution for an illegal activity that other evidence showed he was probably engaged in. At the least, it would alert authorities to the likelihood that the defendant had committed an offense.

Of course the fact that a tax return containing only limited information would not necessarily establish that the taxpayer was engaged in crime does not mean that there is no incrimination in the constitutional sense. Much less is required than that a compelled statement be susceptible only to a criminal interpretation. Recently in *Malloy v. Hogan*[42] the Court restated the test of *Hoffman v. United States:*[43]

---

[42] 378 U.S. 1, 11–12 (1964).   [43] 341 U.S. 479, 486–87 (1951).

"The privilege afforded not only extends to answers that would in themselves support a conviction . . . but likewise embraces those which would furnish a link in a chain of evidence needed to prosecute. . . . [I]f the witness, upon interposing his claim, were required to prove the hazard . . . he would be compelled to surrender the very protection which the privilege is designed to guarantee. To sustain the privilege, it need only be evident from the implications of the question, in the setting in which it is asked, that a responsive answer to the question or an explanation of why it cannot be answered might be dangerous. . . ."

We also said that, in applying the test, the judge must be " '*perfectly clear*, from a careful consideration of all the circumstances in the case, that the witness is mistaken, and that the answer[s] *cannot possibly* have such a tendency' to incriminate."

Indeed, even the failure to file a tax return may be incriminating. If there exists a general requirement that all persons with income above a certain amount file a tax return, except those whose income is from an illegal source, the failure to file would tend to incriminate. It would give rise to a permissible inference, although of course not a compelled inference, that one who did not file was indeed engaged in criminal activity. The incriminating inference arises from inaction rather than from any utterance or active disclosure, but nevertheless there is an inference of a guilty state of mind, from which can be inferred the criminal facts. These inferences are made possible by the general obligation to report income and the exception when the report would result in an incriminating disclosure.

When a witness is subpoenaed to testify before an investigating agency and declines to answer questions on the ground that his answers will tend to incriminate him, a somewhat similar case is presented. The witness' refusal to answer and his invocation of the privilege are themselves incriminating in that they give rise to an inference that he has something to conceal. The inference is made possible by the general obligation to testify and the exception that testimony need not be given when it will tend to incriminate. Even if a person is not under an obligation to appear in response to a subpoena when he believes that any testimony he could give would tend to incriminate, his failure to appear can give rise to an inference of criminality.

In these cases only the abolition of the general requirement to report income, or withdrawal of the general authority to issue subpoenas and compel testimony, would entirely eliminate the danger of incrimination. Only then would a person be relieved of a situation in which he would incriminate himself either by speaking or by remaining silent, by filing a tax return or by not filing one. Such a drastic step is of course not to be considered; the restrictions it would impose upon the revenue-raising and investigatory powers of government would be intolerable. It would forbid a self-reporting system of taxation even as applied to those not engaged in criminal activity, and it would thwart efforts in investigatory proceedings to obtain information even from those whose testimony would not tend to incriminate them. It must be permissible and consistent with the privilege to force a person to incriminate himself at least to the extent that is necessarily incident to the exercise of general investigatory and revenue-raising powers. It must be permissible to compel such incrimination as results from the failure to file an income tax return or the failure to respond to a subpoena.

The question is whether a further step may be taken and a person compelled, in the case of the tax return, to incriminate himself more seriously by filing a tax return but invoking the privilege in the return and withholding certain information. If he files no return at all, he may escape official attention. If he does file a return, however, and claims the privilege, the authorities will be furnished with information that will enable them to draw an incriminating inference. In the case of a witness subpoenaed to testify, the choice between allowing him not to appear at all and requiring him to appear but permitting him to invoke the privilege is not so serious, since in either case the authorities will know of his refusal to co-operate and from it draw an incriminating inference.

It will be recalled that in *Malloy v. Hogan*, from which a passage was just quoted concerning what constitutes incrimination, the defendant in fact appeared before an investigating official and the question was whether or not he was entitled to withhold certain information from that official. It was not a case of a person enjoying anonymity so far as the government was concerned, a person compelled to come forward and identify himself, through explicit invocation of the privilege, as one likely to be engaged in crime. Whether a person enjoying anonymity can be punished for his failure to come forward cannot be answered on the ground that compelling him to come forward is not incriminating, for it surely is. It can only be answered by determining whether the government's interest in raising revenue is sufficiently important to justify some reduction in the protection of the privilege.

Involved here is the general question whether a person is ever entitled to determine for himself, without the intervention of a government official, whether he is privileged. Is it always required that he as least take such action as is necessary to bring his claim of privilege before an official even though this will to some extent incriminate him? It is relevant, perhaps, that in the *Malloy* case, even though the defendant's claim was made before a government official, the decision supports the view that an interrogated person must be left considerable discretion in deciding whether his answers will tend to incriminate, and the official may overrule his decision only if it is patently groundless. Mr. Justice Jackson's concurring opinion in the *Kahriger* case also casts some light on this subject. He was troubled by the Court's decision and only with difficulty brought himself to join in holding that a gambler could be punished for not registering. He observed that:[44]

> Extension of the immunity doctrines to the federal power to inquire as to income derived from violation of state penal laws would create a large number of immunities from reporting which would vary from state to state. Moreover, the immunity can be claimed without being established, otherwise one would be required to prove guilt to avoid admitting it. Sweeping and undiscriminating application of the immunity doctrines to taxation would almost give the taxpayer an option to refuse to report, as it now gives witnesses a virtual option to refuse to testify. . . .

Mr. Justice Jackson is aware here of the argument that a criminal should not have to report his income at all and that what is involved is a direct conflict between the policy of the privilege and other governmental interests. There can be no evasion of this fact by a claim that to file a tax return does not incriminate.

Of course, even if a witness is compelled to respond to a subpoena and a criminal to file a tax return, this does not mean that

---

44 Kahriger v. United States, 345 U.S. 22, 34 (1953).

the resulting disclosure should be available for use against him in connection with a criminal prosecution. As will be discussed later, by insulating the disclosure from prosecutory use, it may be possible both to preserve the essence of the privilege and at the same time give recognition to the government's interest in obtaining information for certain purposes. The implication of the *Sullivan* case could be this: A return of all income must be made whether or not it tends to incriminate. Further information, obviously pointing to criminality and not essential to the determination of tax liability, may be withheld. Self-reporting of income by all is vital to the revenue interests of the government. But whether information contained in the return or the fact that the taxpayer filed an incomplete return may be used in connection with a criminal prosecution is a distinct question.[45]

Another situation in which it is sometimes suggested that there is no incrimination are prosecutions under statutes making it a criminal offense for the driver of a motor vehicle involved in an accident to fail to report the accident. *Commonwealth v. Joyce*[46] is a well-known decision that adopts this rationale. It is clear, however, at least under the *Hoffman-Malloy* test of what constitutes incrimination, that a driver's compliance with these statutes will frequently incriminate him and that a prosecution for failing to report an accident constitutes punishment for refusal to incriminate oneself. If state tests of what constitutes incrimination differ from the *Hoffman* test, they must now, according to *Malloy v. Hogan*, give way before that test.

Assume that a statute requires a driver to report to the police the details of an accident, including his conduct immediately before the collision. Can there be any doubt that in this case there is compelled disclosure of facts that may incriminate? The driver's prosecution and conviction of some criminal offense—driving under the influence of liquor, reckless driving, manslaughter—are rendered more likely. It makes no difference that the facts stated by the driver in his report are susceptible to an interpretation consistent with innocence, or that his report deals with facts relevant to only one element of a possible criminal offense. The privilege

---

[45] *Cf.* Griffin v. California, 380 U.S. 609 (1965) (not permissible to comment on a criminal defendant's failure to take stand).

[46] 326 Mass. 751 (1951).

would be deprived of most of its value if it were held to apply only when a disclosure constitutes a full confession covering all elements of a crime, or is susceptible only to an interpretation of guilt.

Even when a statute requires a person merely to identify himself to the police, the victim, or bystanders as the operator of a vehicle involved in an accident, and not to provide any information about the accident, such identification would seem to constitute incrimination. That his operation of a motor vehicle was causally related to an injury to person or property or to a particular incident on the highway may be crucial in a subsequent criminal prosecution. From other information it may be clear that whoever was driving a given vehicle was guilty of a crime, and the only question is whether the defendant was the operator of that vehicle. Again, so far as incrimination is concerned, it makes no difference that the driver's compelled disclosure of his identity does not cover all the elements of a crime. No one would dispute that it would be compelled incrimination and a violation of the privilege to require a person to come forward and admit that he was present in a bank at a certain hour when from independent information it was known that a robbery took place in the bank at that time.

These motor vehicle accident cases also provide examples of the other principle sometimes put forward as an explanation of why the privilege does not apply in the cases with which we are concerned, but here again the principle is often simply a way of avoiding the necessity of identifying and choosing between conflicting interests. This principle is that the privilege does not apply when the compelled disclosure is not of a communicative or testimonial nature. What is required of a person may provide information about his criminality, but not by way of an inference about his state of mind. This limitation on the privilege has recently received authoritative statement in *Schmerber v. California*,[47] a decision holding that the privilege does not apply to blood tests made to determine intoxication. Familiar earlier examples include fingerprinting, photographing, trying on clothes, standing up to be identified, and so forth. Although it is not entirely clear why the privilege does not apply to these non-testimonial disclosures, it probably must be accepted as firmly established that it does not. There will of course be cer-

[47] 384 U.S. 757 (1966).

tain limitations, deriving from other constitutional principles, such as due process, on the means that may be employed to obtain non-testimonial information from a suspected person and the circumstances under which it may be obtained. The Court's concern with the particular circumstances under which the blood was taken in the *Schmerber* case is evidence of this.

In the automobile accident report cases, what is required of the driver will almost always involve a testimonial use. Usually the driver is required at least to identify himself as the operator of a vehicle involved in an accident. From the driver's identifying statement an inference can be drawn that he believed that he was the operator of such a vehicle, and from this it can be inferred that he in fact was. His communication may be the only source of information on the subject.

If the driver is not required to identify himself, but simply to remain at the scene of the accident until the police arrive, or is required to render assistance to those injured, his conduct in compliance with the statute can still give rise to what could be considered a testimonial inference. It can give rise to an inference concerning the driver's state of mind. Since he is present at the scene of the accident, rendering assistance, he probably believes that he was the operator of a vehicle involved in the accident. From this it can be inferred that he was indeed the operator of such a vehicle. The only difference in this case is that the operator does not act for the purpose of identifying himself as the operator of such a vehicle.

The driver's action can also provide an opportunity for the authorities to obtain non-testimonial evidence, evidence whose value does not depend upon any proposition about the driver's state of mind. If the driver remains at the scene of the accident, it may become possible for witnesses to identify him as the operator of an offending vehicle. An inference that he was the operator need not depend upon any conclusion about his state of mind but simply upon the credibility of the witnesses. The driver's presence may also make it possible for the police to photograph him, take his fingerprints, and conduct various tests on his vehicle that will aid in identifying it as one involved in the accident. Here as in the case of a blood test, the use of the evidence obtained cannot be considered testimonial.

Several questions are suggested. Even if non-testimonial use of a person's conduct is all that is involved, are there limits to the co-operation that the authorities can require of a person in order to obtain the evidence? Can a person be required to engage in conduct that is capable of both testimonial and non-testimonial use? Can a burglar be required to remain at the scene of a crime in order to be fingerprinted? If a driver must comply with a statute to make non-testimonial evidence available, can it be argued that in a prose-cution of the driver for a criminal offense he is entitled to have excluded any testimonial use of his compelled conduct? In any event, as already noted, most of the automobile accident cases can-not be explained on the ground that the evidence sought is non-testimonial. Usually the driver is required to report to the police that he was the driver of a vehicle involved in an accident, and it is obviously contemplated that this identification will be used as a communication justifying the conclusion that the facts the driver states are true. The explanation why the privilege is not available, if there is any, must lie deeper and rest upon more complex con-siderations than that the disclosure required by the statute is not testimonial.

The compulsory production of incriminating records also offers the possibility of arguing that no testimonial incrimination is in-volved. When in certain cases a custodian of records is required to produce them notwithstanding the fact that they will incrimi-nate him, it can be argued that incrimination results from the con-tents of the records and not by way of an inference regarding the custodian's guilty state of mind. This argument must, however, be rejected as an unsatisfactory explanation for many of the record cases. First, in a case like *Shapiro*, which holds that the custodian is not privileged under the circumstances there shown to refuse to produce the records, no distinction is drawn between records made by him and records made by others.[48] The records must be produced

48 And see Wilson v. United States, 221 U.S. 361, 378–79 (1911): "It is at once apparent that the mere fact that the appellant himself wrote, or signed, the official letters copied into the books, neither conditioned nor enlarged his privilege. Where one's private documents would tend to incriminate him, the privilege exists although they were actually written by another person. And where an officer of a corporation has possession of corporate records which disclose his crime, there is no ground upon which it can be said that he will be forced to produce them if the entries were made by another, but may withhold them if the entries were made by himself. The books are no more private books in the latter case than in the former; if they have been held pursuant to the authority of the corporation,

in either case. If records made by the custodian must be produced, the use of their incriminating contents involves an inference about the maker-custodian's state of mind, a testimonial use. If the records are required to be kept, then it makes no difference, so far as compelled testimonial incrimination is concerned, that the maker-custodian recorded his knowledge of incriminating facts sometime before the records were required to be produced. In any case, he is compelled to incriminate himself through a revelation of his state of mind. Second, even though the custodian did not make the records, his act of producing them in response to a subpoena may be of evidentiary value on the issue of his criminality. And this evidentiary value may rest upon an inference from the act of production as to his state of mind: it is not like drawing blood from the custodian's body or taking his fingerprints. Here again, so far as the use of the evidence in a criminal prosecution of the custodian is concerned, there is the possibility of permitting a use that is nontestimonial and prohibiting a use that is testimonial.

In a World War I case involving a prosecution for failure to register for the draft and failure to produce a registration certificate upon demand by a police officer,[49] an argument was made that does not seem to have reappeared in any of the recent cases involving the destruction of registration certificates and related offenses. The argument was that a prosecution for failure to produce a registration certificate violates the privilege against self-incrimination.

The production of the certificate, it might be said, could reveal that the bearer although registered was violating some Selective Service regulation. Or it might identify him as a person wanted for some offense entirely unrelated to the Selective Service laws. Compulsory production of a driver's license or any document of identification may have this effect. Can it be argued that here as in the blood sample and fingerprint cases such incrimination as is involved is not communicative or testimonial? The inference of criminality arises simply from the fact that the bearer has the identifying card, and no conclusion is drawn concerning the bearer's state of mind and his belief in his own identity. Why would he have this

---

that authority is subject to termination. In both cases production tends to criminate; and if requiring him to produce compels him to be a witness against himself in the one case it does so equally in the other."

[49] United States v. Olson, 253 Fed. 233 (W.D. Wash. 1917).

card if he were not the person described in it? It must be recognized, however, that in deciding that a person who carries and presents a card with a certain name and address on it is the person to whom this information applies, we ordinarily rely upon an inference as to the bearer's state of mind. He carries and presents the card because, we believe, he supposes that the information pertains to him. The case is distinguishable from the fingerprint and blood sample cases, or any case in which identification is by some mark or characteristic that a person is powerless to alter. In such cases we do identify a person without any reliance on his state of mind or his belief that the marks identify him.[50]

In the Selective Service case just mentioned it seems likely that the reason the defendant did not produce a registration certificate was that he was not in fact registered and therefore did not have one. A strong argument can be made that the statute that made it an offense to fail to produce a certificate was intended to apply only when a person had a certificate and willfully failed to produce it. If the statute also applies to a person who never had a certificate, though it may facilitate the detection of those who are not registered, its effect is to increase the punishment for the crime of failing to register.

The failure to produce a certificate is evidence that the person who does not produce it is not registered. This is true whether or not it is a distinct offense to fail to produce a certificate. If it is a distinct offense, and persons are required to carry and produce a certificate on demand, the failure to produce is more cogent on the question whether or not one who fails to produce is registered. There is less likelihood that a person who is in fact registered will neglect to carry or refuse to produce his certificate when such conduct is a criminal offense.

Is the incriminating failure to produce a certificate testimonial? In a sense, yes, since in concluding that a person who does not produce is not registered, we assume something about that person's state of mind. We assume that he is not a person who has a

---

[50] Some day, perhaps, the courts will begin to wonder whether there is some connection between testimonial and non-testimonial use of compelled disclosures for purposes of the privilege against self-incrimination and the tangled question of what is hearsay evidence. One would suppose that since different policies are involved, exact congruence of results is not necessarily to be expected.

certificate but for some reason or other has chosen not to produce it. Still, the argument that a non-testimonial use is what is primarily involved is strong, stronger than in the case where from the possession of an identifying certificate we conclude that the bearer is the man described. From the fact that the person does not produce a certificate when there are strong reasons of self-interest for doing so if he can, we conclude that he does not have one and therefore is not registered. The case is close to taking fingerprints or blood samples.

The only way that a non-registrant can be relieved of the situation in which he is identified as a criminal by his inability to produce a certificate is to abolish the whole system of requiring that cards be carried and exhibited. But since the argument that there is a testimonial use of his inability to produce a certificate is so feeble, it seems likely that constitutional objections will have to find some basis other than the privilege against self-incrimination. It is not like the case of the taxpayer engaged in an illegal business who complains of the general requirement that income be reported, because his failure to report gives rise to an inference that his income is from an illegal source. In that case the inference is clearly that he has a guilty state of mind. Of course the taxpayer does not intend by failing to file a return to communicate the idea that his income is from an illegal source.

Boyd v. United States[51] still stands as an obstacle to a flat generalization that the privilege does not apply to non-testimonial disclosures. In that case the privilege was held to cover private papers, and it was not suggested that this depended upon whether the papers had been composed by the plaintiff in error himself rather than by some third person, or upon the possibility that testimonial evidentiary value might be attributed to the act of producing the papers. The privilege relieved the plaintiff in error of the obligation to assist the authorities by producing written statements in his possession, by himself or others, that might tend to incriminate him or lead to a forefeiture of his property. It remains to be seen whether the emphasis in *Schmerber v. California* on testimonial or communicative use has affected *Boyd*'s protection of private papers. Also relevant are recent cases, rules, and statutes dealing with the prosecution's rights of discovery against a criminal de-

---

[51] 116 U.S. 616 (1886).

fendant.[52] Does the emphasis on testimonial use in *Schmerber* mean that the prosecution can compel a defendant to produce for its inspection documents that he has not composed or to assist in obtaining evidence from others? Could such compelled co-operation be found to be testimonial because of the possibility of an inference of a guilty mind from the defendant's admission that he has the evidence or knows that certain persons were witnesses? Or will it be recognized that when a prosecution is actually in progress, the privilege against self-incrimination still entitles a defendant to withhold certain forms of co-operation even though they cannot be considered testimonial?

III. Some Factors Relevant to a Resolution of the Conflict

A. THE FACTOR OF ANTECEDENT CHOICE

If we assume that a disclosure that is sought to be compelled is both incriminating and testimonial, we can now consider the important questions that arise in regard to the application of the privilege in such cases as *Albertson, Shapiro,* the wagering tax cases, and the automobile accident report cases. Among the considerations that have been suggested as rendering the privilege unavailable in some of these cases are the following: (1) The person compelled to incriminate himself had at a certain point in time a way to avoid incriminating himself and made a free choice not to pursue it. Because he had this way out, the incriminating disclosure cannot be considered compelled. (2) The disclosure is only prospectively incriminating and does not reveal past or present crimes. (3) The purpose of the requirement that incriminating information be disclosed is not to prosecute crimes. (4) The social objective to be achieved through compelled disclosure is of very great importance. (5) Unless self-disclosure is required, there is no reasonable way of obtaining information vital to the achievement of an important governmental purpose. (6) The information disclosed will not in fact be used for purposes of criminal prosecution.

In considering the significance of these various factors, it is helpful to examine them as they apply in four rather rough categories

---

[52] See, *e.g.,* Jones v. Superior Court, 58 Cal.2d 56 (1962); Amendments to Fed. R. Crim. Proc., R. 16, 384 U.S. 1097–1100 (1966).

of cases. In discussing the first category, particular consideration will be given to the question of free choice and the fact that there was a way out of the incriminating dilemma that the defendant did not take. The decisions in the wagering tax cases attribute importance to this factor, and so does Wigmore in his discussion of the problem.[53] In fact, an analysis of the significance of free choice and the availability of a way out will in the discussion of each group of cases provide a convenient means of entering into an analysis of all the relevant considerations.

It is clear that the fact of free choice or the failure to take an available way out cannot always result in the loss of the privilege. Take for example a case that seems to involve a frontal assault upon the policy of the privilege. A statute provides that if a person commits a crime, either a crime of a certain kind or any crime, he must report it to the district attorney within a certain period of time. If he does not report, he will be guilty of the distinct and additional offense of failure to report.

On its face the purpose of this statute appears to be to facilitate the detection and prosecution of crime. The reality is probably otherwise. Ordinarily a person who commits a crime will not comply with a reporting requirement. If he does report, he will almost certainly be prosecuted for his offense, whereas if he does not report he may escape punishment both for the primary offense and the offense of failure to report. Although in theory a distinct offense of non-reporting is created, the practical effect of the statute is simply to increase the punishment for the primary offense. Why would a legislature create a distinct offense of non-reporting when it cannot reasonably be expected that anyone will comply with the statute? Why would the legislature not simply increase the punishment for the primary offense? It will be no easier to prove the offense of non-reporting than the primary offense, since to prove the offense of non-reporting it is necessary to establish the commission of the primary offense. Only if a person has committed the primary offense is he bound to report. In some cases it might be possible to prosecute for not reporting when the statute of limitations has run on the primary offense. Or the situation may be the same as that that gave rise to the federal wagering tax statute. The jurisdiction that enacts the reporting requirement considers that it

---

[53] See 8 WIGMORE, EVIDENCE 349 (3d ed. 1940).

has no power directly to punish the primary conduct. Congress believed that there was no federal power directly to punish intrastate gambling. The reporting statute, sometimes tied to a purported revenue purpose, is enacted for the actual purpose of indirectly controlling and punishing conduct that cannot be directly forbidden.

In a few situations a person who has committed a crime might comply with a reporting statute. The penalty for not reporting might be much heavier than the penalty for the primary offense. Also it might be known to the offender that the jurisdiction that has imposed the reporting requirement is efficient and sure in detection and prosecution, and also that there is the possibility that information he reports will not find its way into the hands of officials of the jurisdiction that makes the primary conduct a criminal offense. The federal government for example, might not pass on what it learns to the states.

The argument that the privilege is not available because of defendant's free choice is as follows. The defendant chose to commit the primary offense. If he had not committed the primary offense, he would not be faced with the dilemma of either incriminating himself or committing the distinct offense of not reporting. Since he had this way out, it cannot be considered that the reporting statute compels him to incriminate himself.[54] Not only did the defendant make a choice that subjected him to the reporting requirement, but it was an informed choice. At least it was as capable of being informed as is usually required before serious consequences are visited upon one who makes a choice. At the time the defendant committed the primary offense, the legal consequences of his choice were fixed: he would be liable to punishment for the primary offense and also be faced with the obligation to report the primary offense or be liable to punishment for failure to do so. It might not have been certain that he would actually be detected and punished for not reporting, but practical uncertainty of this kind confronts all those who decide to commit crime.

It is clear that this argument must be rejected and that the privilege cannot be considered forfeited in these circumstances because

---

[54] For language suggesting this argument, see WIGMORE, op. cit. supra note 53. See also Rodgers v. United States, 138 F.2d 992, 995 (6th Cir. 1943).

of the fact of choice. Choice is indeed a factor to which the law frequently attaches consequences, but it does so only when this will aid in achieving some end defined by policy. It does not attach consequences to choice without regard to some objective. The fact of choice alone can hardly ever be considered a sufficient explanation of a legal result. To hold that since the defendant made a choice to commit the primary offense the privilege is lost would be to abolish the privilege in one of its central applications, to abolish it in cases in which it has always historically applied, to defeat its very purpose. The evils intended to be avoided by the privilege would not in fact be avoided. Even though the defendant did make a choice in committing the primary offense, once he did so he was confronted with the dilemma whether to incriminate himself or run the risk of punishment for failure to do so. It is the evils and abuses that inhere in this dilemma that the privilege is intended to avoid, and these evils and abuses are not eliminated simply because of the defendant's antecedent choice. This is true even though the defendant had no right to choose as he did, no right to commit the primary offense. The privilege is designed to provide protection even for those who have chosen to commit crime.

This does not mean that choice can never result in loss of the privilege. A binding waiver of the privilege is possible. For example, when a defendant is actually being prosecuted, he can with the advice of counsel and awareness of his rights waive his privilege to be silent, and the effect of this waiver may extend beyond the particular words that he freely speaks. Thus a defendant in a criminal case who takes the stand can be compelled to answer questions on cross-examination relating to the matter about which he has testified on direct. But the effects of waiver are narrowly limited so as to preserve to a defendant considerable freedom to change his mind. Voluntary testimony at one stage of a criminal proceeding does not result in loss of the privilege to remain silent at a later stage. The right to be silent is preserved because when there is actual, present unwillingness to incriminate oneself, the evils that would arise from compulsion are almost as serious as if there had been no earlier choice to speak.[55]

It has been assumed that the reporting statute under discussion

---

[55] For an illuminating discussion of this problem, see Judge Frank's opinion in United States v. Field, 193 F.2d 92 (2d Cir. 1951).

is expressly aimed at and limited to requiring the disclosure of criminal conduct and that its purpose is either to facilitate the detection and prosecution of crime or to increase the punishment for crime. It is hard to imagine how in such circumstances any argument can be made to turn on the importance of the governmental objective sought to be achieved, or the difficulty of detecting crime without a system of self-reporting, that could constitutionally justify setting aside the privilege. Only the war power, which may have had some influence on the *Shapiro* decision, could conceivably support an argument sufficiently impressive to warrant such a frontal assault on the privilege. The constitutional privilege against self-incrimination expresses a judgment that the evils resulting from compulsory self-incrimination are so serious that they must be avoided even if this involves forgoing the detection of crime in a particularly easy and efficient way.

When the statute requiring a report of criminal conduct is not even in force at the time the defendant commits the crime, there is even less reason to find that the privilege is lost.[56] Even if some significance is ordinarily to be attached to the fact that the defendant chose to commit the primary crime and thus failed to avail himself of a way out of the dilemma of incriminating himself or being liable to punishment for failure to do so, this surely cannot be true when at the time the defendant chose to commit the primary crime, the legal consequences of his action were not fixed. The legislature had not yet imposed a reporting requirement relating to this criminal conduct, and the defendant acted only in the light of the possibility that it might do so. The more uncertain the consequences of choice, the more incomplete the information the actor has at his disposal, the less reason to attach legal significance to his choice. And in any case, the argument regarding the policy of the privilege applies here with equal force. Whether or not the defendant chose to commit the primary crime, the fact is that after he committed the crime he was faced with the dilemma whether to incriminate himself or to expose himself to liability for the offense of non-reporting. The evils in this situation are sufficiently serious to warrant preserving the privilege notwithstanding the defendant's earlier choice.

---

[56] This question of when the reporting statute is enacted is suggested by the language in 8 WIGMORE, EVIDENCE 349 (3d ed. 1940).

It is interesting to consider whether the application of the reporting statute in the case suggested would be invalid under the prohibition against *ex post facto* laws quite apart from the privilege against self-incrimination. The statute is not fully retroactive in that some conduct on the part of the defendant must take place after its enactment before the crime of non-reporting will have been committed. Thus although a conviction for non-reporting could rest on the defendant's commission of the primary offense before the enactment of the reporting statute, it would also require that, following the enactment of the statute, the defendant failed to report the earlier offense. When as a practical matter no one who has committed an offense will report it, however, it can be argued that the actual effect and probable purpose of the reporting statute is to increase the punishment for the primary offense, even if it occurred before the enactment of the reporting statute. If the reporting statute has some purpose other than to increase the punishment for the primary offense, and there is a reasonable likelihood that this purpose can be achieved, then possibly it can withstand an attack as *ex post facto*. In any case, the question need not be answered if the reporting statute is independently invalid because of the privilege against self-incrimination.

Suppose at the time the defendant commits the primary offense there is no statute requiring him to report his crime. There is, however, general authority, vested in certain agencies of government, to make inquiries for the purpose of prosecuting and punishing crime. Pursuant to this general authority, which existed at the time the defendant committed the primary offense, an agency of government calls the defendant before it and questions him concerning his offense. Here, unlike the case where there is a statute requiring the defendant to report his crime, no offense of non-disclosure is committed until the investigating authority puts questions to the defendant and he refuses to answer.

Historically, this is the classic case for the application of the privilege. The High Commission and the Star Chamber, pursuant to general investigatory authority, summoned persons to answer inquiries relating to suspected criminal activities. An argument based on the fact that the defendant made a choice and failed to take a way out, and that his subsequent self-incrimination cannot be considered coerced, certainly cannot be allowed to abolish the privilege in the very situation for which it was primarily designed.

It may be true that here, as in the preceding examples, the defendant did make a choice and could have taken a way out that would have enabled him to avoid subsequent self-incrimination or punishment for contempt. He could have refrained from engaging in the conduct to which the later inquiry is directed. On the other hand, since the facts inquired into by the investigating authority may not in themselves constitute a crime, but merely, under one possible interpretation, be indicative of criminality, it might not at an earlier time have been clear just what it was that the defendant should have avoided doing in order to escape the danger of later incrimination. Here it is not simply a matter of not committing this or that act defined by law as criminal. A large and uncertain range of non-criminal activities may have to be avoided if the defendant is to be entirely safe from the danger of subsequent self-incrimination. And indeed in some cases there may have been nothing that the defendant could have done or refrained from doing that would have relieved him from this danger: the conduct of others or surrounding circumstances over which he had no control, but of which he has knowledge, may weave a web of suspicion around him, and it is as to these facts that the investigating authority may make inquiry.

Even if there is specific conduct from which the defendant could have refrained, the fact that this conduct is not necessarily criminal creates an entirely different problem and raises an additional objection to attaching legal significance to the fact that the defendant did not refrain from engaging in this conduct. It has sometimes been suggested that importance should be attached to the fact that a defendant had no right to engage in the primary criminal conduct.[57] Be that as it may, and in fact the argument that this has significance seems to be largely without merit, if the antecedent conduct was not criminal, then the defendant did, in some sense, have a right to engage in it. It is therefore necessary to ask whether it is desirable in an indirect fashion to burden a person's freedom to engage in non-criminal conduct that may at some future date be seen to have relevance to possible criminality. This question is related to a matter that will be discussed later: whether it is permis-

---

[57] See Lewis v. United States, 348 U.S. 419, 423 (1955).

sible to condition the enjoyment of certain advantages, such as entering or leaving the country, or obtaining employment, upon a person's revealing his past crimes. If choice is claimed to be legally significant, then inquiry must be made into the extent to which that choice is free.

In any case, apart from the questions whether there was a way out for the defendant, whether it was one that was reasonably apparent to a person in his position, whether he was entitled by virtue of other rights not to take the way out, the argument that the privilege survives antecedent choice is as strong here as in the earlier examples. The evils that accompany compelled incrimination, evils that the privilege is designed to avoid, are fully present at the time that the investigating authority seeks to compel the defendant to talk. Indeed, since there is actual questioning of the defendant and not merely the filing of a report by him, there is a greater danger of browbeating, intimidation, and humiliation.

It may be worthwhile to pause here briefly to consider the significance of the distinctions so far as the privilege is concerned between oral testimony, written reports filed with government officials, and records required to be kept and produced on demand. That some importance may attach to these distinctions has already been suggested in the discussion regarding the difficult question of testimonial and non-testimonial incrimination.

It is hard to see why anything should turn on the distinction between compulsory oral testimony and compulsory written reports. Historically, compelled written confessions have been as much condemned as compelled oral confessions. A written confession, made under the pressure of an immediate official demand, is as likely to be a product of intimidation as an oral confession. There is the same potentiality for humiliation of the defendant in one case as in the other, and the dilemma that he confronts is equally painful. In *Albertson* the Court observed that if petitioners were privileged not to testify orally regarding Communist Party membership, it could see no reason why they were not also privileged to refuse to fill out a written registration form containing the same information.[58] Surely in the automobile accident report cases nothing should turn on whether under the particular statute the driver is required to make an oral or a written report to the police.

---

[58] 382 U.S. at 78.

There is authority to the effect that the distinction between oral testimony and written reports required to be filed with a public official on the one hand, and pre-existing records required to be kept and produced on the other, is important.[59] In the *Shapiro* case, where the Court decided that the privilege did not apply to records required to be kept under the Emergency Price Control Act, the Court remarked, without explanation, that of course oral testimony on the same matters covered by the records could not be compelled.[60] Some years before, in *Wilson v. United States*,[61] a case holding that the president of a corporation was not privileged to refuse to produce corporate books even though they might incriminate him, the Court noted that the case did not involve compelling incriminating oral testimony from the defendant.

In *Curcio v. United States*,[62] a union officer was convicted of contempt for refusal to testify on the whereabouts of the union's books. He stated that the books were not in his possession, but refused to testify where they were on the ground that such testimony would tend to incriminate him. The Court recognized that the defendant would be bound to turn over the books if they were in his possession. It held, nevertheless, that he could not be examined as a witness concerning their whereabouts or required to "disclose the contents of his own mind,"[63] and reversed the conviction. The Court did not decide whether a custodian who could be compelled to produce incriminating records could also be required to authenticate them under oath. It pointed out, however, in a manner suggesting that such authentication perhaps could be required, that when a person produces records in response to a *subpoena duces tecum*, there is a tacit assertion by him that these are

---

[59] United States v. Daisart Sportwear, Inc., 169 F.2d 856, 861–62 (2d Cir. 1948), *rev'd on other grounds sub nom.* Smith v. United States, 337 U.S. 137 (1949). The Court of Appeals held in this case that although the defendant, a corporate officer, would have been obligated to produce corporate records required to be kept under the Price Control Act, when according to the defendant's statement the records had been lost or destroyed, he could not be compelled to testify to their contents or the transactions that they covered. Mr. Maguire describes this result as an "embarrassing anomaly," and asks: "Will a man who defies the governmental command to keep records have a privilege which is denied the more docile record maker?" MAGUIRE, EVIDENCE OF GUILT 104 (1959).

[60] 335 U.S. 1, 24 n. 30, 27 (1948).   [62] 354 U.S. 118 (1957).

[61] 221 U.S. 361, 377 (1911).   [63] *Id.* at 128.

the records demanded, and that testimonial authentication of the records would not significantly further incriminate him. The *Curcio* opinion does not make clear whether testimony on the whereabouts of the union records would have incriminated the defendant because it would have led to the discovery of the records and their incriminating contents, or because the very fact that the defendant knew where the records were would incriminate him.

One aspect of the situation when a record is involved is that the incriminating information put into the record may not come to the attention of any government official, and thus no harm may be done to the maker or custodian. Only if the record is inspected will disadvantages follow from the self-incriminating material. Also, some of the evils that the privilege was designed to avoid may not be present when a record is involved. The making of the record probably does not take place under circumstances involving a possibility of intimidation or humiliation. On the other hand, the record maker faces the same hard choice as a witness or a person called upon to file a written report: whether to create evidence of his misdeeds or run the risk of punishment for not doing so. If the privilege protects privacy, that privacy is as much threatened by a requirement that a record be kept and produced as by the compulsion of oral testimony.

To return to an earlier discussion, the difference in treatment of oral testimony and records may rest on the notion that when production of a record is demanded there is no testimonial incrimination. The custodian is simply called upon to produce an already existing document. As has been pointed out, however, and this is recognized in the *Curcio* case, the act of production itself may give rise to an inference of a testimonial nature, an inference about the custodian's state of mind. Also, if the compulsory making of the record is taken into account as well as its compulsory production, the use of the evidence is as much testimonial as is the use of oral testimony or reports required to be filed. The record is used as evidence of the maker's state of mind, and from this are inferred the incriminating facts. If the person ordered to produce the record did not himself make it, then an argument is possible that no testimony is compelled from him. If he did make the record but was not required to do so, and was later required to produce it, then it can be argued that although the evidence is testimonial, it is not in its testimonial aspect compelled.

It may be of importance that in the case of oral testimony, when the witness is faced with the choice of incriminating himself or being punished for contempt, official attention is probably focused upon him in a context of suspected criminality. In the case of a record, however, at the time it is made there may be no official concern with the maker or possible criminality on his part.

It is clear that the mere fact that a record rather than oral testimony is sought is not alone enough to take the case out of the privilege. It may be, however, that when other considerations are also present, one or another of the distinctions that have been suggested will play a part in requiring production of the record when oral testimony on the same matter would not be required.

B. THE FACTOR OF COINCIDENTAL CHOICE

We have spoken of the situation in which a person is required to testify to or keep a record of a prior crime, and have particularly considered the argument that the privilege is lost because the person was free not to commit the crime. A second broad category of cases can now be suggested. This is the situation in which there was a way out that could have been taken other than simply not to commit the crime. If the person had taken this way out, he would not have been faced with the dilemma of incriminating himself or running the risk of punishment for his failure to do so. He could have elected not to engage in an activity or to accept a certain status to which the obligation to report incriminating facts is pendent. An example would be when an applicant for public employment is required to disclose facts that may indicate criminality, and if he accepts employment without disclosing these facts he will be guilty of a distinct offense.

How distinguish this case from the situation that has already been discussed? To abolish the privilege because a person earlier chose to commit a crime is to attack the policy of the privilege directly. Not quite such a clear objection can be raised when the loss of the privilege is made the price of engaging in an activity other than simply committing a crime. Whether making the loss of the privilege turn on engaging in such an activity will have the effect of substantially defeating the purpose of the privilege would seem to depend upon what the activity is and how serious a deprivation is involved in being compelled to forgo it. If the deprivation is so serious as to impair essential freedom, the case is practically indistinguishable from one where a person is required to report a crime simply because he committed it. The deprivation may be as serious as punishment for failure to report the crime.

A provision of the Narcotic Control Act of 1956[64] regulating departure from and entrance into the United States, provides an interesting example of a case involving loss of the privilege upon a person's choice to engage in a non-criminal activity. This statute makes it an offense for a citizen who is a user of narcotics or an addict to leave the United States without registering as such, or to re-enter the United States without registering and surrendering a registration certificate obtained on departure. Such a registration requirement is different from that imposed by the Subversive Activities Control Act in the *Albertson* case in that the requirement is made conditional on the citizen leaving or entering the country. Of course it might be said that the registration requirement in *Albertson* is conditional upon the activity of being in the United States. Petitioners could have escaped the obligation to register by leaving the country before the effective date of the Subversive Activities Control Act or possibly before proceedings were commenced against them. But the Subversive Activities Control Act does not in terms make the requirement to register contingent on any circumstance other than the issuance of an order by the Board.

What strikes one immediately as a possible objection to the provision of the Narcotic Control Act is the seriousness of the deprivation that the addict or user must accept if he is to avoid either incriminating himself or committing the distinct offense of crossing the border without registering. He must stay at home or, if he is outside the United States, stay away from home. That the interest in foreign travel is of great importance and will receive constitutional protection from certain forms of interference has recently been made clear in another context.[65] A very strong governmental interest is necessary to justify putting a person to the choice between forgoing his privilege against self-incrimination and his right to travel.

What indeed is the government's purpose in compelling those who wish to leave the country to disclose that they are addicts or

---

[64] 18 U.S.C. § 1407.

[65] Aptheker v. Secretary of State, 378 U.S. 500 (1964).

users of narcotics? Is there a governmental interest of sufficient strength to overcome the citizen's interest in travel? It surely cannot be a satisfactory answer that the federal government has jurisdiction to regulate the border and may condition entrance and departure upon persons' supplying what information about themselves the government sees fit. Perhaps it can be said that the purpose of the statute is to prevent or control the flow of narcotics into the United States and thus to regulate foreign commerce and enforce treaties relating to the narcotics traffic. Persons who are addicts or users are more likely than others to be carrying narcotics. Registration of such persons will enable the authorities to be particularly watchful about what they are transporting across the border. Actually, if an addict is going to register, he is most unlikely to attempt to smuggle, since he will realize that he will be carefully watched. Under a realistic appraisal, the purpose of the statute can have little to do with prevention of the smuggling of narcotics.

The actual purpose of the statute may be to make life more difficult for users and addicts by depriving them of the advantage of foreign travel, and to create a basis for their prosecution by federal authorities that might not otherwise exist. The latter purpose is not unlike that which underlies the federal wagering tax statute. Would the case be really very different if the Narcotic Control Act provided that on a certain date all users of narcotics must register with the Attorney General? What if the statute provided that any user of narcotics who wished to use the mails must register with the Postmaster General? If the purpose of the Narcotic Control Act is to obtain information from registrants in order to prosecute them for a variety of federal narcotics offenses, how can such a purpose be reconciled with the privilege?[66]

Statutes or regulations making it an offense to bring certain goods into the country without declaring them pose fewer diffi-

---

[66] The constitutionality of the provision of the Narcotic Control Act of 1956 being discussed was upheld in United States v. Eramdjian, 155 F. Supp. 914 (S.D. Cal. 1957). Among the grounds the court suggested were that registration would not be incriminating, *id.* at 925, and that the only incrimination involved was as to a future crime, *id.* at 923–27, a matter to be discussed later in this article. The court stressed the government's power to regulate foreign commerce and spoke of the likelihood that users and addicts would attempt to smuggle narcotics. It also said: "Here the person involved may choose to register and leave the United States or not register and remain." *Id.* at 928. See also Reyes v. United States, 258 F.2d 774 (9th Cir. 1958).

culties. In the first place, declaration will prevent the crime of smuggling from occurring. In some cases it is possible that a declaration will reveal some other offense.[67] Thus if a person declares narcotics, he will thereby reveal possession of narcotics, and possession may be an element of a criminal offense or a link in a chain of evidence leading to proof of another offense. Here the argument that there was a way out reappears. The necessity of revealing the incriminating facts could have been avoided by not seeking to bring the narcotics into the country, and surely the disadvantage of not being able to import certain goods is much less serious than the disadvantage of not being able to enter the country yourself. A reason for requiring that certain goods be declared that does not include the harassment of a particular class of persons or the obtaining of evidence in order to prosecute them can be convincingly stated. The purpose of requiring the goods to be declared is to prevent their importation or to make sure they are not imported without a duty being paid.

A host of other situations can be mentioned in which there is a conflict between a disclosure requirement imposed upon the enjoyment of a particular activity and an individual's desire to withhold particular information that may be incriminating. For example, a requirement that persons operating aircraft identify themselves and give other information before taking off from an airport can in a particular case lead to the identification of a person as one who has committed a crime. Here the information requirement clearly does not exist for the purpose of detecting and prosecuting crime but to assure the safe and orderly conduct of air traffic. This purpose can be achieved even though the information obtained is never used in connection with criminal prosecution. Furthermore, to compel a person to forgo a certain form of transportation if he wishes to avoid incriminating himself is perhaps less onerous that to compel him to forgo various other advantages.

What of local ordinances that require persons who stay at hotels

---

[67] See Rule v. United States, 34 U.S.L. Week 2706 (5th Cir., June 17, 1966) (conviction of importing marihuana without declaring it); Arrizon v. United States, 224 F.Supp. 27 (S.D. Cal. 1963) (same); Pickett v. United States, 223 F.Supp. 695 (S.D. Cal. 1963), cert. denied, 379 U.S. 939 (1964) (same; point made that even if declaration revealed possession of marihuana, that would not be offense, since possession would not have occurred within the United States); United States v. Dalton, 286 Fed. 756 (W.D. Wash. 1923) (liquor).

to register their true name and correct address? The information could be incriminating, and a very likely purpose of the requirement, although there may be others, is to provide the police with information about the whereabouts of those who have committed crimes. Putting your name in a hotel register does not, of course, incriminate to the same extent as putting your signature on a tax return that is not completely filled out.

There is a requirement that aliens register each year with the Attorney General, giving their current address and such other information as may be requested. Criminal prosecution and deportation can result from failure to comply.[68] For a particular person to register may incriminate him. It may reveal that he has entered the country illegally or help identify him as the perpetrator of some other crime. Self-incrimination in this situation, it can be said, is a price the alien must pay for having elected to enjoy the benefit of being in the country. The case is different from the situation first discussed, since choosing to enter the country is different from choosing to commit a crime. But is it not the fact that once the alien has entered the country he no longer has a choice but must register or run the risk of prosecution for not registering? Is he not confronted with the dilemma and the accompanying evils that the privilege was designed to avoid? The situation is different from that under the Narcotic Control Act, for there the option not to leave or enter the country continues right up to the moment when the addict is required to incriminate himself. The alien's way out is lost once he enters the country. As to the purpose of the alien registration requirement, the aim probably is, for a variety of only vaguely perceived reasons, to keep track of a group of persons considered somewhat unreliable. Among the reasons may be acquisition of information useful for criminal prosecutions and deportation.

Conditioning public employment on the disclosure of facts that may be incriminating, for example membership in a particular political organization, has already been mentioned. The problem here is related to that involved when a public employee is dismissed from his job because of a refusal to disclose incriminating information. Exclusion from public employment, especially if this includes firms that do business with the government, is a serious

---

68 8 U.S.C. § 1305 (1964).

deprivation. On the other hand, the purpose of the disclosure requirement is not to detect and prosecute crime, but to assure the
loyalty and competence of public employees. In some cases the
information sought will be irrelevant to the employment, thus
revealing a purpose to punish a particular class of persons by depriving them of the benefit of public employment. But in many
cases the information sought will arguably be pertinent to an applicant's fitness for the job. The policy to be served by requiring
the disclosure is capable of being satisfied without allowing the
information to be used in connection with a criminal prosecution.
If an applicant with incriminating conduct in his past does apply
and does disclose this information, the hiring authority can simply
refuse to employ him, or employ him but take precautions, as he
would in employing a person with a record of conviction.

The automobile accident report statutes can also be analyzed
in terms of imposing upon an activity a requirement that incriminating facts be disclosed. As has already been discussed, the information required of the driver will very often be both incriminating and testimonial. This case is like that of alien registration.
There was once a way out, a way to avoid the dilemma of incrimination or the crime of non-disclosure. But once the choice is made
to engage in the activity—to enter the country or drive an automobile—there is no further way out. A person could have refrained
from driving on the highways, but having done so, and having
become involved in an accident, he now must either incriminate
himself or commit the offense of not reporting the accident. This
aspect of the situation makes these automobile accident report
statutes especially hard to justify. Even if a choice was made earlier, after the accident the driver is in the same position as the
defendant in the first group of cases discussed. He must report
his crime, or run the risk of punishment for not doing so. The
dilemma and the evils that the privilege sought to avoid are present.

What adds to the difficulty of justifying these accident report
statutes is the seriousness of the deprivation involved in not operating a motor vehicle. Under present conditions of life in many
parts of the United States, automobile travel is so vital a part of
normal existence that to impose upon it a forfeiture of the privilege is almost the same as punishing for failure to report a crime,
without regard to the fact that the defendant made an election

to engage in some non-criminal activity. A practical equivalent might be a statute requiring anyone who used the city streets and sidewalks as a pedestrian to report injuries caused in the course of this activity. When early decisions sustained these reporting statutes, automobile travel could perhaps still be looked upon as less than a necessity. But conditions have radically changed, and a rationale is now needed to sustain these statutes that does not emphasize the fact that a free choice was made to operate a motor vehicle. A realization of this need may be what led the Massachusetts court in *Commonwealth v. Joyce*[69] to put forward the unsound explanation that the required disclosure was not incriminating.

Included among the purposes of these accident report statutes is certainly the detection and punishment of crime. On the other hand, some purposes can be achieved without the use of information reported for criminal prosecutions. The information may be useful in determining the cause of accidents for the purpose of judging the adequacy of safety rules, highway construction, and automobile design. Requiring a driver to remain at the scene of an accident and render assistance to the injured obviously has a point apart from criminal prosecution. If it is thought desirable to keep a driver off the highway in the future, this can be achieved, through suspension or revocation of license, without use of the compelled information in a criminal prosecution.

If in justifying these statutes arguments are advanced concerning the great importance of the social interest at stake, one moves onto dangerous ground so far as the continued survival of the privilege is concerned. After all, most of the criminal law expresses social interests of importance, and if the law is not enforced in some manner these interests will suffer. But the importance of the community's interest in detecting and punishing murder or robbery cannot warrant compelling a criminal to report his crime, so long as the privilege remains in the Constitution. If, however, the use to be made of compelled incriminating information stops short of criminal prosecution, it is possible to give more weight to the social interest involved. Society's interest in the regulation of automobile traffic and the prevention of accidents is certainly very great, and in addition, unless a system of self-reporting of accidents is enforced, needed information will in many cases simply not be obtained.

---

[69] 326 Mass. 751 (1951).

A possible analysis of the *Shapiro* case[70] brings it within the class of cases we have been discussing. The obligation to keep and produce records that might contain incriminating information was a condition imposed upon the activity of engaging in the wholesale grocery business. The Court stated that the transactions that the petitioner was required to record were transactions "in which the petitioner could lawfully engage solely by virtue of the license granted to him under the statute."[71] And yet, when the seriousness of the deprivation that must be suffered in order to avoid possible incrimination is as great as it was in the *Shapiro* case—the abandonment of the wholesale grocery business, in which the petitioner had probably been engaged even before price regulation and record keeping were imposed—it is necessary to look beyond free choice for an explanation of why the privilege is not available.

Spevack v. Kline[72] may soon tell us more about how serious a deprivation can be imposed as a price for a refusal to incriminate. In the *Spevack* case an attorney refused to produce records or testify before a referee inquiring into unethical practices of members of the bar. Because of the attorney's refusal, the Appellate Division entered an order of disbarment. This order was affirmed by the New York Court of Appeals on the authority of *Cohen v. Hurley*,[73] an earlier case that also involved the disbarment of an attorney for invoking the privilege in an inquiry into unethical practices, and on the ground that insofar as the production of records was demanded, the case fell within the rationale of *Shapiro*. But the *Cohen* case came before the Supreme Court's decision in *Malloy v. Hogan*,[74] holding that the privilege against self-incrimination is applicable to the states, and was concerned only with a question of fundamental fairness under the Fourteenth Amendment. It is doubtless because of *Malloy* that certiorari has been granted in the *Spevack* case.

Spevack recalls the unusual case of *United States v. Field*,[75] and the illuminating opinions that were written on that occasion. There

---

[70] Shapiro v. United States, 335 U.S. 1 (1948).

[71] *Id.* at 35.

[72] *In re* Spevack, 16 N.Y.2d 1048, (1965), *remittitur amended*, 17 N.Y.2d 490, (1966), *cert. granted sub nom*, Spevack v. Kline, 383 U.S. 942 (1966).

[73] 366 U.S. 117 (1961).

[74] 378 U.S. 1 (1964).   [75] 193 F.2d 92 (2d Cir. 1951).

trustees of a bail fund were found, by reason of their acceptance of this status, to have forfeited the privilege in regard to matters pertaining to the fund. It was considered essential to the performance of their function that they should disclose such matters to the court. The trustees were adjudged in contempt for refusing to answer questions concerning, among other things, the names of persons who had contributed to the fund, information that might have been helpful in locating certain principals under the bail bonds who had fled. Judge Frank, dissenting on the question of the privilege, took the view that even though the trustees in accepting their status had undertaken an obligation to disclose the information requested, this obligation could not be enforced by punishment for contempt. Here as in other cases that have been discussed, at the time the trustees were questioned they had no alternative but to answer and incriminate themselves or suffer punishment for their refusal to do so. The fact that they had earlier accepted the status of trustees and undertaken certain obligations did not eliminate this dilemma or the evils that the privilege was designed to avoid.

C. THE FACTOR OF LEGISLATIVE PURPOSE

If the loss of the privilege cannot be explained on the ground that a person freely chose to engage in an activity to which a reporting requirement is attached, some other explanation must be sought. The conflict between the policy of the privilege and the government's need for information now becomes harsher. Considerations that merely lend support to the argument against the privilege when free choice is deemed legally significant now must provide the entire explanation for its loss. It becomes necessary to distinguish the standard case in which a person is simply required to report his prior crime, where it was said that the privilege must be available.

The purpose of an enactment has frequently been suggested to be relevant. If there is some purpose other than the detection and prosecution of crime, the statute is easier to sustain. If the request for information is stated broadly, and ordinarily would elicit much that is not incriminating, there is very likely a non-prosecutory purpose. The form of classification, however, may be a mere subterfuge to conceal a prosecutory purpose.[76] When the detection

---

[76] See Meltzer, *supra* note 41, at 715.

and punishment of crime is the principal purpose of an enactment, it will be difficult to sustain in the face of the privilege. The usual use of the information disclosed is of course related to the question of purpose. If no use will be made in connection with criminal prosecution, there is a greater possibility of reconciling the government's demand for information with the privilege. Also of significance is the importance of the information to a particular governmental program, and the necessity of self-reporting as a device to obtain this information.

The requirement that persons register for the draft and supply certain information is an example of the sort of case that calls for a weighing of these considerations. For a particular person, the information demanded on the registration form may tend to incriminate him. It may, for example, reveal that he is an alien who has entered the country illegally.[77] Here the statute imposes an unconditional requirement on persons between certain ages to register; there is no way to avoid the dilemma of incrimination or punishment for non-disclosure, no activity the registrant could have forgone. The purpose of the registration requirement is clearly not to detect crime, but to identify those liable to conscription and to obtain information necessary to determine their fitness for military service. The aim is to raise an army, not to punish crime. The purpose is similar to that in the public employment situation, but there one who feared to incriminate himself could refrain from seeking employment. The purpose of the Selective Service registration requirement can be entirely satisfied without allowing the information obtained to be used for the purpose of prosecution. Another example of the situation we are now considering is the census. A person required by law to provide information for the census may find that answers to certain questions will tend to incriminate him.[78] The same arguments about a non-prosecutory purpose and the possibility of limited use can be made here.

Before one concludes that the privilege should not be available whenever the purpose of a statute is non-prosecutory, it is well to recall that it has long been supposed that a witness subpoenaed to testify in court or before an investigatory agency was entitled to

---

[77] Cf. Warszower v. United States, 312 U.S. 342 (1941).

[78] Cf. St. Regis Paper Co. v. United States, 368 U.S. 208 (1961).

refuse to answer questions that would incriminate him, even though the purpose of the inquiry was not to detect criminality on his part, and even though by his refusal to answer important interests of others might be defeated by lack of evidence. But it was perhaps assumed that any answers he gave would, in the absence of a grant of immunity, be available for use against him in a criminal prosecution.

Shapiro v. United States[79] has already been mentioned several times. That case held that the privilege did not prevent compelling a wholesale grocer to produce records required to be kept under the Emergency Price Control Act. Information contained in the records was used to bring about the conviction of the defendant for illegal tie-in sales. As already suggested, the idea of conditioning an activity on the relinquishment of the privilege, the government having the power to exclude entirely from the activity, seems an inadequate explanation of this case. It is probably of significance, however, that the records required to be kept were related to economic activities rather than of a more personal nature.

The *Shapiro* decision relied to some extent on earlier cases that had held, over strong dissent, that a custodian of organizational records, in particular corporate and labor union records, could be required to produce such records even though they tended to incriminate him, at least when the organization was not simply a vehicle for his individual activity.[80] The opinions in these cases justified the loss of the privilege by a variety of arguments. The notion of "public records" was stretched to include corporate records. The government's visitatorial power over corporations was mentioned. A proprietary theory was suggested that seemed to make it important that the custodian did not own the records or hold them in a purely individual capacity. It was also stated that the custodian had voluntarily assumed his position.

This hodgepodge of half-convincing explanations contributed to the shaky foundations upon which the *Shapiro* decision was raised. But in *Shapiro* particular emphasis was placed upon the fact that the records were required by law to be kept. The notion that because a disclosure is required the privilege does not apply, if ex-

---

[79] 335 U.S. 1 (1948).

[80] Wilson v. United States, 221 U.S. 361 (1911); United States v. White, 322 U.S. 694 (1944).

tended to its full logical reach, is capable of entirely destroying the privilege. Disclosure may be required by statute, or it may be required by administrative order issued pursuant to statutory authority. In one case it may be required that records be kept and produced, in another that written reports be filed, in another that oral testimony be given.[81] Required disclosure could even include the situation where a court orders a witness to testify. In one view, the fact that a governmental authority has required an incriminating disclosure appears to be simply a description of what is attempted, that the government seeks to exercise a power possibly denied it under the Constitution, not a reason for finding that the privilege is inapplicable. The fact that the legislature has required that records be kept, however, or has authorized an administrative agency to require it, at least constitutes an authoritative expression of the importance of the governmental interest involved and the necessity of self-reporting to protect that interest.

The purpose of the regulatory program in *Shapiro* was price stabilization, which was considered vital to the war effort. How did the requirement that records be kept and produced promote that purpose? Some uses could be made of the information obtained that would not involve criminal prosecution. Violations of price regulations might be punished by withdrawal of license to do business. Or the information might be used solely as a basis for initiating general legislative and administrative programs aimed at meeting economic problems. But it is clear that the principal purpose of the record keeping requirement was to deter violations of price regulations and to provide evidence of such violations if they occurred. Furthermore, one purpose was to employ evidence of violations thus obtained in criminal prosecutions. At least this was the use to which the evidence was actually put in the *Shapiro* case. If the price control program of World War II was of sufficient national importance to justify compelling incriminating disclosures for the purpose of criminal prosecution, are there not many other federal programs that can be judged of equal importance? And yet it has

---

[81] See the sweeping language of the Uniform Rules of Evidence, Rule 25(e): "[A] public official or any person who engages in any activity, occupation, profession or calling does not have the privilege to refuse to disclose any matter which the statutes or regulations governing the office, activity, occupation, profession or calling require him to record or report or disclose concerning it. . . ."

long been thought that in most of these situations needed information could be obtained only by a grant of immunity.

The decision in the *Sullivan* case,[82] regarding the duty of one engaged in an illegal business to file a tax return, cannot be satisfactorily explained on the ground that the defendant had a free choice and a way out. But the purpose of the requirement that income be reported is obviously not to detect crime and punish criminals, but to raise revenue for the government. In distinguishing *Sullivan* in the *Albertson* case the Court observed that "the questions in the income tax return were neutral on their face and directed at the public at large."[83] This purpose, furthermore, can be achieved without using the information obtained in prosecutions for crimes unrelated to the income tax laws. And a system of self-reporting may well be judged indispensable to the government's revenue-raising program.

It is no doubt difficult to accept a result in these tax cases that gives the criminal a better chance to escape paying taxes than the person who makes his income in a lawful calling. Why should a criminal be free not to report his income? Mr. Justice Jackson remarked in *United States v. Kahriger:* "If the law-abiding must tell all to the tax collector, it is difficult to excuse one because his business is law-breaking."[84] But is there not inherent in the privilege the possibility that in some circumstances the criminal will be better off than the law-abiding citizen?

If the criminal is required to file a tax return,[85] is he also required to give oral testimony? The Court in *Albertson* could see no difference between compelled written disclosure and compelled oral testimony. The *Sullivan* case involved the filing of a tax return, not the production of the taxpayer's records, but this problem is also present, since the Internal Revenue Code requires the keeping

---

[82] United States v. Sullivan, 274 U.S. 259 (1927).

[83] 382 U.S. at 79.

[84] 345 U.S. at 35.

[85] Cases involving tax returns: United States v. O'Mara, 122 F. Supp. 399 (D. D.C. 1954) (contempt for refusal to turn over copy of income tax return to congressional committee; statutory provision making tax return confidential, not privilege against self-incrimination, invoked); Stillman v. United States, 177 F.2d 607 (9th Cir. 1949) (defendant's tax returns used in prosecution for violation of price regulations); Shushan v. United States, 117 F.2d 110, 117–18 (5th Cir.), *cert. denied*, 313 U.S. 574 (1941) (defendant's tax returns used in prosecution for mail fraud).

of such records as the Secretary of the Treasury deems necessary for the determination of tax liability.[86]

One final interesting example may be mentioned. An Air Force regulation required members of the Air Force to report to their superiors attempts by representatives of foreign governments to cultivate their acquaintance for the purpose of obtaining confidential information. In *United States v. Kauffman*,[87] the defendant was convicted by court-martial of failing to notify his commanding officer of contacts by representatives of the Soviet Union and the East German government. In holding that the privilege against self-incrimination was no obstacle to conviction, the military courts took the unsound position that the disclosure required by the regulation would not have incriminated the defendant, because it would not necessarily have shown the commission of a crime by him. An argument was also made that by becoming a member of the Armed Forces the defendant had taken on a status that carried with it the obligation to obey orders, including the order to report. An analogy was drawn with the automobile accident report cases. If it is true that the principal purpose of the regulation was to enable authorities to learn of the activities of foreign agents, not to detect criminal participation in espionage by servicemen, it is also the fact that there was no assurance that the information reported would not be used to prosecute the serviceman.

D. THE FACTOR OF PROSPECTIVE CHOICE

A fourth class of cases must be mentioned. These are cases in which it is made a crime to engage in certain conduct without first

---

[86] 26 U.S.C. § 6001. See Falsone v. United States, 205 F.2d 734, 739 (5th Cir. 1953), *cert. denied*, 346 U.S. 864 (1953) (enforcement of summons to accountant to produce records of client relating to tax liability and to testify on same matter); Beard v. United States, 222 F.2d 84, 93 (4th Cir. 1955), *cert. denied*, 350 U.S. 846 (1955) (in prosecution for tax evasion inference drawn from refusal to produce records).

The decision in Kohatsu v. United States, 351 F.2d 898 (9th Cir. 1965), *cert. denied*, 384 U.S. 1011 (1966), that a special agent of the Internal Revenue Service conducting a criminal investigation need not warn the taxpayer of his right to counsel and of his privilege against self-incrimination may imply that the taxpayer has a privilege of non-disclosure of some scope. *Cf.* United States v. Blue, 384 U.S. 251 (1966).

[87] 33 CMR 748 (Bd. of Review), *aff'd on this question*, 14 USCMA 283, 34 CMR 63 (1963).

having registered. The conduct is independently defined as criminal and proscribed quite apart from the registration requirement. The federal wagering tax statute,[88] a familiar example of this situation, has already been mentioned. This statute makes it an offense to accept wagers without first having registered and paid an occupational tax. Federal law is the source of the obligation to register; state law usually makes the accepting of wagers a crime. In *Lewis v. United States*,[89] federal law itself, as applicable in the District of Columbia, made accepting wagers a crime.

There is an important distinction between these cases and those that have been discussed so far. In the wagering tax cases it can be said that if a person registers when he is supposed to—before he begins to accept wagers—registration does not disclose any past or present criminality. He has not yet committed a crime. True, the registration is incriminating, and in a sense testimonially incriminating, in that it discloses an intention to commit crime, and from this intention it can be inferred that subsequently the registrant did in fact commit the crime. The fact of registration may well be admissible in a subsequent prosecution for gambling, although of course it would not be sufficient, standing alone, to support a conviction. But the registration is not incriminating in the sense of disclosing past or present criminality. This consideration entered into the rationale of decision in the *Kahriger* and *Lewis* cases, where convictions for accepting wagers without having registered were upheld.

Objections to such prospective incrimination cannot convincingly be argued to derive from the privilege against self-incrimination. History does not support such a reading of the privilege. It is true that prior registration increases the likelihood of prosecution and conviction: there is a greater reason for surveillance and additional evidence that the defendant committed a crime. But since there is no disclosure of present or past criminality, the kind of self-degradation and self-inflicted injury that the privilege was designed to prevent does not exist. The registrant does perhaps degrade himself to some extent by revealing an intention to commit crime, and he does expose himself to certain disadvantageous consequences, but the cases upholding the validity of immunity statutes would seem

---

[88] 26 U.S.C. §§ 4401 *et seq.*   [89] 348 U.S. 419 (1955).

to indicate that such consequences are not a sufficient basis for invoking the privilege.

There is language in the *Kahriger* and *Lewis* decisions to the effect that the incrimination involved in registration is not compelled incrimination because there is a way out that will enable the defendant to avoid incriminating himself. He can refrain from accepting wagers. As long as he does not accept wagers the registration requirement is inapplicable. But this does not seem to be the decisive reason why the privilege is inapplicable in the case of prospective incrimination. The decisive reason is that the disclosure does not reveal present or past criminality and therefore does not involve the particular evils that the privilege was designed to avoid, and the fact that the registrant still has a choice not to commit the crime merely points up this aspect of the situation, that as yet no crime has been committed. If it were decided that the privilege did cover prospective incrimination, then the defendant's subsequent choice to commit the crime could not be made a reason for rendering the privilege unavailable without undermining the determination just made concerning its availability. If the privilege were held to shield from an increased likelihood of prosecution for future crime, it would be inconsistent to find that the privilege was lost because of a choice made to commit that crime. Relevant here is what was said earlier in connection with retrospective incrimination, that the fact a person chose to commit a crime in the past cannot be used as a reason for later compelling him to disclose without destroying the policy of the privilege.

A somewhat different case is presented when a statute imposes upon a person an obligation to disclose information which does not necessarily reveal an intention to commit crime but which may later give rise to an inference that a crime was committed. An example of this situation might be a local ordinance that requires a convicted felon to register with the police, notify of change of address and employment, and so forth.[90] This information may prove useful to establish that the person who registered participated

---

[90] See Note, *Criminal Registration Ordinances: Police Control over Potential Recidivists,* 103 U. Pa. L. Rev. 60 (1954). See also Warszower v. United States, 312 U.S. 342 (1942) (information provided in Selective Service registration used to prove that subsequent to the registration the defendant obtained a passport by false statements).

in criminal activity. In this case the felon does not have a way out such as is available to the gambler. His obligation to register is not contingent on his engaging in a future crime. It is based upon his status as a convicted felon and his presence in the community. Nevertheless, the privilege ought also to be considered unavailable here because only prospective incrimination is involved.

Likewise statutes that require a person to provide information as a precondition for engaging in an activity that is ordinarily not criminal—and perhaps the felon registration ordinances should be considered to fall within this category—do not involve the privilege against self-incrimination even though the information disclosed may increase the likelihood of prosecution for a subsequent crime. Information given in registering an automobile or obtaining a driver's license may be useful in establishing that the registrant is a person who later committed a motor vehicle offense. The difference between this situation and the wagering tax case is that here the activity for which registration is made a precondition—automobile driving—does not ordinarily involve criminality but is criminal only if carried on in a particular manner. Similarly a person cannot invoke the privilege against a requirement that he file a flight plan before taking off from an airport because the plan may assist in identifying him as a person who later committed a crime.

That prospective incrimination does not run afoul of the privilege against self-incrimination does not mean that there are not other constitutional difficulties. Principles of free speech and association deriving from the First Amendment, and notions of due process, may interpose barriers to compelling information that will result in police surveillance and facilitate prosecution for future crime. When the information compelled is drawn from a person's mind, the practice may be particularly offensive. The ordinances just referred to that require convicted felons to register may involve serious constitutional questions because of the burden they impose upon a convicted felon's freedom.[91] Open to even more serious objection would be laws requiring all persons engaging in certain conduct, for example entering or leaving a municipality, to make known this fact to the authorities. Nevertheless, since the objections are directed to prospective incrimination and the burden on

---

[91] Cf. Lambert v. California, 355 U.S. 225 (1957).

freedom of action, they do not seem referable to the privilege against self-incrimination.

The validity of such registration laws as tested by constitutional principles other than self-incrimination will doubtless be affected by many of the same considerations that have already been mentioned as having relevance to whether the privilege should give way to pressing governmental needs for information. The seriousness of the evils to be avoided and the necessity of self-disclosure as a means for gathering information must be considered. Consideration must also be given to the extent to which registration acts as a burden on an activity, for example, travel, considered fundamental to freedom. Whether or not there can be any reasonable expectation of compliance with the registration requirement is also important. The purpose of the requirement may be simply to give the prosecutor an additional weapon for harassing a class of persons generally out of favor.

In the opinion in the *Lewis* case it is stated as relevant to the validity of the wagering tax registration requirement that the petitioner had no constitutional right to gamble.[92] Of course he had no right to gamble. That is to say, he could be punished for the act of gambling. But the question is whether it is constitutionally permissible to impose upon the activity of gambling punishment not only for engaging in this activity but such further and particular burdens as arise from requiring disclosure of an intention to gamble. The fact that an activity is already prohibited as criminal does not necessarily mean that any and all means may be used to deter it or to bring about the detection and prosecution of violators. It is not absurd to say that a person who has no right to do an act nevertheless has a right not to answer questions about his intention to do the act when the purpose of the questions is to facilitate his prosecution for doing the act. Is it constitutionally easier or more difficult to sustain a registration requirement when the activity to be engaged in is not necessarily criminal? In such a case other reasons for registration can be suggested than facilitating the prosecution of crime. Can a registration requirement for the operation of a motor vehicle be more easily sustained than a registration requirement for accepting wagers?

92 348 U.S. at 423.

The principal difficulty with what has been suggested regarding the inapplicability of the privilege against self-incrimination to prospective incrimination is that very frequently such incrimination is accompanied by retrospective incrimination. And if there is disclosure of past or present criminality, the obstacle presented by the privilege would not seem overcome or reduced by the fact that prospective incrimination is also present. Thus the records in *Shapiro* in addition to revealing past offenses might well have provided a basis for an inference that the defendant committed price violations after the records were made or perhaps even after they were produced. But this aspect of the case could not lessen the difficulty of deciding whether the privilege barred compulsory disclosure because of incrimination of past offenses.

In the wagering tax cases, retrospective incrimination probably would be avoided only if gambling were not a crime prior to the time that registration was required. Under any other condition, registration could give rise to an inference of earlier gambling, and this inference could arise even though the registrant had not in fact gambled before. If registration is required annually, each year's registration can give rise to an inference of prior gambling. This aspect of the case was pointed out by Mr. Justice Black in his dissent in *United States v. Kahriger.*[93]

Nevertheless, even if one takes into account this possible retrospective incrimination, there is a distinction between the wagering tax case and others that have been considered. There is a way out for the defendant that will enable him to avoid incriminating himself concerning past gambling. He can stop gambling; if he does not go on gambling, he has no obligation to register. This choice was already mentioned in its relevance to the permissibility of compelling prospective incrimination. Here we are concerned with its effect on the privilege so far as retrospective incrimination is concerned. Actually, we have already considered the question whether it is constitutionally permissible to condition the right to engage in an activity not ordinarily criminal on a disclosure of past crimes. Compulsory disclosure of incriminating facts on accepting public employment or leaving the country were mentioned. The peculiarity of the present case is that the activity upon which disclosure of past criminality is imposed is itself criminal.

---

[93] 345 U.S. at 36.

It is too easy to say that if it is permissible to attach to a non-criminal activity the requirement that prior crimes be disclosed, it must be permissible to attach this requirement to activity that is criminal. When the activity is criminal, the purpose of registration is probably to obtain information about prior crimes for the purpose of prosecution, or to facilitate prosecution of future crimes. Or, if compliance with the registration requirement cannot reasonably be expected, the purpose may be to increase punishment for the offense to which the registration requirement is attached, or to provide a way to punish indirectly conduct that cannot be punished directly because of jurisdictional limitations. When the activity upon which the registration requirement is imposed is not ordinarily criminal, it is easier to relate registration to a regulatory purpose not focused upon the detection and prosecution of crime. Do the purposes that, realistically, underlie a requirement that one register before committing a crime justify requiring disclosure of past crimes? Relevant here, perhaps, is what was said earlier, that the fact a person chose to commit a crime cannot be taken as a reason for later requiring him to disclose that crime without destroying the policy of the privilege. Can the same be said of a choice to commit a subsequent crime? We hope soon to have some light on this difficult question from the Court's decision in *Costello v. United States*,[94] a wagering tax case in which certiorari has been granted.

No distinction can be drawn between the wagering tax cases and the *Albertson* case on the ground of prospective and retrospective incrimination. Both forms of incrimination are arguably present in both situations, even though in the wagering tax cases the danger of prospective incrimination is more evident. Registration in *Albertson* incriminates prospectively, since it increases the likelihood that petitioners will be convicted of offenses said to have been committed after their registration. The difference between the cases is not that in one there is prospective incrimination and in the other retrospective incrimination, but, as said before, that in the wagering tax cases there is a way out that is not available in *Albertson*. In the wagering tax cases if a person does not continue to gamble, he has no obligation to register. In *Albertson*, on the other hand, as in the alien

---

[94] 352 F.2d 848 (2d Cir. 1965), *cert. granted*, 383 U.S. 942 (1966), *supra* note 35.

registration and Selective Service cases, the obligation to register is imposed without regard to whether some future activity is engaged in. Petitioners must comply with the Board's order to register or be punished for refusing to do so.

The Court's forthcoming decision in the *Costello* case may see it comparing the purposes of registration in the wagering tax cases and under the Subversive Activities Control Act. The probable purpose of the wagering tax statute has already been discussed. Only with difficulty can one find here a bona fide purpose to raise revenue. Various purposes can be suggested for the registration requirement of the Subversive Activities Control Act. The purpose may have been to facilitate prosecution and conviction of crimes associated with Party membership. Or the purpose may have been to provide the public with information about the membership of organizations deemed inimical to the national interest, and to bring down upon the members of these organizations the disadvantages, governmental and private, that flow from a revelation of Communist association. This purpose, however, as has already been observed, would seem served by the Board's finding of membership, without the further requirement of registration. If voluntary registration or compliance with registration orders cannot reasonably be expected, the purpose of the registration requirement probably is simply to provide another basis for prosecution and to make available punishment for non-registration in addition to whatever punishment is available for crimes associated with Party membership. In any event, no matter how favorably one states the purposes of the registration requirement, *Albertson* stands for the proposition that they are insufficient to justify setting aside the protection of the privilege. Can the purposes of the wagering tax statute be stated more impressively? Of course, in *Albertson* the effect of holding the privilege against self-incrimination applicable is to give protection in an area touching upon political action and opinion. The wagering tax cases have no First Amendment coloration to add strength to the argument based upon the privilege against self-incrimination.[95]

---

[95] The National Firearms Act, 26 U.S.C. §§ 5821 *et seq.*, raises problems that frequently have been discussed in connection with the wagering tax statute, and the many cases that have arisen under the Firearms Act suggest a situation ripe for clarification by the Supreme Court.

Measurement of the provisions of the Act by the standard of the privilege against

IV. COMPULSORY DISCLOSURE FOR LIMITED USE—
A PARTIAL SOLUTION

The foregoing discussion gives some idea of the variety of factors that must frequently be considered in determining the avail-

---

self-incrimination began with Russell v. United States, 306 F.2d 402 (9th Cir. 1962). The defendant was convicted under information that was construed to charge him with a violation of 26 U.S.C. § 5841. Section 5841 required a person possessing a firearm within the meaning of the Act to register the firearm when it was acquired by transfer or importation, if other provisions of the Act were applicable to such transfer or importation and these provisions had not been complied with. In other words, § 5841 required registration when to register would necessarily reveal that there had been a failure to comply with other provisions of the Act. The court held that under the circumstances the application of § 5841 violated the privilege against self-incrimination. The court distinguished *Kahriger* and *Lewis* on the ground that under the wagering tax statute a person was only required to incriminate himself concerning future acts. 306 F.2d at 410. See also United States v. Fleish, 227 F. Supp. 967 (E.D. Mich. 1964); Dugan v. United States, 341 F.2d 85 (7th Cir. 1965).

Section 5851 at the time of the Russell conviction made it an offense to possess a firearm that had been transferred, imported or made without complying with the registration and tax provisions applicable thereto. It did not, however, make it an offense to possess a firearm that had not been registered in compliance with § 5841. For this reason the court held that the information did not charge a violation of § 5851. The court suggested, however, that if the information had stated such an offense, there would be constitutional difficulties if allegations of the defendant's failure to register were deemed essential to the charge made under § 5851. 306 F.2d at 406 n. 7.

After the conviction in the *Russell* case, § 5851 was amended to make it an offense to possess a firearm that had not been registered in compliance with § 5841. In Frye v. United States, 315 F.2d 491 (9th Cir.), *cert. denied*, 375 U.S. 849 (1963), the court affirmed a conviction under § 5851, and distinguished the case from *Russell* on the ground that the defendant was charged not with failure to register but with possession of a gun that was not in fact registered. The notion seemed to be that a charge under § 5851 did not necessarily include an accusation that the defendant had violated § 5841 by failing to register. Section 5851 was violated if a firearm was in the defendant's possession that had not been registered in compliance with § 5841 by anyone. This distinction is extremely thin, especially if the only burden on the government is to show possession of the firearm by the defendant and that it has not been registered, and not to show possession by someone other than the defendant who was under an obligation to register. See also Starks v. United States, 316 F.2d 45 (9th Cir. 1963); United States v. Forgett, 349 F.2d 601 (6th Cir. 1965), *cert. denied*, 383 U.S. 926 (1966).

In the most recent decision in this line of cases, Lovelace v. United States, 357 F.2d 306 (5th Cir. 1966), the court refused to follow *Frye*, or at least distinguished it. The case also involved a charge under § 5851 for possession of a firearm not registered as required by § 5841. The court found that the indictment charged that the defendant was the person who had failed to register the firearm. Does this mean that the government in order to avoid conflict with the privilege need only be careful to draw the indictment vaguely in regard to who failed to register under § 5841?

ability of the privilege in a number of related situations. The opinion in the *Albertson* case gives a misleading impression that it is essentially a simple question to decide whether the privilege applies, simply a matter of determining whether a compelled disclosure tends to incriminate. As soon as one places *Albertson* in a broader framework, however, and attempts to relate it to earlier decisions such as *Shapiro*, the wagering tax cases, automobile accident report cases, cases under the Narcotic Control Act, and so forth, the true difficulty of the problems becomes clear. A large number of factors beyond the question of tendency to incriminate must be considered. Among these are the purpose of the disclosure requirement, the importance of the governmental objective sought to be achieved, and the necessity of self-disclosure as a means of achieving this objective. Also of relevance are the questions whether disclosure is conditioned upon engaging in an activity deemed basic to freedom, whether disclosure is conditioned upon engaging in an activity that is independently criminal, whether incrimination is prospective or retrospective. Finally, there is the question whether the purpose of the disclosure requirement can be achieved without use of the information for criminal prosecution.

This last consideration—whether use of the compelled information can be limited—points perhaps to the best hope of relieving the tension that exists between the policy of the privilege and strong governmental interests in obtaining information. Sometimes it is well that the privilege bend in order that it not break. The essentials of the privilege are not necessarily sacrificed by requiring disclosure of information when the use to which it is put is controlled and limited. Requiring disclosure under such limitations can provide relief from the necessity of choosing between complete protection and no protection at all, between a person's right to remain silent and the government's right to compel incriminating information and to use it for all purposes including criminal prosecution.

The numerous immunity statutes that have been enacted, in various forms, over the past three-quarters of a century, have been one means by which this result of compelled disclosure for limited use has been brought about. The judicial decisions sustaining these statutes have evidenced a recognition of the need to resolve the tension between the privilege and the need for information vital to various governmental programs. They have evidenced a willingness to narrow somewhat the protection of the privilege in order to achieve this end.[96]

Further evidence of the same tendency to compromise is seen in provisions seeking to guarantee the confidentiality of information furnished certain government agencies. Disclosure is prohibited other than for specified purposes and to certain persons, and penalties imposed for violation of the prohibition. Efforts to restrict the use of information can be found in connection with income tax returns,[97] census reports,[98] and numerous other matters. When there is a restriction that precludes use in connection with criminal prosecution, is there any reason not to require disclosure of incriminating information? Is there any reason not to give to such a restriction the effect of an immunity statute? Of course, there is only a restriction on use and not a complete prohibition against prosecution relating to matters revealed in the disclosure.

Also of relevance are authorities stating that when a person is privileged not to disclose incriminating information, but is ordered to do so, and complies, the information disclosed cannot be used in a criminal prosecution.[99] Sometimes it is said that the evidence must be excluded because it was coerced. Once a person has disclosed incriminating information in compliance with an order, the only protection that the Constitution affords, in the absence of an immunity statute, is that the disclosure cannot be used in connection

---

[96] See, *e.g.*, Brown v. Walker, 161 U.S. 591 (1896); Ullman v. United States, 350 U.S. 422 (1956).

[97] See discussion of statutory provision in O'Connell v. Olsen and Ugelstadt, 10 F.R.D. 142 (N.D. Ohio 1949); United States v. O'Mara, 122 F. Supp. 399 (D.D.C. 1954).

[98] 13 U.S.C. §§ 8, 9 (1964); see St. Regis Paper Co. v. United States, 368 U.S. 208 (1961).

[99] See the Court's discussion in Murphy v. Waterfront Commission, 378 U.S. 52, 75–76 (1964), of Adams v. Maryland, 347 U.S. 179 (1954): "The Court, in an opinion joined by seven members, made the following significant statement: 'a witness does not need any statute to protect him from the use of self-incriminating testimony he is compelled to give over his objection. The Fifth Amendment takes care of that without a statute.' . . . This statement suggests that any testimony elicited under threat of contempt by a government to whom the constitutional privilege against self-incrimination is applicable . . . may not constitutionally be admitted into evidence against him in any criminal trial conducted by a government to whom the privilege is also applicable." See also 378 U.S. at 57 n. 6, and 103 (White, J., concurring).

with a criminal prosecution. He is not immunized from all prosecution relating to the matter disclosed.[100]

Two questions are suggested. First, if the Constitution itself requires the exclusion of incriminating evidence given in compliance with an order, why should not the availability of this protection mean that a person must disclose whenever a demand for information is made upon him in the course of an authorized inquiry? Why should he lose his right to remain silent only when there is an immunity statute? The theory of the coerced disclosure doctrine appears to be that the order to disclose was wrongful and that the person was entitled to remain silent, not that he was bound to answer and find his protection in a constitutional exclusionary rule. The importance of this difference in theory is seen in the fact that if the defendant had disobeyed the order and remained silent, he could not have been punished for contempt. It is not maintained that since the evidence will be excluded if the person does speak, he has lost his right to be silent. The right to be silent is lost only if there is an immunity statute.

The second question suggested is why, if a prohibition on prosecutory use satisfies the Constitution when the defendant does disclose incriminating information in compliance with an official demand, such a prohibition does not also satisfy the Constitution when there is an immunity statute? It has sometimes been thought that immunity statutes must protect against all prosecution relating to the matters disclosed and not simply against prosecutory use. If this view is correct, by responding to a demand for disclosure that does not rest upon an immunity statute, a person loses some of the protection that would otherwise be his.

One explanation for the state of the law is that it has seemed unwise to give to a government official, without specific statutory authorization, the power to confer immunity from prosecution. This assumes that immunity from prosecution must be conferred and that a prohibition against prosecutory use is not sufficient. If, however, it is sufficient that prosecutory use be forbidden, one reason at least for not requiring a person to disclose incriminating information when there is an official demand not based on an immunity statute disappears. The protection that the Constitution itself provides, as revealed in the case of a coerced disclosure, would be as full a protec-

---

[100] United States v. Blue, 384 U.S. 251 (1966).

tion as is required in an immunity statute. An official who demands information would not have the power to disable the government from all prosecutions relating to the matter disclosed. Prosecutory use of the information disclosed and its fruits would alone be forbidden, and the government would be no worse off in regard to prosecution than if the information had never been compelled.

In addition to the argument that an official should not have power to immunize from prosecution in the absence of specific statutory authorization, there is the notion that before a person is compelled to incriminate himself, he is entitled to such assurance of protection as is provided by the existence of an immunity statute. But if it is clearly settled by judicial decision that the information disclosed cannot be used for prosecutory purposes, does this not give equally satisfactory assurance of protection?[101]

Finally, when it comes to so serious a matter as compelling a person to make an incriminating disclosure, it has perhaps been thought desirable that the legislature make a judgment that the governmental objective sought to be achieved is of sufficient importance to warrant this action, and that self-disclosure is an essential means to obtain needed information. These judgments of importance and necessity ought not to be left in the hands of administrative officials even though it may be true that when an immunity statute is enacted there is administrative discretion about when it shall be applied.

Returning to the matter of immunity from prosecution as against a prohibition on prosecutory use, there are some indications, in addition to those implicit in the coerced disclosure cases, that there may in fact be no requirement of immunity from prosecution. In *Murphy v. Waterfront Commission*,[102] a demand for incriminating information was made by an interstate agency. Immunity from prosecution under state law was assured. The Supreme Court held that this protection was not enough and that the privilege also required protection from the consequences of incrimination under federal law. The Court held, however, that when disclosure is compelled

---

[101] Under the decision in Murphy v. Waterfront Commission, 378 U.S. 52 (1964), petitioners are compelled to incriminate themselves on the strength of the Supreme Court's assurance that their testimony cannot be used against them in a federal criminal prosecution.

[102] 378 U.S. 52 (1964).

by a state, neither the information disclosed nor its fruits can be used in connection with a federal prosecution. This protection derives from the Fifth Amendment itself. Furthermore, it is all the protection that the Fifth Amendment provides; it does not provide absolute immunity from federal prosecution relating to the matters disclosed.

The *Murphy* decision sought to resolve conflicting state and federal interests, a state interest in acquiring information and a federal interest in not being precluded from prosecuting violators of federal law. It does not follow that because the *Murphy* result is appropriate in the adjustment of federal-state relations that it will also apply when only a single jurisdiction is involved. *Murphy* did not hold that it would satisfy the privilege if the jurisdiction demanding incriminating information only gave assurance that it would not make prosecutory use of the information, and did not give immunity from prosecution for the matters disclosed. There is, however, some language in the opinions suggesting the possibility of rejecting the requirement that immunity from prosecution be granted.[103] Similar suggestions were included some years earlier in language in *Ullman v. United States*,[104] suggestions that *Counselman v. Hitchcock*[105] and *Brown v. Walker*[106] can perhaps be interpreted never to have imposed a requirement of absolute immunity from prosecution.

The Supreme Court is unlikely to move further in the direction of holding that a prohibition against prosecutory use is a sufficient substitute for the right to remain silent, or that an official has the right to compel disclosure even in the absence of an immunity statute, without first having had considerable experience regarding the actual effects of the rule against prosecutory use in those few situations to which it now applies. As indicated, these situations include those where federal-state relations are involved and where a

---

[103] See especially the Court's description, 378 U.S. at 78–79, of the holding in Counselman v. Hitchcock, 142 U.S. 547 (1892). In his concurring opinion, Mr. Justice White explicitly stated: "In my view it is possible for a federal prosecution to be based on untainted evidence after a grant of federal immunity in exchange for testimony in federal criminal investigation." 378 U.S. at 106. His interpretation of the holding in *Counselman v. Hitchcock*, is consistent with this view. *Id.* at 104–06.

[104] See 350 U.S. 422, 437 (1956).

[105] 142 U.S. 547 (1892).   [106] 161 U.S. 591 (1896).

person submits to an official demand for incriminating information that he was entitled to withhold. It may turn out that the theory of protection from prosecutory use is simply a cloud of words behind which the substance of the privilege is lost. This may be true even though it is laid down that in any prosecution brought against a person who was required to disclose incriminating information, the government has the burden of showing that its evidence was obtained independently of the compelled disclosure.[107] As a practical matter, will it be possible to determine whether the government's evidence was obtained independently? Suppose the evidence used to convict has no causal connection with the compelled disclosure other than that it provided the reason for commencing an investigation? It can of course be said that an investigation could have resulted from the mere fact that a person invoked the privilege and declined to answer questions. But when an incriminating disclosure has actually been made, a subsequent investigation is, realistically, likely to be more focused. The upshot of a rule restricted to forbidding prosecutory use may be that a person is in fact much worse off in regard to the danger of prosecution and conviction than if he had remained silent.

If it were held that a prohibition against prosecutory use was sufficient to satisfy the privilege, or that an official was entitled to compel disclosure of incriminating information even in the absence of an immunity statute, this would presumably be true in all cases to which the privilege presently applies. The decisions sustaining immunity statutes do not suggest that such statutes are valid only if directed to subjects of a certain importance or when self-disclosure is an especially necessary source of information. It is for the legislature to decide in what situations information is worth the price of immunity. There still would be the necessity, however, to decide which cases fall entirely outside the privilege, so that information required to be disclosed could be used for all purposes including criminal prosecution.

The further development of this subject of limited use has great significance for the course of decision in the group of cases that we have considered, represented by *Albertson, Shapiro,* and the wagering tax cases. If the compromise is extended that deprives a person of the right to remain silent but gives protection from prosecutory

---

[107] See Murphy v. Waterfront Commission, 378 U.S. at 79 n. 18 (1964).

use, pressure will be greatly reduced to find that in particular circumstances records, reports, or required testimony fall entirely outside the privilege. *Shapiro* stands as an example of what can happen when the government's demand for information becomes particularly insistent, and it is not a case that commends itself as providing a reasoned explanation for its result. The extension of compromise may take the form of an increasing number of immunity statutes directed at particular areas of governmental regulation, or the enactment of a single federal immunity statute available in any case in which an authorized official makes a determination of necessity. Or it may take the form of an increase in the number of situations in which protection from prosecutory use is found to be constitutionally sufficient. Most radically, it could take the form of a determination that the right to silence is lost whenever there is an official demand for information, even in the absence of an immunity statute, since there is constitutional protection against prosecutory use.

When the problems touched upon earlier in this article are recalled, and it is appreciated how various and complex are the factors that arguably must be taken into account in deciding whether the privilege to remain silent should stand in spite of impressive governmental needs for information, the path of compromise seems particularly attractive. In addition to the problem of which of the various factors that have been considered should be determinative in a given case, there is the very real danger that through the process of weighing competing interests the subtle but important values represented by the privilege will gradually be lost to sight. Of course, if the only use that can be made of incriminating information is in connection with criminal prosecution, there is an irreconcilable conflict between the policy of the privilege and the government's desire for information. But in a great many situations, as has been suggested, use of incriminating information for purposes other than prosecution will satisfy the reason for compelling disclosure. Advantage should be taken of this fact to reduce the conflict between the privilege and other governmental policies.

MONRAD G. PAULSEN

KENT V. UNITED STATES: THE

CONSTITUTIONAL CONTEXT OF

JUVENILE CASES

A Children's Hour has come to the Supreme Court of the United States. It has been a long time coming. The original juvenile court act of Illinois, a model quickly followed in almost every state, was approved by the governor of Illinois on April 21, 1899. Until March 21, 1966, the Supreme Court had never passed upon the legality of juvenile court procedures or of police practices respecting juveniles. Sixty-seven years after the passage of the seminal legislation, the Court decided one juvenile's case arising from the District of Columbia[1] and agreed to hear two more, these arising from the states.[2] The long delay is the more remarkable because the Court in its recent past has displayed only modestly its traditional concern for judicial self-restraint.

Unlike some of the Court's recent actions, the decision to concern itself with justice for juveniles is deserving of general approval. The constitutional principles applicable to juvenile courts cry out—not for clarification but for enunciation. The relevant questions

Monrad G. Paulsen is Professor of Law, Columbia University.

[1] Kent v. United States, 383 U.S. 541 (1966).

[2] Miller v. Rhay, 384 U.S. 902 (1966); *In re* Gault, 384 U.S. 997 (1966). The *Miller* case was remanded for further consideration by the Washington Supreme Court. 384 U.S. 892 (1966).

are, for the most part, questions of fairness of legal procedures, issues upon which the Court has as much wisdom and experience to offer as upon any issue the Court decides.

The problems are exceedingly important even if they are measured only in terms of the number of families touched by them. The most recent official report of juvenile court statistics estimates that 591,000 children were, informally or formally, respondents in juvenile court delinquency cases in 1964.[3] In addition, the report hazards that one child in nine "will be referred to juvenile courts for an act of delinquency (excluding traffic) prior to . . . [his] eighteenth birthday."[4] Considering boys alone we find the situation alarming indeed: about one boy in six will be involved with such a court. For girls, the chances are one in twenty-three. Furthermore, dependency and neglect cases in the juvenile courts in the United States totaled 150,000 in 1964.[5]

Thus great numbers of Americans have had their most vital interests in freedom and in the right to the custody and control of their children adjudicated by courts employing procedures of debatable constitutional validity. Today no one can state with authority whether a respondent to a juvenile court delinquency petition is entitled to the right to counsel; if so, in what cases and at what stage of the proceedings; whether such youngsters may invoke the privilege against self-incrimination; whether a juvenile's lawyer has the right to inspect the social service record compiled by the court staff to assist the judge in making disposition of the case; whether a child in juvenile court has the right to a jury trial; whether the full reach of the Fourth Amendment applies to children in the same manner as to adults; whether the limitations on police interrogation which must be observed in criminal cases after *Miranda v. Arizona*[6] are also to be observed in cases of youths headed for Children's Court. This list offers only a few of the multitude of questions that a parade of juvenile court cases would put to the Justices.

I. The Aims and Claims of Juvenile Courts

Where the juvenile court movement really began is not easy to say. Australia, Denver, and Chicago each have filed claims, but

---

[3] U.S. Dept. of Health, Education, and Welfare, Children's Bureau, Juvenile Court Statistics 1 (1965).

[4] *Ibid.*   [5] *Id.* at 6.   [6] 384 U.S. 436 (1966).

certainly the Illinois legislative model was pivotal in the United States. Thirty state legislatures acted similarly within six years after its enactment. The Illinois reformers were prototypes of those throughout the nation who prodded and worried legislators until a juvenile court act had been put on the books. They were concerned not only with helping children but also with improving society at many levels, with prison reform, with women's suffrage, with the moral and spiritual uplift of the poor. Jane Addams, for example, was a vigorous supporter of the group active in Chicago. "The juvenile court," wrote Herbert Lou in 1927, "is conspicuously a response to the modern spirit of social justice."[7]

In particular, the reformers generally rejected deterrence and retribution as adequate notions to justify criminal sanctions. A criminal law based on such principles had failed to suppress crime and was cruel to individuals because of its failure to individualize treatment. Certainly such a harsh, poorly conceived system should no longer be applied to children. The reformers saw and were appalled by the facts: youngsters (over the age of seven) could be given long prison sentences; branded for life with the stigma of criminality; mixed in jails, penitentiaries, and prisons with hardened adult offenders; offered no opportunity for social and moral re-education. The rules of criminal responsibility, based on what seemed to be an outmoded conception of "free will," were thought unsuited to the progress appropriate to the new century, and certainly could have no proper application to children. The reformers knew that society, not the individual, is the source of crime.

Children were considered educable and reformable. The criminal law did nothing to form good character; quite the contrary, it worked a great deal of harm. Even leniency on the part of criminal court judges was not to be welcomed. An act of such "generosity" to a child might simply be a lost opportunity for corrective education. "[T]he significant fact which must not be overlooked is that, even if [he was] 'let off' by the justice . . . no constructive work was done in the child's behalf. . . . [W]hatever was done in the case was necessarily done with little or no relation to the child's history or surroundings."[8]

---

[7] Lou, Juvenile Courts in America 2 (1927).

[8] Lathrop, *Introduction*, in Breckinridge, The Delinquent Child and the Home 2 (1912).

"The Juvenile Court," wrote Miriam Van Waters, a referee in a California juvenile court, "is conceived in the spirit of the clinic."[9] Leaders of the juvenile court movement believed, in general, that in the behavioral sciences and the medical arts there was available a body of scientific information which, if applied to an erring child, could work beneficial change in him. The social and economic setting in which delinquency flourished was well understood, but consideration of this matter played not nearly so great a role in the discussions of reform as did medicine, psychology, and biology. To better the environment presented too vast an undertaking, and moreover such a long-range task had no relevance to a little delinquent boy presently before the cruel bar of justice.

Considerations such as these lay behind the creation of a new court for juveniles, a court to which Judge Julian Mack would give the most awesome charge:[10] "The problem for determination by the judge is not, Has this boy or girl committed a specific wrong, but What is he, how has he become what he is, and what had best be done in his interest and in the interest of the state to save him from a downward career." This court was to meet a delinquent child's "needs" and to serve his "best interests," not to punish him.

Not only was the aim of a court for children to differ from that of the criminal court; its way of going about things was to be changed as well. Procedure had to be "socialized." "The purpose of the juvenile court is to prevent the child's being tried and treated as a criminal; all means should be taken to prevent the child and his parents from forming the conception that the child is being tried for a crime."[11] The respondent to a petition filed in his own interest replaced the defendant to a criminal charge filed in the interest of the state. Trials by jury should be permitted "under no circumstances," because "they are inconsistent with both the law and the theory upon which children's codes are founded."[12] Hearings were not to be "public trials" lest youngsters be damaged by publicity. Little or no need would be found for the respondent to

---

[9] Van Waters, *The Socialization of Juvenile Court Procedure*, in HOAG & WILLIAMS, CRIME, ABNORMAL MINDS AND THE LAW 158 (1923).

[10] Mack, *The Juvenile Court*, 23 HARV. L. REV. 104, 119–20 (1909).

[11] CHILDREN'S BUREAU (Pub. No. 121), JUVENILE COURT STANDARDS 5 (1923).

[12] *Id.* at 6.

have a lawyer; "the judge represents both parties and the law."[13]
The proceedings were to be "informal," or, as the original Illinois
act put it:[14] "The Court shall proceed to hear and dispose of the
case in a summary manner." The rules of evidence governing criminal cases were not to be strictly followed. In part, they were to
be rejected because the inquiry was to be broader than the relatively
simple question: "Did the child do it?" The inquiry was also to
consider medical and psychological information, the "impressions
of trained observers,"[15] in order to understand the Reason Why.
In part, evidentiary rules of exclusion were to be rejected because
they derived from considerations of extraneous policy. For example,
the rule excluding illegally obtained evidence would simply block
information that might be essential to child rescue. The methods
of the "old common law" were to be abandoned and replaced by
"instruments forged by a jurisprudence which realizes that law, like
medicine, is social engineering."[16] In short, the ordinary protections
of a person accused of crime were hindrances to the achievement
of juvenile court goals, not milestones on the path of human ad-
vancement.

Not to be overlooked is another aspect of the insistence on in-
formality in court. The community has never been much concerned with the impact of criminal procedure on the feelings of an
accused. If he is terrified by the courtroom scene, so much the better.
A malefactor might thus be convinced never to return. The reformers, on the other hand, sought to dispel the fear that can
accompany a child's day in court. They perceived the appearance
before the juvenile court judge as the beginning of the treatment
process, a beginning that should not make the total job of serving a
child's needs more difficult. If the state is to act like a father, its
representative, the judge, should act like one at the hearing. The
respondent child, Judge Mack said, should "be made to feel that
he is the object of [the court's] care and solicitude. The ordinary
trappings of the court-room are out of place in such hearings. The
judge on a bench, looking down upon the boy standing at the bar,

---

[13] FLEXNER, OPPENHEIMER, & LENROOT, THE CHILD, THE FAMILY AND THE COURT
(Children's Bureau Pub. No. 193) 4 (1929).

[14] Juvenile Court Act, § 5, Ill. Laws 1899, p. 131.

[15] FLEXNER, OPPENHEIMER, & LENROOT, op. cit. supra note 13.

[16] Ibid.

can never evoke a proper sympathetic spirit. Seated at a desk, with the child at his side, where he can on occasion put his arm around his shoulder and draw the lad to him, the judge, while losing none of his judicial dignity, will gain immensely in the effectiveness of his work."[17]

The juvenile court would achieve its purposes through the work of a well-chosen judge and a qualified staff, particularly the staff of probation officers. The judge would see to it that the "socialized" procedure disadvantaged no one. He was to adjudicate whether the respondent child had performed the acts alleged in the petition and to decide, with the help of his staff, what the child's needs were and how they could be met. The specifications for the ideal judge resulted in a tall order. Miriam Van Waters, writing in the early twenties, demanded, in addition to legal training, "a thorough knowledge of psychology, mental hygiene, sociology and anthropology, at least those branches of anthropology that deal with criminology, cultural history of the race and racial traits and capacities. . . ."[18] Judge Mack asked for a thoroughly trained lawyer, one who was willing and patient to search out the causes of misbehavior and to formulate a plan by which cure may be effected. "He must, however, be more than this. He must be a student of and deeply interested in the problems of philanthropy and child life, as well as a lover of children."[19]

For many reformers, including Judge Mack, "Probation is, in fact, the keynote of juvenile-court legislation."[20] Through the probation staff a child's re-education could be pursued with vigor, wisdom, and consistency. The institution of probation enabled the court to leave a child in his home while a treatment plan was followed. In short, probation performed the social casework that a child and his family might need.

One final point. The hearings in courts, the detention centers, the training institutions, were all to be quite separable from those employed for adults. The mixing of delinquents with adult offenders at any level was universally condemned.

How could the reformers create this kind of court within a constitutional framework that insisted upon many of the institutions and procedures then thought to be irrelevant or subversive of the

17 Mack, *supra* note 10, at 120.   19 Mack, *supra* note 10, at 119.

18 Van Waters, *supra* note 9, at 160.   20 *Id.* at 116.

job of protecting children? First, because most of the objectionable constitutional provisions applied only to criminal cases, they could be avoided by insisting that the proceedings in juvenile court were "civil" and not "criminal." Second, the inventive Illinois group invoked a variant of a well-established principle of the courts of equity. The writers of a Children's Bureau pamphlet of the 1920's described the idea:[21] "The conception that the State owes a duty of protection to children that it does not owe to adults was established by the old courts of equity.... The crown was *parens patriae* and exercised its prerogative to aid unfortunate minors through the great seal." Never mind that the doctrine of the crown as *parens patriae* had been applied only to protect children in respect to their property against the acts of greedy adults or to assure a child a proper upbringing but never to immunize a child against the consequences of criminal conduct. It was close enough to do a job. "In short, the Chancery practice was substituted for that of the criminal procedure."[22]

The reformers did more than change labels and invoke history. After all, some of them pointed out, they were dealing with children, and children are naturally subject to many restraints, some of them quite arbitrary and not to be suffered by mature persons. An early Pennsylvania case upholding the constitutionality of that state's first juvenile court act argued:[23] "The natural parent needs no process to temporarily deprive his child of its liberty by confining it in his own home, to save it and to shield it from the consequences of persistence in a career of waywardness; nor is the state, when compelled, as *parens patriae*, to take the place of parents for the same purpose, required to adopt any process as a means of placing its hands upon the child to lead it into one of its courts." Most important of all was the point that the criminal courts and the juvenile courts differ radically in respect to purposes and consequences. The aim of the criminal process is the imposition of stigma and pain for the purposes of punishment, deterrence, or

---

[21] FLEXNER & OPPENHEIMER, THE LEGAL ASPECTS OF THE JUVENILE COURT (Children's Bureau Pub. No. 99) 9 (1922).

[22] Hurley, *Origins of the Illinois Juvenile Court Law,* in THE CHILD, THE CLINIC AND THE COURT 328 (1925).

[23] Commonwealth v. Fisher, 213 Pa. 48, 53 (1905).

reformation. The aims of the new juvenile process were protection, education, and salvation:[24]

> The child was not to be convicted, but was to be found dependent, delinquent or truant or discharged. The child was not to be sentenced to a reformatory or prison, but committed to the care of a probation officer or to the care of a friendly institution. . . . [T]he effort being first, to find out what was the best thing to be done for the child, and secondly, if possible, to do it. It will be seen at once that this procedure contemplated a complete change; instead of punishment and reformation is formation. The procedure contemplated care, attention and formation rather than reformation.

To such beneficent purposes constitutional guarantees had little or nothing to contribute. Why should the fundamental law hamstring the state in its attempt to to good?

The reformers were well pleased with their creation. Nor did the approval fade in a day. Herbert Lou, in 1927, wrote:[25] "[I]n this new court we tear down primitive prejudice, hatred, and hostility toward the lawbreaker in that most hidebound of all human institutions, the court of law, and we attempt, as far as possible, to administer justice in the name of truth, love and understanding." Miriam Van Waters also used the superlative:[26] "[The] devoted pioneers of Chicago and Denver . . . devised the best plan for the conservation of human life and happiness ever conceived by civilized man." Hardly anybody paid mind to the point of view of Judge Waite of Minneapolis:[27] "The Court which must direct its procedure even apparently to do something *to* a child because of what he *has done*, is parted from the court which is avowedly concerned only with doing something *for* a child because of what he *is* and *needs*, by a gulf too wide to be bridged by any humanity which the judge may introduce into his hearings, or by the habitual use of corrective rather than punitive methods after conviction."

Though the United States Supreme Court has never passed on the basic constitutional issues presented by the juvenile court acts, over forty state supreme courts have upheld the local variants of

---

[24] Hurley, *supra* note 22.   [25] Lou, *op. cit. supra* note 7, at 2.

[26] Van Waters, *Organization of Family Courts*, in THE CHILD, THE CLINIC AND THE COURT 266 (1925).

[27] Waite, *How Far Can Court Procedure Be Socialized without Impairing Individual Rights*, 13 J. AM. INST. OF CRIM. L. & CRIM. 339, 340 (1922).

such laws against the claim that the statutes violated both state and federal constitutions in each case.[28] In each of the cases, a child, or his guardian, urged that he had been committed to a training school or placed under some authoritative regime without the basic rights of a person accused of crime. In most instances the child was charged with an act that would have been a crime save for the juvenile court statute. To the child and his family the imposition of authority or commitment to a training school seemed little different from the consequence of a criminal conviction. How could it be, they asked, that the legislature could take away the right to jury trial, to a public hearing, the right to appear and defend in person, the right to counsel, and the rest? The state courts answered by echoing the arguments of the reformers. The proceedings are civil and not criminal. In one of the leading early cases, *Commonwealth v. Fisher*,[29] the Supreme Court of Pennsylvania wrote that, of course, no act of the legislature could take away rights guaranteed by the state's Bill of Rights whether the person be young or old, "if he is to be tried for a crime against the commonwealth. But there was no trial for any crime here. . . ." Children are generally subject to control that is not based on law. The purpose of the legislation is to help the child and to attend to his needs:[30] "Its object is to confer a benefit both on the child and the community in the way of surrounding the child with better and more elevating influences and of educating and training him . . . thereby saving him to society and adding a good and useful citizen to the community." A parent who complained that his right to his child's custody had been violated when the child was sent to training school as the result of an act of delinquency was met with the argument that the delinquent act of the child substantially established the parent's unfitness for custody.[31]

In whatever way the Supreme Court of the United States may

---

[28] Some of the leading cases are: Lindsay v. Lindsay, 257 Del. 328 (1913); *In re* Sharp, 15 Idaho 120 (1908); Wissenberg v. Bradley, 209 Iowa 813 (1929); Commonwealth v. Fisher, 213 Pa. 48 (1905); Mill v. Brown, 31 Utah 473 (1907).

[29] Commonwealth v. Fisher, 213 Pa. 48, 53 (1905).

[30] *In re* Sharp, 15 Idaho 120, 127 (1908).

[31] A case note in 19 Harv. L. Rev. 374 (1906) is surely the first law review student commentary on juvenile court legislation. In it the author argued that a father's "failure to develop this boy into a law abiding citizen is at least some evidence of his incompetence."

ultimately resolve the issues presented by the juvenile court acts, we can be confident, after the Court's opinion in its first juvenile court case, *Kent v. United States*, that the Court's future work in the juvenile field will not take much inspiration from these state judgments that uncritically reflect the optimism of a more hopeful day.

II. KENT v. UNITED STATES

The fingerprints of Morris A. Kent, Jr., aged 16, were found in the apartment of a woman who had been raped and relieved of her wallet by an intruder. Kent was already on probation under an order of the District of Columbia's Juvenile Court following an indication of delinquency based upon "several housebreakings and an attempted purse snatching."[32] Taken into custody and interrogated by the police, he admitted that he was, indeed, the intruder and, further, he "volunteered information as to similar offenses involving housebreaking, robbery and rape."[33] Because of his age Kent was subject to the exclusive jurisdiction of the District's Juvenile Court. He could be tried on criminal charges only if the juvenile court judge "waived" jurisdiction after a "full investigation."[34]

Kent's mother retained counsel to represent him. Counsel promptly conferred with the social service director of the court and was told that the court might waive jurisdiction, thus sending Kent to criminal court for trial. Opposing waiver, Kent's lawyer asked for a hearing on the question and moved that he be given access to the social service file that the court staff had accumulated during Kent's probation, an item that the judge would have before him when he decided whether to turn Kent over to the criminal court for trial. In support of his motion for a hearing, counsel filed a psychiatrist's affidavit recommending hospitalization for psychiatric examination and certifying that Kent "is a victim of severe psychopathy."[35] Counsel also offered to prove that if petitioner were given adequate treatment in a hospital under the aegis of the Juvenile Court, he would be a suitable subject for rehabilitation.

The judge, pressed by an overcrowded docket,[36] was probably

---

[32] 383 U.S. at 543.

[33] *Id.* at 544.

[34] D.C. Code § 11-1553 (Supp. IV, 1965).

[35] 383 U.S. at 545.

[36] "It should be noted that at this time the statute provided for only one Juvenile Court judge. Congressional hearings and reports attest the impossibility of the burden which he was supposed to carry." *Id.* at 546 n. 5.

convinced that an adversary hearing would be pointless because Kent's record of repeated, serious offenses against persons and property would, in any event, require a decision to waive. He did not expressly rule on any of the motions made. He did not confer with Kent, his parents, or his lawyer before announcing the decision. He made no findings and gave no reasons for his action. The judge merely entered an order reciting that "after full investigation, I do hereby waive" jurisdiction.

In fairness to the judge it should be remarked that his decision was made in September, 1961, and the action that he took probably satisfied the standards then set by the Court of Appeals for the District of Columbia. In *Wilhite v. United States*,[37] a decision handed down in 1960, a panel of the Court of Appeals had ruled that no formal hearing was required under the District statute's waiver provision. The "full investigation" by the Juvenile Court of which the statute speaks need only be whatever "is needed to satisfy that court as to what action should be taken on the question of waiver."[38] It will little comfort the juvenile court judge who still sits in the District to be told by the Supreme Court of the United States, citing cases from 1964 and 1965, that "The authority of *Wilhite* . . . is substantially undermined by other, more recent decisions of the Court of Appeals."[39]

It is to the validity of this waiver "proceeding" that the opinion in *Kent* is addressed. In the criminal prosecution following the waiver decision the youth was found "not guilty by reason of insanity" of the charges of alleged rape but found guilty on six counts of housebreaking and robbery.[40] Kent was sentenced to a total of 30 to 90 years in prison: 5 to 15 years on each of the six counts.

Before the trial, Kent's counsel had moved to dismiss the indictment on the ground of the impropriety surrounding the transfer

---

[37] 281 F.2d 642 (D.C. Cir. 1960).

[38] *Id.* at 643.

[39] 383 U.S. at 558. The Supreme Court referred to Black v. United States, 355 F.2d 104 (D.C. Cir. 1965), and Watkins v. United States, 343 F.2d 278 (D.C. Cir. 1964).

[40] The Court in *Kent* explained this astonishing verdict on the hypothesis that the robberies had taken place before the rapes and the robberies and housebreakings "were not the product of his mental disease or defect, while the rapes were produced thereby." 383 U.S. 550 n. 10.

of the case. The District Court denied the motion on grounds
which, as we have said, explain the juvenile court judge's summary
handling of the matter. " '[T]he Courts have held . . . with reference to full investigation, that that does not mean a quasi judicial
or judicial proceeding. No hearing is required.' "[41] In an opinion,
flavored much like many of the state cases raising constitutional
issues presented by juvenile court acts, the Court of Appeals[42] upheld the District Court. The Supreme Court reversed in a five-to-
four decision. The vote of the Court requires a word of explanation.
The four dissenters did not dissent from or express objection to
the main thrust of the Court's opinion. Mr. Justice Stewart, speaking for his colleagues Justices Black, Harlan, and White, noted the
Court's general practice of leaving undisturbed decisions of the
Court of Appeals for the District concerning the meaning of legislation designed to govern the District. Moreover, he pointed out,
two cases decided by the Court of Appeals after the Court of Appeals' *Kent* opinion "may have considerably modified the court's
construction of the statute."[43] The dissenters would therefore have
vacated the judgment and remanded to the Court of Appeals "for
reconsideration in the light of its subsequent decisions."[44] From
the brief Stewart opinion there is no way of knowing whether the
dissenters have any views respecting the issues in *Kent* different
from those of Mr. Justice Fortas, who wrote for the Court.

III. The Context of the Constitution

An amicus curiae brief filed with the Court by a group of
lawyers and law teachers, mostly from the District of Columbia
area, urged that "The present case not only provides an opportunity
for the necessary definition of constitutional standards in juvenile
courts but indeed demands it."[45] But the Court purportedly declined the invitation to reach for the broad issues. "The Juvenile
Court Act and the decisions of the United States Court of Appeals
for the District of Columbia provide an adequate basis for the decision of this case, and *we go no further*."[46]

The Court did not go "further" in that the Justices refused "to

---

[41] *Id.* at 549.

[42] 343 F.2d 247 (D.C. Cir. 1964).

[43] 383 U.S. at 568.

[44] *Ibid.*

[45] Brief of Amicus Curiae, p. 7.

[46] 383 U.S. at 556.

rule that constitutional guaranties which would be applicable to adults charged with the serious offenses for which Kent was tried must be applied in juvenile court proceedings. . . ."[47] But neither did the Court simply give a statute an interpretation that the legislature might readily change.

A waiver of jurisdiction by the juvenile court, Mr. Justice Fortas wrote, "is a 'critically important' action determining vitally important statutory rights of the juvenile."[48] In the juvenile court the youngster is shielded from publicity; he may be detained only until he is twenty-one; he is protected from the stigma of a criminal conviction, and so forth. For Kent, the juvenile court presented the danger of a possible five years of confinement; the criminal court threatened with a death penalty maximum. The waiver decision, of such high practical importance, must be preceded by "a hearing, including access by his counsel to the social records and probation or similar reports which presumably are considered by the court, and to a statement of reasons for the Juvenile Court's decision."[49] The respondent must also be offered counsel. All this, the Court said, flowed from the statute, "read in the context of constitutional principles relating to due process and the assistance of counsel."[50] It would be rash to conclude that hereafter any similar waiver statute, state or federal, will be upheld under the Constitution unless it had been similarly interpreted "in the context of constitutional principles." "[T]here is no place in our system of law for reaching a result of such tremendous consequences without ceremony—without hearing, without effective assistance of counsel, without a statement of reasons."[51]

A statutory provision for a "full investigation" read in the context of constitutional principles requires a hearing and "access by the child's counsel to the social records of the child"[52] made up of probation or similar reports, at least if the judge is to receive and rely on such material in making a waiver decision. This reading of the law will touch off an uproar among social workers when the news reaches them. It is not likely that the required disclosure to counsel will be limited to waiver cases. A decision respecting dis-

---

[47] *Ibid.*   [48] *Ibid.*   [49] *Id.* at 557.

[50] *Ibid.* "The Court of Appeals has held in *Black* and we agree, that counsel must be afforded to the child in waiver proceedings."

[51] *Id.* at 554.   [52] *Id.* at 562.

position determining whether or not a boy goes to training school is surely also a decision of "critical importance." If a judge may not receive and rely on "*ex parte* analyses" and "secret information"[53] in deciding whether to transfer a case to a criminal court where, after all, the respondent can have a full trial, it ought to be equally improper for him to rely on the same secret reports in relation to an immediate decision to commit. Further, once the report must be made available to respondent's counsel for any purpose, most of the force behind the argument for confidentiality will be dissipated.

The portion of the opinion giving counsel access to hitherto confidential reports fails to consider the principal reasons usually given for keeping the material closely held inside the juvenile court itself. There is a footnote referring to the fact that Kent's lawyer had, in fact, seen the confidential material at a stage in the proceedings after the waiver decision. In that footnote, Mr. Justice Fortas quipped:[54] "Perhaps the point of it is that it again illustrates the maxim that while non-disclosure may contribute to the comfort of the staff, disclosure does not cause the heavens to fall." To which many experienced probation officers would respond: "Not right away perhaps." The arguments that the Court failed to acknowledge are these: To get information, especially of an intimate sort, the social investigator must be able to give firm assurances of confidentiality; if people generally learn that supplying information will bring them to court or plunge them into a neighborhood feud, they will no longer share their knowledge and impressions; information destructive of the youngster's chances at rehabilitation may leak back to him.

Mr. Justice Fortas' insistence on disclosure is rooted in his estimate of counsel's role and the lawyer's need for information. In its opinion below, the Court of Appeals had said that the lawyer's proper task in juvenile court is "to present to the court anything on behalf of the child which might help the court in arriving at a decision; it is not to denigrate the staff's submissions and recommendations."[55] Mr. Justice Fortas insisted, "on the contrary, if the staff's submission includes materials which are susceptible to challenge or impeachment, it is precisely the role of counsel to

---

[53] *Id.* at 563.

[54] *Id.* at 564 n. 32.   [55] 343 F.2d at 258.

'denigrate' such matter."[56] It is counsel's job to subject such material "to examination, criticism and refutation."[57] Without access to the records at this hearing the right to counsel is "an illusion, a mockery —unless counsel is given an opportunity to function."[58]

The Supreme Court does no service by maintaining silence in respect to the arguments of those who support the position that would withhold some information. They are arguments seriously advanced and deserve a considered reply. The shortcoming of the opinion in this respect may be a by-product of narrowing the issues that the Court chose to decide. By focusing on the validity of a waiver under a District of Columbia statute, the Court did not have to face the question whether disclosure would have a bad general effect on the operation of juvenile courts.

The impact of this not-fully-addressed question is great, if "the constitutional principles of due process and the assistance of counsel" require that state statutes be read in ways similar to *Kent*. Decisions reading statutes in the "context" of constitutional principles sometimes establish constitutional law. Should *Kent* be setting constitutional standards for the states, almost every juvenile court in the land will have to change its ways respecting the confidentiality of some staff material. Let me not leave a false impression about my own view. On balance, I think counsel must be given the right to probe and test the materials used in decision with, perhaps, some ultimate discretion in the court to withhold reports in very special circumstances. My point is that the Supreme Court has marched ahead without so much as a nod toward the reasons that support present general practice.

In this regard *Kent* has significance beyond the area of juvenile court procedure. Are the presentence reports of convicted persons now to be examined by counsel as a matter of right established by the "constitutional context" which must shape the meaning of legislation authorizing that the reports be made and presented to the sentencing judge? Certainly someone will make the challenge tomorrow or the next day. The *Kent* opinion encourages the claim. A decision about sentencing is of "critical importance"; the defendant has the right to counsel; a lawyer's task is to subject the bases of such decisions "to examination, criticism and refutation." And one cannot test that of which he does not know.

---

[56] 383 U.S. at 563.   [57] *Ibid.*   [58] *Id.* at 561.

A statute providing for waiver from juvenile court to criminal court requires that the deciding judge give the reasons for his decision when the statute is "read in the context of constitutional principles of due process." Reasons are required because otherwise effective appellate review is impossible. "Meaningful review requires that the reviewing court should review."[59] The judge's statement need not be a formal opinion but it should demonstrate that the question "has received the careful attention of the Juvenile Court."[60] If this requirement truly flows from the constitutional context, it will change practice for the many juvenile court judges who do not spell out the reasons for important decisions. Indeed, many courts, even high courts, dealing with adults do not give a statement of reasons concerning all important matters they determine. If *Kent* has significance for adult cases as well as juvenile, and there is no reason to think that it does not, more judges will write more opinions than ever before. A horrific prospect.

As one reflects upon the *Kent* case there is a certain irony produced. The amicus curiae brief and Kent's counsel were eager to bring the constitutional law of adults to children's cases. The Court, in interpreting a statute in its "constitutional context," may have brought protections to the adult criminal from a juvenile case.

The purpose of waiver provisions is to give the juvenile court discretion to send those youngsters to criminal court who are unlikely to be successful candidates for the rehabilitative efforts of the juvenile court. The exercise of discretion at that point may now require a form of adversary hearing, although one is not yet constitutionally required when the prosecutor exercises his discretion to prosecute or not.[61] Grand jury procedure would not pass muster under the *Kent* text. Parole board actions need not offer a full hearing or conclude with a statement of reasons. Counsel is not

---

[59] *Ibid.*   [60] *Ibid.*

[61] An interesting problem is presented under the new Illinois Juvenile Court Act. According to Smith-Hurd, Ill. Rev. Stat. ch. 37, § 702-7 (1965 Cum. Ann. Pocket Part), the state's attorney, in the case of a child over 13 who has committed a criminal offense, "shall determine the court in which . . . [a] minor is to be prosecuted" with a proviso that the chief judge of the circuit shall decide the issue by which court the youngster is to be tried if the juvenile court judge disagrees with the prosecutor's choice. Must the prosecutor now hold a hearing if *Kent* has announced constitutional principles?

generally provided a parole applicant and the information on which
the board acts is generally secret. The opinion, of course, limits
itself to stating the requirements of judicial decision-making. "The
Juvenile Court is governed in this respect by the established principles which control courts and quasi-judicial agencies of the Government."[62] Are prosecutors, parole boards, and grand juries not
also engaged in judicial or quasi-judicial functions?

In each situation suggested in the preceding paragraph, the
decision may be "a result of tremendous consequences" to the
person affected. Does the *Kent* opinion look toward such radical
innovation as to implant an adversary hearing in all official decision-
making that may work "a result of tremendous consequences" to
individuals in respect to their freedom? Perhaps not yet, but the
question is worth putting. The basic requirements of the accusa-
torial-adversary process have found their way into the police
station. Little in the present day of racial crises and of the discon-
tented poor argues for the extension of discretionary power. Legal
norms and forums in which a man can state his point of view,
argue his case, and hear the reasons for his fate have an attractive
look in 1966. The opinion in *Kent* is another small step in a per-
ceptible movement toward the "legalization" of official decision-
making wherever it intimately affects the individual.

IV. THE CONSTITUTION ITSELF

Though the Court's opinion in *Kent* does not actually hurl
constitutional thunderbolts at the nation's juvenile courts and
police practices respecting juveniles, it does raise a warning of
turbulent weather ahead. Mr. Justice Fortas noted that *Kent* presented a "number of disturbing questions concerning the administration by the police and the Juvenile Court authorities of the
District of Columbia laws relating to juveniles."[63] He warned that
a juvenile court judge's exercise of the power *parens patriae* was
limited by the rule of law: "the admonition to function in a
'parental' relationship is not an invitation to procedural arbitrari-
ness."[64] Courts have permitted legislatures to classify juvenile
court proceedings as "civil" rather than "criminal" because the
objectives of the court were rehabilitative and protective, designed

---

[62] 383 U.S. at 563.   [63] *Id.* at 542–43.   [64] *Id.* at 555.

to educate rather than to punish. At its most ominous, the opinion contrasts such hope and promise with performance:[65]

> While there can be no doubt of the original laudable purpose of juvenile courts, studies and critiques in recent years raise serious questions as to whether actual performance measures well enough against theoretical purpose to make tolerable the immunity of the process from the reach of constitutional guarantees applicable to adults. There is much evidence that some juvenile courts, including that of the District of Columbia, lack the personnel, facilities and techniques to perform adequately as representatives of the State in a *parens patriae* capacity, at least with respect to children charged with law violation. There is evidence, in fact, that there may be grounds for concern that the child receives the worst of both worlds: that he gets neither the protections accorded to adults nor the solicitous care and regenerative treatment postulated for children.

The lightning may indeed strike during the 1966 Term. On June 20, 1966, the high court noted probable jurisdiction in the appeal of Gerald Francis Gault[66] from a decision of the Supreme Court of Arizona.[67] Gault and his parents launched a broadside attack on the constitutionality of the Arizona juvenile court law. They argue, *inter alia*, that they had been given insufficient notice of the allegations against the youth, that they had not been advised of their right to counsel, that they had been denied important constitutional rights because of the informal hearing afforded in the juvenile court.

The Arizona Supreme Court took Gault's case as an opportunity to unburden itself in regard to a whole range of issues and at the same time to approach the constitutional issues in a cautious manner. Instead of insisting that the whole catalogue of the rights of accused persons must be applied in juvenile courts or that the proceedings are "civil" and hence have no relation to guarantees applicable to defendants in criminal cases, the Arizona judges said:[68] "Our task is to determine the procedural due process elements to which an infant and his parents are entitled in a juvenile hearing and decide whether our statute may be construed to in-

---

[65] *Id.* at 555–56.   [66] 384 U.S. 997 (1966).

[67] Application of Gault, 99 Ariz. 181 (1965).

[68] *Id.* at 189.

clude them." The opinion makes the point in another way by speaking of "the proper balance between the infant's right[s] . . . and the state's interest in avoiding or erasing the stigma of delinquency. . . ."[69] The best approach to the constitutional issue, thus, is to ask, "What does fairness or justice require in a special court for children alleged to be delinquent or neglected?"[70]

Using this "fairness to the juvenile" yardstick,[71] the Arizona court took a number of positions. "[T]he infant and his parent or guardian will receive a petition only reciting a conclusion of delinquency."[72] At "the initial hearing they must be advised of the facts involved in the case" and "they must be given a reasonable time to prepare" a response.[73] Due process did not require a right to counsel:[74] "the parent and the probation officer may be relied upon to protect the infant's interests." Nor that a youth be advised of a privilege against self-incrimination:[75] "the necessary flexibility for individualized treatment will be enhanced by a rule which does not require [it]. . . ." Nor the right to confrontation:[76] "the relevancy of confrontation only arises where the charges are denied." So it went. The juvenile court might consider hearsay if it were of the kind "on which reasonable men are accustomed to rely in serious affairs,"[77] but sworn testimony should be required of all witnesses including police officers, probation officers, and other members of the court's staff. The judge should make a finding of delinquency only if he is persuaded by clear and convincing evidence that the child has committed a delinquent act.

The Arizona court's disposition of all the issues will not satisfy everybody, but an approach of this kind offers a defensible way of resolving the fundamental constitutional questions presented by the juvenile court acts. Thus, the Supreme Court could avoid insisting that the juvenile court apply every right held by accused persons, especially if a given protection is not central to a fair determination of the questions that the court must resolve or if it seriously interferes with the juvenile court's function. Recognizing that all the rights of an accused are applicable to children

---

[69] Id. at 190.

[70] Paulsen, Fairness to the Juvenile Offender, 41 MINN. L. REV. 547, 563 (1957).

[71] 99 Ariz. at 189.   [74] Id. at 191.

[72] Id. at 190.   [75] Ibid.

[73] Ibid.   [76] Ibid.   [77] Id. at 192.

in delinquency cases would mean offering a right to trial by jury, the right to a public trial, the standard of proof beyond a reasonable doubt, and the privilege of refusing to give information. Present-day friends of the juvenile court movement vigorously deny that there is so little remaining of the juvenile court dream that the Supreme Court should fasten this yoke on juvenile courts throughout the land.

The standards applied by the Arizona court leave much to the subjective judgment of the judges, but the due process concept has traditionally done just that. Even in the process of "selectively incorporating" the Bill of Rights into the Due Process Clause, the Supreme Court has not required that the states charge adults by grand jury indictment. Few would argue that grand jury indictment is necessary to a fair trial. Indeed, the indictment process, involving secret proceedings and an *ex parte* presentation, is widely thought to be quite at odds in many ways with essential justice. If the Court can selectively "absorb" portions of the Bill of Rights in adult criminal cases it can do so for children's matters in juvenile court.

It is probably true that some of the adult protections that the reformers sought to avoid could be introduced into the juvenile court without completely hampering its operation. The right to a jury trial is preserved in some states and the juvenile courts still function with jury trials, although, in fact, the right is usually waived. A constitutional right to a public trial has rarely been invoked. If a child properly advised by parents and counsel, wishes a public trial, why should he not have it? In my view the reformers, in their desire to distinguish sharply between juvenile and criminal proceedings and in the hope that children would be processed as patients in a clinic or given social education as in a school, put too much emphasis on the need for informal procedure. The child and his parents are under no illusion. They know they are in court, not in school or at a doctor's office. To find a court acting like a court may only bear out the expectations derived from television. Certainly, too, the reformers were mistaken about the opportunity for treatment presented by a few minutes in court. Not many today would agree that a judge who put his arm around a boy gains "immensely in the effectiveness of his work." If our methods work changes in the characters of delinquent children, they must embrace more sustained measures over a period of time. Medical and psychiatric treatment programs, skillful probation services, soundly conceived "friendly institutions" (if any exist), may do the work of character building. But the experience at the hearing will be quickly forgotten in most cases.

Without doubt the most important issue before the Supreme Court will be whether counsel must be offered in juvenile court cases, and, if so, in what cases. The issue did not arise in *Kent* because the boy's mother had retained counsel. In any event, the right to counsel at the waiver hearing had previously been recognized by the Court of Appeals for the District of Columbia as a matter of statutory interpretation.[78] Yet the opinion in *Kent* is relevant. As we have seen, it interprets the District of Columbia statute "in the context of constitutional principles relating to due process and the assistance of counsel." Mr. Justice Fortas referred with approval to the Court of Appeals case establishing the right to counsel in waiver proceedings.[79] At another point he wrote:[80] "The Statute does not permit the Juvenile Court to determine in isolation and without the participation of the child or any representative of the child the 'critically important' question whether a child will be deprived of the special protections of the Juvenile Court Acts." And finally, to repeat a phrase already quoted, "there is no place in our law for reaching a result of such tremendous consequences without ceremony—without hearing, without effective assistance of counsel. . . ."

Gault squarely presents the issue of the right to counsel in juvenile cases. I predict that such a right will be recognized by the Court under the Fourteenth Amendment,[81] though the scope of the right is less clearly revealed by the crystal ball into which I gaze. The right to counsel in juvenile cases can be derived from a simple extrapolation from *Gideon v. Wainwright*,[82] holding that the right to counsel exists in adult criminal cases. The lower courts have shown no disposition to limit *Gideon*'s reach save in the most

---

[78] 383 U.S. at 555.   [79] *Id.* at 562.   [80] *Id.* at 553.

[81] The prediction is not made more difficult by another three sentences of the Fortas opinion: "The right of representation by counsel is not a formality. It is not a grudging gesture to a ritualistic requirement. It is of the essence of justice." *Id.* at 561.

[82] 372 U.S. 335 (1963). It will be recalled that Mr. Justice Fortas, before joining the Court, had served as Gideon's lawyer in the Supreme Court. See Lewis, Gideon's Trumpet (1964).

petty of criminal matters. The very heart of juvenile court "philosophy"—i.e., that after an adjudication the question for decision is not what a child has done but what he needs—implies that there are clearly no "petty" delinquency cases. A child found to have committed even a minor offense may be found to "need" commitment to a training school. *Gault* is a case in point. The offense there was the use of obscene language to a woman over the telephone in violation of an Arizona statute.[83] Presumably because of a prior record, Gault was sent to the Arizona Industrial School, where he might not be released until twenty-one. In criminal court his offense would have been "punishable by a fine of not less than five nor more than fifty dollars, or by imprisonment in the county jail for not more than two months."[84]

A juvenile's right to counsel may also exist by an extension of the equal protection cases, *Griffin v. Illinois*[85] and *Douglas v. California*.[86] Without question those who can pay for counsel have a right that a lawyer attend them in juvenile court. If the poor have no access to legal assistance, the law may have created an "invidious discrimination" between rich and poor in the administration of justice.

A decision recognizing the state's duty to provide counsel for children will be welcome for the excellent reasons that exist for bringing lawyers into the juvenile court. Elsewhere I have attempted to state some of them:[87]

> A court without lawyers leaves only the judge to perform the triple role of prosecutor, defense lawyer, and impartial arbiter. These functions, necessary to a full hearing of both sides to a dispute, ought not to be joined. To Americans arguments about the facts forming a basis for a judicial decision ought to be submitted to a tribunal which tests evidence through cross-examination. In fact, in lawyerless juvenile court proceedings the judge cross-examines the witness; the very skill and energy which he brings to the task of pushing witnesses to tell the truth may present a frightening picture to a child looking to the judge for help in one of life's difficult moments.
> Both at the point of intake and at a dispositional hearing an

83 Ariz. Rev. Stat. § 13-377.   85 351 U.S. 12 (1956).

84 *Ibid.*   86 372 U.S. 353 (1963).

87 Paulsen, *Juvenile Courts, Family Courts and the Poor Man*, 54 CALIF. L. REV. 694, 704 (1966).

attorney may present arguments for the point of view which parents might assert, were they gifted with communication skills. Every juvenile court act requires that parents be notified of hearings, requirements which are thought so central that the court is without power to proceed if they are not satisfied. Why is so much importance attached to the notice requirement? Surely, the reason must be that the parents are expected to participate in some meaningful way. Yet any observer of a big city court knows how few parents come forward with argument and how ineptly those few go about it. A lawyer experienced in speaking up and making points clearly can be of enormous help to a vulnerable, poorly educated parent and to the youngster. Further the judge may find lawyers useful because, through them, they may be able better to explain to the parents the aims of the court and the purposes underlying a particular decision.

Where will the right to counsel begin and where does it end? The *Kent* case puts its emphasis on the stages of the proceedings that decide "critically important" questions. That would certainly include a fact-finding hearing, the main dispositional hearing, and, probably, at least first appeals. A juvenile court typically involves a number of court appearances at which progress is reviewed. Will lawyers be required at all of them or only in those at which a change-in-treatment plan will be recommended? The intake decision, deciding whether a given case shall go on to court, can be very important to a child. Must counsel be made available at that stage? The Court will surely find the Children's Hour a crowded time.

The most nettlesome question, raised on the facts but not decided in *Kent*, is whether the full reach of the limitations on police interrogation and search and seizure practice will extend to juveniles. These limitations enforced by the exclusionary evidence principle doubtless allow some guilty persons to go free. While we may agree, with general deterrence in mind—full enforcement of the law is not required for the law to have a deterrent effect—that it is better for many of the guilty to go unpunished than for an innocent person to be convicted, do we embrace the same attitude where children are concerned? There are at least two important points of difference. Almost no one regards an accused who is not convicted as an unlucky man. In the case of children it is possible to view a dismissal in juvenile court as a missed opportunity for correction and training. Second, is not the moral education, derived from a juvenile court experience, corruptive rather than regenerative if a youngster "beats the rap" because of what will seem like a "technical" rule—a loophole?

In so far as doctrine still moves judges to conclusions, much will turn on whether the Justices decide that youngsters subject to juvenile proceedings have a right to silence. The plan for police questioning laid out in *Miranda v. Arizona* requiring that interrogation in custody proceed only after the arrested person is cautioned that he need not speak and told that he may have access to counsel before answering—at public expense if necessary—is based on the need to protect a suspect's privilege against self-incrimination. If children possess the privilege or some sort of juvenile court analogue, it would be wrong not to give offending children the same immunity as murderers. Recognition of a juvenile's constitutional right to silence will shape not only consideration of the rules of police interrogation but also the handling of the question whether the exclusionary evidence rule is to be applied in juvenile court. The latter point arises from the opinion in *Malloy v. Hogan*,[88] which links, once more, the Fifth Amendment's right to silence with the exclusionary evidence principle.

In my view the full force of the Fourth and Fifth Amendments ultimately will be brought to bear on children's cases. It will seem more and more outrageous that the police may treat children more harshly than adult offenders. In *Kent*, Mr. Justice Fortas was plainly disturbed that the respondent had been detained in violation of the juvenile court statute and had not been brought before a judge for prompt arraignment in the manner required by the Federal Rules in adult cases.[89] If a mature offender and a stripling aged 16 rob a bank together, will we actually countenance a system that provides the oldster with counsel during questioning and the youngster with none? It should also be remembered that the rules respecting search and seizure and interrogation have the function of guiding the police, and the police will benefit from a single set of rules. They are not easily able to read the suspect's age at a distance. It should be added that the Constitution will certainly not be unresponsive to the claims of children. The Arizona Supreme Court has held that a children's officer may constitutionally enter a parents' house without a warrant to search for a seriously injured

[88] 378 U.S. 1 (1964).   [89] See 383 U.S. at 544 n. 1.

child in a case where the officer had probable cause to know of the child's condition.[90] Surely the issue is correctly decided. My point is only that the Justices will not adopt a dual system of control of police work, with the system applicable to children offering less protection than the system applicable to adults.

Again, it is not likely to be so disruptive to extend adult constitutional norms to children's cases as many active in the juvenile court movement believe. Significant in-custody interrogations characterize the investigation of only our most serious offenses—usually involving adults. The greatest difficulty of the police in living with the search and seizure rules lies in the area of the vice crimes. The greater proportion, by far, of juvenile offenses are offenses against property (41 per cent), many of them petty; offenses against public order (11 per cent); offenses applicable to juveniles only (truancy, curfew, running away, etc., 27 per cent). In 1964 less than one-tenth of juvenile offenses were offenses against the person.[91]

V. The Limits of the Constitution

What can a court and a constitution do about the treatment of juvenile delinquents? Most of the truly important issues respecting facilities, treatment methods, and the adequacy of staff are, indeed, as Mr. Justice Fortas indicated, "not within judicial competence."[92] The Court can introduce more formality into juvenile court procedure; it can require that counsel be made available; it can extend the constitutional limitations on police practices to children; but little else. I have argued that the coming "legalization" of juvenile court power will not destroy the court, but will it benefit children? It is agreed that something will be gained by the extension of the right to counsel. The involvement of lawyers in juvenile court may even improve facilities because of the higher "visibility" of the court's problems gained by bringing them to the attention of an influential group. It may help a youth to have an advocate and a mediator. But is the lot of a wayward child improved by public trials, jury trials, or the right to silence in court?

---

[90] State v. Hunt, 2 Ariz. 2d 6 (1965).

[91] U.S. Dept. of Health, Education, and Welfare, op. cit. supra note 3, at 3.

[92] 383 U.S. at 541.

The point is that tearing the "socialized" procedure out of our system is not a great leap forward. But some of the things the judges cannot give us might be, *e.g.*, an adequately staffed, well-trained probation service. For children who are receiving "the worst of both worlds,"[93] it is no great achievement to brighten the one that may not matter as much to them.

---

[93] *Id.* at 556.

JEROLD H. ISRAEL

ELFBRANDT V. RUSSELL: THE DEMISE OF THE OATH?

In *Elfbrandt v. Russell*,[1] the Supreme Court, in a 5-to-4 decision, declared unconstitutional Arizona's requirement of a loyalty oath from state employees. At first glance, *Elfbrandt* appears to be just another decision voiding a state loyalty oath on limited grounds relating to the specific language of the particular oath.[2] Yet, several aspects of Mr. Justice Douglas' opinion for the majority suggest that *Elfbrandt* is really of far greater significance:[3] it may sharply

---

Jerold H. Israel is Professor of Law, University of Michigan.

[1] 384 U.S. 11 (1966).

[2] Immediate reaction generally placed the case in this category. The *New York Times*, for example, made the following comments in describing *Elfbrandt*: "The decision avoided sweeping terms that might also have invalidated loyalty oaths of other states. But it continued the high court's recent tendency to resolve all constitutional doubts against loyalty oath laws. . . .

"In the early nineteen-fifties the Supreme Court upheld loyalty oaths relating to Los Angeles city employees, teachers in New York State, and candidates for public office in Maryland. But in recent years without overruling the principle that public employees can be required to sign such oaths, it has struck down several, finding that they were improperly drafted." N.Y. Times, April 19, 1966, p. 1, col. 6; p. 1, col. 4. See also Chicago Tribune, April 19, 1966, p. 3, cols. 1–3; NEWSWEEK 21 (May 2, 1966).

[3] Even if the *Elfbrandt* ruling were limited to the particular language of the Arizona statute, it would still have a significant impact on the laws of several states since the Arizona provision is based on Maryland's widely copied "Ober Act." See MD. ANN. CODE, art. 85a, §§ 1, 10, 11 (1965 Supp.); FLA. REV. STAT., tit. 44, ch. 876, §§ 22, 24, 25 (1965 Supp.); MISS. CODE ANN., tit. 17, ch. 10, §§ 4064-01, 4064-02, 4064-03 (1964 Supp.); N.H. REV. STAT. ANN., ch. 588, §§ 1, 9 (1965 Supp.); OKLA. STAT.

limit the scope and coverage of loyalty oaths generally and, indeed, may presage a ruling invalidating all such oaths. Of course, only the Supreme Court can determine this. In the meantime, some evaluation by others seems appropriate, particularly in light of the numerous attacks against loyalty oaths currently being mounted in various state courts and legislatures.[4]

I. THE ELFBRANDT OPINIONS

A. THE BACKGROUND

In form, if not in substance, the Arizona loyalty oath considered in *Elfbrandt* was unusual. For its language contained none of the negative disclaimers of affiliation or advocacy that mark the test oath.[5] The employee merely swore to "support and defend the constitution of the United States against all enemies, foreign and domestic"; that he would "bear true faith and allegiance to the same"; and that he would "well and faithfully discharge the duties of [his] office."[6] An oath in this form had been required of Arizona's public employees since 1901.[7] In 1961, however, the legislature, in adopting Arizona's version of the Communist Control Act,[8] put a gloss on the 1901 oath that, in effect, turned it into a more typical loyalty oath. Section 5 of the Arizona Communist Control Act made it a crime "subject to all the penalties for perjury" for any employee, having taken the positive oath of allegiance, thereafter "knowingly and willfully" (1) to "commit or aid in the commission of any act to overthrow [the state government] by force or violence," (2) to advocate the overthrow of the state government by such means, or (3) to "become or remain a member of the Communist party, its subordinate organizations, or any

---

ANN., tit. 21, ch. 52, §§ 1266.4, 1266.6 (1965 Supp.); PA. STAT. ANN., tit. 65, ch. 11, §§ 212, 213, 214 (1965 Supp.); see also IND. STAT. ANN., tit. 10, ch. 52, §§ 10-5203, 10-5207 (1965 Supp.).

[4] See ACLU, Feature Press Service Bulletin, § 2266, May 16, 1966.

[5] See BROWN, LOYALTY AND SECURITY 92–95 (1958); Koenigsberg & Stavis, *Test Oaths: Henry VIII to the American Bar Association*, 11 LAW. GUILD REV. 111 (1951). See generally HYMAN, TO TRY MEN'S SOULS (1960).

[6] ARIZ. STAT. § 38-231 (1965 Supp.).

[7] ARIZ. REV. STAT. § 222 (1901). The oath was originally adopted while Arizona was still a territory, and consequently was amended in several respects when Arizona was admitted to statehood.

[8] Ariz. Laws 1961, c. 108, § 1-9.

other organization having for one of its purposes the overthrow by force or violence of the [state] government" where the employee "had knowledge of said unlawful purpose of said organization or organizations."[9] To supplement § 5, the Arizona act also required all government employees to resubscribe to the oath of allegiance as interpreted in the light of the new section.[10]

Petitioner Elfbrandt, a teacher in the Tucson public schools, refused to take the oath and brought suit in the Arizona state courts to have the state oath requirement declared unconstitutional.[11] That litigation lasted five years and was twice taken to the United States Supreme Court before the Arizona statute was finally held unconstitutional.[12]

---

[9] That section amended § 38-231 to read as follows: "E. Any officer or employee as defined in this section having taken the form of oath or affirmation prescribed by this section, and knowingly or wilfully at the time of subscribing the oath or affirmation, or at any time thereafter during his term of office or employment, does commit or aid in the commission of any act to overthrow by force or violence the government of this state or of any of its political subdivisions, or advocates the overthrow by force or violence of the government of this state or of any of its political subdivisions, or during such term of office or employment knowingly and wilfully becomes or remains a member of the communist party of the United States or its successors or any of its subordinate organizations or any other organization having for one of its purposes the overthrow by force or violence of the government of the state of Arizona or any of its political subdivisions, and said officer or employee as defined in this section prior to becoming or remaining a member of such organization or organizations had knowledge of said unlawful purpose of said organization or organizations, shall be guilty of a felony and upon conviction thereof shall be subject to all the penalties for perjury; in addition, upon conviction under this section, the officer or employee shall be deemed discharged from said office or employment and shall not be entitled to any additional compensation or any other emoluments or benefits which may have been incident or appurtenant to said office or employment."

All references to § 5 in the text of this article refer to this provision, now ARIZ. REV. STAT. § 38-231E (1965 Supp.).

[10] ARIZ. REV. STAT. § 8-231(c) (1965 Supp.).

[11] Although the Arizona act requires all employees to take the oath, the only sanction provided for failure to do so is denial of compensation. Consequently, the petitioner retained her job and simply continued to teach without pay. This aspect of the case attracted at least as much attention from the press as did the Court's opinion. See, e.g., NEWSWEEK, supra note 2. The back pay accumulated by petitioner and her husband, a fellow teacher who also refused to take the oath, amounted to over $60,000, but apparently the school boards involved were not entirely sure of the Elfbrandts' right to the money even after the Supreme Court decision. Ann Arbor News, June 23, 1966, p. 7, cols. 2–5.

[12] The Arizona Supreme Court later found in an opinion as yet unreported that the petitioner still was required to take the oath, although the special gloss of

On the first appeal to the Supreme Court, an Arizona Supreme Court decision upholding the oath was vacated,[13] and the case was remanded for reconsideration in the light of *Baggett v. Bullitt*.[14] In *Baggett* the Supreme Court had found unconstitutionally vague a Washington oath that contained language very much like that found in the first clause of § 5.[15] On remand, however, a majority of the Arizona court found that *Baggett* was inapplicable since the reference in § 5 to activity aiding an act designed to overthrow the government had a much narrower and more traditional scope than did a similar reference in the Washington oath.[16] One member of the Arizona court, Justice Bernstein, dissented on the ground that *Baggett* was controlling.[17] The dissent was not based on the first clause of § 5, however, but was tied entirely to the third clause of that section, which prohibits an employee from knowingly becoming a member of any organization "having for one of its purposes the overthrow by force or violence of the government."[18] Justice Bernstein found that this clause failed adequately to identify the nature of the organization in which membership was barred, and, therefore, that it was unconstitutionally vague. As an illustration, he pointed to the university scientist, who, he said, "could not know whether membership is prohibited in an international scientific organization which includes members from neutralist nations and Communist bloc nations—the latter admittedly dedicated to the overthrow of our government and which control the organization. . . . Though all might agree that the principal purpose of such organization is scientific, the statute makes [the scientist's] membership a crime if any subordinate purpose is the overthrow

---

§ 38-231E was no longer applicable. See Ann Arbor News, June 23, 1966, p. 7, cols. 2–5.

[13] 378 U.S. 127 (1964), *vacating* 94 Ariz. 1 (1963).

[14] 377 U.S. 360 (1964).

[15] Washington required public employees to swear that they were not subversive persons as defined by statute: " 'Subversive person' means any person who commits, attempts to commit, or aids in the commission, or advocates, abets, advises or teaches by any means any person to commit, attempt to commit, or aid in the commission of any act intended to overthrow, destroy or alter, or to assist in the overthrow, destruction or alteration of the constitutional form of the government of the United States, or of the state of Washington or any political subdivision of either of them by revolution, force, or violence. . . ." Wash. Laws 1955, c. 377.

[16] 97 Ariz. 140 (1965).   [17] *Id.* at 147.   [18] See note 9 *supra*.

of the state government." "The vice of vagueness here," he concluded, "is that the scientist cannot know whether membership in the organization would result in a prosecution for violation of [§ 5] or in honors from his university for the encyclopedic knowledge acquired . . . in part through his membership."[19]

B. THE MAJORITY OPINION

On review of the Arizona decision, Mr. Justice Douglas, speaking for himself, the Chief Justice, and Justices Black, Brennan, and Fortas, agreed with Justice Bernstein that the invalidity of the third or so-called membership clause of § 5 rendered Arizona's oath requirement unconstitutional. In reaching this conclusion, however, the majority opinion, though quoting extensively from Justice Bernstein's dissent, did not rely upon the "void for vagueness" rationale that he had used.[20] Rather, Mr. Justice Douglas' opinion was based squarely on the ground that the membership clause of § 5 violated a basic principle restricting the scope of statutes affecting First Amendment rights. Quoting from *Cantwell v. Connecticut* and *Shelton v. Tucker*, Mr. Justice Douglas described that principle as follows:[21]

> "[A] statute touching . . . protected rights must be narrowly drawn to define and punish specific conduct as constituting a clear and present danger to a substantial interest of the state." . . . Legitimate legislative goals "cannot be pursued by means that broadly stifle fundamental personal liberties when the end can be more narrowly achieved."

Mr. Justice Douglas found that the Arizona statute failed to meet this standard because it applied to employees who might knowingly join organizations favoring violent overthrow of the government but who themselves might not subscribe to that goal. In including such persons, § 5 necessarily relied, said Mr. Justice Douglas, on an improper theory of "guilt by association" and the section therefore had "infringe[d] unnecessarily" on protected First Amendment rights.[22]

The crux of the reasoning that led Mr. Justice Douglas to this

---

[19] 97 Ariz. at 147–48.   [20] 384 U.S. at 14–15.

[21] *Id.* at 18, quoting from Cantwell v. Connecticut, 310 U.S. 296, 311 (1940), and Shelton v. Tucker, 364 U.S. 479, 488 (1960).

[22] 384 U.S. at 19.

conclusion is found in several paragraphs toward the end of his opinion.[23] First, he noted that in *Scales v. United States*,[24] the Court had recognized that " 'a blanket prohibition of association with a group having both legal and illegal aims' would pose 'a real danger that legitimate political expression or association would be impaired.' "[25] Accordingly, the Court in *Scales* had carefully limited the application of the membership clause of the Smith Act to those members of organizations advocating overthrow who were both "active" in their membership and had the "specific intent of assisting in achieving the unlawful ends of the organization."[26] The constitutional significance of the "specific intent" requirement imposed by *Scales* had been clearly established in *Aptheker v. Secretary of State*[27] when the Court voided a statute prohibiting the issuance of passports to members of "Communist organizations" precisely because that statute "covered membership which was not accompanied by a specific intent to further the unlawful aims of the organization."[28] The Arizona "oath and accompanying statutory gloss suffer from an identical constitutional infirmity" as the statute in *Aptheker*[29] Under § 5 a state employee who knowingly joins an organization "which has as 'one of its purposes' the violent overthrow of the government is subject to immediate discharge and criminal penalties" even though he "does not subscribe to the organization's unlawful ends."[30] As a result, here, as in *Baggett v. Bullitt*, persons risk prosecution by engaging in "knowing but guiltless" activity. Illustrative might be the teacher who attends the Pugwash Conference or "joins a seminar group predominantly Communist and therefore subject to control by those who are said to believe in the overthrow of the government."[31] Surely, Mr. Justice Douglas continued:[32] "Those who join an organization but do not share its unlawful purposes and who do not participate in its unlawful activities pose no threat, either as citizens or public employees." A law which encompasses such persons "impose[s], in effect, a conclusive presumption that the member shares the unlawful aims of the organizations," and for that reason alone is clearly unconstitutional.[33] Summarizing the Court's position at the conclusion of the opinion, Mr. Justice Douglas wrote:[34]

---

[23] *Id*. at 15–18.
[24] 367 U.S. 203 (1961).
[25] 384 U.S. at 15.
[26] *Ibid*.

[27] 378 U.S. 500 (1964).
[28] 384 U.S. at 16.
[29] *Ibid*.
[30] *Ibid*.

[31] *Id*. at 17.
[32] *Ibid*.
[33] *Ibid*.
[34] *Id*. at 19.

A law which applies to membership without "the specific intent" to further the illegal aims of the organization infringes unnecessarily on protected freedoms. It rests on the doctrine of "guilt by association" which has no place here. . . . Such a law cannot stand.

C. THE DISSENTING OPINION

Mr. Justice White's dissenting opinion, joined by Justices Clark, Harlan, and Stewart, noted at the outset that "[a]ccording to unequivocal prior holdings of this Court, a state is entitled to condition public employment upon its employees abstaining from knowing membership in . . . organizations advocating the violent overthrow of the government which employs them," and "the state is [also] constitutionally authorized to inquire into such affiliations and . . . discharge those who refuse to affirm or deny them."[35] The dissent cited eight previous decisions in support of this proposition, and noted that Mr. Justice Douglas' opinion "does not mention or purport to overrule these cases."[36] Neither does the majority opinion, as Mr. Justice White read it, "expressly hold" that a state "must retain" as employees those who knowingly hold membership in organizations aiming at violent overthrow. "It would seem, therefore," he concluded, "that the Court's judgment is only aimed at the criminal provisions of the Arizona law which exposes an employee to a perjury prosecution if he swears falsely about membership when he signs the oath or if he later becomes a knowing member while remaining in public employment."[37]

Mr. Justice White then argued that the distinction the Court appears to have drawn between criminal and civil sanctions is invalid. The right to punish for intentional falsification is clear from prior cases. As for the punishment of employees who later join an organization of the proscribed type:[38] "If a State may disqualify for knowing membership . . . , it is likewise within its

---

[35] *Ibid.*

[36] *Id.* at 20. Six cases were cited directly: Gerende v. Board of Supervisors, 341 U.S. 56 (1951); Garner v. Board of Public Works, 341 U.S. 716 (1951); Adler v. Board of Education, 342 U.S. 485 (1952); Beilan v. Board of Education, 357 U.S. 399 (1958); Lerner v. Casey, 357 U.S. 468 (1958); Nelson v. County of Los Angeles, 362 U.S. 1 (1960). The dissent cited as "see also" two other cases: Wieman v. Updegraff, 344 U.S. 183 (1952); Slochower v. Board of Education, 350 U.S. 551 (1956).

[37] 384 U.S. at 20.   [38] *Id.* at 21.

powers to move criminally against the employee who knowingly engages in disqualifying acts during his employment." "The crime provided by the Arizona law," Mr. Justice White emphasized, "is not just the act of becoming a member of an organization but it is that membership plus concurrent public employment."[39]

The dissent also argued that "there is nothing in *Scales . . .* or *Aptheker . . .* dictating the result reached by the Court."[40] *Scales* involved the general criminal provisions of the Smith Act and therefore was not in point. Neither was *Aptheker,* since the statutory provision involved there applied to members who actually lacked knowledge of the organization's illicit purpose. In fact, *Speiser v. Randall,*[41] another case cited by the majority, had "carefully preserved" *Gerende v. Board of Supervisors*[42] and *Garner v. Board of Public Works,*[43] two cases upholding test oaths for employees that were based on the same principles as the Arizona oath. Finally, Mr. Justice White suggested that even if one were to accept the majority's position and were to hold that Arizona may not take criminal action against employees who are knowing members of organizations aiming at violent overthrow of the government, the appropriate remedy would not be to invalidate the Arizona oath requirement as the majority had done, but to remand the case to the state court to determine the severability of the criminal provisions of the Arizona statute.

D. THE IMPLICATIONS OF SILENCE

When viewed in light of the dissent, two aspects of Mr. Justice Douglas' opinion immediately stand out. Both deal, not unsurprisingly, more with what the opinion left unsaid than with what it said. The first is the complete absence of any reply to the dissent, either with respect to its narrow characterization of the majority ruling or with respect to the cases Mr. Justice White cited as clearly controlling if the majority had sought to rely on a broader ground. The second is the absence in both opinions, but particularly in the majority opinion, of any meaningful discussion of the nature of the state's interests in the loyalty oath requirement. These omissions are significant for more than the light they may shed

---

39 *Ibid.*

40 *Id.* at 22.

41 357 U.S. 513 (1958).

42 341 U.S. 56 (1951).

43 *Id.* at 716.

on the professional quality of the Court's opinion. The inferences to be drawn from the opinion's silence on these matters probably will determine what impact *Elfbrandt* will have upon the permissible scope and coverage of loyalty oaths.

II. The Significance of the Criminal Sanction

Dissenting opinions are hardly the best source for determining the breadth of a majority ruling. This is particularly true when a case is decided by a close vote as *Elfbrandt* was, and when the dissent is concerned with the next case and the possibility of accomplishing a shift in the Court's position not inconsistent with the immediate decision. Nevertheless, Mr. Justice White's characterization of the Court's ruling as grounded solely on Arizona's use of criminal sanctions finds just enough support in the majority opinion that it cannot be dismissed out of hand as simply a dissenter's tactic.

First, there is the fact that the majority made no effort to reply to Mr. Justice White's statement of its ruling. Admittedly Mr. Justice Douglas' opinion does not place primary emphasis on the criminal sanctions imposed by § 5, although it does make frequent mention of these sanctions.[44] It is also true, as will be seen later, that the cases cited by Mr. Justice White as otherwise controlling are distinguishable on grounds other than Arizona's reliance on criminal sanctions in § 5.[45] Still, since it would have taken so little flatly to reject Mr. Justice White's interpretation, it is difficult to understand why this was not done. Perhaps Mr. Justice Douglas, who had dissented in several of the cases cited by Mr. Justice White, felt that any attempt to distinguish those cases would give them undue recognition.[46] Perhaps the majority's failure to reply to the dissent reflects no more than the often criticized tendency of members of the present Court to engage "in separate monologues rather than a dialogue."[47] Yet the absence of any reply to an obvious attempt to limit a majority opinion is unusual, and a

---

[44] See 384 U.S. at 16–17.

[45] See text *infra*, at section III.

[46] Mr. Justice Douglas dissented in five of the eight cases cited by Mr. Justice White: *Garner, Adler, Beilan, Lerner,* and *Nelson.* See note 36 *supra.*

[47] Shapiro, *The Supreme Court and Constitutional Adjudication: Of Politics and Neutral Principles,* 31 Geo. Wash. L. Rev. 587, 591 (1963).

possible inference therefrom is that at least one member of the majority accepted Mr. Justice White's interpretation of its ruling.

Another element that may be cited in support of Mr. Justice White's interpretation is the fact that the two cases on which Mr. Justice Douglas relied most heavily, *Scales* and *Aptheker,* both involved criminal statutes.[48] Moreover, insofar as *Scales* was concerned, it was commonly recognized that the Court there had employed a standard of review far different from that used in previous loyalty oath cases, such as *Garner* and *Gerende.*[49]

Nevertheless, Mr. Justice White's interpretation of the majority's ruling is most difficult to accept because such a decision would be unsupportable in either precedent or logic. Admittedly, the Court has generally distinguished statutes imposing criminal sanctions on speech or association, such as the Smith Act, from statutes imposing more "limited" sanctions, such as disqualification from employment under a state loyalty program. No matter whether the standard has been described in terms of balancing, overbroadness, or defining protected speech, the Court has always given considerably more leeway to a legislature's non-criminal sanctions.[50] Thus, in the Hatch Act case, *United Public Workers v.*

---

48 *Scales* involved a criminal prosecution under the Smith Act. 18 U.S.C. § 2385. *Aptheker* involved a suit for a declaratory judgment in which the Court was asked to declare unconstitutional a criminal provision of the Subversive Activities Control Act, 50 U.S.C. § 785 (1964).

49 Although the Court had not actually discussed *Scales* as it related to the loyalty oath cases, the First Amendment issues in *Scales* were resolved largely on the basis of Dennis v. United States, 341 U.S. 494 (1951). *Dennis* involved a considerably more restrictive standard of review than the loyalty oath cases. See, *e.g.,* Konigsberg v. State Bar, 366 U.S. 36, 49–51 (1961); Speiser v. Randall, 357 U.S. 513, 527–28 (1958).

50 In Konigsberg v. State Bar, 366 U.S. 36 (1961), Mr. Justice Harlan described this distinction—actually based on the function of the restriction on speech—in terms of the difference between those cases in which the Court determines whether "the speech . . . [is] outside the scope of constitutional protection" and those in which the Court applies what is commonly referred to as the "balancing" test. *Id.* at 49–51. Unfortunately, the wide-ranging debate over use of "balancing" in First Amendment cases has tended to obscure the distinction drawn by Mr. Justice Harlan. Certainly, all decisions in this area, whether phrased in terms of balancing or defining the scope of "protected" speech necessarily involve an evaluation of competing interests. See Nutting, *Is the First Amendment Obsolete?* 30 GEO. WASH. L. REV. 167 (1961); Karst, *Legislative Fact in Constitutional Litigation,* [1960] SUPREME COURT REVIEW 75, 95. It is also true that the Court may sometimes speak in terms of balancing even in dealing with restrictions upon borderline classes of speech. See,

Mitchell,[51] the Court sustained the power of the federal government to discharge employees who engaged in certain political activities, although a criminal statute inhibiting such action by the general public clearly would be unconstitutional.[52] The distinction drawn in *Mitchell* and similar cases has not, however, rested on the nature of the sanction employed by the legislature, but on the purpose of the legislation.[53] Criminal sanctions gener-

---

e.g., Dennis v. United States, 341 U.S. 494, 510 (1951), dealing with speech advocating illegal activity. But the type of balancing referred to by Mr. Justice Harlan in *Konigsberg* rests upon an entirely different approach, if not a different process, than that balancing involved without recognition in the obscenity cases and with recognition in *Dennis*. See generally Kalven, *The New York Times Case: A Note on "The Central Meaning of the First Amendment,"* [1964] SUPREME COURT REVIEW 191, 213–17. But see Frantz, *The First Amendment in the Balance*, 71 YALE L. J. 1424, 1429–32 (1962).

Unlike *Dennis* and other cases involving direct restraints, the Court in *Elfbrandt* does not proceed from the premise that there is a central core area of clearly protected speech and the relation of the legislatively proscribed speech to that core will, in large measure, determine the constitutionality of the proscription. See Kalven, *supra*, at 204–11. See also Dennis v. United States, 183 F.2d 201, 207 (2d Cir. 1950). Since the legislative restriction on speech in Mr. Justice Harlan's second category of cases is an incidental aspect of a general regulation, the nature of the speech involved obviously becomes less significant, and the basic assumption is that "compelling" state interest will justify an incidental restriction imposed even on speech within the central core area. See generally Bates v. Little Rock, 361 U.S. 516, 524 (1960). Accordingly, the Court's approach to "weighing" competing interests in this class of cases is much more akin to the normal standard of substantive due process than is the evaluation of the nature of the speech and the legislative interest in cases of direct restraints on speech, such as *Dennis*, or New York Times v. Sullivan, 376 U.S. 254 (1964).

[51] 330 U.S. 75 (1947).

[52] *Id.* at 101–04. The political activity involved in the case before the Court was participation "as [an] executive committeeman and a worker at the polls." *Id.* at 103.

[53] Although the Court in *Mitchell* did not attempt to distinguish cases involving restrictions aimed directly at the content of speech, it did emphasize that the congressional purpose in the Hatch Act was to preserve the efficiency of the federal service and not to restrict political activities. See 330 U.S. at 101–04. The distinction between cases like *Mitchell* and those involving direct restraints on speech was clearly stated in later cases. In Konigsberg v. State Bar, 366 U.S. 36, 49–51 (1961), the Court described that distinction as follows: "Throughout its history this Court has consistently recognized at least two ways in which constitutionally protected freedom of speech is narrower than an unlimited license to talk. On the one hand certain forms of speech, or speech in certain contexts, have been considered outside the scope of constitutional protection. See, *e.g.*, *Schenck v. United States*, 249 U.S. 47; *Chaplinsky v. New Hampshire*, 315 U.S. 568; *Dennis v. United States*, 341 U.S. 494; *Beauharnais v. Illinois*, 343 U.S. 250; *Yates v. United States*, 354 U.S. 298; *Roth v. United States*, 354 U.S. 476. On the other hand, general regulatory

ally have been used in legislation aimed directly at suppressing a particular class of speech, either because of disagreement with its content or concern for its impact upon an audience.[54] The more limited sanctions, such as disqualification from public office or the denial of permission to use public streets for political rallies, are usually found in legislation aimed at the prevention of certain conduct other than that produced by the speech.[55] The regulation of speech in these circumstances imposes what the Court describes as an "indirect" restriction on speech, an "incidental" by-product of the prohibition of undesirable conduct.[56] Thus, the purpose of the Hatch Act was not to suppress political activities, but to prevent a situation conducive to the administrative evils of a spoils system.[57] Similarly, prohibitions against the employment of persons who advocate the overthrow of the government have traditionally been looked upon as an "indirect" restriction on speech because the legislation is aimed not at the content of the speech,

statutes, not intended to control the content of speech but incidentally limiting its unfettered exercise, have not been regarded as the type of law the First or Fourteenth Amendments forbade Congress or the state to pass, when they have been found justified by subordinating valid governmental interests, a prerequisite to constitutionality which has necessarily involved a weighing of the governmental interest involved. See e.g., *Schneider v. State*, 308 U.S. 147, 161; *Cox v. New Hampshire*, 312 U.S. 569; *Prince v. Massachusetts*, 321 U.S. 158; *Kovacs v. Cooper*, 336 U.S. 77; *American Communications Ass'n v. Douds*, 339 U.S. 382; *Breard v. Alexandria*, 341 U.S. 622." See also American Communications Ass'n v. Douds, 339 U.S. 382, 396, 399 (1950). But cf. United States v. Brown, 381 U.S. 437, 456–60 (1965).

[54] See, e.g., the first group of cases cited by Mr. Justice Harlan in the excerpt from *Konigsberg* quoted in note 53 *supra*.

[55] See, e.g., American Communications Ass'n v. Douds, 339 U.S. 382, 396 (1950): "But the question with which we are here faced is not the same one that Justices Holmes and Brandeis found convenient to consider in terms of clear and present danger. Government's interest here is not in preventing the dissemination of Communist doctrine or the holding of particular beliefs because it is feared that unlawful action will result therefrom if free speech is practiced. Its interest is in protecting the free flow of commerce from what Congress considers to be substantial evils of conduct that are not the products of speech at all. Section 9(h), in other words, does not interfere with speech because Congress fears the consequences of speech; it regulates harmful conduct which Congress has determined is carried on by persons who may be identified by their political affiliations and beliefs." See also Speiser v. Randall, quoted *infra* note 58.

[56] See Konigsberg v. State Bar, 366 U.S. 36, 49–51 (1961); Speiser v. Randall, 357 U.S. 513, 527 (1958); American Communications Ass'n v. Douds, 339 U.S. 382, 396, 399 (1950).

[57] 330 U.S. at 102–03.

but at the potential performance of the speaker in public office. The reference to the speech of a particular content is viewed, in effect, merely as a means of identifying a person who is more likely to engage in undesirable conduct as an employee.[58]

While not all the members of the Court have agreed that statutes restricting government employment on the basis of speech or association should be characterized as indirect restraints on speech, generally they all do recognize that the key to such characterization must be the purpose of the legislation, not the nature of the sanction used to implement that purpose.[59] The Court has

---

[58] See note 56 *supra*. See also Speiser v. Randall, 357 U.S. 513, 527 (1958): "The appellees, in controverting this position, rely on cases in which this Court has sustained the validity of loyalty oaths required of public employees, *Garner v. Board of Public Works*, 341 U.S. 716; candidates for public office, *Gerende v. Board of Supervisors*, 341 U.S. 56, and officers of labor unions, *American Communications Assn.* v. *Douds, supra*. In these cases, however, there was no attempt directly to control speech but rather to protect, from an evil shown to be grave, some interest clearly within the sphere of governmental concern. The purpose of the legislation sustained in the *Douds* case, the Court found, was to minimize the danger of political strikes disruptive of interstate commerce by discouraging labor unions from electing Communist Party members to union office. While the Court recognized that the necessary effect of the legislation was to discourage the exercise of rights protected by the First Amendment, this consequence was said to be only indirect. The congressional purpose was to achieve an objective other than restraint on speech. Only the method of achieving this end touched on protected rights and that only tangentially. The evil at which Congress had attempted to strike in that case was thought sufficiently grave to justify limited infringement of political rights. Similar considerations governed the other cases. Each case concerned a limited class of persons in or aspiring to public positions by virtue of which they could, if evilly motivated, create serious danger to the public safety. The principal aim of those statutes was not to penalize political beliefs but to deny positions to persons supposed to be dangerous because the position might be misused to the detriment of the public."

But *cf*. United States v. Brown, 381 U.S. 437, 456–60 (1965). *Brown* possibly could be extended further to undermine this line of analysis. The Court there suggested that the legislative purpose to prohibit misuses of office could constitute "punishment" for the purposes of the bill of attainder prohibition. Whether the Court would then use the clause to invalidate a restriction stated in terms of a class larger than the membership of a particular organization remains to be seen. Certainly the opinion in *Brown* and certain aspects of *Elfbrandt* indicate it would not. 381 U.S. at 461–62; see text *infra*, at note 111–14.

[59] Of the present Justices who were then sitting, only Justices Black and Douglas did not join in the characterization of the loyalty oath cases as indirect restraints in *Konigsberg* or *Speiser, supra* note 56. Both Justices have rejected the application of the "balancing" test in these cases, but this stems from their belief that loyalty oaths are not really aimed at preventing misuse of conduct, but are "direct" restrictions designed primarily to punish speech. See Konigsberg v. State Bar, 366

recognized that indirect restraints *e.g.*, a limitation on the use of sound amplifiers, may be enforced by criminal sanctions.[60] The Court has also recognized that direct restraints need not always take the form of criminal prohibitions, as is illustrated by the restriction on the receipt of mail recently invalidated in *Lamont v. Postmaster*,[61] and the denial of a veterans' tax exemption voided in *Speiser v. Randall*.[62] To be sure, the purpose of the legislation has not always been clearly identified as the important factor in distinguishing between direct and indirect restraints.[63] As a result, there has been occasional confusion in the lower courts,[64] as indeed was exhibited by the Arizona Supreme Court in its first consideration of the *Elfbrandt* case.[65] But the Supreme Court itself has consistently recognized the basis of the distinction, although there has often been disagreement over its application.[66] Accordingly, whatever limitation *Elfbrandt* imposes upon the use of political association as a basis for restricting employment should, according to precedent, be applicable irrespective of whether the state implements its policy by discharging the employee or by imposing penal sanctions. Moreover, precedents aside, a different result would make little sense in terms of any theory of First Amendment

---

U.S. 36, 56, 68–70 (1960); Barenblatt v. United States, 360 U.S. 109, 134, 141–53 (1959); Beilan v. Board of Education, 357 U.S. 399, 412, 414–15 (1958); Wieman v. Updegraff, 344 U.S. 183, 192 (1952). It is not entirely clear whether their view is based primarily on the history of loyalty oaths or on a general suspicion of any standard that operates with reference to the content of speech. Compare *Wieman* and *Barenblatt, supra,* with *Konigsberg.* In any event, it is clear that both Justices recognize the special nature of incidental restrictions on speech where it is clear that the restriction is not "aimed at speech" and does not "depend for its application upon the content of speech." Konigsberg v. State Bar, *supra,* at 70. See also Barenblatt v. United States, *supra;* Viereck v. United States, 318 U.S. 237, 249, 250–51 (1942).

60 See Kovacs v. Cooper, 336 U.S. 77 (1949). See also Cox v. New Hampshire, 312 U.S. 569 (1941); Prince v. Massachusetts, 321 U.S. 158 (1944).

61 381 U.S. 301 (1965), especially at 307–08 (Brennan, J.).

62 357 U.S. 513 (1958).

63 See, *e.g.,* Adler v. Board of Education, 342 U.S. 485, 492 (1952); Brotherhood of Railroad Trainmen v. Virginia Bar, 377 U.S. 1, 7–8 (1964).

64 See, *e.g.,* Brown v. United States, 334 F.2d 488, 492–96 (9th Cir. 1964), *affirmed on other grounds,* 381 U.S. 437 (1965); Weaver v. Jordan, 49 Cal. Rptr. 537, 543 (1966); In re Schlessinger, 404 Pa. 584 (1961).

65 94 Ariz. at 9–10.

66 See Kalven, *supra* note 50, at 216.

protection, especially in view of the fact that, as the Court itself often has recognized, non-criminal sanctions may often pose more of a danger to the preservation of protected rights than criminal sanctions.[67]

In the light of this background, Mr. Justice White's interpretation of the majority ruling may be nothing more than an artfully employed "straw man." The failure of the majority opinion to reply to the dissent on this point probably can be attributed to Mr. Justice Douglas' views on the art of opinion writing.[68] The citation of *Scales* without mention of the difference in the nature of the statute there involved can probably be similarly explained. Mr. Justice Douglas has never been willing to accept the premise that loyalty oath cases should be treated as indirect restrictions on speech,[69] and, in large degree, he has been unwilling even to acknowledge that previous decisions have drawn a distinction between statutes like the Smith Act and employment disqualification provisions.[70] Also, since *Aptheker*, a case involving an indirect restraint under the traditional view, had already drawn upon reasoning similar to that employed in *Scales*, the distinction between the Smith Act and the Arizona legislation may well have been viewed as without importance for the purpose of applying *Scales* to this case.[71]

III. THE SCOPE OF ELFBRANDT: SUB SILENTIO OVERRULING

The rejection of Mr. Justice White's interpretation of the Court's ruling does not eliminate all the problems presented by the majority's failure to respond to the argument of the dissent. There remains in particular the several cases cited by Mr. Justice White as generally controlling if the majority opinion were not

---

[67] See *e.g.*, New York Times Co. v. Sullivan, 376 U.S. 254, 277–78 (1964); Garrison v. Louisiana, 379 U.S. 64 (1964); see also *In re* Sawyer, 360 U.S. 622 (1959).

[68] See generally Rogat, *Mr. Justice Pangloss*, N.Y. Rev. of Books, Oct. 22, 1964, pp. 5–7; see also Kurland, *Foreword, "Equal in Origin and Equal in Title to the Legislative and Executive Branches of the Government,"* 78 HARV. L. REV. 143, 167–68 (1964).

[69] See note 60 *supra*.

[70] See, *e.g.*, Killian v. United States, 368 U.S. 231, 261 (1961) (dissenting opinion) (relying on *Scales* and *Yates* in a loyalty test case).

[71] Aptheker v. Secretary of State, 378 U.S. 500, 511–12 (1964); *cf.* United States v. Brown, 381 U.S. 437, 456 (1965).

narrowly based on Arizona's use of criminal sanctions to implement its loyalty oath.

Six of the eight cases cited by the dissent can be distinguished without serious difficulty. Four, *Lerner v. Casey*,[72] *Beilan v. Board of Education*,[73] *Nelson v. County of Los Angeles*,[74] and *Slochower v. Board of Education*,[75] deal solely with the right of federal or state officials to require an employee to reveal any past or present membership in organizations advocating violent overthrow of the government.[76] The determination that state and federal authorities had this power in no way established that such membership alone is an adequate basis for denying employment. The Court's rulings only indicated that the subject of the state's inquiry could be relevant to some valid standard for disqualification.[77] Since a question is relevant if it relates to any aspect of the state's standard, inquiry about membership in an organization advocating overthrow clearly would be relevant even under a standard that, consistent with *Elfbrandt*, was limited to exclusion only of those members who had a specific intent to further the illegal aims of the organization.

Both *Wieman v. Updegraff*[78] and *Adler v. Board of Education*[79] deal directly with use of speech and association as a basis for denying government employment, but they too can be distinguished. In *Wieman*, the Court voided an Oklahoma loyalty oath on the ground that it indiscriminately barred from employment all members of organizations advocating violent overthrow regardless of whether the members were aware of the organization's illegal

---

[72] 357 U.S. 468 (1958).   [74] 362 U.S. 1 (1960).

[73] 357 U.S. 399 (1958).   [75] 350 U.S. 551 (1956).

[76] In *Slochower* the Court found that the state acted arbitrarily in discharging the petitioner solely because he relied upon the Fifth Amendment privilege against self-incrimination to refuse to answer an inquiry concerning past membership in the Communist party. *Beilan, Lerner,* and *Nelson* all upheld discharges under somewhat similar circumstances when the state based the discharge upon the employee's general lack of co-operativeness in failing to answer the inquiries, rather than upon his use of the privilege. See, *e.g.*, Nelson v. County of Los Angeles, 362 U.S. 1, 6–8 (1960).

[77] See, *e.g.*, Lerner v. Casey, 357 U.S. 468, 474, 477 (1958), where the Court specifically noted that it need not determine whether the particular standard employed by the state in that case was valid. See also Beilan v. Board of Education, 357 U.S. 399, 405 (1958); Nelson v. County of Los Angeles, 362 U.S. 1, 8 (1960).

[78] 344 U.S. 183 (1952).   [79] 342 U.S. 485 (1952).

purpose. While the opinion did not mention that the oath also
failed to except the member who knew of, but did not share, that
purpose, little significance can be attached to that omission, since
the Court had no reason to consider the need for a "specific intent" requirement once the statute was found unconstitutional on
other grounds.[80] In *Adler,* the Court sustained the New York
loyalty program for teachers under the Feinberg Law. The Court's
opinion dealt primarily with a provision making knowing membership in an organization advocating violent overthrow "prima facie
evidence" of disqualification for employment.[81] Although the
Feinberg Law was supposedly designed to implement a statute
that denied employment to all knowing members of such organizations,[82] the Court's opinion indicates that it assumed, probably
on the basis of a lower court opinion,[83] that an employee could
successfully rebut the prima facie case by showing that he did
not share the illegal aims of the organization.[84]

 Gerende v. Board of Supervisors[85] and *Garner v. Board of*

---

[80] The arguments advanced by the Court in rejecting the Oklahoma oath related
solely to the member who was unaware of the organization's illegal objectives and
were not readily applicable to the knowing member who did not subscribe to the
organization's illegal goals. See 344 U.S. at 190–91.

[81] N.Y. EDUC. LAW § 3022.

[82] The Feinberg Law does require the removal of all "subversive persons from
the public school system," but it does not define "subversive persons." The Act
defines subversive organizations, however, as those that advocate, advise, embrace,
or teach the doctrine of violent overthrow. The N.Y. CIVIL SERVICE LAW § 12(a),
the Act that the Feinberg Law was designed to implement, see 342 U.S. at 487–
89, provides for the disqualification from public employment of any person who
"becomes a member of any . . . group . . . which teaches or advocates that the
government of the United States or of any state . . . shall be overthrown by force
or violence. . . ." Accordingly the significance of the provision making membership in such organizations constitute only prima facie evidence of disqualification
is not entirely clear from the face of the statute.

[83] See L'Hommedieu v. Board of Regents, 97 N.Y.S.2d 443, 452–53 (App. Div. 3d
Dept. 1950), *aff'd,* 301 N.Y. 476 (1950). *L'Hommedieu* was a companion case to
Adler.

[84] See 342 U.S. at 495–96, emphasizing the individual's opportunity to rebut the
prima facie presumption arising from knowing membership. See also *id.* at 492,
noting that only "unexplained" knowing membership in an organization advocating
overthrow constituted a basis for removal under the New York statute.

 The decision in Nostrand v. Little, 368 U.S. 436 (1962), apparently was based
on the same assumption as *Adler.* See 362 U.S. 474 (1960); 58 Wash.2d 111 (1961).

[85] 341 U.S. 56 (1951).

Public Works[86] also deal directly with the state's power to deny employment to individuals solely on the basis of their associations, but these cases are difficult to distinguish from *Elfbrandt*. In *Gerende,* a unanimous Court, including Justices Black and Douglas, upheld a Maryland requirement that every candidate for political office "make oath that he is not a person who is engaged 'in one way or another in the attempt to overthrow the government by *force or violence,*' and that he is not knowingly a member of an organization engaged in such an attempt."[87] Although the Maryland oath made no exception for knowing members who lacked the specific intent to support the organization's illegal goals,[88] the Court sustained the state oath requirement in a one-paragraph per curiam opinion that made no mention of the specific intent question. *Gerende* can nevertheless be distinguished from *Elfbrandt* on two grounds. First—and this ground will be discussed more fully—the oath in *Gerende* was limited to officials with policy-making functions.[89] Second, the Maryland oath might be interpreted as applying only to membership in organizations engaged in a present attempt to overthrow the government. Knowing membership in such a group could be distinguished from membership in a group that had merely advocated violent overthrow sometime in the future, on the ground that the immediate danger presented by the first type of organization so clearly established the individual's support for the organization's illegal objective that inquiry into his "specific intent" was unnecessary. Such a narrow interpretation of the Maryland oath, however, is subject to question. The oath applies to attempts "in one way or another" to overthrow the government, and this might well require no more than advocacy itself, especially when it is remembered that

---

[86] 341 U.S. 716 (1951).

[87] *Id.* at 56–57. (Emphasis in original.)

[88] Moreover, there was nothing in the opinion of the Maryland Court of Appeals to suggest that a requirement of "specific intent" had been read into the state statute. See Shub v. Simpson, 196 Md. 177 (1950).

[89] See *infra,* at section VI. Although it is possible that not all elected officials would possess the type of discretionary authority that might be manipulated to serve an organization seeking violent overthrow, certainly the group as a whole can be classified as having such authority. Perhaps, a separate ground of distinction might be found in the very fact that these officials are elected. See Douglas, The Right of the People 130 (1958). But there is nothing in the subsequent treatment of *Gerende* that indicates the Court considered this an important factor.

the concept of advocacy used in this area is that of urging future action in language "reasonably and ordinarily calculated to incite persons to such action."[90] If this broad interpretation of the Maryland oath is accepted, then *Gerende* presents, aside from the first ground of distinction, the same difficulty in reconciliation with *Elfbrandt* as *Garner.*

In *Garner,* the Court upheld a statute denying employment to any person who within five years had been a knowing member of any organization that "advised, advocated, or taught the overthrow by force or violence" of the state or federal government.[91] Although no mention of the point was made in either the majority or dissenting opinions (including those of Justices Black and Douglas),[92] the statute in *Garner* clearly would exclude from employment knowing members who lacked the specific intent to further the organization's unlawful aims.[93] *Garner* therefore seems, at least on the surface, to be in direct conflict with *Elfbrandt.* Yet, cases are not ordinarily overruled sub silentio,[94] and Mr. Justice

---

[90] See Yates v. United States, 354 U.S. 298, 316 (1957); Dennis v. United States, 341 U.S. 494, 511–12 (1951). The same standard is ordinarily applied to loyalty oaths. See, *e.g.,* 94 Ariz. at 8. Of course, *Gerende* was decided before *Dennis* and *Yates,* but this would not have prevented the Court from viewing "*Yates*-style" advocacy as constituting an attempt "in one way or another to overthrow the government by force and violence."

[91] 341 U.S. at 717–18.

[92] The dissenting opinion of Mr. Justice Douglas, joined by Mr. Justice Black, concentrated entirely on the contention that the Los Angeles ordinance was a bill of attainder. See 341 U.S. at 731–33. Mr. Justice Black's short dissenting opinion briefly mentioned the First Amendment issue, but discussed it in general terms. *Id.* at 730–31. Both Mr. Justice Frankfurter's separate opinion and Mr. Justice Clark's opinion for the Court did discuss that issue, however, in connection with the possible application of the ordinance to members who were unaware of an organization's illegal activity, the majority assuming that the statute incorporated a requirement of scienter, and Mr. Justice Frankfurter finding the statute unconstitutional because that assumption reasonably could not be made. *Id.* at 720–21, 723–24, 724.

[93] But see Horowitz, *Report on the Los Angeles City and County Loyalty Programs,* 5 STANFORD L. REV. 233, 244 (1953), possibly suggesting that the element of scienter read into the ordinance in *Garner* might make the ordinance inapplicable to the "employee [who] was a member of the organization but continually fought against policies of overthrow." The language of *Garner,* however, quite clearly discussed scienter strictly in terms of knowledge rather than intent. 341 U.S. at 723–24. This was reaffirmed in Wieman v. Updegraff, 344 U.S. 183 (1952).

[94] See Israel, *Gideon v. Wainwright: The "Art" of Overruling,* [1963] SUPREME COURT REVIEW 211, 214 n. 15, 215–26.

Douglas' opinion failed to mention the *Garner* case. It could reasonably be assumed that there was a basis for reconciling the two cases, and that *Garner* remains controlling precedent until explicitly overruled.[95]

A ground for reconciling *Garner* and *Elfbrandt* in fact can be found, if not without difficulty. The *Garner* statute applied to membership in organizations that were actively engaged in the advocacy of violent overthrow, and the Court obviously treated it as aimed at the Communist party or similar organizations that made the overthrow of the government a dominant organizational goal.[96] *Elfbrandt*, on the other hand, involves a statute prohibiting employee membership in an organization that has the violent overthrow of the government merely as "one of its purposes."[97] As Justice Bernstein noted in the Arizona court, the Arizona statute would encompass an organization for which overthrow was merely a "subordinate purpose."[98] Both Justice Bernstein and Mr. Justice Douglas mentioned the possible application of the Arizona statute to a teacher's membership in a seminar group dominated by Communist scientists. Certainly, a member of such a group cannot be compared to a member of an organization like the Communist party, either in terms of his contribution to the potential violent overthrow of the government or his lack of dedication to the present form of government.[99] The Court could have adopted the position that membership in such an organization does not justify employment disqualification without a showing of the individual's support for the policy of violent overthrow, although knowing membership in an organization like the Communist party would be sufficient justification for disqualification. In any event, the argument might continue, since *Elfbrandt*

---

[95] *Cf.* United States *ex rel.* Vajtauer v. Commissioner of Immigration, 273 U.S. 103, 112 (1927), noting the need for caution in drawing "inferences from silence."

[96] See 341 U.S. at 719–20. The oath was combined with a requirement that every employee execute an affidavit stating whether he had ever been a member of the Communist party. *Ibid.*

[97] See note 9 *supra*.   [98] 97 Ariz. at 148; see text *supra*, at note 19.

[99] It might also be argued that a restriction extending to any organization that might have violent overthrow as "one of its purposes" would impose a greater deterrent to free association because the employee would have greater concern about not being able to recognize all the subordinate organizational purposes. The statute in *Elfbrandt* was limited to members with knowledge, but the impact of that safeguard upon the individual's willingness freely to join various organizations is questionable.

went no further than to declare invalid a law covering the first situation, *Garner* still remains a valid precedent until the Court faces a statute dealing solely with membership in groups actively advocating overthrow.

Support for this view of the limited scope of the *Elfbrandt* opinion can be found in various portions of Mr. Justice Douglas' opinion. Justice Bernstein's dissent, which was based entirely on the "subordinate purpose" theme, is quoted at length in the majority opinion.[100] Mr. Justice Douglas also added his own discussion of the same point, including his hypotheticals concerning teacher participation in such events as the Pugwash Conference. Finally, throughout the majority opinion, Mr. Justice Douglas spoke solely in terms of organizations with an illegal "purpose" or "aim." No reference is made to membership in an organization presently advocating overthrow.[101] Nevertheless, although these elements of the majority opinion give this reading of the Court's ruling far more support than that suggested by Mr. Justice White, it too should be rejected.

If *Elfbrandt* is viewed as going no further than to invalidate a statute so broad as to encompass membership in a scientific seminar dominated by Communists, it becomes very difficult indeed to understand why the case was not clearly controlled by *Baggett v. Bullitt*,[102] and, if so, why (1) two members of the *Baggett* majority dissented in *Elfbrandt*[103] and (2) the majority relied primarily on *Scales*, and *Aptheker* rather than *Baggett*. In *Baggett*, the Court, with only Justices Clark and Harlan dissenting, held unconstitutional a Washington statute that barred from public employment all persons, *inter alia*, who "aid[ed] in the commission of any act intended to overthrow, destroy, or alter or assist in the overthrow, destruction, or alteration" of the state or federal government.[104] While Mr. Justice White's opinion for the Court was based on the ground that the statute was unduly vague, this rationale was keyed to the impact of the statute on First Amendment rights. The vagueness in the Washington statute entered the picture primarily because a

---

[100] 384 U.S. at 14–15. The quotation included the entire discussion by Justice Bernstein of the "scientist" hypothetical.

[101] See, *e.g.*, 384 U.S. at 16, 17.   [102] 377 U.S. 360 (1964).

[103] The majority in *Baggett* included Justices White and Stewart, both of whom dissented in *Elfbrandt*.

[104] 377 U.S. at 362.

literal interpretation of the statute so clearly imposed on protected speech that the Court assumed that a somewhat narrower, but less well defined, compass was intended.[105] In listing the obviously impermissible bases for denial of employment that could fall within the state statute if literally interpreted, Mr. Justice White offered an illustration almost identical to that cited by Mr. Justice Douglas in *Elfbrandt*—the denial of employment to a scholar who "attends and participates in an international convention of mathematicians and exchanges views with scholars from Communist countries."[106] Mr. Justice White's discussion of this and other illustrations clearly indicated that the state could not deny employment to an individual simply because he unintentionally lent indirect aid to the "cause" of violent overthrow by engaging in lawful activities that he knew might add to the power of persons supporting illegal overthrow.[107] Thus, although the Washington statute, when read literally, was much broader in scope than the statute in *Elfbrandt*, the basic principle expressed in the *Baggett* opinion clearly would control *Elfbrandt* if that case were viewed as concerned primarily with the application of the Arizona statute to such matters as membership in a Communist-dominated scientific seminar.

While the Court's opinion in *Elfbrandt* does cite *Baggett v.*

---

[105] *Id.* at 366–68. The opinion of the Court does not clearly express the interrelationship of the vagueness doctrine and the overbreadth of the statute when it is read literally. This point is given more explicit recognition, however, in a subsequent opinion that relied primarily on *Baggett*. See Dombrowski v. Pfister, 380 U.S. 479, 486–87, 490–92, 493–94 (1965); see also Aptheker v. Secretary of State, 378 U.S. 500, 515–16 (1964); United States v. National Dairy Corp., 372 U.S. 29, 36 (1963); N.A.A.C.P. v. Button, 371 U.S. 415, 432–33 (1963); Shelton v. Tucker, 364 U.S. 479, 491–92 (1960) (dissenting opinion); Amsterdam, *The Void for Vagueness Doctrine,* 109 U. PA. L. REV. 67 (1960).

[106] 377 U.S. at 369.

[107] Although the Court's opinion in *Baggett* raises some question concerning the nature of the individual's awareness that his acts would aid those seeking overthrow, the opinion also indicates that the activity discussed would be protected even if the individual knew "that his aid or teaching would be used by another and that the person aided has the requisite guilty intent." The discussion relating to the possible ambiguity in the oath's scienter requirement was discussed as a supplementary point. See 377 U.S. at 368–69. See also Dombrowski v. Pfister, 380 U.S. 479, 492–93. *Dombrowski* also indicates that the protection afforded by *Baggett* would be equally applicable to the person who is a member of an organization that itself lends indirect and unintended aid to those supporting overthrow by participating for other purposes in legal activities that will strengthen the position of such groups. *Ibid.*

Bullitt in connection with the discussion of the hypotheticals concerning scientific conferences, it does not rely heavily on that decision.[108] Both the citation and the hypotheticals seem to serve merely to supplement the argument for requiring an element of "specific intent" by presenting an extreme example of what could happen when a loyalty oath contained no exemption of members who lacked such intent. The primary emphasis in *Elfbrandt* is on *Scales* and *Aptheker*, both of which involved membership in the Communist party.[109] Reliance on these decisions, when *Baggett* was otherwise sufficient precedent, indicates that the Court's rejection of employment disqualification based solely on knowing membership in an organization supporting the violent overthrow of the government extends to all such organizations, including those in which violent overthrow is a matter of primary emphasis. *Garner v. Board of Public Works* must, therefore, be viewed as overruled. Admittedly, the assumption that the Court overruled an earlier precedent sub silentio is not to be lightly indulged. But two recent opinions by Mr. Justice Douglas seem to overrule several other cases in this manner.[110] And certainly the thrust of the majority opinion, as well as the cases cited therein, indicates that *Garner* was intended to share the same fate.

Actually, there are a few statements in *Elfbrandt* suggesting that a statute like that in *Garner* would be deficient on not one but two grounds. While Mr. Justice Douglas' several statements of the Court's ruling in the majority opinion consistently refer only to the improper disqualification of the knowing member who lacks "a 'specific intent' to further the illegal aims of the organization," a few comments in the opinion suggest that even a statutory restriction on employment limited to members with "specific intent" would not be valid. For example, in citing the *Scales* case, Mr. Justice Douglas noted that the majority there read the Smith Act "membership clause" to require not only that the member have the requisite intent but also that he be an "active" member.[111] At another point, the opinion might be taken to suggest that even "active" participation in the group's activities would not be enough

[108] 384 U.S. at 16–17.   [109] See 367 U.S. at 205–06, 378 U.S. at 504–05.

[110] See Kurland, *supra* note 68, at 150, 167–68, discussing Gray v. Sanders, 372 U.S. 368 (1963), and Schneider v. Rusk, 377 U.S. 163 (1964).

[111] 384 U.S. at 15; see 367 U.S. at 222–24, 255 n. 29.

if the activities involved were all legal. Mr. Justice Douglas stated that those "who join an organization but do not share its unlawful purposes and who do not participate in its unlawful activities surely pose no threat to society."[112] While this could be viewed as suggesting alternative requirements, it may indicate that the Court will not allow employment disqualification to be based on political association absent a showing of specific intent to promote the violent overthrow of the government plus previous participation in illegal activities serving that end. Some support for this second requirement might also be found in Mr. Justice Douglas' statement that a statute denying employment on the basis of speech-related activities must be "narrowly drawn to define and punish specific conduct as constituting a clear and present danger to a substantial interest of the state." The clear-and-present-danger standard, especially as viewed by Mr. Justice Douglas, could easily be taken to require prior participation in illegal activity.[113]

If these statements do not in themselves impose any additional requirements, they lay the foundation for a future decision to that effect.[114] Whether the Court's ruling will be expanded to require active membership or even actual participation in illegal activities will depend in large part on the precise nature of the considerations that led the Court to reject Arizona's reliance upon knowing membership as an appropriate basis for denying government employment. The nature of those considerations will also have considerable bearing on whether *Elfbrandt* will be applied to a statute requiring loyalty oaths of only a limited group of employees, such as those in sensitive positions. Unfortunately, however, the identification of these relevant considerations is hidden to a large degree

---

112 384 U.S. at 17.

113 See, *e.g.*, Dennis v. United States, 341 U.S. 494, 581 (1951) (dissenting opinion).

114 The dissent at one point suggested that the majority did impose a requirement of active membership. See 384 U.S. at 22–23: "[T]he Court errs in holding that the act is overbroad because it includes state employees who are knowing members but who may not be active and who may lack the specific intent to further the illegal aims of the Party."

The majority opinion, however, refers to an "active" membership requirement only in connection with its general description of the *Scales* case. *Id.* at 15. The discussion of *Aptheker*, the reference to the possible scope of the statute, and the summary of the Court's ruling at the end of the opinion speak only of the element of "specific intent." *Id.* at 16–19.

by the manner in which the *Elfbrandt* opinion utilized the rule against overbroadness as the basis for its ruling.

IV. Overbroadness and the Nature of the State's Interests

The rule against overbreadth in legislation affecting First Amendment rights is a doctrine very much favored by the present Court.[115] In large part, this is probably due to the fact that it represents one of the few common meeting grounds for the variant views of the meaning of the First Amendment.[116] But, as one might expect of a doctrine serving this function, the rule is frequently used in different ways by different Justices in writing opinions for the Court. Thus, in some cases, the Court would seem to have rejected legislation as overbroad primarily because the means employed by the state bore little or no relationship to the interests it sought to implement.[117] In other cases, the Court has acknowledged the presence of a substantial relationship, but has still found the legislation invalid because the state interest could be attained by an alternative means that would impose less severe restrictions on the individual's personal liberty.[118] In still other cases, the Court seemed to reject legislation because, whatever the possible alternative

---

[115] See, *e.g.*, Aptheker v. Secretary of State, 378 U.S. 500 (1964); N.A.A.C.P. v. Alabama, 377 U.S. 288, 307–08 (1964); N.A.A.C.P. v. Button, 371 U.S. 415, 432–44 (1963); Louisiana v. N.A.A.C.P., 366 U.S. 293 (1961); Shelton v. Tucker, 364 U.S. 479 (1960); Talley v. California, 362 U.S. 60, 62–64 (1960).

[116] Shapiro, Freedom of Speech: The Supreme Court and Judicial Review 140–41 (1966). *Compare* Justices Douglas' and Black's joining opinion for the Court in Shelton v. Tucker, *supra* note 115, *with* their use of a separate concurring opinion in Bates v. Little Rock, 361 U.S. 516, 527 (1960).

[117] See, *e.g.*, N.A.A.C.P. v. Button, *supra* note 115; Talley v. California, *supra* note 115; Lovell v. Griffin, 303 U.S. 444 (1938). Frequently, as in *Lovell* and, perhaps, *Talley*, there is the further suggestion that the restriction upon speech was so significant that the statute would not be sustained even if it did bear a relationship to some state interest. In fact, the decisions probably rested on this ground, since the state's use of an absolute prohibition against the distribution of all literature, as in *Lovell*, or all anonymous handbills, as in *Talley*, does serve the state's interest in eliminating obscene or libelous publications in the sense that the flat prohibition against distribution obviously is considerably easier to administer than one that attempted to specify what literature might fall in the obscene or libelous category. *Cf.* Note, *The Supreme Court, 1959 Term*, 74 Harv. L. Rev. 97, 130 (1960).

[118] See, *e.g.*, Aptheker v. Secretary of State, *supra* note 115; Shelton v. Tucker, *supra* note 115; Saia v. New York, 334 U.S. 558, 562 (1942).

means, the state interest served by the legislation was deemed insufficient to justify the extensive restriction it imposed upon protected speech or association.[119] While these varying uses of the "overbroadness" doctrine all rest on the same basic process of evaluating competing interests, the differences in underlying rationale may be relevant in determining the degree to which the rejection of legislation as "overbroad" might preclude an attempt to satisfy the same state interest through different means. Yet, opinions relying upon the "overbroadness" rule often provide no more indication of the Court's analysis than a conclusionary statement that a particular aspect of the statutory infringement on speech was overly broad as it applied to the particular interest that the state advanced in that case.[120] The majority opinion in *Elfbrandt* fits this pattern and, indeed, is more delinquent, since the Court failed in large part even to identify the state interest against which the legislation was balanced.

Mr. Justice Douglas' opinion starts with a description and evaluation of the interest of the individual in joining organizations having both legal and illegal objectives, and, except for one or two sentences, it never leaves that aspect of the case. Although the opinion states in conclusion that the Arizona statute "infringes unnecessarily on protected freedoms," it never clearly defines the state interests in relation to which the infringement was deemed "unnecessary."[121] The lack of any extended discussion of the state's interest is not surprising in an opinion by Mr. Justice Douglas, who generally seeks to avoid creating any impression that the Court might be engaged in "balancing" individual rights against a state's interests.[122] In the area of the legislation involved in *Elfbrandt*,

---

[119] See, *e.g.*, N.A.A.C.P. v. Alabama, *supra* note 115; Louisiana v. N.A.A.C.P., *supra* note 115. See also Shelton v. Tucker, *supra* note 115, at 493 n. 3 (dissenting opinion).

[120] See, *e.g.*, Louisiana v. N.A.A.C.P., *supra* note 115; Talley v. California, *supra* note 115.

[121] 384 U.S. at 19. Although relying upon *Aptheker* for other purposes, the opinion ignores the statement in *Aptheker* that application of the rule against overbroadness requires examination of the state's interest. See Aptheker v. Secretary of State, *supra* note 115, at 508.

[122] Consider, for example, his treatment of the state's interest in the following description of *N.A.A.C.P. v. Alabama* and *Bates v. Little Rock*, as they relate to the power to compel disclosure of membership lists: "We deal with a constitutional right, since freedom of association is included in the bundle of First Amendment rights made applicable to the states by the Due Process Clause of the Four-

however, this omission takes on special significance, since at least three different state interests are commonly advanced to justify disqualification of individuals from public employment on the basis of membership in organizations advocating the violent overthrow of the government: (1) The elimination of persons who present a potential for sabotage, espionage, or other activities directly injurious to national security. (2) The elimination of persons who are likely to be either incompetent or untrustworthy in the performance of their duties. (3) The elimination of persons who, aside from any question of danger or fitness, simply are not considered deserving of a government position because they oppose the basic principles on which the government is founded. The *Elfbrandt* opinion contains no reference to any of these interests aside from a single ambiguous sentence. In that sentence, Mr. Justice Douglas emphasized that members who do not share an organization's unlawful purposes and never participate in its unlawful activities "surely pose no threat, either as citizens or as public employees."[123] The nature of the "threat" to which Mr. Justice Douglas is referring is not entirely clear, but the context of the sentence indicates that he was probably making reference only to the possibility of sabotage or similar activities. Since all three state interests were advanced in justification of the Arizona legislation, however, either in the briefs or in the opinions below,[124] it must be assumed that the Court found the statute unnecessarily broad as applied to all of them. And, as previously noted, the considerations that led the Court to reject these interests will determine the possibilities for the extension of the *Elfbrandt* ruling to loyalty oaths more limited than Arizona's.[125]

---

teenth Amendment . . . [citations omitted]. And where it is shown, as it was in *N.A.A.C.P.* v. *Alabama, supra*, 462–463, that disclosure of membership lists results in reprisals against and hostility to the members, disclosure is not required. And see *Bates* v. *Little Rock, supra*, 523–524." Louisiana v. N.A.A.C.P., *supra* note 115, at 296.

[123] 384 U.S. at 17.

[124] Although the respondent's brief placed emphasis upon the first of the state interests mentioned above, the opinion of the lower court made reference to the other two. See Brief for Respondent, pp. 8, 13; 94 Ariz. at 6, 10–11. See also the *Report of the Arizona Judiciary Committee in Support of the Committee Amendment to H.B. 115*, reproduced as Appendix B in Respondent's brief.

[125] Of course, even if the opinion had clearly identified the state's interest and explained why the statute was overbroad in relation to those interests, the Court

V. The Denial of Support to Disloyal Groups

It has frequently been argued that persons who lack "fidelity to the very presuppositions of our scheme of government" should be denied public employment simply because the government need not support those who oppose it.[126] Taxpayers' funds," so the argument goes, "should not be spent to support . . . a person of doubtful loyalty to the very governmental system for which he wants to work."[127] Or, to look at it from the other side, the state should be allowed to promote loyalty to our basic institutions by employing only those who accept those institutions.[128]

Although this argument probably serves as the primary basis for much of our "loyalty" legislation,[129] the state interest it advances has not always been recognized as separate from that of excluding

---

need not have committed itself on the weight of those interests in the case of a modified statute. See Karst, *The First Amendment and Harry Kalven: An Appreciative Comment on the Advantages of Thinking Small*, 13 U.C.L.A. L. Rev. 1, 15–17 (1965). Yet that would be the inevitable result of reliance upon several of the possible grounds for judgment that are discussed in the next three sections of this article.

[126] Garner v. Board of Public Works, 341 U.S. 716, 725 (1951) (concurring opinion). See Brown, *op. cit. supra* note 5, at 205, 333, 335, 337; Linde, *Justice Douglas on Freedom in the Welfare State*, 39 Wash. L. Rev. 39 (1964) (both noting the argument, but not supporting it).

[127] Linde, *supra* note 126, at 39. As used in this argument, "disloyalty" means only the denial of the basic premises on which the government is founded. In the case of persons believing in violent overthrow, it is the denial of the premise that change in government can take place only through the democratic means provided by the Constitution. See Brown, *op. cit. supra* note 5, at 6–7, 389.

Another concept of loyalty sometimes advanced in connection with this argument rests on the individual's alleged subservience to a foreign nation. See, *e.g.*, Ariz. Rev. Stat., tit. 16, ch. 2, § 16-205 (1965 Supp.) (Arizona Communist Control Act). This concept, however, does not relate to all groups advocating overthrow of the government, and it has been employed primarily in connection with Communist Control Acts. It could provide an entirely separate basis for denial of support through employment disqualification. See People v. Crane, 124 N.Y. 154, 161, 164 (1915), *aff'd*, 239 U.S. 195 (1915). But it would present essentially the same difficulties as *Elfbrandt* with respect to the need for a showing that the individual member owed his allegiance to a foreign country.

[128] *Cf.* First Unitarian Church v. County of Los Angeles, 48 Cal.2d 419, 438–39 (1957), *rev'd*, 357 U.S. 545 (1958).

[129] See Willcox, *Invasions of the First Amendment through Conditioned Public Spending*, 41 Cornell L.Q. 12, 48 (1955); Linde, *supra* note 126, at 39; Brown, *op. cit supra* note 5, at 337, 340.

potentially unreliable and incompetent employees. The two interests do often overlap, but they are distinct in one important respect.[130] The state's interest in obtaining fit employees relates to the individual's potential performance in public employment, while its interest in denying support to "disloyal" persons may relate only to the individual's attitude toward basic principles of constitutional government.[131] Thus, associational ties that might not be adequate to establish the likelihood that a person will act improperly in office may nevertheless be sufficient to show a lack of "loyalty," for example, in the individual's acceptance of a general theory that the violent overthrow of government is preferable to the constitutional processes for change provided in the Constitution.

The Court in *Elfbrandt* obviously found that the state interest in denying support to "disloyal" persons could not justify the Arizona loyalty oath. That conclusion may have been based on at least two distinct approaches, each furnishing somewhat different implications of the future effect of the decision. On the more limited approach, the Court may have agreed that the state has an interest in denying support to "disloyal" persons but still have found that the Arizona statute was not sufficiently related to that interest. Since, under the state's theory, the basis for denial of employment turns on the individual's rejection of the basic principles of constitutional government, the loyalty oath, to implement that theory, logically should exclude only those members who themselves subscribe to the illegal objective of violent overthrow.[132] The Arizona statute, as related to this state interest, could very properly be described as unnecessarily broad. A ruling based on this analysis would go no further than to require that the element of "specific intent" be added to the "membership clause" of § 5. The addition of an element of active participation in the organization's affairs would not be needed, since, as noted, "disloyalty" for the purpose of this theory need not be related to action.

---

130 See BROWN, *supra* note 5, at 205. See also 94 Ariz. at 6, 10–11.

131 See note 127 *supra*. See also Sacks, *Federal Civilian Employees Security Program: An Analysis of the Wright Commission Report*, 52 Nw. U. L. Rev. 715, 719 (1958).

132 The Court adopted a similar view in interpreting the requirement of "attachment to the principles of the constitution" under the Nationality Act of 1906. See Nowak v. United States, 356 U.S. 660 (1958); Maisenberg v. United States, 356 U.S. 670 (1958).

This analysis would not in itself answer the argument, suggested by the dissent, that the individual by lending "his name and influence" to the organization automatically aided its illegal objectives, whatever his intent, and that the state could, therefore, exclude him from employment as a means of denying support to a "disloyal" organization.[133] On this point, the Court would be required to answer that the state's justification for a loyalty oath must relate directly to the denial of support to the individual, rather than to the organization, since it is the individual who suffers the brunt of the restriction. Some support for this position may be found in *Wieman v. Updegraff*,[134] where the Court held that the state could not deny employment to members of organizations advocating overthrow who were not aware that the organization had this objective. Certainly, a member in that category could give the organization as much aid by lending it "his name and influence" as the knowing member who did not share the organization's purpose.[135] While there is a significant difference in the fact that the member in the second case has knowledge of the organization's illegal goals, *Baggett v. Bullitt* indicates that, at least in the case of somewhat more indirect assistance such as united activity in support of a joint political objective, it matters not that the individual realizes that his assistance will indirectly further the organization's illegal objectives.[136] Membership in an organization actually advocating overthrow may, of course, constitute a much more direct contribution to its illegal objectives. But when the importance *Wieman* attached to freedom of association is also considered, the Court might well conclude that the state's interest in shutting off this additional element of organizational support was insufficient to outweigh the restriction on individual freedom. In sum then, under this first approach, the Arizona oath would be rejected because (1) the state's interest in denying support to "disloyal" persons is not sufficient so long as the individual does not himself subscribe

---

133 384 U.S. at 20. This argument was also suggested in the Arizona Supreme Court. See 94 Ariz. at 10–11.

134 344 U.S. 183 (1952).

135 The Court has recognized that an individual can be an active member of an organization and still not be aware of its illegal objective. See Nowak v. United States, *supra* note 132; Maisenberg v. United States, *supra* note 132; *cf.* Rowoldt v. Perfetto, 355 U.S. 115 (1957).

136 See text at note 107 *supra*.

to an organization's illegal goals, and (2) the state's interest in denying the organization whatever support comes from the membership of a person who does not favor its illegal ends is not sufficient to justify restricting that individual's right to join that organization in order to work for a legal objective he does favor.

A second and more far-reaching approach to both aspects of this problem would hold that the state's interest in denying support to "disloyal" persons or organizations is never a proper basis for employment disqualification, except possibly where the grounds of disqualification are limited to speech or association that could be directly proscribed under the Constitution. At the outset, it should be noted that the Court never has had occasion directly to accept or reject the principle that a state can base a loyalty test on its desire to deny employment to those persons who reject the basic principles of constitutional government. Scattered statements in one or two opinions might be taken as recognizing the state's interest in this regard, but these opinions dealt primarily with other state goals.[137] Moreover, these opinions were written before *Speiser v. Randall*.[138]

---

[137] See Garner v. Board of Public Works, 341 U.S. 716, 725 (1951) (concurring opinion); Adler v. Board of Education, 342 U.S. 485, 492–93 (1952). The statements in *Adler* are ambiguous because the Court never defines the term "loyalty" when it speaks of determining "fitness and loyalty." Moreover, the various statements in *Adler* emphasizing the so-called privilege rationale were sharply limited only a year later in Wieman v. Updegraff, 344 U.S. 183 (1953).

[138] 357 U.S. 513 (1958). One post-*Speiser* statement that could be bracketed with the cases cited in note 137 is found in Flemming v. Nestor, 363 U.S. 603 (1960). The Court there sustained a statutory provision disqualifying from social security benefits persons who "had been deported on several grounds, including membership in the Communist Party." The Court noted that a rational justification for the statute might rest on the deportee's inability to aid the domestic economy by spending the benefits locally. The opinion then went on to make the following statements: "For these purposes, it is, of course, constitutionally irrelevant whether this reasoning in fact underlay the legislative decision, as it is irrelevant that the section does not extend to all to whom the postulated rationale might in logic apply. . . . Nor, apart from this, can it be deemed irrational for Congress to have concluded that the public purse should not be utilized to contribute to the support of those deported on the grounds specified in the statute."
It is not entirely clear whether the last sentence refers to the fact that the deportee would be residing abroad or whether it establishes a right to deny support simply because alien Communists are not "deserving" of benefits. See Linde, *supra* note 126, at 17, suggesting the latter interpretation. In any event, subsequent cases, apparently viewing *Flemming* as based entirely on the first rationale, have treated *Speiser* and *Flemming* as consistent in the general principle each applied. See, *e.g.*, Sherbert v. Verner, 374 U.S. 398, 404–05, 409 n. 9 (1963).

In *Speiser* the Court held unconstitutional a California statute requiring every applicant for a veteran's tax exemption to swear that he was not presently advocating the violent overthrow of the federal or state government. The California statute was based on essentially the same state interest as is advanced to deny employment to "disloyal" persons. It was designed to "encourage . . . loyalty to our institutions" by denying support of persons who advocated the violent overthrow of those institutions.[139] Unlike the Arizona loyalty oath, however, the standard for denial of benefits was limited to speech that had been held to be outside the protection of the First Amendment.[140] The Court, therefore, did not have to deal directly with the question whether the denial of tax benefits could have been based on speech that could not be directly prohibited under the Constitution. Nevertheless, the Court's opinion indicated quite clearly that if such exemptions can be denied on the basis of speech at all, it must be on the basis of "proscribed speech for which [the individual] might be fined or imprisoned."[141] In particular, the opinion emphasized that legislation serving the function of the California statute constituted a direct restraint on speech, since it was "frankly aimed at the suppression of dangerous ideas," rather than the control of particular conduct relating to the benefit granted.[142] The Court carefully distinguished prior loyalty oath cases, such as *Gerende*, on the ground that the "principal aim of those statutes was not to penalize political beliefs but to deny positions to persons supposed to be dangerous because the position might be misused to the detriment of the public."[143] Finally, the Court, relying in part on *Wieman v. Updegraff*, rejected the argument that tax exemptions constituted a privilege and therefore were not subject to constitutional limitations upon the infringement of speech.[144]

In light of *Speiser*, a loyalty oath justified solely in terms of the state's interest in denying support to "disloyal" persons, as opposed to an interest in insuring employee reliability, must be viewed as a

---

[139] 357 U.S. at 527. See also statement of Clark, J., dissenting: "The interest of the State . . . is dual in nature, but its primary thrust is summed up in an understandable desire to insure that those who benefit by tax exemption do not bite the hand that gives it." *Id*. at 543.

[140] *Id*. at 519–20.   [142] *Id*. at 519.

[141] *Id*. at 520.   [143] *Id*. at 527.   [144] *Id*. at 518–19.

direct restraint on speech. It follows that the only permissible standard for an oath serving that interest would be one tied, as in *Speiser*, to speech or association that might generally be made criminal under such legislation as the Smith Act.[145] Moreover, even if the standard employed were to meet the requirements of the *Scales* case, for example, there still might be some question about its validity when used in the context of a loyalty oath. *Speiser* only assumed *arguendo* that a state could deny benefits solely on "disloyalty" grounds where the speech involved was directly punishable.[146] The opinion then went on to reject the California statute because, in any event, it improperly shifted the burden of proof. In reaching this result, *Speiser* compared the California provision to a statute imposing a penalty for a crime.[147] Extending this reasoning, the Court might well rule, if forced to meet the issue, that a loyalty requirement "frankly aimed at suppressing speech," even if limited to constitutionally prohibitible speech, would still be invalid because it fails to afford the safeguards of the Sixth Amendment.[148] This would, in effect, reject any state employment test designed as a means of denying support to "disloyal" persons or organizations unless the standards under that test were relevant also to the quality of the employee's performance on the job.

Even if *Speiser* is not extended to its logical extreme, its application to the area of government employment still presents the problem of distinguishing (or rejecting) two "practical" precedents that are often cited to justify loyalty qualifications for government employees. The first is the traditional practice of hiring and firing under the spoils system that was so prevalent in this country before the advent of civil service (and is still not unheard of today).[149] If Republicans can deny employment to Democrats simply because they are Democrats, why not, it is asked, permit both parties to exclude persons who believe in the overthrow of the government?

[145] See Thompson v. Gleason, 317 F.2d 901, 906 (D.C. Cir. 1952); *cf.* Danskin v. School Board, 28 Cal.2d 536 (1946); United States v. Schneider, 45 F. Supp. 848 (E.D. Wisc. 1942).

[146] 357 U.S. at 519–20.

[147] *Id.* at 525, citing Lipke v. Lederer, 259 U.S. 557 (1922).

[148] Cf. Kennedy v. Mendoza-Martinez, 372 U.S. 144, 184 n. 39 (1963) (relying on Lipke v. Lederer, *supra* note 147).

[149] See Bailey v. Richardson, 182 F.2d 46, 59–60, 62–63 (D.C. Cir. 1950), *aff'd by equally divided court*, 341 U.S. 918 (1951) (collecting sources).

A possible answer could be that the spoils system was basically a product of a different era in which the characterization of employment as a privilege carried far more weight than it does today.[150] But the better answer is that the patronage system of employment has operated behind the Court's general refusal to examine the basis of the government's employment decisions unless the grounds for those decisions are clearly announced.[151] If the basic premise of the spoils system, insofar as it is not related to fitness, were clearly stated in statute or regulation, it would be rejected as arbitrary. This point seems clear from *United Public Workers v. Mitchell*, where the Court noted that "none would deny" that "Congress may not enact a regulation providing that no Republican, Jew, or Negro shall be appointed to federal office."[152]

The second precedent relied upon is the general requirement that government employees take an oath swearing to "bear true faith and allegiance" to the government, to "support and defend the Constitution against all enemies, foreign and domestic," and to "faithfully discharge the duties of [public] office."[153] An "affirmative" oath of this nature has been required of federal employees in the executive branch since 1884,[154] and a somewhat similar oath is required of the President by Article II of the Constitution. The contents of the oath, particularly the general requirement of defense of the Constitution, seems to indicate that it extends to matters beyond the individual's performance in office. Accordingly, it is argued that a requirement that employees believe in democratic processes for change, as opposed to violent overthrow, merely restates in a more specific fashion the employee's affirmative duty to defend the Constitution and to bear true allegiance to the government formed under the Constitution.[155] The short answer here

---

150 See generally Willcox, *supra* note 129, at 12–15, 37–44. *Compare* Heim v. McCall, 239 U.S. 175, 191 (1915), *with* Wieman v. Updegraff, 344 U.S. 183, 192 (1952). See also Powell, *The Right To Work for the State*, 16 Colum. L. Rev. 99 (1916).

151 See, *e.g.*, Cafeteria and Restaurant Workers Union v. McElroy, 367 U.S. 886 (1961).

152 330 U.S. at 100.

153 5 U.S.C. § 16 (1964). See Constanzo, *Loyalty Oath Affidavit*, 37 U. Det. L. J. 718, 728 (1960); Willcox, *supra* note 129, at 49.

154 See 5 U.S.C. § 16 (1964); 23 Stat. 22 (1884).

155 The fact that the affirmative oaths refer to future conduct and therefore would not likely be enforced by a perjury prosecution would not in itself serve as an

is that the affirmative oath of allegiance refers only to positive acts
in violation of a constitutionally imposed legal duty. In *In re Summers*,[156] for example, the Court, in finding that a person unwilling
to bear arms could not conscientiously take the oath to "support
the Constitution," specifically rested its conclusion on the assumption that the draft exemption for conscientious objectors was not
constitutionally required and that the failure of a conscientious
objector to bear arms could validly be made a crime. Similarly,
the affirmative oath, if it applies to speech at all, creates a duty to
abstain only from such seditious speech or association as could be
directly prohibited consistent with the Constitution. This would
be entirely consistent with at least the more limited view of *Speiser
v. Randall* as restricting the basis for the denial of benefits "to
proscribed speech for which [the individual] might be imprisoned
or fined."[157]

As previously noted, the Court's opinion in *Elfbrandt* does not
clearly indicate why it found the state's interest in denying support to "disloyal" persons insufficient to justify the Arizona loyalty
oath. The Court probably did not advance beyond the first approach suggested above, that membership without specific intent
to further illegal objectives bore an insufficient relationship to the
state interest. The more broadly based ground would have required
a discussion of *Speiser*, and that case was cited only once and for
a different point.[158] On the other hand, four members of the *Elfbrandt* majority had previously urged a very broad interpretation

---

adequate basis for distinguishing the loyalty oath. See Baggett v. Bullitt, 377 U.S.
360, 374 (1964): "Without the criminal sanctions, it is said, one need not fear
taking this oath. . . . This contention ignores not only the effect of the oath on
those who will not solemnly swear unless they can do so honestly and without
prevarication and reservation, but also its effect on those who believe the written
law means what it says."

156 325 U.S. 561, 569–73 (1945). *Summers* involved the duty to support the
state constitution (Illinois), but, at that time, a similar construction had been placed
upon the requirement of support of the federal constitution in the oath of allegiance
required by the Naturalization Act of 1906. See United States v. Schwimmer,
279 U.S. 644 (1929); United States v. MacIntosh, 283 U.S. 605 (1931), *overruled*
by Girouard v. United States, 328 U.S. 61 (1945). The *Girouard* case found that
Congress had not intended to make willingness to bear arms an absolute prerequisite
to citizenship.

157 See note 141 *supra*.

158 384 U.S. at 17–18.

of *Speiser* in another context.[159] Perhaps they viewed *Speiser* as so clearly rejecting this interest that no discussion was necessary. If this is true, *Elfbrandt* will have bearing beyond the employment situation and may, along with *Speiser,* provide the basis for rejecting such loyalty restrictions as that imposed under the recent Medicare legislation.[160]

VI. The State's Interest in Insuring the Fitness of Its Employees

The ruling in *Elfbrandt* indicates also that the Arizona oath requirement could not be sustained by the state's interest in insuring the fitness of its employees. Here again the significance of the decision will depend in large degree on which of two somewhat different rationales led the Court to this conclusion.

The first rationale would be based primarily on the total coverage of the Arizona statute. Although petitioner in *Elfbrandt* happened to be a teacher, the Arizona oath was required of all state and local employees, including janitors, street cleaners, and others with purely ministerial functions.[161] As applied to persons in these positions, the case for determining the prospective employee's potential performance on the basis of his membership in an organization advocating overthrow is very weak. The traditional argument for denying state employment to members of such organizations has rested on the likelihood that they would use their positions to strengthen the organization's ability eventually to attempt violent overthrow by (1) promoting the organization's influence through favoritism in the distribution of governmental benefits to those groups sympa-

159 See Konigsberg v. State Bar, 366 U.S. 36, 75–80, 80–81 (1961) (dissenting opinions). See also the concurring opinion of Mr. Justice Douglas, joined by Mr. Justice Black, in *Speiser.* 357 U.S. at 532, 535–38.

160 See 79 Stat. 333 (1965), 42 U.S.C. § 427 (note) (Supp. 1965). This section generally extends hospital benefits to persons not insured under Social Security or Railroad Retirement, but makes an exception for a member of any organization ordered by the Subversive Activities Control Board to register as a Communist organization under the Internal Security Act of 1950. See also the various provisions cited in Note, *Unconstitutional Conditions,* 73 Harv. L. Rev. 1595, 1601–02 (1960).

161 Ariz. Rev. Stat. § 38-231 (B), (C) (1965). The Arizona oath was required of "any person elected, appointed or employed, either on a part-time or full-time basis by the state or any of its political subdivisions or any county, city, town, municipal corporation, school district, public educational institution, or any board, commission or agency of any of the foregoing." *Ibid.*

thetic to the organization's goals and (2) using government power to achieve social and economic conditions that are prerequisites to a successful attempt at revolution.[162] Typical examples offered in support of this position are the employees of legislative committees who attempted "to manipulate hearings so as to favor the friends of the party and depreciate its enemies,"[163] and the public school teachers who used their position to indoctrinate students through the teaching of "a prescribed party line."[164] While the Court has previously accepted the state's interest in preventing such misuse of office as an appropriate basis for imposing loyalty restrictions on teachers[165] and lawyers,[166] it would seriously strain this reasoning to sustain restrictions upon numerous positions that do not allow the employee sufficient discretion to permit any significant manipulation to benefit the organization. Nevertheless, the strained reasoning has been offered in several arguments supporting the application of loyalty tests to all government positions.

One such argument defends total coverage on the ground that it

---

162 See SELZNICK, THE ORGANIZATIONAL WEAPON 215–24 (1960); BROWN, *op. cit. supra* note 5, at 215–18, 336–38. A special danger frequently mentioned in connection with employment of Communist party members is their tendency "to influence specific [policy] decisions, especially on matters of less than central interest to the target government which may help a communist faction abroad or may increase vulnerability to Soviet diplomacy." SELZNICK, at 220. This possibility presents basically the same type of problems in devising an appropriate scope for loyalty oath requirements as the two types of misuse of position mentioned in the text.

163 SELZNICK, *op. cit. supra* note 162, at 222, citing statements by former Senator R. M. La Follette, Jr., concerning the activities of "pro-communist elements" on the staffs of congressional committees.

164 N.Y. Laws 1949, c. 360 (legislative findings supporting the Feinberg Law). See also HOOK, HERESY YES—CONSPIRACY NO 184–87 (1953); THOMAS, THE TEST OF FREEDOM 90–93 (1954).

165 Adler v. Board of Education, 342 U.S. 485, 489–93 (1951). See also Beilan v. Board of Education, 357 U.S. 399 (1958).

166 Konigsberg v. State Bar, 366 U.S. 36 (1961). Although the primary issue before the Court in the second *Konigsberg* case concerned the state's power to compel a bar applicant to answer an inquiry concerning membership in the Communist party, the Court did indicate that the standard for disqualification to which the inquiry related—advocacy of violent overthrow—was constitutionally valid. See *id.* at 51–52: "It would indeed be difficult to argue that a belief firm enough to be carried into advocacy, in the use of illegal means to change the form of the State or Federal government is an unimportant consideration in determining the fitness of applicants for membership in a profession in whose hands so largely lies the safekeeping of this country's legal and political institutions."

is not administratively feasible to identify those positions in which the opportunity for misuse of office in favor of organizational objectives is either nonexistent or negligible.[167] This is a difficult position to sustain in the light of the ability of the federal government, for example, to distinguish between sensitive and non-sensitive positions under the employee security program and between discretionary and ministerial functions under the Federal Torts Claims Act.[168] Also, it seems particularly unlikely to appeal to a Court that itself has undertaken the task of distinguishing between different state positions in order to determine which persons are "public officials" for the purpose of the *New York Times Co. v. Sullivan* rule.[169]

Another argument favoring total coverage rests on the thesis that the employment of members of groups advocating overthrow, no matter what the individual's position, will give the government service a bad public image and therefore impair its general effectiveness. Assuming that such public reaction is a reality,[170] decisions like *Wieman v. Updegraff*[171] would seem to foreclose its use for imposing a restriction upon constitutionally protected association. Although *Wieman* deals with the member of an organization who is unaware of its illegal objectives and *Elfbrandt* with the knowing member who merely does not support those objectives, the difference in the two is unlikely to be significant insofar as public reaction to employment of such persons is concerned. Except in unusual cases, the member's lack of awareness of the organization's objectives is unlikely to be a matter of public knowledge, and where it is, it will often be disbelieved.[172] Similarly, although *Wieman*, unlike

---

[167] *Cf.* Brief for Respondent, pp. 36–43, 56–60; Garner v. Board of Public Works, 341 U.S. 716 (1951).

[168] See Cole v. Young, 351 U.S. 536 (1956); Dalehite v. United States, 346 U.S. 15 (1953). This is not to say that either of these distinctions is satisfactory for determining which positions might easily be misused to support organizational objectives, but only to suggest that the process of classifying government jobs for this purpose is no more difficult than drawing the distinctions required under the Federal Security program or the Federal Torts Claim Act.

[169] See Rosenblatt v. Baer, 383 U.S. 75 (1966).

[170] See STOUFFER, COMMUNISM, CONFORMITY AND CIVIL LIBERTIES 39–45 (1955).

[171] 344 U.S. 183 (1952).

[172] See generally Mowitz, *Michigan—State and Local Attack on Subversion,* in THE STATES AND SUBVERSION 184, 206–15, 228–30 (1952) (Gellhorn ed.); STOUFFER, *op. cit. supra* note 170, at 39.

Elfbrandt, concerned membership in "front" organizations as well
as those directly advocating overthrow, the Court has clearly indicated that the ruling there is applicable to members of either type of
organization.[173] The negative impact upon free association is, of
course, presumably less in *Elfbrandt* than in *Wieman* because the
Arizona statute does include the element of "scienter." Yet this difference hardly seems likely to alter what might well be viewed in
Wieman as a total rejection of public reaction as a factor that may
be used in determining employment qualifications.[174] Adverse public
reaction may justify otherwise irrational government action in other
areas,[175] but the Court is not willing to give such reaction any
weight where it would affect the exercise of a constitutionally protected right. As Mr. Justice Frankfurter stated in his separate opinion in *Garner:*[176] "[S]urely a government could not exclude from
public employment members of a minority group merely because
they are odious to the majority." This seems equally true whether
the minority is defined in terms of race, religion, or politics.

Finally, the Court in *Garner* sustained the total coverage of a
loyalty oath requirement on the ground that membership in a group
such as the Communist party might be viewed as likely to affect the
individual's performance in all government positions, "both high
and low."[177] Unfortunately, the Court's opinion concentrated primarily on other issues and offered little explanation of its conclusion on this point.[178] The opinion does suggest that the Court viewed

[173] See Aptheker v. Secretary of State, 378 U.S. 500, 510 (1964); Schware v. Board
of Bar Examiners, 353 U.S. 232, 239 (1957); see also Sweezy v. New Hampshire, 354
U.S. 234, 247–48 (1957).

[174] 344 U.S. at 190–91; see also *id.* at 194–97 (concurring opinion). Although the
Court did not specifically mention the possible impact upon the public image of
government service, the opinion clearly recognized the community attitude about
persons discharged on loyalty grounds and emphasized that there was no state
interest that justified imposing that burden on the "innocent" member. *Id.* at 191.

[175] *Cf.* NEWSWEEK, *supra* note 2 (improper sexual activities); Scott v. Macy, 349
F.2d 182 (D.C. Cir. 1965).

[176] 341 U.S. at 724.   [177] *Id.* at 720.

[178] The Court devoted only two paragraphs to this issue, the first dealing primarily
with the state's power to require that employees disclose by affidavit any past membership in the Communist party: "We think that a municipal employer is not dis-
abled because it is an agency of the State from inquiring of its employees as to
matters that may prove relevant to their fitness and suitability for the public service. Past conduct may well relate to present fitness; past loyalty may have a reasonable relationship to present and future trust. Both are commonly inquired into

the individual's willingness to support illegal overthrow of the government as a reasonable indication of a general lack of "integrity." It also has been suggested that members of such organizations tend to be inefficient and easily disgruntled employees because of their strong opposition to the government for which they work.[179] Additionally, their intense psychological involvement in the organization's "cause" allegedly makes them less able to devote their full efforts to their work.[180] All these points have relevance, however, only to the person who is deeply involved with the organization's purpose. Although there are obviously some hard core members ("cadres") of whom it may be true,[181] certainly membership with knowledge of the organization's illegal purpose would hardly indicate in itself that the individual falls in that category.[182] Accordingly, even if the Court gave full recognition to this argument, it could still reject a loyalty requirement applicable to all knowing members of an organization advocating overthrow irrespective of their purpose in joining the organization or their degree of participation in the organization's activities.[183]

---

in determining fitness for both high and low positions in private industry and are not less relevant in public employment. The affidavit requirement is valid.

"2. In our view the validity of the oath turns upon the nature of the Charter amendment (1941) and the relation of the ordinance (1948) to this amendment. . . . We assume that under the Federal Constitution the Charter amendment is valid to the extent that it bars from the city's public service persons who, subsequent to its adoption in 1941, advise, advocate, or teach the violent overthrow of the Government or who are or become affiliated with any group doing so. The provisions operating thus prospectively were a reasonable regulation to protect the municipal service by establishing an employment qualification of loyalty to the State and the United States. Cf. *Gerende* v. *Board of Supervisors of Elections*, 341 U.S. 56 (1951). Likewise, as a regulation of political activity of municipal employees, the amendment was reasonably designed to protect the integrity and competency of the service. This Court has held that Congress may reasonably restrict the political activity of federal civil service employees for such a purpose, *United Public Workers* v. *Mitchell*, 330 U.S. 75, 102–103 (1947), and a State is not without power to do as much." 341 U.S. at 720–21.

[179] BROWN, *op. cit. supra* note 5, at 336–37; ALMOND, THE APPEALS OF COMMUNISM 103, 260–62 (1954).

[180] BROWN, *op. cit. supra* note 5, at 337; ALMOND, *op. cit. supra* note 179, at 258–59.

[181] MEYER, THE MOULDING OF COMMUNISTS 132–52, 161–65 (1961); ALMOND, *op. cit. supra* note 179, at 232–33.

[182] SELZNICK, *op. cit. supra* note 162, at 83–85; MEYER, *op. cit. supra* note 181, at 105–31.

[183] In *Garner*, the total coverage of the Los Angeles oath was emphasized only in the ACLU brief as amicus curiae, p. 8. Respondent's reply simply brushed over

The Court's rejection of the state's interest in insuring employee fitness thus could have been based, in large part, upon the total coverage of the Arizona oath. Yet, although Mr. Justice Douglas does not in any sense reject this as the ground for decision, it seems likely that the *Elfbrandt* decision was intended to have a much greater reach. While the opinion does note that the Arizona statute applies to all employees, it places no emphasis on this factor.[184] On the other hand, the point on which Mr. Justice Douglas placed the greatest stress, the denial of employment to members lacking "specific intent," would seem to have significance no matter what the coverage of the statute. Thus, although it is far from clear, the opinion indicates that the Court would have reached the same conclusion had the Arizona oath been limited to employees, such as teachers, whose jobs were clearly capable of being manipulated to serve the interests of an organization advocating violent overthrow. If that is true, the Court's ruling is of considerably more significance, from a doctrinal as well as a practical viewpoint.

On a test oath limited to employees with discretionary authority, the state's argument for the exclusion of all knowing members of an organization advocating violent overthrow would rest essentially on the recognized tendency of these organizations to "promote" the "misuse" of such authority. As the Court at one time recognized in a related context, even members of such organizations who have no interest in promoting the overthrow of the government may be induced to misuse public power to achieve organizational objectives.[185] Thus, it has been suggested that teachers belonging to the Communist party will use their classes to advance the party line, not because they necessarily believe in overthrow, but because they be-

---

this objection as an administrative matter on which the state's judgment must be respected. Respondent's brief, p. 66. Other than this the briefs concentrated almost entirely on the bill of attainder argument. Very little attention was given to the membership clause, and there was no mention of the absence of a requirement of specific intent to support the organization's illegal objective.

[184] 384 U.S. at 12. The Court mentioned the total coverage only in the general description of the facts of the case.

[185] See American Communications Ass'n v. Douds, 339 U.S. 382, 387–89 (1950). The Taft-Hartley provision sustained in *Douds* extended to all members of the Communist party, irrespective of the individual's attitude toward its illegal objectives. Of course, *Douds* has been undercut to a great extent by United States v. Brown, 381 U.S. 437 (1965), and though *Brown* rejects the *Douds* analysis primarily on other points, the opinion there suggests that the Court also would reject this aspect of the *Douds* reasoning. See *id.* at 455–56.

lieve in the legal objectives of the party and because the party strongly urges its members to engage in this activity as a means of achieving those objectives.[186] The statute in *Elfbrandt* was not, of course,
limited in application to the Communist party, but the manipulation of public offices in the manner previously described would be
an essential ingredient of the program of any organization that
hoped to overthrow the government. In sum, the argument would
be that even members who do not subscribe to the organization's
illegal ends pose a danger because (1) the organization imposes
great pressure on its members to build group strength through the
employee's manipulation of discretionary authority, and (2) the
nature of the manipulation is sufficiently related to the group's
legal objectives to encourage participation by members who favor
only those objectives. The first factor, the constant stress on manipulation, also serves to distinguish the state's regulation here from
the possibly unconstitutional denial of employment to members
of other groups that might profit by manipulation of public power.
Thus, it provides the answer to the argument that the exclusion of
Communist teachers logically would also permit the exclusion of
Catholic clergy teaching in public schools because they too engaged in classroom indoctrination.[187] Although members of some
other groups may occasionally misuse their public position to aid
the group, only organizations advocating overthrow have actively
promoted such activity, as logically they must if they are to achieve
their basic goal.[188]

The opinion in *Elfbrandt* does not clearly indicate whether the
Court considered this argument or, if so, on what grounds it rejected
it. Certainly, the majority's reliance on the prohibition against
"guilt by association" would not be an adequate ground. The denial
of employment to all knowing members does not rest on a "conclusive presumption that the member shares the unlawful aims of
the organization,"[189] but rather on the potential danger presented

---

186 See generally HOOK, *op. cit. supra* note 164, at 181–86; BROWN, *op. cit. supra*
note 5, at 340–41.

187 See Zeller v. Huff, 236 P.2d 949 (N.M. 1951); see also HOOK, *op. cit. supra*
note 164, at 219–20.

188 HOOK, *op. cit. supra* note 164, at 219–20; see also SELZNICK, *op. cit. supra* note
162, at 221–24.

189 384 U.S. at 17.

by the member even when he does not share these aims. In fact, the Court's reliance on this argument might well indicate that it did not appreciate the state's position in this regard.

On the other hand, the Court relied heavily on *Aptheker v. Secretary of State*,[190] which does provide an adequate basis for rejecting the state's argument. In *Aptheker* the Court held unconstitutional a section of the Securities Activities Control Act that made it a crime for any member of an organization found to be a "communist organization" to seek a United States passport.[191] The congressional purpose in enacting this provision had been to prevent travel abroad that could further the organization's relationship with the "world Communist movement" through the exchange of secret communiqués, the training of local leaders, and similar activities.[192] The Court majority there, including four members of the *Elfbrandt* majority,[193] held the statute unconstitutional because, as in *Elfbrandt*, the legislature had sought to achieve its objective "by means that sweep unnecessarily broadly and thereby invade the area of protected freedom."[194] The unnecessary breadth came from Congress' failure to take into consideration several factors that were considered relevant to "the likelihood that travel by such a person would be attended by the type of activity which Congress sought to control."[195] The Court particularly emphasized that the statute automatically denied the member's right to travel without regard to his knowledge of the organization's improper purpose, "his commitment to its purpose," "his degree of activity in the organization," his "purposes" for wishing to travel, and "the security-sensitivity of the areas in which he wishes to travel."[196]

Despite certain differences, a strong analogy can be drawn between *Aptheker* and *Elfbrandt*. Although the holding in *Aptheker* was framed in terms of the Fifth Amendment right to travel,[197] various references in the opinion indicate that the decision was

---

[190] 378 U.S. 500 (1964).

[191] 64 Stat. 993, 50 U.S.C. § 785 (1964).

[192] 378 U.S. at 526–27 (dissenting opinion).

[193] The Chief Justice and Justices Black, Douglas, and Brennan. Mr. Justice Fortas, the fifth member of the *Elfbrandt* majority, was not then a member of the Court.

[194] 378 U.S. at 508, quoting from N.A.A.C.P. v. Alabama, 377 U.S. 288, 307 (1964).

[195] 378 U.S. at 510.   [196] *Id.* at 510, 512.   [197] *Id.* at 505–07, 514, 517.

grounded on the restriction upon free association. The Court relied in large part on First Amendment cases,[198] and specifically analogized the restrictions on the issuance of passports to loyalty restrictions on government employment.[199] Also, although the legislation extended to "Communist front" organizations and therefore included groups in which a large majority of members were unlikely to be aligned with the "world Communist movement,"[200] the Court's opinion did not refer to this fact, and it made no effort to distinguish between members of "Communist front" and "Communist action" organizations. Thus, despite Mr. Justice White's objection that "*Aptheker* did not deal with the government employee,"[201] the ruling in *Aptheker* clearly was entitled to significant consideration in determining the validity of an employment test imposing a similar type of restriction upon the individual's right of association.

Mr. Justice White also distinguished *Aptheker* on the ground that the statute involved there applied to members who were unaware of the organization's ties to the "world Communist movement."[202] The *Aptheker* opinion indicates, however, that the addition of this element of knowledge would not have altered the result in that case. The opinion placed great stress on the legislature's failure to consider the individual's "activity, commitment, and purpose in the places for travel."[203] Perhaps, the Court's reliance upon one of these factors, the member's commitment to the organization's purposes, could be distinguished in the situation presented by *Elfbrandt*. Unlike the prospect of manipulation of public office, the activities that Congress sought to inhibit in the passport legislation

---

198 See, *e.g.*, *id.* at 517, 525; see also Note, 78 HARV. L. REV. 143, 195–99 (1964).

199 378 U.S. at 508, 510, 513–14.

200 Communist front organizations are those (1) "substantially directed, dominated, or controlled by a Communist action organization," and (2) "primarily operated for the purpose of giving aid and support to a Communist-action organization . . . or the world Communist movement." 64 Stat. 989, 50 U.S.C. § 785 (1964). See American Committee for the Protection of the Foreign Born v. S.A.C.B., 331 F.2d 63 (D.C. Cir. 1962), *vacated*, 380 U.S. 503, 505 (1965).

201 384 U.S. at 22.   202 *Ibid.*

203 *Id.* at 514. "In addition to the absence of criteria linking the bare fact of membership to the individual's knowledge, activity or commitment, § 6 also excludes other considerations which might more closely relate the denial of passports to the stated purpose of the legislation." *Id.* at 511.

would be undertaken only by members who shared the organization's goal of promoting the "world Communist movement." But the stress that *Aptheker* places on the other factors of activity and purpose of travel, especially when viewed in the light of the administrative burdens involved in considering those factors,[204] suggests a general policy, equally applicable to *Elfbrandt*, against the use of knowing membership as an indicator of an individual's tendency to act improperly on behalf of an organization. Surely, if this policy required legislative consideration of so many factors beyond the element of scienter in *Aptheker*, it could easily make similar demands of Arizona.

Reliance upon *Aptheker* becomes more difficult, however, if *Elfbrandt* is viewed as establishing a standard that would be applicable to a loyalty oath requirement limited to employees with discretionary authority. Although the *Aptheker* Court stated that several factors were relevant to the congressional purpose in restricting travel, it did not state that a legislative standard necessarily must include every one of these factors. In fact, it clearly avoided this conclusion when it stated that there was no need to consider the constitutionality of the passport regulation as applied to the petitioners—both very active high officials of the party—because the petitioners could, in any event, attack the legislation on its face.[205] Certainly the opinion left open the possibility that Congress might condition the issuance of passports on most of the factors mentioned, yet exclude others as not equally significant. Thus,

---

[204] The Court did not mention the obvious administrative difficulties involved in considering all of these factors. The reference to the federal employees loyalty program, however, apparently constituted its answer to this problem. Whether the problems could be handled by an administrative program is uncertain. Could an administrative hearing determine, for example, whether Aptheker's purpose was *merely* to travel and lecture abroad, to visit the Bodleian library, etc.? In any event, the increase in administrative burden would obviously be great. But this factor was not considered worthy of discussion.

[205] See, *e.g.*, 378 U.S. at 514–17. One of the major questions presented in *Aptheker* was whether the Court should consider the lack of statutory recognition of such elements as scienter and active membership when the petitioners themselves clearly met those requirements. This question would have been irrelevant if, for example, the "purposes and places of travel" were factors that the legislature had to take into consideration. If that were the case, the statute would clearly be unconstitutional even as it related to the petitioners. The Court, however, did not rule on the statute as it applied to the active member, but held that the petitioners had standing to attack the validity of the statute "on its face." *Id*. at 515.

it might provide that all knowing members of "communist organizations," would be denied passports to visit the U.S.S.R. or the "satellite" countries except in connnection with very limited purposes. Whether the Court would reject this provision because it was not also limited to active members committed to the organization's illicit purposes is not settled by *Aptheker*. The validity of a loyalty oath based on knowing membership, but limited in application to a specific group, such as teachers, would present a roughly similar question. If *Elfbrandt* was intended to control in this situation, then it clearly has proceeded, albeit without discussion, beyond the position taken in *Aptheker*. This is not to suggest that the general tenor of the opinion in *Aptheker* might not furnish some support for such an extension. Certainly the basic thrust of Mr. Justice Goldberg's opinion in *Aptheker* might be viewed as indicating that legislation characterizing individuals according to membership will be accepted only when the class of members is so sharply limited by consideration of all relevant facts that the tendency ascribed to the group is shown to be an almost uniform characteristic of each member.[206] Under this premise, of course, *Elfbrandt's* requirement of "specific intent" is easily sustainable without regard to the limited nature of the positions covered by the oath requirement.

This view of *Aptheker* would also lend support to the suggestion in *Elfbrandt* that an appropriate loyalty oath would require that the excluded individual be an "active" member of the organization. Requiring this additional element would mean, in effect, that the constitutional limits imposed upon an indirect restraint aimed at preventing improper manipulation of public office would be identical, in the end, with the constitutional limits presently imposed under *Scales* on direct restraints on association.[207] Actually, as previously noted, the *Elfbrandt* opinion at one point suggests that the constitutional restrictions on the loyalty oath standard might be taken one step further to require membership with "specific intent"

---

[206] Acceptance of this view of *Aptheker* might place the legislature on the horns of a dilemma, since legislation limited to such a specific class could present difficulties under the newly expanded concept of "bills of attainder" as presented in United States v. Brown, 381 U.S. 437 (1965). See also note 58 *supra*.

[207] See Scales v. United States, 367 U.S. 203 (1961); Noto v. United States, 267 U.S. 290 (1961).

plus past participation in the organization's unlawful activities. This proposal reflects the views of Justices Black and Douglas that "government can concern itself only with the actions of men, not with their opinions or beliefs."[208] If this position were applied literally to government employment, the Court would probably be forced to overrule all the cases cited in the *Elfbrandt* dissent, including the *Gerende* decision in which Justices Black and Douglas joined.[209] Moreover, the standard suggested would obviously extend beyond the security area and raise a serious question of the validity of common employment criteria, *e.g.*, personality profiles that are based in large part upon the individual's general attitudes and viewpoints.[210] It seems unlikely that the single reference in *Elfbrandt* to the individual's past participation in illegal action reflected the willingness of the majority as a whole to take this step. Chief Justice Warren and Mr. Justice Brennan, in particular, have carefully avoided joining those Black and Douglas dissents that suggest such a position.[211] The reference in *Elfbrandt* may reflect a possible change of heart on their part, but similar language found in Mr. Justice Black's opinion in *Schware* turned out to have little consequence.[212]

---

[208] Beilan v. Board of Education, 357 U.S. 399, 412, 415 (1958) (Black and Douglas, JJ., dissenting); see also Speiser v. Randall, 357 U.S. 513, 535–36 (1958) (same). But *cf.* DOUGLAS, *op. cit. supra* note 89, at 118–19.

Justices Douglas and Black have on several occasions argued that participation in the organization's illegal activities should be a prerequisite for employment disqualification. See, *e.g.*, Killian v. United States, 368 U.S. 231, 258 (1961); Beilan v. Board of Education, 357 U.S. at 412–16; Adler v. Board of Education, 342 U.S. at 511. Mr. Justice Douglas also has suggested that such activity is a constitutional prerequisite for the deportation of aliens. See Carlson v. Landon, 342 U.S. 524, 568–69 (1952) (dissenting opinion).

[209] But see DOUGLAS, *op. cit. supra* note 89, at 130.

[210] See generally, Mirel, *The Limits of Governmental Inquiry into the Private Lives of Government Employees*, 46 B.U. L. REV. 1 (1966); Creech, *Psychological Testing and Constitutional Rights*, [1966] DUKE L.J. 332.

[211] See, *e.g.*, Beilan v. Board of Education, 357 U.S. 399, 411, 417 (1958) (dissenting opinions); Speiser v. Randall, 357 U.S. 513 (1958). Mr. Justice Brennan has been particularly consistent in this regard. See, *e.g.*, Konigsberg v. State Bar, 366 U.S. 36, 80 (1961); Wilkinson v. United States, 365 U.S. 399, 429 (1961); Braden v. United States, 365 U.S. 431, 446 (1961); Barenblatt v. United States, 360 U.S. 109, 166 (1959).

[212] Schware v. Board of Bar Examiners, 353 U.S. 232, 245–46 (1957); Konigsberg v. State Bar, 353 U.S. 252, 267 (1957).

VII. The State's Interest in Protecting Internal Security

The Court's ruling in *Elfbrandt* also constituted a rejection of the state's interest in preserving internal security as a justification for the Arizona oath. The problems presented by this aspect of the Court's decision are basically the same as those discussed in connection with the rejection of the state interest in insuring employee reliability. Here also, the significance of the decision depends in large part on how the Court viewed the state's interest as presented in *Elfbrandt*.

The Court has asserted that the state's interest in guarding against acts injurious to internal security, such as sabotage, espionage, or the unintentional release of confidential information, will be given substantial weight in justifying indirect restrictions upon speech.[213] The difficulty in *Elfbrandt*, once again, was that Arizona's oath requirement applied to all state employees. The decision in *Cole v. Young*,[214] although not based on constitutional grounds, certainly indicates that little, if any, weight will be given to the state's alleged interest in preserving internal security where no effort has been made to separate the sensitive from the non-sensitive position. The Court in *Cole* held that a federal statute authorizing summary discharge of employees "in the interest of national security"[215] could not properly be applied to all government positions. The dissent had argued that total coverage was necessary because "one never knows just which job is sensitive."[216] The majority concluded, however, that the task of distinguishing between jobs on the basis of task, access to information, and similar factors was not so difficult as to suppose that Congress meant to include all federal positions under an extraordinary procedure that denied the employee the normal safeguards of civil service procedures. Certainly, with First Amendment rights involved, the Court would expect the states to be equally capable of distinguishing between positions. Accordingly, insofar as the state's interest in protecting against subversion is concerned, a loyalty restriction encompassing all state employees might easily be characterized as using "means that broadly stifle

---

213 See, *e.g.*, Communist Party v. S.A.C.B., 367 U.S. 1, 93–96 (1961); Barenblatt v. United States, 360 U.S. 109, 127–29 (1959).

214 351 U.S. 536 (1956).

215 64 Stat. 476, 5 U.S.C. § 22 (1964).   216 351 U.S. at 569.

fundamental personal liberties when the end can be more narrowly achieved."

As previously noted, however, there is little to indicate that the Court in fact based its decision on the total coverage of the Arizona oath requirement. On the other hand, as Mr. Justice White emphasized in his dissent, the majority opinion nowhere "expressly holds that a state must retain, even in its most sensitive positions, those who lend such support as knowing membership entails to those organizations, such as the Communist party, whose purposes include the violent destruction of democratic government."[217] The nature of the test oath is such, however, that it is unlikely to be used as a primary security device for the "most sensitive position," nor, for that matter, is the state government likely to have many such positions.[218] Nevertheless, a loyalty requirement of the type employed in *Elfbrandt* might well be imposed for a limited group of persons, such as state civil defense workers, police officers, and others who would occupy particularly important positions in time of emergency.[219] As limited to such positions, a state could defend a standard excluding all knowing members of organizations urging violent overthrow on at least two grounds that have considerable support in practice under state and federal security programs.

First, the state might argue that the importance of its interest in safeguarding against potential subversion justifies exclusion of all knowing members as the most effective administrative means of insuring complete exclusion of these knowing members who do

---

[217] 384 U.S. at 20.

[218] Loyalty oaths are usually required of general classes of employees, *e.g.*, all teachers and civil defense workers. Those state employees who have access to classified information will usually constitute only a small group of upper-level officials within a department, *e.g.*, senior officers within the state militia. These people will often be subject to federal clearance, and the state is unlikely to single them out as the subjects for a special loyalty oath.

[219] See generally BROWN, *op. cit. supra* note 5, at 92–109, 235–53, 470–71. Various states presently require civil defense workers to take an oath patterned after the federal civil defense oath. 64 Stat. 1256, 50 U.S.C. § 2255 (1964). See, *e.g.*, CONN. REV. STAT. § 28-12 (1965 Supp.); ILL. ANN. ST., ch. 127, § 286 (1966 Supp.); MISS REV. STAT. 38610-18 (1964). A 1965 compilation of state statutes listed thirty states with special civil defense oaths. FUND FOR THE REPUBLIC, DIGEST OF THE PUBLIC RECORD OF COMMUNISM 347–82 (1955). Although these oaths vary in context, they all require a denial of membership in any group that advocates the overthrow of the government.

share the organization's illegal objectives.[220] The effectiveness of a provision like § 5 of the Arizona statute depends upon the deterrence potential of possible criminal prosecution for improperly subscribing to the state loyalty oath. Yet, while most knowing members arguably do support the organization's illegal objectives, proof of "specific intent" as it relates to a particular individual may often be very difficult.[221] Accordingly, to make the loyalty requirement an effective device, the state must be given administrative leeway to encompass an area of membership somewhat larger than that which is the direct source of the supposed evil. Admittedly, administrative leeway of this sort is not ordinarily accorded in areas affecting free association, but here, where the statute is appropriately limited to sensitive positions, the impact of the restriction on association is also limited and the state's need is greater. Any indication in previous cases that only knowing members may be automatically excluded even from sensitive positions in no way constitutes a rejection of this position.[222] Failure to require that the member at least be aware of the organization's illegal goals would vastly increase the area of associational freedom that would be subject to restraint. Moreover, the element of knowledge, so the argument goes, is not nearly so difficult to prove as that of specific intent to further the organization's illegal purposes.[223]

The state may also argue that the exclusion of all knowing members is justified because even the knowing member who does not share the organization's objective of violent overthrow may present a threat to internal security. As the Court has recognized on several occasions, security requirements for sensitive positions extend far beyond the individual's loyalty to his government.[224] A person who does not favor violent overthrow of the government but nevertheless joins an organization supporting that objective, either does not

[220] See BROWN, op. cit. supra note 5, at 235–43, 265.

[221] See Noto v. United States, 367 U.S. 290 (1961).

[222] E.g., Wieman v. Updegraff, 344 U.S. 183 (1952). Wieman, of course, involved an oath required of all state employees and could be distinguished on that ground. See Willcox, supra note 129, at 12, 50 n. 158.

[223] See Killian v. United States, 368 U.S. 231, 244–58 (1961). See also HOOK, op. cit. supra note 164, at 89; GELLHORN, INDIVIDUAL FREEDOM AND GOVERNMENT RESTRAINTS 135 (1956).

[224] See, e.g., Cafeteria and Restaurant Workers v. McElroy, 367 U.S. 886, 898–99 (1961); Lerner v. Casey, 357 U.S. 468, 478 (1958); Cole v. Young, 351 U.S. 536 (1956).

consider that organization a serious threat or considers the achievement of other values more important than possibly increasing the risk of overthrow. In either case, the individual indicates a lack of appropriate concern for security measures.[225] Similarly, it might also be argued that anyone who associates with potential subversives necessarily puts himself in a position where he becomes a more likely subject of coercive pressure to join a subversive activity.[226] While both these arguments have an Orwellian air about them, the state could cite experience under the federal loyal security program to support their use in the case of employees who occupy sensitive jobs.[227]

Assuming the Court in *Elfbrandt* meant to reject all arguments of this type, the basis for its conclusion, at least as indicated by the majority opinion, again would rest primarily on *Aptheker*. The *Aptheker* decision seems to be relevant here in much the same sense as it would be in the situation where the state seeks to insure against possible misuse of public office by excluding knowing members from positions carrying considerable discretionary authority.[228] The difference in the nature of the interest in safeguarding against subversion is not likely to be controlling. *Aptheker*, after all, was itself presented to the Court as a case involving national security.[229] An argument could be made that the state's security interest is so greatly sharpened when only sensitive positions are involved that a policy announced in connection with the general restriction on travel voided in *Aptheker*, even if equally applicable to more limited restrictions concerning other state interests, would not be applicable here. Both past decisions and *Elfbrandt* itself suggest, however, that the *Elfbrandt* majority would not be receptive to such an argument, if for no other reason than that they would refuse to attach any special significance to the state interest in safeguarding against subversion by such groups as the police or civil defense workers.

The Chief Justice, and Justices Black, Douglas, and Brennan

---

[225] *Cf.* Atomic Energy Commission, In the Matter of J. Robert Oppenheimer (1954). See Hook, *op. cit. supra* note 164, at 225.

[226] See Brown, *op. cit. supra* note 5, at 254–61, 272; Selznick, *op. cit. supra* note 162, at 70–72.

[227] See Brown, *op. cit. supra* note 5, at 37, 254–79.

[228] See text at notes 204–07 *supra*.   [229] 378 U.S. at 509.

all have indicated that they draw an important distinction between government positions classified as "sensitive" because of special access to confidential information and those placed in that category simply because of their potential significance during a period of national emergency. In fact, for Justices Black and Douglas, the state's interest in protecting against subversion by employees in the latter situation will rank no higher than its interest generally in preventing other types of misuse of position. Thus, in *Lerner v. Casey*,[230] Mr. Justice Douglas' dissent, joined by Mr. Justice Black, clearly gave no special weight to the fact that the employee, a New York subway conductor, was classified as working in a "sensitive" position under the New York Risk Law. Mr. Justice Douglas treated the question of the state's power to discharge the conductor on the basis of his speech or association as no different from its power to discharge the teacher involved in a companion case from Pennsylvania.[231] In response to the state's argument that the conductor's access to an important transportation facility placed him in an especially sensitive position, Mr. Justice Douglas quoted a lower court opinion noting that vast numbers of persons throughout the economy had access to prime sites for sabotage, that the imposition of restrictive security regulations on all such persons would be constitutionally impermissible, and therefore "in the event of war" we may just have to take our chances with the possibility of "Black Tom explosions on every waterfront, poison in our water systems, and sand in all important industrial machines."[232] Mr. Justice Douglas has recognized, on the other hand, that special considerations may require more flexibility in permitting the discharge of persons who have access to classified information or restricted locations.[233] Mr. Justice Brennan, along with the Chief Justice, also

---

[230] 357 U.S. 468 (1958).

[231] 357 U.S. at 415–16.

[232] *Id.* at 416–17, quoting Judge Pope in Parker v. Lester, 227 F.2d 708, 721 (9th Cir. 1955). See also Black v. Cutter Laboratories, 351 U.S. 292, 300, 303–04 (1956) (dissenting opinion).

[233] See DOUGLAS, THE RIGHT TO BE LET ALONE 118, 121 (1958). Although recognizing the importance of the security interest in this situation, Mr. Justice Douglas still opposes any type of administrative program that might involve "labeling." He would prefer that the executive in charge have absolute discretion to discharge men and women in "sensitive jobs for good reasons or for no reasons at all." *Id.* at 121. Exactly what would happen to the normal civil service protection of employees in this category is not stated, but the loss of that safeguard is apparently deemed to be the lesser of two evils.

has recognized this distinction, although it is not clear that they would go quite so far as Mr. Justice Douglas in their treatment of the fact that a particular government position provides the potential to cause substantial harm in an emergency situation.[234] While the remainder of the Court has not spoken to this point, it seems likely that at least Mr. Justice Fortas, who was in the majority in *Elfbrandt*, would also be reluctant to attach any substantial weight to the state's interest in preventing subversion as it related to jobs with particular security significance only under the "remote risk of a mass breakdown."[235]

VIII. The Practical Significance of Elfbrandt and the Future of Loyalty Oaths

In terms of the legal limits upon loyalty oaths, the ultimate significance of *Elfbrandt* will depend upon how the Court answers various questions left unanswered by Mr. Justice Douglas' opinion: whether the *Garner* case has been overruled; whether the Court has rejected the state's interest in denying support to "disloyal" persons as an appropriate basis for a test oath; whether the addition of an element of "specific intent to further the illegal aims of the organization" would be required in an oath limited in application to employees in positions that could easily be manipulated to serve organizational ends; whether the same would be true of an oath applicable only to employees in positions classified as "sensitive" from the standpoint of protecting internal security; and, finally, whether, wherever the specific intent element must be added, the Court will also insist upon a requirement of active participation in the organization's affairs, or even participation in illegal activities. On the other hand, in terms of its practical significance, the impact of *Elfbrandt* will be much the same whether these questions are answered in one way or in another.

Obviously, many oaths, no matter what view of *Elfbrandt* is taken, will survive litigation, at least temporarily. State courts, taking a page from the *Scales* case,[236] may "read into" the mem-

---

234 Lerner v. Casey, 357 U.S. 468, 417, 421–22 (1958).

235 Brown, *op. cit. supra* note 5, at 248.

236 367 U.S. 203 (1961). The Court there interpreted the Smith Act membership clause to require both "active" membership and "specific intent" to support violent overthrow, although neither element was mentioned in the statute. State courts have followed this pattern in the past with respect to the element of scienter. See Adler v. Board of Education, 342 U.S. 485, 494 n. 8 (1952).

bership clause of state oaths the requirements of specific intent and perhaps even active membership. In other instances, while the membership clause may be held unconstitutional, the state court will retain as properly severable that clause dealing with the individual's own advocacy of overthrow.[237] Even where the entire oath is voided, the likelihood is that the legislature will swiftly re-enact it in appropriately modified form. For the combination of cold war exasperation, fear, and chauvinism that produces community support for loyalty tests apparently is still present in most parts of the country. While Congress was repealing the loyalty affidavit requirements of the Defense Education Act and Economic Opportunity Act,[238] it was adopting a new loyalty requirement in the Medicare Act,[239] and the Office of Economic Opportunity was adding still another loyalty requirement for antipoverty workers.[240] Similarly, on the state level, organized efforts to gain legislative repeal of oaths have been noticeably unsuccessful.[241]

It is equally clear that the ardent opposition to the oaths will be only slightly mollified, if at all, by the addition to the oaths of such requirements as the member's "specific intent" to support the organization's illegal objectives. In the past that opposition has gone primarily to the basic concept of the loyalty oath, rather than to the specific standards employed in the oaths.[242] Resentment of individuals at being singled out as government employees or teachers to swear to such oaths will remain.[243] As for those employees whose associations might have been determined in part by the fear of a possible prosecution or loss of job, the addition of the elements of "specific intent" and "active membership" is unlikely to provide great comfort—especially when the Court itself warns that both prosecutors and juries are only "human" and may therefore have a

---

[237] Cf. Cramp v. Board of Public Instruction, 137 So. 2d 828 (Fla. 1962).

[238] 76 Stat. 1070 (1962); 79 Stat. 973 (1961). See N.Y. Times, Oct. 12, 1962, p. 13, col. 3; N.Y. Times, Oct. 18, 1962, p. 1, col. 2.

[239] 79 Stat. 333, 42 U.S.C. § 427 (note). See note 160 supra. This requirement has been implemented by the use of an oath.

[240] ACLU, Feature Press Service Bulletin, § 2265, May 9, 1966.

[241] See note 4 supra.

[242] See Byse, A Report on the Pennsylvania Loyalty Act, 101 U. PA. L. REV. 480, 486 (1953).

[243] See N.Y. Times, March 11, 1966, p. 9, cols. 3, 4.

tendency to "label as Communist [any] ideas which they oppose."[244]

In light of these facts, it is not surprising that current legal attacks against loyalty oaths frequently are concentrated not on standards used in the oaths, but on the alleged invalidity of any and all loyalty oaths, no matter what standards they employ.[245] The main argument being advanced is that, assuming the state may utilize some form of loyalty test based upon certain classes of speech and association to serve the legitimate interests of protecting internal security and insuring employee reliability, the loyalty oath is invalid because it is a totally inappropriate means of serving those interests. Thus, the petitioner in *Elfbrandt* based his argument in part on the alleged ineffectiveness of loyalty oaths in keeping undesirable persons out of government employment.[246] In support of this position, petitioner cited several commentators who have noted that oaths have been most ineffective in disclosing potential subversives.[247] The only employees who have objected to newly imposed oaths have been those with conscientious objections to the oath. On the other hand, "the really dangerous 'Reds,' the unidentified plotters, are unlikely to stickle at taking the oaths."[248] Mr. Justice Douglas took a similar extrajudicial view of the loyalty oath.[249] And the *Elfbrandt* opinion quotes an Arizona legislative report that notes the ineffectiveness of oaths against "the Communist trained in fraud and perjury."[250] The report appears to have been used to make another point,[251] however, and it seems unlikely that the Court as a whole would be willing to base its judgment in any large degree upon the alleged ineffectiveness of the

---

244 384 U.S. at 16–17. See also Adler v. Board of Education, 342 U.S. 485, 509 (1952).

245 See note 4 *supra*.   246 Brief for Petitioner, 6, 27–28.

247 *Id*. at 28, citing Horowitz, *supra* note 93; Byse, *supra* note 242; Elson, *People, Government and Security*, 51 Nw. U. L. Rev. 83 (1956); O'Brian, *New Encroachments on Individual Freedom*, 66 Harv. L. Rev. 1 (1952).

248 Gellhorn, *op. cit. supra* note 223, at 367–68, quoted in Byse, *supra* note 242, at 485.

249 Douglas, *op. cit., supra* note 89, at 135–36.

250 384 U.S. at 18, quoting from the report of the Arizona Judiciary Committee, Journal of the Senate, 1st Reg. Sess., 25th Legislature of Arizona 424 (1961).

251 The remainder of the quotation dealt with the impact of the oath upon public employees generally, and the report was cited to emphasize Mr. Justice Douglas' argument on that point. See 384 U.S. at 17–18.

oaths. Since the effectiveness of the oaths depends in large degree upon the fear of a possible prosecution for false swearing,[252] any attempt to evaluate its operation is necessarily speculative. Individuals who openly refuse to take the oath afford no basis for judgment.[253] The active member of an organization who might potentially misuse his office or even engage in subversion to assist the organization is not likely to announce that he is leaving government employment because he fears a possible criminal prosecution for false swearing. In the end, the effectiveness of the loyalty oath in forcing such persons out of government remains in large part a matter of conjecture.[254]

A more substantial argument supporting the rejection of all oaths could be based on the rationale of *Aptheker* and *Elfbrandt*, that the oath constitutes an unnecessarily restrictive means of accomplishing the state's objectives. First, it might be argued that the only legitimate objective of a loyalty oath is the exclusion of persons who might engage in undesirable conduct as an employee. This would require that the Court expand upon the theme of *Speiser* and find that the denial of employment for reasons unrelated to the employee's prospective performance in office constitutes punishment and cannot be imposed without the procedural guarantees afforded by the Sixth Amendment.[255] With this point established, it could be argued that the loyalty oath constituted an unnecessarily broad and rigid means of judging the employee's potential performance. The determination that an individual is likely to misuse his public position in order to aid a subversive organization or to engage in subversion cannot rest on the automatic application of any set criterion. Several factors, it could be argued, must be considered, and each is a variable that must be viewed in the light of the others. Even, for example, the individual's commitment to

---

[252] A substantial number of prosecutions for false swearing were brought on the basis of the Taft-Hartley loyalty oath sustained in American Communications Ass'n v. Douds, 339 U.S. 382 (1950). See 1 EMERSON & HABER, POLITICAL AND CIVIL RIGHTS IN THE UNITED STATES 472 (1954). At least one criminal prosecution relating back to the Taft-Hartley oath is still pending. See Dennis v. United States, 384 U.S. 855 (1966).

[253] On the other hand, it is relevant in determining the impact of the restriction on the free exercise of the right of association. See Byse, *supra* note 242, at 484–85.

[254] See BROWN, *op. cit. supra* note 5, at 94–95.

[255] See text at notes 138–52 *supra*.

the illegal goals of an organization and his active membership in the organization cannot be treated as sufficient. The state must also examine the nature of the position involved, the employee's past attitude toward his work, and the nature of the "subversive" organization to which he belongs. All of these are factors that must be considered and weighed on an individual basis. The oath is not sufficiently flexible to permit this and, as a result, may easily exclude a person who, upon consideration of all the relevant factors, would be found not to present a potential for either direct subversion or misuse of office. Accordingly, the argument would conclude, the loyalty oath constitutes a means of achieving a legitimate state end that "broadly stifle[s] fundamental personal rights when the end can be more narrowly achieved."[256]

Support for this argument could come from both *Aptheker* and *Elfbrandt* in so far as both cases suggest that multiple factors must be considered in administrating an employment standard related to speech or association. *Aptheker* also lends some support for the position that these factors cannot be weighted automatically by a loyalty oath. In striking down a statutory prohibition against the issuance of passports to members of "communist organizations," the Court in *Aptheker* specifically pointed to the Federal Employee Loyalty program as an analogous illustration of a "less drastic" means of achieving the congressional purpose of safeguarding national security.[257] The same federal program illustrates that here also the state's interests "can be adequately protected by means which, when compared with [the loyalty oath] are more discriminately tailored to the constitutional liberties of the individual."[258]

Although this position may indeed find a fair degree of support in *Aptheker* and *Elfbrandt*, its acceptance by the Court would be most unfortunate. It would ignore the fact that the rule prohibiting a state from using means that "broadly stifle fundamental rights when the end can be more narrowly achieved" represents a judicial, not a legislative, standard, and it is to be applied within the limits of the judicial function in reviewing legislation. As noted by Mr. Justice Frankfurter:[259]

---

[256] Shelton v. Tucker, 362 U.S. 479, 488 (1961).

[257] 358 U.S. at 512–14.

[258] *Id.* at 514.

[259] 364 U.S. at 493–94.

The consideration of feasible alternative modes of regulation
... [does] not imply that the Court might substitute its own
choice among alternatives for that of a state legislature or that
the states ... [are] to be restricted to the narrowest workable
means of accomplishing an end. ... The issue remains whether,
in light of the particular kind of restriction upon individual
liberty which a regulation entails, it is reasonable for a legislature to choose that form of regulation rather than others less
restrictive. To that determination, the range of judgments easily open to a legislature in considering the relative degrees of
efficiency of alternative means in achieving the end it seeks is
pertinent.

The argument for total rejection of loyalty oaths simply fails to
give weight to these pertinent factors. To suggest that the loyalty
oath is unconstitutional because a loyalty program will provide less
rigid standards and, therefore, will reach more appropriate results
in an individual case is to ignore all considerations of cost, of administrative ease,[260] and perhaps even of the over-all impact on society in its exercise of associational rights. For one can easily argue
that a loyalty program has a far greater restrictive impact on
speech than does the loyalty oath. Admittedly, the program offers
the individual a chance to explain his position, and therefore should
produce a decision in which the individual would have more confidence. But loyalty programs also permit broad-ranging investiga-
tions of an individual's beliefs and background, involve considerably
more delay and expense to the individual, and offer far greater
opportunity for serious injury to his reputation.[261] In any event,
irrespective of which type of regulation in fact constitutes a more
serious deterrent to the exercise of individual rights, this hardly
seems to be the type of judgment that the Court can adequately or
appropriately make.

The relative merits or demerits of the loyalty oath and loyalty
program point up the practical limits of a decision that would go
so far as to find all loyalty oaths invalid. As noted, the public concern over security and loyalty matters still runs strong. The rejec-

260 The costs of administration here are obviously far more substantial than in
Shelton. See KALVEN, THE NEGRO AND THE FIRST AMENDMENT 103–05 (1965). See also
Karst, *supra* note 125, at 15–18; BICKEL, THE LEAST DANGEROUS BRANCH 113–17
(1962).

261 See Adler v. Board of Education, 342 U.S. 485, 508 (1952) (dissenting
opinion); Vitarelli v. Seaton, 359 U.S. 535, 540–45 (1959); BROWN, *op. cit. supra*
note 5, at 21–61, 183–201, 235–83. But see Green, *Q-Clearance: The Development
of a Personnel Security Program*, 20 BULL. ATOMIC SCIENTISTS 9 (1964).

tion of loyalty oaths might only produce a new series of loyalty programs. The Court has directly considered the constitutionality of a loyalty program only in *Adler*,[262] and even then it
scrutinized only a part of the program. Nevertheless, the nature of
the response by both majority and dissent to earlier cases involving
the federal program indicates that with appropriate procedure and
labels an administrative loyalty program limited in application to
special groups of employees will be sustained.[263] Admittedly, administrative programs cost more to administer than loyalty oaths and
consequently will not be used as extensively.[264] Yet it seems likely
also that loyalty programs will be used in connection with those
positions, such as public school teachers, where the programs can
do the greatest damage to the spirit of free inquiry. In the end,
looking to the impact on free association throughout the society,
one must wonder which is the lesser evil. It must be recognized,
however, that the loyalty oath and loyalty program can be, and
sometimes are, cumulative and not alternative devices. In this light,
a prohibition against oaths might well appeal to the Court as affording some diminution of the total restriction that may be imposed
upon speech by loyalty measures.

IX. CONCLUSION: THE ELFBRANDT OPINION

At last, a few comments should be made concerning the
Elfbrandt opinion, not as it reflects upon the future of loyalty
oaths, but simply as it reflects on the art of opinion writing as practiced in the Supreme Court. If one were asked to pick that opinion
in the 1966 Term that best lends support to the recent criticism
of the Court's opinions,[265] there is no doubt that *Elfbrandt* would

---

[262] Adler v. Board of Education, 342 U.S. 485 (1952).

[263] See Greene v. McElroy, 360 U.S. 474 (1959); Vitarelli v. Seaton, 359 U.S. 539
(1959); Peters v. Hobby, 349 U.S. 331 (1955). While Justices Black and Douglas have
not hesitated in other cases to go beyond the procedural issue presented and find the
entire state or federal program invalid, see, *e.g.*, Carlson v. Landon, 342 U.S. 524,
568 (1952); Lerner v. Casey, 357 U.S. 468, 512 (1958), they have not suggested here
that the entire federal program is invalid. Mr. Justice Brennan and the Chief Justice
clearly have been willing to assume that a program would be valid provided the
proper procedures were followed and employees were not categorized as disloyal.
See Beilan v. Board of Education, 357 U.S. 399, 417, 422 (1958).

[264] The New York experience shows, however, that they are hardly so expensive
as to be out of the state's reach. See also Horowitz, *supra* note 93.

[265] See Shapiro, *supra* note 47, at 591 (collecting sources); Kurland, *supra* note 68,
at 144–45.

rank at least among the quarter finalists. Certainly this is an opinion that ignores past precedent, that fails to define carefully the interests involved in the case, and that fails even to attempt to rebut the arguments of its opponents. Perhaps these features are a product of compromise among five Justices who could not agree, for example, on just how *Garner* should be handled and therefore decided that the best treatment was silence. Yet it seems likely from comparison with other opinions that *Elfbrandt* was less the product of compromise than the product of Mr. Justice Douglas' general approach to the writing of opinions. That approach, a reflection of what has been described as Mr. Justice "Douglas's relentless effort to simplify our understanding of the world,"[266] is rather nicely analyzed by Yosal Rogat as follows:[267]

> As presented by Justice Douglas, not a single case is hard enough to perplex a right thinking man; a case does not present a tangle of competing principles, but a single transcendent principle—for instance, free speech or religious freedom—which need only be identified for the solution to be plain. In this way, he avoids the task, so basic to legal analysis, of reconciling competing principles. Instead, he substitutes simple labels and lines. . . .

Obviously opinions of this type will hardly qualify Mr. Justice Douglas for membership in Holmes's Society of Jobbists,[268] a position to which Mr. Justice Douglas undoubtedly does not aspire.[269] Still, opinions like *Elfbrandt* seemingly also would leave a good deal to be desired for those who, like Mr. Justice Douglas, are interested in "results," not craftsmanship. Opinions that fail to resolve the competing issues, that ignore precedent and speak in generalities, are also opinions that are easy to distinguish. They provide stepping stones for moving backward or sideward as well as forward. Such opinions constitute "the law" for only so long as their author has the ready votes. To some degree this is always true, but Mr. Justice Douglas to the contrary notwithstanding, the weight of precedent does have a significant effect even in the area of constitutional law. To have such effect, however, an opinion should at least explore fully the issues before the Court and clearly and carefully resolve them.

---

266 Rogat, *supra* note 68, at p. 5, col. 1.

267 *Id*. at p. 6, col. 2.   268 Kurland, *supra* note 68, at 144–45.

269 *Cf*. Brennan, *Charles Fahy*, 54 Geo. L. J. 1, 2 (1965).

ALFRED KAMIN

THE UNION AS LITIGANT: PER-SONALITY, PRE-EMPTION, AND PROPAGANDA

The Supreme Court, during the 1965 Term, was again called on to examine the legal notions that are uncomfortably described by the phrase, "exclusive primary jurisdiction of the National Labor Relations Board," or the equally unhelpful word, "pre-emption." The pre-emption issue involves "the potential conflict of two law-enforcing authorities, with the disharmonies inherent in two systems, one federal the other state, of inconsistent standards of substantive law and differing remedial schemes."[1] Parties to litigation of this nature, however, are more concerned with the immediate problems in their mundane conflict than with the elucidation of the niceties of dividing power in a federal system. Pre-emption of state regulation often establishes a practical immunity for the union whose behavior is protected or prohibited by the National Labor Relations Act. Although the considerations advanced by counsel and the Court deal with the question who should regulate labor relations, the real issue, in many instances, is whether certain labor activities should be regulated at all.

Alfred Kamin is Professor of Law, Loyola University (Chicago).

[1] San Diego Bldg. Trades Council v. Garmon, 359 U.S. 236, 242 (1959).

I. The Labor Union as a Corporation: Steelworkers v. Bouligny

The case of *Steelworkers v. R. H. Bouligny, Inc.*[2] offers a helpful introduction to the problem of union immunity. Bouligny, a North Carolina corporation, sued the United Steelworkers of America, "an unincorporated association," in a North Carolina county court, sitting at Charlotte,[3] for writing, publishing, and delivering to many persons in Charlotte, particularly to employees of the plaintiff, certain pamphlets and circulars alleged to contain false and defamatory statements about the plaintiff. Bouligny sought actual damages of $100,000 and punitive damages of an equal amount.

North Carolina, under a 1955 statute, permits suits by or against an unincorporated association in its common name.[4] After service was obtained upon the union in North Carolina, the union removed the action to the United States district court at Charlotte. The union's removal petition asserted the existence of diversity jurisdiction on the ground that it was a citizen of Pennsylvania, where the United Steelworkers of America had its principal headquarters.[5]

The plaintiff moved to remand, claiming that diversity of citizenship was lacking because the defendant was an unincorporated association that had members who were citizens of North Carolina, domiciled and residing therein.[6] The district court, finding that the union was a juridical person of Pennsylvania "citizenship" as fully and completely as if it were organized as a corporation, refused to remand.[7] The trial judge recognized that the overwhelming weight

---

[2] 382 U.S. 145 (1965).   [3] Record, pp. 1–3.

[4] "All unincorporated associations, organizations or societies, foreign or domestic, whether organized for profit or not, may hereafter sue or be sued under the name by which they are commonly known and called, or under which they are doing business, to the same extent as any other legal entity established by law and without naming any of the individual members composing it. Any judgments and executions against any such association, organization or society shall bind its real and personal property in like manner as if it were incorporated. This section shall not apply to partnerships or co-partnerships which are organized to engage in any business, trade or profession." N.C. Gen. Stats. ch. 545, § 1-69.1 (Supp. 1965). For a discussion of the difficulties encountered in suits against unions in North Carolina prior to the quoted statute, see Youngblood v. Bright, 243 N.C. 599 (1956).

[5] Record, pp. 4–5.

[6] *Id.* at 6.   [7] L.R.R.M. 2574 (1963).

of precedent was to the contrary, but he was impressed by treatises urging the absence of any good reason for treating an unincorporated national union differently from a corporation.

The court of appeals reversed[8] on the authority of *Chapman v. Barney*,[9] which had held that for diversity purposes the citizenship of an unincorporated association is determined by the actual citizenship of each of its members.

The case involved a practical problem candidly posed to the Supreme Court by counsel for the union. The federal forum was desired because it would be more receptive to the union's contention that such libel suits are pre-empted by the National Labor Relations Act.[10] This argument involved abandonment of a more venerable theory for union immunity—the proposition that a union is not a suable legal entity.

II. BACKGROUND OF BOULIGNY

The forms available in American law for early labor organizations were limited by what Cardozo called "the tyranny of concepts."[11] A labor union could operate either as an aggregation of individuals, barely tolerated as an exception to the criminal law of conspiracy, or as a legal unit with legislative authority to function as a duly chartered corporation.[12]

---

[8] 336 F.2d 160 (4th Cir. 1964).

[9] 129 U.S. 677 (1889).   [10] 382 U.S. at 147 n. 2.

[11] PARADOXES OF LEGAL SCIENCE 61 (1928). Cf. "A fertile source of perversion in constitutional theory is the tyranny of labels." Snyder v. Massachusetts, 291 U.S. 97, 114 (1934).

[12] British legal scholars have been more prodigious than their American counterparts in efforts to articulate a workable theory of the law of unincorporated associations. Problems arising from the corporate concept fascinated Maitland. Fisher, *Maitland's Theory of Corporate Personality*, in THE FREDERICK WILLIAM MAITLAND READER 201–02 (1957). Laski dealt with the problem in *The Personality of Associations*, 29 HARV. L. REV. 404 (1916); *The Early History of the Corporation in England*, 30 HARV. L. REV. 561 (1917); see 1 HOLMES-LASKI LETTERS 29 (Howe ed. 1953). LLOYD, THE LAW RELATING TO UNINCORPORATED ASSOCIATIONS (1938), is an excellent treatise. Lloyd has mildly modified his earlier formulations. See *The Law of Associations*, in LAW AND OPINION IN ENGLAND IN THE 20TH CENTURY (Ginsberg ed. 1959). A valuable work has been written by an Australian scholar. FORD, UNINCORPORATED NON-PROFIT ASSOCIATIONS (1959). A comprehensive treatment of the adaptation of the law of unincorporated associations to trade union affairs in the United Kingdom is afforded by GRUNFELD, MODERN TRADE UNION LAW (1966). The most celebrated American writings are: WARREN, CORPORATE ADVANTAGES

In the post–Civil War period, union leaders, including Samuel Gompers, sought legislation to permit union incorporation under state and federal law. They believed that official recognition of the legality of unions by the government of the United States would help persuade employers to recognize unions and deal with them. Federal incorporation was also regarded as an efficient and economical method of avoiding multistate enrollment.[13] For a time American employers successfully thwarted union efforts to secure the privileges of incorporation,[14] but in 1886 a law providing for federal incorporation of trade unions was enacted.[15] At the

WITHOUT INCORPORATION (1929); Dodd, *Dogma and Practice in the Law of Associations*, 42 HARV. L. REV. 977 (1929); Sturges, *Unincorporated Associations as Parties to Actions*, 33 YALE L.J. 383 (1924). For treatment of labor unions as legal entities, see Witmer, *Trade Union Liability: The Problem of the Unincorporated Corporation*, 51 YALE L.J. 40 (1941); Forkosch, *The Legal Status and Suability of Labor Organizations*, 28 TEMP. L.Q. 1 (1954); *Unions as Juridical Persons*, 66 YALE L.J. 712 (1957); HART & WECHSLER, THE FEDERAL COURTS AND THE FEDERAL SYSTEM 965–68 (1953).

[13] 2 COMMONS et al., HISTORY OF LABOUR IN THE UNITED STATES 324–25, 329–30 (1918); PERLMAN, HISTORY OF TRADE UNIONISM IN THE UNITED STATES 112, 152 (1922); SIMONDS & McENNIS, THE STORY OF MANUAL LABOR 644 (1887). Senate Report No. 857, 48th Cong., 1st Sess. (1884), recommended passage of a bill "to legalize the incorporation of national trades unions . . . [because] the labor organizations of the country justly complain of the deprivation of important privileges and facilities in the prosecution of the benevolent and educational and other essential purposes for which they are established, by reason of the existing necessity that their organizations be made under State laws only." For a summary of various Senate hearings on labor problems in 1883–86, see PERLMAN, LABOR UNION THEORIES IN AMERICA 247–64 (1958).

[14] 2 COMMONS, *op. cit. supra* note 13, at 66–67; Patch, *Responsibility of Labor Unions*, 1 EDITORIAL RESEARCH REPORTS (No. 3) 41 (1937); BONNETT, HISTORY OF EMPLOYERS' ASSOCIATIONS IN THE UNITED STATES 104 (1956).

[15] Act of June 29, 1886, ch. 567, 24 Stat. 86. The House Committee on Labor had recommended passage because "the request for the legalizing by incorporation of trades unions comes from the organizations themselves. . . . [W]ith a view of ascertaining the real sentiment of the working people upon this subject, each witness was asked if he favored the legalization of trades unions. But one witness in two hundred gave a negative answer." Reference was made to Gompers, as the chairman of the International Federation of Trades Unions of the United States and Canada who had "strongly urged the passage of the bill in its present shape, regretting that its scope could not be increased." *Incorporation of National Trades Unions*, H.R. Rep. No. 2699, 49th Cong., 1st Sess. (1886). His youthful advocacy of union incorporation must have embarrassed Gompers in his later career. His autobiography omits all references to the incorporation demands of early union action programs. SEVENTY YEARS OF LIFE AND LABOR (1925). Three histories of the American Federation of Labor are similarly silent on the subject of union incor-

founding convention of the American Federation of Labor, held in the same year, the legislation was lauded as a recognition of "the principle of the lawful character of Trade Unions, a principle we have been contending for years."[16] Disappointment was expressed only because "the law is not what was desired, covering only those organisations which have, or may remove their headquarters to the District of Columbia, or any of the Territories of the United States."[17]

One year after passage of the National Trade Union Act, the Interstate Commerce Act was passed[18] and in 1890 the Sherman Act became law.[19] Early experience under both statutes and with state court injunctions made labor leaders fearful of judicial regulation of their affairs.[20] The *Taff Vale* decision in 1901,[21] holding

---

poration. LORWIN, THE AMERICAN FEDERATION OF LABOR: HISTORY, POLICIES AND PROSPECTS (1933); TAFT, THE A.F. OF L. IN THE TIME OF GOMPERS (1957); TAFT, ORGANIZED LABOR IN AMERICAN HISTORY (1964).

[16] Quoted in 1 COMMONS, *op. cit. supra* note 13, at 409–10.

[17] *Ibid.* No labor union was ever incorporated under the federal act. It was repealed in 1932 to thwart fraudulent insurance companies which had registered as unions to avoid state regulation. MAGNUSSON, GOVERNMENT AND UNION-EMPLOYER RELATIONS 22 (1945). Some bona fide unions were incorporated under state laws. See CARSEL, A HISTORY OF THE CHICAGO LADIES' GARMENT WORKERS' UNION 23–24 (1940). For a description of efforts in 1886 of the Illinois State Labor Association, predecessor to the Illinois State Federation of Labor, to secure passage of a state law to permit union incorporation, see BECKNER, A HISTORY OF ILLINOIS LABOR LEGISLATION 21–22 (1929). For a discussion of the subsequent statutory exclusion by Illinois of labor unions from a right to corporate franchise, see People *ex rel.* Padula v. Hughes, 296 Ill. App. 587 (1938).

[18] 24 Stat. 379 (1887).   [19] 26 Stat. 209 (1890).

[20] A labor injunction based upon the Interstate Commerce Act was issued by William Howard Taft in Toledo. A.A. & No. Mich. Ry. v. Pennsylvania Co., 54 Fed. 730 (C.C. N.D. Ohio 1893). See 1 PRINGLE, THE LIFE AND TIMES OF WILLIAM HOWARD TAFT 130–32 (1939). The first labor injunction under the Sherman Act was issued in United States v. Workingmen's Amalgamated Council, 54 Fed. 994 (C.C. E.D. La. 1893), aff'd, 57 Fed. 85 (5th Cir. 1893). See BERMAN, LABOR AND THE SHERMAN ACT 58–60 (1930). Witte states that the first known civil suit against a labor union in the United States was filed in 1834. "There were at least thirty-three damage suits against unions or their members before 1900, including eleven in which the plaintiffs recovered damages." THE GOVERNMENT IN LABOR DISPUTES 139 (1932). See also 3 MILLIS & MONTGOMERY, ORGANIZED LABOR 651–61 (1945).

[21] Taff Vale Ry. v. Amalgamated Soc'y of Ry. Servants [1901] A.C. 426. The Trade Disputes Act, 1906, aimed at undoing *Taff Vale* barred actions against unions for tortious acts, but did not alter the legal status or personality of a registered union. *Taff Vale* is frequently coupled by legal scholars with the first *Coronado*

that registered unions in Britain were suable and their treasuries subject to damage judgments, obliterated any prospect of voluntary incorporation of American labor organizations. The unions began to resist demands for their compulsory incorporation. For while the unincorporated union had legal disabilities, it enjoyed legal immunities which were believed to outweigh the disabilities. Incorporation had become synonymous with regulation.[22]

So thoroughly accepted was the notion that a labor organization was not a legal entity that in the *Danbury Hatters* litigation, which commenced in 1902 and terminated in 1917,[23] civil liability for treble damages under the Sherman Act was not imposed upon the labor organization but only upon individual officers and members

case, discussed in the text accompanying notes 25–34, *infra.* See LLOYD, *op. cit. supra* note 12, at 158–64; WARREN, *op. cit. supra* note 12, at 648–69. A contemporary British labor law scholar even today expresses deep anguish over the *Taff Vale* holding. WEDDERBURN, THE WORKER AND THE LAW 218–23 (1965).

[22] See MITCHELL, ORGANIZED LABOR ch. 26 (1903). For updated, but pre–Taft-Hartley discussions of the subject, see DAUGHERTY, LABOR PROBLEMS IN AMERICAN INDUSTRY 455–56 (1938); HARRIS, AMERICAN LABOR 416–19 (1938); 3 MILLIS & MONTGOMERY, *op. cit. supra* note 20, at 657–61 (1945). Louis D. Brandeis accepted the rigid categorical alternatives that a union must be either a corporation or a legal nonentity. In debate with Gompers in 1902, Brandeis argued: "This practical immunity of the unions from legal liability is deemed by many labor leaders a great advantage. To me it appears to be just the reverse. It tends to make officers and members reckless and lawless, and . . . creates on the part of the employers a bitter antagonism. . . ." *Shall Trade Unions Be Incorporated?* 15 GREEN BAG 11, 13 (1903). See also MASON, BRANDEIS: A FREE MAN'S LIFE 142 (1946). The response of Gompers might be gathered from a report of the AFL convention in the same year: "[W]hen we bear in mind the fact that often judges have deep-seated prejudice against organizations of labor; that the farfetched interpretation in the Taff-Vale case, where an organization of labor in Great Britain was mulcted in damages . . . under the law passed by the British Parliament as a 'concession to labor,' and that the enunciation of judicial principles is mutually interpreted and held by the judiciary of all English-speaking countries, it is not difficult to divine the purpose that the advocates of compulsory incorporation of trade unions have in view. They would mulct or outlaw our unions, the organizations which are the factors in our modern life to work for human progress by natural, rational, peaceable and evolutionary means." AMERICAN FEDERATION OF LABOR, HISTORY ENCYCLOPEDIA REFERENCE BOOK 244 (1919).

A specification of the Colorado Labor Peace Act requiring incorporation of all unions operating in the state was declared unconstitutional. A.F. of L. v. Reilly, 113 Colo. 90 (1944).

[23] See Loewe v. Lawlor, 208 U.S. 274 (1908); Lawlor v. Loewe, 235 U.S. 522 (1915). For a blow-by-blow description of this long-drawn exercise in legal maneuvering, see ROBINSON, SPOTLIGHT ON A UNION ch. 5 (1948).

of the United Hatters of North America who could be located in the federal judicial district in which the action was commenced.[24]

In the first *Coronado* case[25] in 1922, the way was opened for judicial treatment of labor unions as legal entities. The United Mine Workers of America and branch organizations in Arkansas were named as defendants in a proceeding brought under the Sherman Act for damages suffered by certain coal-mining companies through violence in a labor dispute. Special appearances and motions to quash service of summons were filed on behalf of the labor unions on the ground that they were "in law a myth."[26]

The nonentity claim was stressed by Charles Evans Hughes,[27] counsel for the union, in his brief to the Court:[28]

> It is well settled that it must appear that an association, if it is not a corporation, has received by appropriate legislation a legal status so that it, or its members, may be sued in the name of the group. Where, however, an unincorporated association or a group of individuals have not received any such legal status, they are nothing but individuals, however related to each other, and can only be sued as such.

The court of appeals had held that the term "associations" in § 8 of the Sherman Act did not refer only to "an association having a

---

[24] LIEBERMAN, UNIONS BEFORE THE BAR 60 (1960).

[25] United Mine Workers of America v. Coronado Coal Co., 259 U.S. 344 (1922).

[26] Typical of the grounds of the motions to quash were those of the international union: "The United Mine Workers of America is not a corporation, citizen of any state or country, or legal entity, or person; . . . it is in law a myth, being an unincorporated association composed of many persons, who are engaged in laboring as coal miners, and being the name by which such laborers are designated; . . . it can neither sue or be sued, and there is no authority of law for issuing a summons against it, and no authority of law for serving a summons upon it." 1 Record, 87.

[27] The first *Coronado* case was handled by a remarkable array of legal talent. Besides Hughes, two other unsuccessful presidential candidates took part as attorneys. Alton B. Parker, represented the union in the second court of appeals case. 258 Fed. 829 (8th Cir. 1919). John W. Davis was company counsel and appeared on the petition for rehearing. Merlo J. Pusey, biographer of Hughes, on August 21, 1963, answered my inquiry about the existence of papers dealing with his representation of the United Mine Workers of America: "[T]he record was rather meager on this part of his career. I do know, however, from his statements to me when I was working on his biography, that he was very proud of his work for the U.M.W.A. He felt that it gave balance to his legal career, and he was always pleased to represent some people who might be unpopular with the entire country."

[28] Brief for Plaintiffs-in-Error, p. 82.

legal entity by force of law," but included unincorporated labor unions as well.[29] Hughes addressed himself to this question:[30]

> It is at once apparent that Congress did not attempt to provide a new remedy against all unincorporated groups or associations. Congress provided no designation of officers or agents upon whom process might be served. It made no provision as to the effect of the judgment to be recovered, or limiting execution thereon to common property or property jointly held through the group or association. If it was the intent of Congress to provide that any unincorporated group, association or labor union could be sued in its name, Congress undoubtedly would have said so and would have provided the rules of procedure for a practice of such scope.

Hughes also sought comfort in the knowledge that in the *Danbury Hatters* case the suit was brought only against individuals.[31]

The Court, through Chief Justice Taft, held that unincorporated organizations such as labor unions could be sued, *eo nomine*, in the federal courts in civil actions under the Sherman Act,[32] and

---

[29] Dowd v. United Mine Workers of America, 235 Fed. 1 (8th Cir. 1916).

[30] *Supra* note 28, at 83. Hughes may have remembered this argument when the Federal Rules of Civil Procedure were drafted during his service as Chief Justice. Rule 17(b) seems the belated answer. See note 34 *infra*.

[31] *Supra* note 28, at 91: "The present case, as an endeavor to reach the association by a suit against it in its name, instead of proceeding against alleged offending members as in *Loewe v. Lawlor*, has no precedent whatever."

[32] The opinion of the Chief Justice confounded and meandered. The UMWA had a large membership, great unity of action, and union government power was centralized. 259 U.S. at 383–85. Embezzlement of union funds was a crime under state laws. *Id.* at 386. The union label, a form of trade-mark, was given legal protection. *Ibid.* Modern equitable procedure had recognized the representative suit. *Id.* at 387. "It would be unfortunate" if a great union "could assemble its assets for economic action, yet be free from liability for injuries caused by such action." *Id.* at 388–89. A suit against each of 400,000 persons would leave a plaintiff "remediless." *Id.* at 389. The *Taff Vale* decision was predicated upon a registration statute of England which "did not create" unions but merely "recognized their existence and regulated them in certain ways." *Id.* at 390. Many federal statutes, including the federal incorporation act, recognized the legality of unions. *Id.* at 391. "In this state of federal legislation . . . [unions] are suable." *Ibid.* Moreover, the term "associations" in §§ 7 and 8 of the Sherman Act included unincorporated labor unions. *Id.* at 392. And in any event the whole problem is in essence a procedural matter. *Id.* at 390.

The controversy between Professors Warren and Dodd, *supra* note 12, was typical of the disputation in the profession over the meaning of *Coronado*. *Compare* also FORD, *op. cit. supra* note 12, at 109–10, *with* LLOYD, *op. cit. supra* note 12, at 161–63.

Was *Coronado* merely a holding that a union was an "association" within the

that "funds accumulated to be expended in conducting strikes are subject to execution in suits for torts committed by such unions in strikes."[33]

In 1938, the *Coronado* principle was incorporated into Rule 17(b) of the Federal Rules of Civil Procedure so that an unincorporated association lacking legal capacity under applicable state law could sue or be sued in its common name in a federal court "for the purpose of enforcing for or against it a substantive right existing under the Constitution or laws of the United States."[34]

The status of unincorporated labor unions, as litigants in federal courts, was next briefly considered by the Court in *Hague v. C.I.O.*[35] Unincorporated unions and the American Civil Liberties Union, a membership corporation, and individual citizens had obtained an injunction against suppression of meetings in streets and parts of Jersey City. The Court observed that "natural persons, and they alone, are entitled to the privileges and immunities which § 1 of the Fourteenth Amendment secures for 'citizens of the United States.' Only the individual respondents may, therefore, maintain this suit."[36]

United States v. White[37] illustrates the continuing difficulty encountered by the Court in the formulation of a theory about the legal entity of labor unions. A union official was charged with contempt for refusal to produce union books and records in re-

---

meaning of the Sherman Act? Or was it a declaration that a union was a legal entity for other purposes in federal courts? Justice Sanford, about two years after *Coronado*, described it as a holding "in which unincorporated labor unions were held to be 'associations' within the meaning of the Anti-Trust Law." Hecht v. Malley, 265 U.S. 144, 157 (1924).

[33] 259 U.S. at 391. Gompers paid his compliments to the Court: "This decision means that big business has won its objective in its long campaign for trade-union incorporation." Quoted in WITTE, *op. cit. supra* note 20, at 137.

[34] In hearings before the House Committee on the Judiciary, March 2, 1938, on the final phases of introduction of the federal Rules of Civil Procedure, testimony was given by Joseph A. Padway, AFL General Counsel, Merle D. Vincent, ILGWU attorney, and Lee Pressman, CIO General Counsel. Padway was mildly in favor of the adoption of Rule 17(b), but Vincent and Pressman fudged their positions. All three labor lawyers were opposed to Rule 4(c)(3) describing *inter alia* how service of process on unincorporated associations should be made. Hearings before the House Committee on the Judiciary, 75th Cong., 3d Sess., ser. 17 (1938). Excerpts from Padway's statement appear in Busby v. Electric Utils. Employees Union, 147 F.2d 865 (D.C. Cir. 1945).

[35] 307 U.S. 496 (1939).   [36] *Id.* at 514.   [37] 322 U.S. 694 (1944).

sponse to a grand jury subpoena. He claimed, on behalf of the union, its officers, and members, and on his own behalf, the immunity granted under the Fourth and Fifth Amendments. The court of appeals held that if the defendant was a member of the union he could avail himself of the privilege against self-incrimination if the documents tended to incriminate him. The Government's claim that a union could be analogized to a corporation was found unpersuasive. "A corporation is a creature of the state legislature. . . . The present-day status of [the union] is quite different. It does not derive its existence from any charter granted by the state."[38]

The Supreme Court disagreed, and held, in an opinion by Justice Murphy, that the privilege against self-incrimination could not be invoked on behalf of the labor union because it was so impersonal an organization that it could not be said to embrace the purely private or personal interests of its constitutents, but only their common or group interests:[39]

> Structurally and functionally, a labor union is an institution which involves more than the private or personal interests of its members. It represents organized, institutional activity as contrasted with wholly individual activity. This difference is as well defined as that existing between individual members of the union. The union's existence in fact, and for some purposes in law, is as perpetual as that of any corporation, not being dependent upon the life of any member. . . .
> Both common law rules and legislative enactments have granted many substantive rights to labor unions as separate functioning institutions.

After illustrating the applicability of the first *Coronado* case, and detailing the many state and federal statutes upon which Chief Justice Taft relied to establish suability of the Mine Workers Union, Justice Murphy continued:[40]

> Even greater substantive rights have been granted labor unions by federal and state legislation subsequent to the statutes enumerated in the opinion in [the *Coronado*] case.
> Outstanding examples of federal legislation enacted subsequent to the *Coronado* case giving recognition to union personality are the National Labor Relations Act . . . the Railway

---

[38] 137 F.2d 24, 26 (3d Cir. 1943).   [39] 322 U.S. at 701–03.

[40] *Id.* at 703, and n. 5. *Cf.* dissent of Judge Sparks in the *Pullman Standard* case, *infra* note 47.

Labor Act . . . the Norris-LaGuardia Act. . . . The Anti-Racketeering Act . . . excepts certain types of activity by labor unions, thereby recognizing them as entities capable of violating the Act. The War Labor Disputes Act evidences a similar recognition.

The first formal requirement for annual registration of trade unions was imposed by the Revenue Act of 1943. Annual filing of financial information by labor unions was made a condition of continued exemption from federal income taxes.[41]

The process of treating labor unions as entities in federal courts was further extended in § 301 of the Labor-Management Relations Act.[42] In the Labor-Management Reporting and Disclosure Act of 1959, Congress continued to define the legal personality of labor unions.[43] Every labor union must register and file annual financial reports with the Secretary of Labor.[44] Union relationships with members are regulated. An elaborate code for union fiscal affairs must be followed. Fiduciary standards are imposed upon union officers. Derivative actions to recover misused or converted funds may be brought by members against union officers.[45]

Enactments in many states authorize actions by or against a labor organization in its common name.[46] Despite the trend toward establishing a capacity to sue or be sued in federal law and in state enactments, in states where the common law of nonentity still prevails, unions seek immunity from suit by the same kinds of procedures and arguments that were attempted in the trial court in the first *Coronado* case. Where federal court jurisdiction is predicated upon

---

[41] 26 U.S.C. § 6033.

[42] 61 Stat. 136 (1947).   [44] 29 U.S.C. § 431 (1964).

[43] 73 Stat. 519 (1959).   [45] 29 U.S.C. §§ 411, 501–03 (1964).

[46] See Forkosch, *supra* note 12; the Labor Relations Expediter, LRX 139 (1966). But suability of labor unions pursuant to statute does not necessarily abrogate the common-law notion that vicarious liability may not be imposed upon an unincorporated association unless all of its members are individually liable for the wrong giving rise to the action. Illustrative is Martin v. Curran, 303 N.Y. 276 (1951), a libel action against union officers in their representative capacities. "[T]he Legislature has limited such suits against association officers, whether for breaches of agreement or for tortious wrongs, to cases where the individual liability of every single member can be alleged and proven. Despite procedural changes, substantive liability in such cases is still, as it was at common law, 'that of the members severally' . . . : 'In the kind of association now under consideration, only those members are liable who expressly or impliedly with full knowledge authorize or ratify the specific acts in question.'" 303 N.Y. at 282.

diversity grounds only, union defendants seek dismissal because unions are not juridical entities under the common-law rule of the state in which the federal district court functions.[47] The *Bouligny* case must be considered against the background of stratagems utilized by labor organizations. When it is to the advantage of the union litigant to claim that it is an entity possessed of quasi-corporate status, it will do so. But when a practical immunity can be derived from application of the ancient notion of the nonentity of unincorporated associations, that theory will be invoked. The same union, through the same lawyers, will play one tune or the other as the occasion requires.[48]

---

[47] Pullman Standard Car Mfg. Co. v. Local 2928, United Steelworkers of America, 152 F.2d 493 (7th Cir. 1945), was a diversity case for alleged libel in a union newspaper. Following Busby v. Electrical Utils. Employees Union, 323 U.S. 72 (1945), the majority applied local law and concluded that decisions of the Illinois Appellate Court barred tort actions against unincorporated labor unions because of their lack of legal entity. The dissenting judge would have read the Illinois cases to allow such actions and also urged that such treatment was demanded by the Wagner Act. "If this be not true then Congress is placed in the unenviable attitude of authorizing a non-entity to carry out the provisions of the Act. . . ." 152 F.2d at 498. In 1966, in *Bouligny*, Steelworkers' counsel used the dissenter's rationale. See text at notes 49–52, *infra*. Cf. Judge Wyzanski: "In this United States District Court, sitting in a matter in which it is alleged that there is diversity jurisdiction, the law of Massachusetts is controlling in determining the capacity of the parties and their suability at law. It is settled by a line of cases . . . that in Massachusetts a labor union is not a corporate entity, may not be sued as a person, and may not be subjected to any decree." Worthington Pump & Machinery Corp. v. United Electrical Radio & Machine Workers, 63 F. Supp. 411, 413 (D. Mass. 1945).

[48] See Fahy, *The Union in Court*, 37 ILL. B.J. 203 (1949). In Price v. Mine Workers, 336 F.2d 771 (6th Cir. 1964), *cert. denied*, 380 U.S. 913 (1965), the union sought to abate federal pendent jurisdiction because "a voluntary unincorporated labor organization may not be amenable to process in its common name in Kentucky." 336 F.2d at 775. In Illinois State Bar Ass'n v. United Mine Workers of America, No. 39642, Supreme Court of Illinois, March Term 1966, *pending on rehearing*, but unofficially reported in full, 54 ILL. B.J. 922 (1966), the trial court had enjoined the union from engaging in unauthorized practice of law. The amicus brief of the Illinois State Federation of Labor and Congress of Industrial Organizations asserted, that as a voluntary, unincorporated association, District 12 does "not constitute a legal entity separate and apart from the members who compose the association." But in May, 1966, the labor press hailed the opinion of the general counsel of the Equal Employment Opportunity Commission, 34 U.S.L. WEEK 2640, that a labor union is a "person aggrieved," entitled to institute a Commission proceeding on its own behalf charging racial discrimination in a bargaining unit. Auto Workers v. Scofield, 382 U.S. 205 (1965), permitting a union to intervene as a party in NLRB enforcement and review proceedings in a court of appeals, was similarly praised in the union press. For a comment on the irony that twentieth-century unions

III. The Bouligny Decision

In determining whether to apply for certiorari in *Bouligny*, union counsel had to consider the consequences to their client and other unions, if they should succeed in the Supreme Court. While a victory would permit removal to federal courts of cases not otherwise removable on federal question grounds, it would also permit unions to be sued in federal courts, on the basis of diversity, in states where unions might prefer to be heard in a state court. Indeed, a broad essay by the Supreme Court on juridical theories of labor organizations might destroy existing benefits of practical immunity obtained in many state courts, and in some diversity cases in federal courts, through assertion of nonentity arguments. Union counsel apparently concluded that more was to be gained by the labor movement than lost, should the Supreme Court be persuaded to reverse.

The union attorneys argued that in the first half of the twentieth century the labor union had undergone a legal transformation as dramatic as that of the corporation a century earlier. "By statute and by judicial reformation of the common law, the union has emerged with a legal personality as complete as the corporation's. . . ."[49] *Coronado, White,* and observations of the NLRB and Justice Frankfurter were cited as establishing the legal personality of the union separate and apart from its members.[50] The Labor-Management

---

should rely upon their illegality at early common law as a defense to actions brought against them, see GRODIN, UNION GOVERNMENT AND THE LAW 13 (1961).

Trade-union desire for the immunities of nonentity are not confined to Anglo-American organizations. "With the abolition of the Fascist corporative regime, which took place in November 1944, trade unions, which prior to this time had the status of a public agency, re-acquired the legal status of 'non-recognized' or '*de facto*' private associations which they had possessed before the advent of Fascism. This happened in spite of several attempts to introduce particular forms of registration and recognition." Giugni, *The Legal Status of Collective Bargaining in Italy,* in LABOUR RELATIONS AND THE LAW 92 (Kahn-Freund ed. 1965). But see Savatier, *Internal Relations between Unions and Their Members: French Report,* 18 RUTGERS L. REV. 375 (1964): "Regularly constituted trade unions [in France] possess civil personality and may thus own property and bring actions at law. . . . [T]his legal status is of advantage not only to unions composed of individuals but also to federations composed of unions."

[49] Brief for Petitioner, p. 33.

[50] *Id.* at 34–36. The NLRB reference was International Longshoremen's Union, 79 N.L.R.B. 1487, 1508 n. 40 (1948). Justice Frankfurter's comment was that: "the

Relations Act of 1947, and the Labor-Management Reporting and Disclosure Act of 1959 were cited as extensive catalogues of rights and duties which made legal entities of labor unions. Analogies were drawn between the obligations and duties of union officers imposed by these federal statutes and similar responsibilities of corporate officers.[51] Indeed, urged the union, in two respects a union has a life distinct from its members that exceeds the separation of the corporation from its shareholders: first, a union may have involuntary members under union shop contracts; second, the union is required by law to represent members and non-members alike. "What better evidence that the labor union has a personality distinct from its members than that it may have members who would prefer not to belong, and that it must represent persons who do not belong?"[52]

The union argued less convincingly on the ultimate issue about which the Court had to be persuaded. The plaintiff employer who claimed to have been libeled could not argue that the union lacked legal personality. It was suing the international union as a legal entity. Its process was directed at the international union, and the relief it sought was a money judgment, payable out of the general treasury of the international union. For plaintiff's purposes the union's legal personality under North Carolina law was sufficient. With the case precedent heavily in its favor, the plaintiff urged that legal personality and citizenship were not necessarily synonymous. In response, union counsel had to demonstrate that every legal entity, corporate or unincorporate, chartered or unchartered, was a "citizen" under Art. III, § 2 of the Constitution. This was the main thrust of the union's argument and, presumably, what it hoped would be its constructive contribution to American labor law. An attribution of citizenship to the parent labor organization would extend the scope of union methods for maintenance of immunities and exemptions in the American legal system. But in this effort the union failed, even though the Court believed its position to be meritorious:[53]

> [I]t is not good judicial administration, nor is it fair, to remit a labor union or other unincorporated association to vagaries of jurisdiction determined by the citizenship of its members and

law regards a union as a self-contained, legal personality." International Ass'n of Machinists v. Street, 367 U.S. 740, 808 (1961) (dissenting).

[51] Brief for Petitioner, pp. 36–38.   [52] *Id.* at 38.   [53] 382 U.S. at 150.

to disregard the fact that unions and associations may exist and have an identity and a local habitation of their own.

The Court found appealing the union's argument that one of the main reasons for the diversity jurisdiction of the federal courts, the protection of the non-resident defendant from local prejudice, was especially applicable in this day to labor organizations. It was sympathetic to the union's suggestion that diversity jurisdiction should be extended to labor organizations because:[54]

> [It] would make available the advantages of federal procedure, Article III judges less exposed to local pressures than their state court counterparts, juries selected from wider geographical areas, review in appellate courts reflecting a multistate perspective, and more effective review by this Court.

The Court concluded, however, that "pleas for extension of the diversity jurisdiction to hitherto uncovered broad categories of litigants ought to be made to the Congress and not the courts."[55] It recited difficulties encountered by the Court and Congress in handling diversity jurisdiction claims of corporations. The Court described *Marshall v. Baltimore & O. R.R.*[56]—a compromise that endured until 1958—as promulgating a fiction that although a corporation was not itself a citizen for diversity purposes, there would be a conclusive presumption that all of its shareholders were citizens of the state of incorporation.[57]

Finally, the Court asserted that "the doctrinal wall" of *Chapman v. Barney*,[58] upon which the court of appeals had relied, had not been breached by *Puerto Rico v. Russell & Co.*,[59] wherein an unincorporated business society, "an exotic creation of the civil law,"[60] called a *sociedad en comandita*, was held to be a citizen domiciled in Puerto Rico under Puerto Rican law, although its members resided elsewhere. Paying tribute to the intrinsic merits

---

[54] *Ibid.*   [55] *Id.* at 150–51.   [56] 16 How. 314 (1853).

[57] By 72 Stat. 415 (1958), codified in 28 U.S.C. § 1332(c), "a corporation shall be deemed a citizen of any State by which it has been incorporated and of the State where it has its principal place of business."

[58] *Supra* note 9, and accompanying text.   [59] 288 U.S. 476 (1933).

[60] Reference to civil law evokes the conflicting theories of group personality about which British and Continental scholars debate so eloquently. See Maitland, *Introduction*, in GIERKE, POLITICAL THEORIES OF THE MIDDLE AGES (1900); Barker, *Introduction*, in GIERKE, NATURAL LAW AND THE THEORY OF SOCIETY (1934); LLOYD, THE IDEA OF LAW 300–09 (1964); and LLOYD, *op. cit. supra* note 12, at 1–27.

of the union's arguments and acknowledging widespread support for treatment of labor unions as juridical entities, the Court sent it elsewhere for relief.[61]

The Court, no doubt, reached the correct result under the applicable precedents. But congressional clarification merely of the status of a union's citizenship for resolution of problems in diversity jurisdiction would do but a fraction of the job. Needed is a general congressional declaration that labor unions representing employees in industries affecting commerce are federal quasi-corporations, full legal entities for all purposes, without theoretical disabilities or immunities derived from the persistence of ancient and erroneous legal theories.[62] It is high time to stop applying to union organizations legal theories derived from judicial precedents affecting wine clubs, coal clubs, churches, convents, monasteries,

---

[61] 382 U.S. at 153. But in Swift & Co. v. Wickham, 382 U.S. 111 (1965), decided the same day as *Bouligny*, the Court was quite responsive to commentators' criticisms of its *Kesler* doctrine announced only in 1962, and declared that an important procedural principle "should not be kept on the books in the name of stare decisis once it is proved to be unworkable in practice," *id*. at 116, and concluded that a three-judge court was not required where the only challenge to the constitutionality of a state statute was based upon the Supremacy Clause.

[62] Although registered labor unions in the United Kingdom may be parties plaintiff and may be sued for non-immunized conduct under *Taff Vale*, there are unregistered unions which represent many workers. Most employers' associations, which are treated as trade unions under British law, are also unregistered. Obviously they have opted to forgo the slight advantages of registration in favor of procedural immunity. There is a striking analogy between the state of British and American law on the legal personality of labor unions. Registered unions in the United Kingdom are like American unions involved in proceedings governed by *Coronado*, *White*, Rule 17(b) of the Federal Rules of Civil Procedure, and special state laws. Unregistered unions of the United Kingdom are free to utilize the nonentity ploy as are American unions when sued in Illinois, Massachusetts, and other states that still follow the nonentity theory of unincorporated associations, *supra* note 46. This problem is discussed in submissions to the Royal Commission on Trade Unions and Employers' Associations. Professor K. W. Wedderburn, in his Memorandum of Evidence to the Commission, proposes that: "[A] procedural code should be enacted whereby the now outmoded difficulties of the 'representative action' could be swept aside in respect of *all* quasi-corporate bodies. Bodies which own property or funds, employ staff and engage in business transactions should in legal action be represented by the name of the association. In effect, for trade unions, this would mean that procedural difficulties for the unregistered union would be solved at a stroke. . . ." Mimeographed copy of Evidence, at 46–47 (January, 1966).

The complexities of the legal status of American unions will not be solved at a legislative stroke. But neither will they be solved in a single decision of the Court, as *Bouligny* so poignantly discloses.

library societies, joint stock associations, partnerships, and trusts.[63] The Anglo-American dilemma is described by an English scholar:[64]

> Trade unions have been placed by English law in the jurispru-
> dential category of voluntary unincorporated associations.
> However, with their gradual growth and movement to the
> centre of the industrial organisation and economic structure of
> the country, trade unions have begun, at this point and at that,
> to break out of the simple original classification. Today, they
> are associations which are neither purely voluntary nor purely
> unincorporated; although there is as yet little discernible in-
> clination on the part of the courts or Parliament to re-enumer-
> ate the legal entities which English law recognises in order to
> accommodate the peculiarities displayed by trade unions.

IV. Freezing and Thawing on the Great Lakes: Hanna Mining v. Marine Engineers

If *Bouligny* presages an end to the long-lived nonentity fiction, *Hanna Mining Co. v. Marine Engineers Ass'n*[65] suggests a
delimitation on the immunity device of greatest practical significance to unions: the use of the pre-emption doctrine to prolong
picketing that might otherwise be proscribed by state authority.

Declarations of pre-emption in American labor law were slow
in developing. The National Labor Relations Act of 1935 (Wagner Act) dealt with unfair labor practices of employers and with
questions of representation that state law had not regulated. After
passage of the Wagner Act, efforts by states to control one of the
union's principal organizational devices—the peaceful picket line
—were thwarted by an equation of peaceful picketing with constitutionally protected speech.[66] Unqualified constitutional immunity of peaceful picketing from state regulation did not last long.
By the time of the Taft-Hartley debates in the Eightieth Congress
in 1947, the coupling of every variety of peaceful picketing with
constitutionally protected speech had been substantially loosened,
and by 1952 had become practically a dead issue in American

---

[63] See Ford, Unincorporated Non-Profit Associations (1959).

[64] Grunfeld, Modern Trade Union Law 14 (1966).

[65] 382 U.S. 181 (1965).

[66] Thornhill v. Alabama, 310 U.S. 88 (1940); Carlson v. California, 310 U.S. 106 (1940).

labor law.[67] In a thorough overhauling of national labor policy, the Labor-Management Relations Act (Taft-Hartley)[68] extended federal regulation to several types of previously unregulated union activities, including various forms of peaceful picketing.[69]

The Taft-Hartley Act, denounced by trade unionists as a "slave labor act,"[70] was passed over a presidential veto accompanied by a scathing message.[71] Never was political hyperbole so unjustified. The Taft-Hartley Act and the Landrum-Griffin amendments in 1959 nationalized labor relations and displaced state power as thoroughly as any regulatory scheme ever formulated by Congress.[72] Unions cheerfully subordinated their First Amendment arguments and urged the Commerce and Supremacy Clauses to thwart state court regulation of their activities. Building on a few earlier labor pre-emption cases,[73] they soon succeeded in persuading the Court that when non-violent picketing, alleged to violate state law, was either protected or prohibited by the National Labor Relations Act, the labor dispute was within the exclusive primary jurisdiction of the National Labor Relations Board.[74]

---

[67] For cases and materials on the rise and fall of the *Thornhill-Carlson* doctrine, see Kamin, *Residential Picketing and the First Amendment*, 61 Nw. U. L. Rev. 177, 184–97 (1966). For a contrary view, see St. Antoine, *What Makes Secondary Boycotts Secondary?* Proc. Eleventh Ann. Inst. on Labor Law 5 (1965).

[68] *Supra* note 42.

[69] Particularly by new § 8(b), which defined and proscribed union unfair labor practices, 29 U.S.C. § 158(b) (1964), and § 301, 29 U.S.C. § 185 (1964), which transformed labor agreements into federal contracts.

[70] John L. Lewis gave voice to the strongest denunciation: "The Taft-Hartley statute is the first ugly, savage thrust of fascism in America. . . ." Alinsky, John L. Lewis: An Unauthorized Biography 337 (1949).

[71] See 1 N.L.R.B., Legislative History of the Labor Management Relations Act, 1947 915 (1948).

[72] "The nationalization of industrial relations was the single most important consequence of the Taft-Hartley amendments." Cox, Law and the National Labor Policy 18 (1960).

[73] *E.g.*, Hill v. Florida, 325 U.S. 538 (1945); Bethlehem Steel Co. v. New York Labor Rel. Bd., 330 U.S. 767 (1947); see Cox, *Federalism in the Law of Labor Relations*, 67 Harv. L. Rev. 1297 (1954), and Meltzer, *The Supreme Court, Congress and State Jurisdiction of Labor Relations*, 59 Colum. L. Rev. 6, 269 (1959).

[74] Garner v. Teamsters Union, 346 U.S. 485 (1953). The "arguably subject" formulation was made six years later in San Diego Bldg. Trades Council v. Garmon 359 U.S. 236 (1959). *Garner*, however, had declared: "It is not necessary or appropriate for us to surmise how the National Labor Relations Board might have decided

State courts were banned from regulating peaceful picketing, even though it might be true that the federal remedy was "inadequate, as a practical matter, because the slow administrative processes of the National Labor Relations Board could not prevent imminent and irreparable damage."[75] Any exercise of state power to give redress by way of an award of damages for peaceful picketing was also barred. "Even the States' salutary effort to redress private wrongs or grant compensation for past harm cannot be exerted to regulate activities that are potentially subject to the exclusive federal regulatory scheme."[76] When peaceful union "activity is arguably subject to § 7 or § 8 of the Act, the States as well as the federal courts must defer to the exclusive competence of the National Labor Relations Board."[77]

For practical purposes, exclusive NLRB regulation means no immediate control over union conduct. The filing of a charge against a union with a regional office of the NLRB lacks the chastening impact upon the charged party that normally attends the filing of injunctive papers. The NLRB seeks to vindicate enunciated public policy and not private rights.[78] During the investi-

---

this controversy had petitioners presented it to that body. The power and duty of primary decision lies with the Board, not with us." 346 U.S. at 489-90.

State regulation has been pre-empted in labor matters in which picketing was not under challenge. Automobile Workers v. O'Brien, 339 U.S. 454, 45 (1950), held unconstitutional a strike-vote provision of a Michigan statute. "Congress occupied this field and closed it to state regulation." Street, Electric Railway & Motor Coach Employees v. Wisconsin Employment Relations Board, 340 U.S. 383, 394 (1951), declared invalid a Wisconsin statute barring strikes by public utility employees and imposing economic arbitration procedures: "[W]here . . . the state seeks to deny entirely a federally guaranteed right which Congress itself restricted only to a limited extent in case of national emergencies . . . , it is manifest that the state legislation is in conflict with federal law." Teamsters v. Oliver, 358 U.S. 283, 295-96 (1959), blocked an Ohio injunction against enforcement of a clause of a labor agreement found to be violative of state antitrust law. Bargaining on the subject through union representatives was a right of the employees protected by § 7 of the National Labor Relations Act: "To allow the application of the Ohio anti-trust law here would wholly defeat the full realization of the congressional purpose." In the 1966 Term, in Vaca v. Sipes, 384 U.S. 969, the Court will review a holding of the Supreme Court of Missouri that pre-emption does not bar a member's damage action against a union for wrongful failure of its officials to take his discharge grievance to impartial arbitration.

[75] 346 U.S. at 487.   [76] 359 U.S. at 247.   [77] Id. at 245.

[78] Amalgamated Util. Workers v. Consolidated Edison Co., 309 U.S. 261, 265 (1940).

gatory phases of a Board proceeding, the union has no formal adversary. Union counsel can discuss a pending charge with Board agents at a level of reciprocal respect and mutual expertise in an ambience of intellectual dispassion.

The charge matures into an adversarial proceeding only after the regional director of the Board concludes that the investigation of his staff justifies the issuance of a formal complaint.[79] The union activity sought to be halted by the charging party continues while the investigation and the discussions go forward. In the ordinary case involving primary and non-recognitional activity, the union has no practical inducement to terminate its activity until after formal complaint has been issued.[80] In these circumstances the Board may in its discretion seek a temporary injunction from a United States district court to halt the unfair labor practice until a final administrative determination is made and formally enforced.[81] But if no § 10 (j) injunction is sought, the union is legally free to carry on its activity until formal and final judicial enforcement by decree of an adverse Board order.[82]

When charges are made of union misconduct through proscribed secondary activity, seeking or enforcing a "hot cargo" agreement or engaging in unlawful recognition picketing, the Board's regional director is required to give priority to the investigation of the charge, and if he concludes that there is basis for issuance of a complaint he is under a statutory mandate to apply forthwith to a federal district court for injunctive relief in aid of the projected administrative proceeding.[83] But even under the statutory mandate for expeditious handling of such matters, the respondent union has sufficient time to enjoy at least temporary immunity from curtailment of its peaceful, but unlawful, conduct. The official report of the Board shows that a median of eight weeks elapses from filing

---

[79] N.L.R.A. § 10(b), 29 U.S.C. § 160(b) (1964).

[80] The only effective inducement for a union to capitulate at this stage of the proceeding is avoidance of the expense of litigation.

[81] N.L.R.A. § 10(j), 29 U.S.C. § 160(j) (1964). In the fiscal year ending June 30, 1965, 18 proceedings for § 10(j) injunctions were commenced, although 2498 complaints were issued. NLRB, THIRTIETH ANNUAL REPORT 181, 214 (1966).

[82] "No power to enforce an order is conferred upon the Board. To secure enforcement, the Board must apply to a Circuit Court of Appeals for its affirmance." Myers v. Bethlehem Shipbldg. Corp., 303 U.S. 41, 48 (1938).

[83] N.L.R.A., § 10(1), 29 U.S.C. § 160(1) (1964).

of a charge to issuance of a complaint.[84] The objectives of union pressure, peaceful but illegal, are ordinarily won or lost within a few days. No comparable delay would be likely in the issuance of a state court injunction. The exclusive forum of the NLRB is patient and benevolent, and never a tyrannical or arbitrary forum.[85] Labor unions that thrive and grow through picketing bask in the security of the pre-emption doctrine much as employers once did under the doctrine of substantive due process.[86]

From 1953 to the 1965 Term of the Court, union attorneys enjoyed an almost unbroken string of successes in persuading the Court that state courts had acted improperly in taking jurisdiction in labor disputes involving non-violent union activity and in refusing to defer to the exclusive primary jurisdiction of the NLRB.[87] *Hanna*, however, reveals a growing awareness that, in many instances, pre-emption may mean immunity. In an opinion by Mr. Justice Harlan, the Court concluded that union activity designed

---

[84] NLRB, *op. cit. supra* note 81, at 11.

[85] "We are, by statute, essentially custodians of the public interest. You [lawyers] are, by the nature of your calling, entrusted essentially with the protection of the rights of your clients. The difference, however, is not as great as it might appear. Indeed, I believe, there is in the real sense no basic antithesis at all. The interests of your clients, collectively considered, coincide with the public interest." *The Litigant's Role and the Public Interest* 2–3, an address by Arnold Ordman, General Counsel, NLRB, before the Labor Law Section of the State Bar of Wisconsin, February 21, 1964.

[86] *Cf.* McCloskey, *Economic Due Process and the Supreme Court: An Exhumation and Reburial,* [1962] SUPREME COURT REVIEW 34.

[87] Radio & TV Union v. Broadcast Serv., Inc., 380 U.S. 255 (1965); Hattiesburg Bldg. & Trades Council v. Broome, 377 U.S. 126 (1964); Liner v. Jafco, Inc., 375 U.S. 301 (1964); Local 438 Constr. Union v. Curry, 371 U.S. 542 (1963); Marine Engineers Ass'n v. Interlake S.S. Co., 370 U.S. 173 (1962); Plumbers Local 298 v. County of Door, 359 U.S. 354 (1959); Hotel Employees Union v. Sax Enterprises, Inc., 358 U.S. 270 (1959); Local 429 I.B.E.W. v. Farnsworth & Chambers Co., 353 U.S. 968 (1957); and Weber v. Anheuser-Busch, Inc., 348 U.S. 468 (1955).

Recent examples of state court deference in peaceful picketing cases to the exclusive primary jurisdiction of the NLRB are: Baltimore Bldg. and Constr. Trades Council v. Maryland Port Authority, 238 Md. 232 (1965); Colorado Council of Carpenters v. District Court, 155 Colo. 54 (1964); Directors Guild v. Superior Court, 45 Cal. Rptr. 246 (1965); Kitchens v. Doe, 172 So.2d 896 (Fla. Ct. App. 1965); Local 675, Int'l Union of Operating Eng'rs v. Acme Concrete Corp., 168 So.2d 697 (Fla. Ct. App. 1964); Gust G. Larson & Sons, Inc. v. Radio and TV Broadcast Eng'rs Union, 66 Ill. App.2d 146 (1965); Painters Local 567 v. Tom Joyce Floors, Inc., 398 P.2d 245 (Nev. 1965); Trifoam Sleep Products, Inc. v. Local 140, Bedding Workers, 56 L.R.R.M. 2414 (N.Y. Sup. Ct. 1964).

to secure the organization of supervisors,[88] or union recognition in their behalf, was outside the scope of § 7 and § 8 of the National Labor Relations Act and was subject to state regulation.

The union, a labor organization within the meaning of the Act,[89] had represented a unit of supervisory employees, licensed marine engineers in the plaintiff's fleet of cargo vessels, under a labor agreement that terminated on July 15, 1962. While negotiations for a new contract were under way and after contract expiration, a majority of its marine engineers informed the employer that they did not wish to be represented by the union. The employer then advised the union that it would not negotiate until the union's majority status was confirmed by a secret ballot. The union responded by picketing ships of the employer in Superior, Wisconsin, and other ports. Dock workers reacted to the picketing by refusing to unload the employer's ships at Duluth, Minnesota.

Benefiting from the experience of another maritime employer, whose state court efforts in a similar dispute had recently come to naught in the Supreme Court,[90] the plaintiff immediately petitioned a regional director of the Board to hold an election among its engineers to prove or disprove the union's majority status. The petition was promptly dismissed on the regional director's conclusion that the engineers were "supervisors" under the Act and thus excluded from the definition of "employees." On intra-agency review the Board approved the regional director's determination. The employer also filed charges with a regional director alleging

---

[88] By a Taft-Hartley amendment in 1947, a "supervisor," as defined in § 2 (11) of the Act, 29 U.S.C. § 152 (11) (1964), is excluded from the term "employee" in § 2 (3) thereof, 29 U.S.C. § 152 (3) (1964).

[89] For a discussion of what is a labor organization within the meaning of the Act, of the Board's exclusive primary jurisdiction to determine the question, and of the means for unions that represent both rank-and-file workers and supervisors to exploit pre-emptive immunity and the "supervisor" issue, see generally Marine Engineers Beneficial Ass'n v. Interlake Steamship Co., 370 U.S. 173 (1962). For a dramatic example of a case in which the Board and employers were given a litigative run-around on the issue whether union conduct is immune from NLRB regulation because the persons for whom the union acts are "supervisors," see Master, Mates & Pilots v. N.L.R.B., 351 F.2d 771 (D.C. Cir. 1965). Cf. Marino v. Ragen, 332 U.S. 561, 657 (1947): "[T]he Illinois procedural labyrinth is made up entirely of blind alleys, each of which is useful only as a means of convincing the federal courts that the state road which the petitioner has taken was the wrong one."

[90] Marine Engineers Beneficial Ass'n v. Interlake Steamship Co., 370 U.S. 173 (1962).

that the union had engaged in secondary activity proscribed by the Act by inducing work stoppages by the dock workers at Duluth. These charges were dismissed, and the dismissal was approved by the general counsel of the NLRB, because the director had concluded after investigation that the picketing complained of did not exceed the Board's lawful picketing standards. The employer's final effort to secure redress through the NLRB was a charge that the union had engaged in recognition picketing in violation of the Act. This charge, too, was dismissed with subsequent approval by the general counsel on the ground that the union's activities were not covered because it sought by its picketing to represent "supervisors" and not "employees" as defined in the Act.[91]

The dispute was interrupted by the end of the navigation season on the Great Lakes. After the thaw in the spring of 1963, both shipping and picketing were resumed. The company then sought an injunction in a Wisconsin court to restrain picketing at Superior. State precedents would have permitted the issuance of an injunction if local law controlled,[92] but following *Garmon* carefully and literally, the trial court dismissed for lack of jurisdiction and the state supreme court affirmed.[93] With the help of a sympathetic memorandum from the Solicitor General, who thought the state court had erred, the company obtained certiorari.[94]

Conceding in the Supreme Court that efforts to unionize supervisory employees are not arguably prohibited or protected by the Labor Act, the union sought to construe § 14(a)[95] as a declaration of a federal policy of *laissez faire* toward supervisors, which would oust state, as well as federal authority. This argument was rejected. The Court also concluded that the supervisory status of the company's engineers had been settled "with unclouded legal significance"[96] by the Board's statement of reasons for refusal to order

---

[91] The chronology of the various filings is set out in 382 U.S. at 184–86.

[92] Vogt, Inc. v. Int'l Brotherhood of Teamsters, 270 Wis. 315 (1956), *aff'd*, 354 U.S. 284 (1957).

[93] 23 Wis.2d 433 (1964).   [94] 380 U.S. 941 (1965).

[95] "Nothing herein shall prohibit any individual employed as a supervisor from becoming or remaining a member of a labor organization, but no employer subject to this sub-chapter shall be compelled to deem individuals defined herein as supervisors as employees for the purpose of any law, either national or local, relating to collective bargaining." 29 U.S.C. § 164(a) (1964).

[96] 382 U.S. at 190.

a representation election pursuant to the employer's petition. Finally, the Court deemed irrelevant an inquiry whether the union's picketing at Superior might arguably have been unlawful secondary activity. "[E]ven if a § 8(b) (4) (B) violation were present, central interests served by the *Garmon* doctrine are not endangered by a state injunction when, in an instance such as this, the Board has established that the workers sought to be organized are outside the regime of the Act."[97]

Hanna considered the adjudicatory effects of the Board's administrative non-judicial action upon a petition or charge filed with a regional office. The employer's representation petition was dismissed by the regional director on the jurisdictional ground that the Board may not conduct elections among supervisory employees.[98] The NLRB approved this decision.[99] No hearing was ever held. The administrative investigation and conclusion not to proceed were treated by the Court as a form of jurisdictional adjudication:[100] "We hold that the Board's statement accompanying its refusal to order a representation election does resolve the question with the clarity necessary to avoid preemption." On the charge of recognition picketing, allegedly violative of § 8(b) (7), a regional director, with the concurrence of the general counsel, refused to issue a complaint because a field investigation showed that the picketing was directed to organizing supervisors and not employees.[101] The latter determination was not expressly treated as a form of jurisdictional adjudication in the Court's statement:[102] "[T]he Board's decision on the supervisory question determines ... that none of the conduct is arguably protected...." The Court's evaluation of the regional director's disposition of the employer's § 8(b) (4) (B) charge of unlawful secondary activity, however, seems to give adjudicatory effect to an explicated administrative determination to dismiss a charge because the field investigation discloses that the union conduct was not prohibited by the Act:[103]

> Hanna's claim that there is no arguable violation rests, of course, on the finding made by the Regional Director and General Counsel in declining to issue a complaint under § 8(b)(4)(B) with respect to MEBA's 1962 picketing. The

---

[97] *Id.* at 192–93.

[98] *Id.* at 184–85.   [100] *Id.* at 190.   [102] *Id.* at 193.

[99] *Ibid.*   [101] *Id.* at 186.   [103] *Id.* at 191–92.

Wisconsin Supreme Court refused to credit this finding because of this Court's comment in *Garmon* that the "refusal of
the General Counsel to file a charge"[104] is one of those dispositions "which does not define the nature of the activity with
unclouded legal significance." . . . This language allows more
than one interpretation, but we take it not to apply to those re-
fusals of the General Counsel which are illuminated by explanations that do squarely define the nature of the activity. The
General Counsel has statutory "final authority, on behalf of the
Board, in respect of the investigation of charges and issuance
of complaints," . . . and his pronouncements in this context are
entitled to great weight. The usual inability of the charging
party to contest the General Counsel's adverse decision in the
courts . . . does to be sure create a slight risk if state courts
may proceed on this basis, but in the context of this case we
believe the risk is too minimal to deserve recognition.

Notwithstanding this statement, it cannot be generalized that
hereafter an agency conclusion, whether purely administrative with
explications or formally adjudicative after a full hearing, that union
picketing is neither protected nor prohibited by the Act will clear
the way for state action. The Court reiterated in *Hanna*[105] its earlier
announcement in *Teamsters Union v. Morton*[106] that the ambit of
pre-empted labor disputes is by no means limited to union activity
which is either protected by § 7 or prohibited by § 8. There still
remains an undefined range of union activities that are neither protected nor proscribed by federal labor legislation but nonetheless
closed to state regulation.[107] The Court stated that there is a hier-
archy of pre-empted causes:[108]

> Most importantly, the Board's decision on the supervisory
> question determines . . . that none of the conduct is arguably
> protected nor does it fall in some middle range impliedly with-
> drawn from state control. Consequently, there is wholly absent

---

[104] Justice Frankfurter erred slightly in the phrase quoted from *Garmon*. A
"charge" is field by a party. If field investigation shows that there is NLRB jurisdiction and merit in the charge, a complaint may be issued by the general counsel,
or his representative, who usually is the appropriate regional director. §§ 3 (d) and
10 (b), 29 U.S.C. §§ 153(d) and 160(b) (1964).

[105] 382 U.S. at 189, 193 n. 14.   [106] 377 U.S. 252, 258–60 (1964).

[107] "For a state to impinge on the area of labor combat designed to be free is quite
as much an obstruction of federal policy as if the state were to declare picketing free
for purposes or by methods which the federal Act prohibits." Garner v. Teamsters Union, 346 U.S. 485, 500 (1953).

[108] 382 U.S. at 193–94.

the greatest threat against which the *Garmon* doctrine guards, a State's prohibition of activity that the Act indicates must remain unhampered.

Nor is this a case in which the presence of arguably prohibited activity may permit the Board to afford complete protection to the legitimate interests advanced by the State. . . .

The employer's prolonged agonies and ultimate victory in *Hanna* should reshape practice in cases where a labor organization utilizes the pre-emptive issue without letup to impede state court action. A predicate for state court action is now clearly established when the complaining party secures from a Board regional director a dismissal of his petition for representation on jurisdictional grounds, and exhausts intra-agency procedures for review of the dismissal at the regional level, eliciting thereby a restatement of absence of Board jurisdiction over the essential dispute. A similar predicate for the state court action may result from a dismissal of an unfair labor practice charge on the ground that the activity complained of is not prohibited by the Act.

The *Garmon* doctrine, which had been uncritically and routinely applied by the Court, received in *Hanna* a sorely needed clarification:

1. Union conduct protected by § 7 of the Act is also protected from state limitation. Preclusion of state action against protected conduct is the essential reason for the pre-emption doctrine.

2. Union conduct arguably within a prohibition of § 8 must first be submitted to the Board for adjudication. Informal determination by a regional director that the Board lacks jurisdiction in a representation proceeding, confirmed by the Board itself, and similar treatment of an unfair labor practice charge, confirmed by the general counsel, with a clear statement of jurisdictional reasons in each case for refusal to proceed, is advice to a state court that the union conduct is not subject to Board regulation. The way is cleared for state action because the internal administrative determinations, when fully explained, are treated as adjudicatory.

3. When a violation of § 8 by a union is investigated by a regional director or his agents in behalf of the general counsel, and a final internal administrative determination is made that the union conduct involved is not prohibited by the Act, a refusal to issue a complaint, "illuminated by explanations," is equivalent to an adjudication to that effect. After such an administrative determination, the state

tribunal is free to proceed, unless the conduct is protected by § 7 or is of a character that Congress intended to be unregulated by either federal or state power.

V. Linn v. Plant Guards: A Pinkerton "Maneger" Is Libeled

In *Hanna* reference was made to a middle range of prohibited activity arguably within Board competence. *Garmon* had decided that the courts should not anticipate the Board's action on the merits of a case,[109] and in *Hanna* the Court expressly did "not retreat from *Garmon*."[110] But what about a middle range of prohibited activity which the Board, through its general counsel, has declined to regulate because an investigation discloses that a particular charge cannot be supported by evidence? This problem appeared in *Linn v. Plant Guards*.[111] Also present was the issue latent in *Bouligny*, whether a civil action under state law for defamation during a union organizing campaign was pre-empted by the exclusive primary jurisdiction of the NLRB.[112]

The second question was answered in *Linn* by a 5-to-4, self-conscious, qualified, and tentative negative. A private remedial action under state law is available for libel committed by a union or an employer during a union organizing drive, when "the complainant can show that the defamatory statements were circulated with malice and caused him damage."[113] But, if experience demonstrates that a more complete curtailment of state libel remedies, "even a total one, should be necessary to prevent impairment of [national labor] policy, the Court will be free to reconsider today's holding."[114]

The Court treated the problem of regulation of conduct falling within the "middle range impliedly withdrawn from state control"[115] almost as if *Hanna* had never been written.

There were ironic twists to *Linn*. The case arose out of efforts to organize Pinkerton plant guards, successors of the Pinkerton Protective Patrol whose activities for so long had occupied a high

---

[109] 359 U.S. at 245, especially n. 4.

[110] 382 U.S. at 194.

[111] 383 U.S. 53 (1966).

[112] Text at note 10, *supra;* 382 U.S. at 147 n. 2.

[113] 383 U.S. at 65.

[114] *Id.* at 67.

[115] 382 U.S. at 193.

place in the demonology of trade unionists. In the Taft-Hartley revisions of 1947, Congress restricted the representation of guards to specialized unions, segregated from labor organizations representing other kinds of employees.[116] Late in 1962, a local of the independent United Plant Guard Workers of America was endeavoring to organize employees of Pinkerton's National Detective Agency, Inc. A Pinkerton employee, whom the NLRB's regional director later administratively decided was not a union agent, distributed a leaflet to his fellows which said, *inter alia:*[117]

> The men in Saginaw were deprived of their *right to vote* in three N.L.R.B. elections. Their names were not summited [*sic*]. . . . These Pinkerton guards were *robbed* of pay increases. The Pinkerton manegers [*sic*] were *lying* to us all the time the contract was in effect. No doubt the Saginaw men will file criminal charges. Somebody may go to jail!

Pinkerton filed charges with the Board's regional director claiming that union distribution of the leaflet coerced its employees in violation of § 8 (b) (1) (A).[118] The regional director refused to issue a complaint on the basis of an investigation showing that the Pinkerton employee who had circulated the leaflet was neither an officer, a member, nor an agent of the Plant Guards local union. The administrative determination against issuance of a complaint was sustained by the general counsel.[119]

While the Board matter was pending, the plaintiff, a Pinkerton manager who was a citizen of Ohio, brought suit in federal court in Michigan against the local union, two of its officers, and the employee, attributing citizenship in Michigan to the local union, all of its members, and the three individual defendants.[120] He alleged that the leaflet referred to him and that the statements were "false, defamatory and untrue" to the defendants' knowledge.[121] The district court granted the motion to dismiss on the ground that, if the local union or its officers had distributed "a false and defamatory publication which would tend to affect adversely the relations between Pinkerton's and its employees, this would arguably constitute an unfair labor practice under Section 8 (b) of

---

[116] § 9(b) (3), 29 U.S.C. § 159(b) (3) (1964).   [117] 383 U.S. at 56.

[118] "It shall be an unfair labor practice for a labor organization or its agents . . . (1) to restrain or coerce (A) employees in the exercise of rights guaranteed in Section 7. . . ." 29 U.S.C. § 158(b) (1) (A) (1964).

[119] 383 U.S. at 57.   [120] Record, pp. 3–4.   [121] *Id.* at 5.

the National Labor Relations Act, a fact which Pinkerton's has tacitly admitted in requesting the Regional Director of the NLRB to issue a complaint."[122] *Garmon* was the principal authority cited by the district court.[123] The court of appeals affirmed, assuming, but not deciding, that the statements were false, malicious, libelous, and damaging to the plaintiff, but relevant to the union's organizing campaign.[124] With an assist from the Solicitor General of the United States, certiorari was granted.[125]

The Supreme Court reversed in an opinion by Mr. Justice Clark that followed, in its principal outline, the amicus brief of the United States. The Government's brief urging reversal, advised the Court that the question presented was not controlled by its pre-emption decisions as the district court and the court of appeals had believed. The Government read the pre-emption decisions before and after *Garmon* as a bar only to state action directly affecting labor relations. It declared that affording a remedy for defamation under state law would not directly regulate labor relations. It asserted that *Garmon* should not be read to limit state intervention in labor disputes affecting commerce only to curtailment of violence. It concurred in the plaintiff's analogy between the tort of defamation and the tort of assault. The Court was advised that the NLRB's supervision of campaign utterances was highly permissive, and that false and defamatory utterances were generally neither a ground for setting aside a representation election nor a basis for an unfair labor practice finding. The Government asserted that one of the traditional justifications for furnishing a remedy for defamation is to thwart breaches of the peace which might be provoked by defamatory statements.

The Government argued further that neither complete preclusion of nor complete freedom for defamation suits could be implied from federal labor laws. Complete freedom would severely undermine the federal regulatory scheme. Complete prohibition would give insufficient weight to substantial state interests and would not be necessary to effectuate the policies of the Act. Thus state courts, and federal courts in diversity cases, should be barred from entertaining defamation suits based upon statements arising

---

[122] Petition for certiorari, pp. 24–25.

[123] *Id*. at 25.

[124] 337 F.2d 68 (6th Cir. 1964).

[125] 381 U.S. 923 (1965).

from labor disputes, unless the defamation was made with a willful disregard for truth and gravely injured the plaintiff's reputation.

The middle ground proposed for a federal defense to a state defamation action might, it was suggested, be derived by analogy from the *Times* libel case.[126] By such analogy, liability should not attach, urged the Solicitor General, unless the defamatory statement was known to be false or was made with reckless indifference to its truth. Liability should be limited to grave, and not trivial, injuries to the plaintiff's reputation, because labor campaigns often generate a high level of abuse, exaggeration, and name-calling. Conventionally defamatory words like "scab," "liar," "crook," "skunk," and similar epithets would not involve a social interest sufficient to justify redress. State libel actions, the Government believed, should be confined to such grave defamations as statements charging the commission of a felony, sexual misconduct, espousing of treasonable or disloyal views, or engaging in "other misconduct which the community regards as infamous."[127] Finally, the Solicitor General advocated that punitive damages should not be allowed in state actions for defamation arising from a labor dispute affecting commerce.

The opinion by Mr. Justice Clark found an overriding state interest in redressing libel arising from labor disputes. An exercise of state jurisdiction in such matters would be "a merely peripheral concern of the Labor-Management Relations Act," if limited to redressing libels "published with knowledge of their falsity or with reckless disregard of whether they were true or false."[128] Either attitude accompanying a defamatory statement is "malicious" within the criteria of the *Times* case,[129] the standards of which were

[126] New York Times Co. v. Sullivan, 376 U.S. 254 (1964).

[127] Brief for the United States as Amicus Curiae, p. 45.

[128] 383 U.S. at 65.

[129] By adhering to the "reckless disregard" standard for malice announced in the *Times* case, *supra* note 126, at 279–80, the Court adhered to a concept that is the bane of torts and criminal law teachers. In discussing the *Times* case, Willard H. Pedrick has observed: "To attempt to define 'reckless disregard' is to attempt the impossible as anyone with a casual acquaintance with the automobile guest cases will confirm. . . . The state court libel cases will not supply much guidance in the application of the 'reckless disregard' objective standard for 'malice.'" *Freedom of the Press and the Law of Libel: The Modern Revised Translation*, 49 CORNELL L.Q. 581, 597 (1964).

adopted by analogy in labor disputes affecting commerce, and not under constitutional compulsion.[130]

Proof of actual damage to the plaintiff is a predicate for recovery. Two suggestions of the Government, as amicus curiae, were rejected. The Court would not limit liability to "grave" defamations, such as language charging criminal, homosexual, treasonable, or other infamous conduct. Such limitations were rejected as artificial characterizations that would encroach too heavily upon state jurisdiction.[131] Similarly, the Court rejected the Government's suggestion that punitive damages should be barred in labor libel cases. It held, however, that the defamed party must prove compensable harm as a prerequisite to recovery of additional damages.[132] With the frank declaration that it was experimenting and might impose a more complete curtailment of labor libel actions, or even their abolition,[133] the Court reversed with the direction that the plaintiff be given leave to amend his complaint to meet the requirement of the opinion.[134]

Mr. Justice Black, dissenting, would read the congressional intent of the National Labor Relations Act as eschewing any "purpose to try to purify the language of labor disputes or force the disputants to say nice things about one another."[135] Libel suits, he felt, conflict with the basic purposes of the Act, which are to end labor disputes and not aggravate them. Mr. Justice Black also restated his thesis that libel suits are inconsistent with the Constitution.[136]

---

[130] The limitations upon the state cause of action enunciated in *Linn* are based upon the Court's construction of the NLRA. In its brief, at page 40, the Government asked the Court "to fashion, from the design and policies of federal labor law and the principles of federalism, a reasonably clear and certain standard that will afford a federal defense to some but not all defamation suits growing out of labor disputes." No authority for modification of a state cause of action by a federal defense was supplied to the Court. No authority is offered by the Court except its own statement: "We apply the malice test to effectuate the statutory design with respect to pre-emption." 383 U.S. at 65. Cf. *Exceptions to Erie v. Tompkins: The Survival of Federal Common Law*, 59 HARV. L. REV. 966 (1946); Maryland Casualty Co. v. Cushing, 347 U.S. 409 (1954); Tungus v. Skovgard, 358 U.S. 588 (1959).

[131] 383 U.S. at 65 n. 7.   [133] *Id*. at 67.

[132] *Id*. at 66.   [134] *Id*. at 66.

[135] *Id*. at 69. Cf. Cahn, *Justice Black and the First Amendment "Absolutes": A Public Interview*, 37 N.Y.U. L. REV. 549 (1962).

[136] 383 U.S. at 68.

Mr. Justice Fortas wrote a dissent joined by the Chief Justice and Mr. Justice Douglas. He would read *Garmon* as permitting state remedies in labor disputes affecting commerce only when there is a compelling public interest in preventing violence or the threat of violence. He deplored the majority's opening of "a major breach in the wall which has heretofore confined labor disputes to the area and weaponry defined by federal labor law, except where violence or intimidation is involved."[137] If *Hanna* stripped unions of a practical immunity they had been abusing, *Linn* may give unions an effective organizing weapon heretofore rarely utilized.

The Court was seriously misled about the significance of libel in organizing campaigns. Defamatory statements are not weapons of significance in the attainment of short-range or long-range objectives of unions. The American labor movement lacks revolutionary goals. Its outlook is pragmatic and business unionism is its dominant ideology.[138] An established union is constantly engaged in organizational efforts either to expand its base or to make up for membership lost through business failures, plant removals, mergers, technological displacement and, on occasion, raids from other labor organizations. In an organizing campaign, even when illegal picketing is attempted, the union assumes that its relationship with management will become permanent. Whatever may be the metaphor of an organizing venture, the union must eventually develop a firm and trustworthy relationship with the managers of the employing company. Malicious libel, of the kind proscribed by *Linn*, is not likely to be uttered by experienced labor organizers. If there is any inducement to go all out in the use of defamatory language, it is on the side of the employer, whose goal in combating union organization is often the avoidance of any long-term relationship with the adversary.

It is safe to predict, however, that libel actions, with allegations adequate under *Linn*, will be plentiful. These actions will not be filed to serve some state interest in suppressing defamatory utterances, especially since interposition of a federal defense drastically shrinks that interest. They will be filed for their immediate tactical

---

137 383 U.S. at 69.

138 See BELL, THE END OF IDEOLOGY 209–21 (1960); Mills, *The Labor Leaders and the Power Elite*, in POWER POLITICS AND PEOPLE 97–109 (Horowitz ed. 1963); Lipset, *Trade Unions and Social Structure*, 1 IND. REL. 89 (1962).

effect in aid of or in opposition to organizational campaigns or other
union activities.

To my mind, the Court majority has erred seriously in permitting
such suits, and the Board exhibited an utter lack of comprehension
of its own procedures under § 9[139] when it urged the Court to do
so. Even as clarified by *Hanna*, the *Garmon* test for excluding state
regulation of union conduct protected by § 7 or prohibited by § 8
of the Act is not coextensive with the range of subject matter to
be regulated only by federal law.[140] Section 9 of the Act precludes
parallel or conflicting state action on questions of employee representation.[141] The Board's administration of § 9 is plenary and un-
reviewable except under highly restricted circumstances.[142] Because
the Board's powers are so broad, its action under § 9 usually has
sharper impact upon the parties than any § 8 order, except those
of reinstatement and back pay. The draftsmen of the Board's amicus
brief ignored the details of § 9 proceedings as viewed and handled
in regional offices.[143]

---

[139] 29 U.S.C. § 159 (1964). Although my criticism of *Linn* is based upon the
plenary power of the Board over pre-election propaganda under § 9, I believe that
a strong case can be made for exclusive federal regulation of union libel, under
§ 8(b)(1)(A). Proponents of that section were "less concerned with actual acts
of violence than . . . with . . . false statements . . . by which employees are coerced
by union organizers and interfered with in their free choice of representatives.
. . ." 93 Cong. Rec. 4137 (April 25, 1947). Senator Taft favored the amendment
because, under the Wagner Act, "if a union . . . issues defamatory statements mis-
representing the facts that is not an unfair labor practice, and in no way invalidates
the election." *Id.* at 4142.

[140] See note 74 *supra.*

[141] Bethlehem Steel Co. v. New York Labor Rel. Bd., 330 U.S. 767 (1947);
La Crosse Telephone Corp. v. Wisconsin Employment Rel. Bd., 336 U.S. 18 (1949).

[142] *Cf.* Leedom v. Kyne, 358 U.S. 184 (1958); Boire v. Greyhound Corp., 376 U.S.
473 (1964); N.L.R.B. v. Metropolitan Life Ins. Co., 380 U.S. 438 (1965). Courts of
Appeals have denied enforcement of Board bargaining orders based upon § 9 cer-
tifications obtained through improper election propaganda by the victorious union.
Note 154 *infra* and accompanying text.

[143] In 1959, § 3(b) of the Act was amended to authorize the Board to delegate its
full powers in representation cases to regional directors, except for limited review
powers. 29 U.S.C. § 153(b) (1964). The delegation was made in 1961, NLRB, Rules
and Regulations, ser. 8, rev. Jan. 1, 1965, §§ 102.60–102.72. In the fiscal year ending
June 30, 1965, 1,521 elections were ordered by the regional directors and only 88 by
the Board itself. Board personnel who specialized in supervising representation
matters for the Board in Washington were transferred to the various field offices
to perform the same functions for the regional directors.

A union's organizing campaign, aimed at a certification under § 9, divides into two distinct phases. In the first phase, the union must secure the necessary number of written authorizations or other signatory evidence of interest in the labor organization. Ordinarily 30 per cent of the employees in the bargaining unit must exhibit such an interest in being organized before the Board will proceed.[144] While this portion of the organizing campaign is not subject to the considerable sanctions of § 9, but only to the general provisions of § 8, it is in fact the most delicate. Most often the campaign for signatures is quiet and undercover.[145] The Board has laid down rules for free oral communication among employees inside the plant, on non-productive time, both in work areas and in non-work areas.[146] There is no practical likelihood of malicious utterances by union organizers in this frangible portion of the campaign. It is assumed that union bombast would frighten away potential signers of the much-coveted authorization cards. And it is greatly to a union's advantage to obtain more than the minimum 30 per cent of unit signatures. A campaign that produces a majority of signers in the bargaining unit may be a predicate for compulsory union recognition in some circumstances, even though the union should lose the election.[147]

The second phase of a campaign occurs after a union has obtained the necessary number of authorizations. When a union has filed a petition under § 9 supported by sufficient authorizations, Board jurisdiction attaches to the entire campaign and election. The Board has set aside elections for reasons that would appear unrealistic if not irrelevant to a political scientist.[148] Misconduct that would justify the nullification of an election need not be so gross as to constitute an independent unfair labor practice.[149] Though the

---

[144] NLRB, Rules and Regulations, *supra* note 143, § 101.18.

[145] BARBASH, THE PRACTICE OF UNIONISM 37–44 (1956); GITELMAN, UNIONIZATION ATTEMPTS IN SMALL ENTERPRISES: A GUIDE FOR EMPLOYERS 18–33 (1963).

[146] Stoddard-Quirk Mfg. Co., 138 N.L.R.B. 615 (1962).

[147] Bernel Foam Products Co., 146 N.L.R.B. 1277 (1964).

[148] See Bok, *The Regulation of Campaign Tactics in Representation Elections under the National Labor Relations Act*, 78 HARV. L. REV. 38 (1964); Allied Electric Products, Inc., 109 N.L.R.B. 1270 (1954) (prohibiting use of marked facsimile sample ballots).

[149] General Shoe Corp., 77 N.L.R.B. 124 (1948).

Board may have been "highly permissive"[150] in the past and has not set aside elections solely because of maliciously defamatory utterances, it has power to do so.[151] A Board policy of controlling malicious campaign defamation by § 9 sanctions would contribute much more to the maintenance of a uniform national labor policy, than would the implementation of *Linn* by a proliferation of tactical state lawsuits, most of them frivolous. The penalty of forfeiture of an election victory through appropriate Board action is a far more effective safeguard of truth and decency in election propaganda than fear of responding in damages to a state court defamation action.

Moreover, the Board's statutory task of policing the environment and incidents of election campaigns is complicated by *Linn*. It is a commonplace that lawsuits and charges of unfair labor practices during organizing campaigns are propaganda maneuvers, not unlike libel suits filed during contests for political office. The pleading in the lawsuit or the charge before the Board is often merely

---

[150] Brief for the United States as Amicus Curiae, p. 27.

[151] "Congress has entrusted the Board with a wide degree of discretion in establishing the procedure and safeguards necessary to insure the fair and free choice of bargaining representatives by employees." N.L.R.B. v. Tower Co., 329 U.S. 324, 330 (1946).

The Board has constructed a complete jurisprudential system around § 9 without any express statutory mandate. It has full power to curtail malicious speech or even abusive speech in election contests. Stricter standards for propaganda are consistent with its own summary of the range of its control: "Section 9(c)(1) of the Act provides that if, upon a petition filed, a question of representation exists, the Board must resolve it through an election by secret ballot. The election details are left to the Board. Such matters as voting eligibility, timing of elections, and standards of election conduct are subject to rules laid down in the Board's Rules and Regulations and in its decisions. Board elections are conducted in accordance with strict standards designed to assure that the participating employees have an opportunity to determine, and to register a free and untrammeled choice in the selection of, a bargaining representative. Any party to an election who believes that the standards have not been met may file timely objections to the election with the regional director under whose supervision it was held." NLRB, *op. cit. supra* note 81, at 51.

"In election proceedings, it is the Board's function to provide a laboratory in which an experiment may be conducted, under conditions as nearly ideal as possible, to determine the uninhibited desires of the employees. It is our duty to establish these conditions; it is also our duty to determine whether they have been fulfilled. When, in the rare extreme case the standard drops too low, because of our fault or that of others, the requisite laboratory conditions are not present and the experiment must be conducted over again." General Shoe Corp., 77 N.L.R.B. 124, 127 (1948).

another form of pamphleteering, with the added advantage that it may be reported in the newspapers or on radio and television.[152] The Board may be compelled to set aside elections or find unfair labor practices when an employer or a union has won with the substantial aid of a frivolous lawsuit. A few examples will suffice.

In the course of a pending election contest involving one hundred employees, the union distributes a leaflet critical of the employer, which to a libel lawyer is obviously outside the purview of *Linn*. The employer sues for $1 million actual damages and $1 million punitive damages. Employees are told by employer representatives that if the union wins the forthcoming election, the employees will become parties to a judgment debt of $2 million as a union liability. The union loses the election under circumstances where it is clear that but for the lawsuit and the ensuing propaganda it would have won. The Board may then be asked to inquire into the merits of a pending state case to ascertain whether the litigative allegations that the union had maliciously made of defamatory utterances damaging to the employer were meritorious or frivolous. The Board's inquiry might be limited under § 9 to whether the election results should be set aside and a new election ordered. Or, the union may demand that the *Bernel Foam*[153] doctrine be invoked. The employer's lawsuit and comments thereon must then be evaluated as a factor in the anti-union campaign that is supposed to have led to the diminution of the union's majority. Upon either kind of inquiry, confusion in state-federal relationships is unavoidable.

Or add to this illustration an element making the facts more closely resemble *Linn*. Assume that a libel action of doubtful factual merit, set forth in an adequate pleading, is filed by a company official during the pendency of the Board election and produces a union defeat. There follow similar post-election requests by the union for Board action, aimed either at a new election or an order to bargain under the *Bernel Foam* doctrine. Now the Board must determine whether the filing of the lawsuit, which clearly affected the election results, was employer-inspired or was wholly an inde-

---

152 Two-thirds of all charges of unfair labor practices filed with the Board are found to be without merit after investigation, and are either dismissed by the regional director or withdrawn by the charging party. NLRB, *op. cit. supra* note 81, at 10.

153 *Supra* note 147 and accompanying text.

pendent act of the plaintiff in no way imputable to the employer.

To reverse the parties in this parade of horribles, assume that a large union is undertaking to organize a unit of one hundred employees in an enterprise owned by a major publicly held corporation. In a pending election campaign, the plant manager sends a letter to employees containing unkind remarks about the union, its officers, and its system of internal government. The union responds with an action for $1 million actual damages and $1 million punitive damages because of malicious libel. Then the union organizers tell employees that the parent union, plaintiff in the action, really does not want the money. They say the lawsuit was filed "as a matter of principle," and therefore that all money recovered, the full $2 million, if collected, will be cheerfully turned over to the new plant local union if the union wins the election. The union wins under circumstances clearly showing that the promise of local administration of a potential fund of $2 million was a material factor in its victory. What is the Board to do with the employer's election objections?

The supervisory role of the federal courts of appeals in their review of NLRB bargaining orders will also be made more difficult by *Linn*. Courts of appeals have denied enforcement to bargaining orders of the Board where certified labor unions have won elections through improper propaganda techniques.[154] The same questions

---

[154] In N.L.R.B. v. Schapiro & Whitehouse, 356 F.2d 675 (4th Cir. 1966), enforcement was denied to a Board order to bargain with a union that won an election based upon "propaganda [which] is deplorable. . . . Besides their utter irrelevance, the leaflets appear to this court as highly inflammatory. . . ." *Id.* at 679. In N.L.R.B. v. Bonnie Enterprises, 341 F.2d 712, 714 (4th Cir. 1965), enforcement was similarly denied to an order to bargain with a union that won the Board election by use of a circular that "went far beyond the bounds of permissible hyperbole sometimes indulged in during pre-election campaigns." Enforcement was similarly denied in N.L.R.B. v. Gilmore Industries, Inc., 341 F.2d 240 (6th Cir. 1965), because of improper union propaganda concerning waiver of initiation fees. In N.L.R.B. v. Trancoa Chemical Corporation, 303 F.2d 456, 460–62 (1st Cir. 1962), in denying enforcement of a bargaining order, the Court rebuked the Board for a "sorry record" of supervision of union campaign propaganda: "We do not think that the Board's view of what impairs freedom of choice is more sacrosanct than its other fact-finding powers. . . . If the Board tolerates low standards that is where they will stop. The Board twice asserts that it does not 'condone' untruthfulness but standards will be set by what it does, not by what it says." Improper union campaign propaganda was also the basis for denial of enforcement of orders to bargain with a union that had been certified pursuant to NLRB election in N.L.R.B. v. Houston Chronicle Publishing Co., 300 F.2d 273 (5th Cir. 1962); Celanese Corpora-

that I have propounded for the Board may also be argued in the courts of appeals.

Aside from its inherent unsoundness as a normative technique in labor relations, *Linn* also disrupts the maintenance of a uniform national labor policy. The cause of action for defamation, preempted in large measure by a federal defense, is enforceable only in states in which the union is subject to vicarious liability for acts in which less than all of its members participate and may sue or be sued as a legal entity.[155]

Linn adds more confusion to the administration of national labor policy than will be engendered by the tactical litigative devices of competing unions and employers under *Hanna* and the uncertainty of juridical entity and liability of labor unions in the various states underlined by *Bouligny*. In *Hanna*, administrative refusal to issue a complaint, based upon field investigation showing no illegal conduct under federal law and fully "illuminated by explanations" of the regional director and the general counsel was treated as a form of adjudication that could be a predicate to state court action in an appropriate case.[156] But in *Linn* the refusal to issue a complaint on the employer's charges was based upon a field investigation that exculpated the union. The adjudicatory nature of this determination, recognized by the district court, was ignored by the Supreme Court.

When is the fully exhausted administrative process, truncated because of an explicated field investigation showing no factual merit to the charge, to be treated as adjudicatory so as to bar state action? In *Hanna* a refusal to proceed for jurisdictional reasons was held to be a predicate for state action. *Hanna* and *Linn* are inconsistent in appraising the adjudicative effect to be given an internal administrative determination that forecloses a formal hearing and order.

---

tion of America v. N.L.R.B., 291 F.2d 224 (7th Cir. 1961); Allis Chalmers Manufacturing Company v. N.L.R.B., 261 F.2d 613 (7th Cir. 1958); Cross Company v. N.L.R.B., 286 F.2d 799 (6th Cir. 1961); Kearney & Trecker Corp. v. N.L.R.B., 210 F.2d 852, *cert. denied*, 348 U.S. 824 (7th Cir. 1964). (None of the cases discussed in this footnote was cited in the Goverment's brief in *Linn*.)

The courts of appeals are under directions not to deny enforcement of otherwise valid bargaining orders based upon elections marred by "trivial irregularities of administrative procedure." N.L.R.B. v. Mattison Machine Works, 365 U.S. 123 (1961); N.L.R.B. v. Celanese Corporation of America, 365 U.S. 297 (1961).

155 See note 46 *supra*.   156 See notes 97–102 *supra*, and accompanying text.

Moreover, in its conclusion that the Board cannot give relief to a defamed party, the Court forgot its frequently announced and often followed practice of deference to the primary jurisdiction of the Board. The Court decided for itself the status of disputed activities.[157] In *Linn*, the regional director treated Pinkerton's charge as one upon which a remedy might be predicated if field investigation yielded enough evidentiary support to sustain a formal complaint. The refusal to issue a complaint was based upon an explanation, in which the general counsel later concurred, that the employee who had composed and circulated the leaflet was not an agent of the union. Refusal to go further with the charge was explicated as in *Hanna*. But yet it was a refusal to act further for inadequate evidence, not for jurisdictional reasons, and not because the conduct complained of was irremediable under the Act, by virtue of being outside the ambit of §§ 7, 8, or 9. Indeed, the very fact that a field investigation was conducted at all is convincing proof that on its face the charge was arguably within the purview of § 8.[158]

By usurping the functions of the Board, and deciding for itself the general proposition that all malicious defamation is outside the ambit of the Act, the Court has undertaken primary adjudication of the meaning and application of the National Labor Relations Act, a process which it expressly eschewed in *Garmon*. It is to be hoped that the Court will soon take advantage of the "reopening clause" of its opinion in *Linn* to restore the balance in American labor law that the decision has so unwisely disturbed.

---

[157] In earlier labor pre-emption cases, *e.g.*, U.A.W. v. Wisconsin Employment Rel. Bd., 336 U.S. 245 (1949), the Court itself determined whether the federal statute governed the disputed conduct. In *Garner,* the Court said, "It is not necessary or appropriate for us to surmise how the National Labor Relations Board might have decided this controversy had petitioners presented it to that body. The power and duty of primary decision lies with the Board, not with us." 346 U.S. at 489. In *Garmon* the "arguably subject" test was enunciated. In so doing the Court referred to *U.A.W. v. Wisconsin Employment Rel. Bd.*, and said: "The approach taken in that case, in which the Court undertook for itself to determine the status of the disputed activity, has not been followed in later decisions, and is no longer of general application." 359 U.S. at 245 n. 4.

The tactic of inviting an amicus brief and oral argument, to delineate for the Court the full scope of NLRB regulation, smacks of an *ad hoc* original declaratory proceeding in the Supreme Court on an abstract or hypothetical case. A fast answer obtained by such obvious suppression of normal administrative and judicial processes, in my view, must prove a wrong answer.

[158] See note 139 *supra*.

E D M U N D   W.   K I T C H

GRAHAM V. JOHN DEERE CO.: NEW

STANDARDS FOR PATENTS

In the 1964 Term, it was news of importance to the patent bar, though of little note elsewhere, that the Supreme Court had, for the first time in fifteen years,[1] undertaken to review some patent cases turning on the issue of invention.[2] The Court had granted certiorari to consider the effect of the standard of non-obviousness imposed by § 103 of the Patent Act of 1952[3] on theretofore judicially developed tests of invention.

The interest of the patent bar derived from a widespread concern that the Court might use § 103 as a basis for promulgating more rigorous standards of invention than had yet been utilized. Indeed, after the Court had granted certiorari in *Graham v. John*

Edmund W. Kitch is Assistant Professor of Law, The University of Chicago.

[1] The Court last considered the issue in Great Atl. & Pac. Tea Co. v. Supermarket Equip. Corp., 340 U.S. 147 (1950).

[2] Graham v. John Deere Co., 379 U.S. 956 (1965); United States v. Adams, 380 U.S. 949 (1965); Calmar, Inc. v. Cook Chemical Co., 380 U.S. 949 (1965); Colgate-Palmolive Co. v. Cook Chemical Co., 380 U.S. 949 (1965).

[3] 35 U.S.C. § 103 (1964): "A patent may not be obtained though the invention is not identically disclosed or described as set forth in section 102 of this title, if the differences between the subject matter sought to be patented and the prior art are such that the subject matter as a whole would have been obvious at the time the invention was made to a person having ordinary skill in the art to which said subject matter pertains. Patentability shall not be negatived by the manner in which the invention was made."

Deere Co.,[4] in order to resolve a conflict between the Fifth[5] and Eighth[6] Circuits, the Solicitor General had invited the Court "to consider pressing problems relating to the administration of the patent laws in a variety of contexts and in broad perspective."[7] This language took on an ominous sound when the Court accepted the invitation and granted certiorari in *United States v. Adams*[8] and the twin cases of *Calmar, Inc. v. Cook Chemical Co.* and *Colgate-Palmolive Co. v. Cook Chemical Co.*[9]

The Court was inundated with a shower of amicus curiae briefs revealing an apprehension that the Court would utilize the new statutory language as a valve to cut down the flow of patents that pour forth from the Patent Office each year.[10] The worry of the patent bar was perhaps expressed most frankly in an amicus brief filed by Professors E. Ernest Goldstein and Page Keeton of the University of Texas patronizingly entitled "Brief Amicus Curiae in Support of 35 USC 103." Such a brief was necessary, wrote these self-appointed defenders of the statute, "because some writings by some Justices of this Court[11] and the opinions by the Court of Appeals in this case, appear to put the practical operating life of the patent system at stake, and to put the whole socio-economic functioning of the entire patent system at issue."[12]

The decisions that the Court has rendered may assuage this fear. They expressly purport to follow the earlier decisions and to turn

---

[4] 383 U.S. 1 (1966).

[5] The Fifth Circuit had found the patent valid in Graham v. Cockshutt Farm Equip. Co., 256 F.2d 358 (5th Cir. 1958), and Jeoffroy Mfg. Inc. v. Graham, 219 F.2d 511 (5th Cir. 1955).

[6] The Eighth Circuit had held the patent invalid. John Deere Co. v. Graham, 333 F.2d 529 (8th Cir. 1964).

[7] Petition for Certiorari, pp. 15–16, United States v. Adams.

[8] 383 U.S. 39 (1966).   [9] 383 U.S. 1 (1966).

[10] The amicus curiae briefs were filed by the American Bar Association, the New York Patent Law Association, the Illinois State Bar Association, the State Bar of Texas, and the School of Law of the University of Texas.

[11] In a concurring opinion in the *Supermarket* case, note 1 *supra*, Mr. Justice Douglas, joined by Mr. Justice Black, had observed "how far our patent system frequently departs from the constitutional standards" and accused the Patent Office of having "placed a host of gadgets under the armor of patents." 340 U.S. at 154, 158.

[12] Amicus Curiae Brief of the School of Law of the University of Texas, pp. 1–2, Graham v. John Deere Co.

toward neither leniency nor harshness. "We believe," wrote Mr. Justice Clark for the Court, "that the revision [in 1952] was not intended by Congress to change the general level of patentable invention."[13] And, if actions speak louder than words, the Court held a patent valid for the first time in twenty-two years.[14] The opinions leave the impression that the decisions represent a mere ripple in the long stream of the law of invention and that the Court will now leave that complicated and hopelessly technical subject to the care of the courts of appeals for another fifteen years. But in fact the cases may, indeed, foreshadow an important doctrinal clarification of what has been a needlessly confused concept.

The petitioner in *Deere* eschewed the arguments offered by the amici curiae and asserted instead that "there can be no doubt that Congress has spoken and has defined for the first time a statutory requirement for patentable invention. The wording of the statute is clear and should be followed."[15] In essence, he argued that the Court of Appeals for the Eighth Circuit had erroneously used a standard of invention that required proof of a new or different result in order to sustain the validity of the patent. The patent involved in *Deere* was on an improved clamp whose structure is difficult to describe but simple to understand from a diagram. The clamp was designed to provide a strong connection between the shank of a plow and the implement frame. The important feature of the clamp was that it permitted the shank to pivot upward when the plow point struck rocks, preventing damage. The patented clamp was an improvement on an earlier clamp that functioned in the same way and was also developed and patented by Graham. By having the shank pass under instead of over the pivot point and providing a rigid connection between the end of the shank and the clamp, Graham had designed a clamp that would perform better because of less wear and because it offered minutely greater freedom of movement along the whole length of the shank.

The Eighth Circuit had rejected this as a ground of patentability because "the inversion of the parts so as to allow the

---

[13] 383 U.S. at 17.

[14] United States v. Adams, 383 U.S. 39 (1966) (8–1). The Court last held a patent valid in Goodyear Tire & Rubber Co. v. Ray-O-Vac Co., 321 U.S. 275 (1944) (5–4).

[15] Brief of Petitioner Graham, p. 25, Graham v. John Deere Co.

shank to flex downwardly away from the plate above it did
not bring about a significantly new or different result."[16] On
this issue it differed from the Fifth Circuit, which had found the
patent valid because of the rule "long recognized by this Court,
that an improvement combination is patentable even though its
constituent elements are singly revealed by the prior art, where,
as here, it produces an old result in a cheaper and otherwise more
advantageous way."[17] A concern with "result" as a test for invention has venerable origins in American patent law, but the petitioners in *Deere* argued with complete persuasiveness that "nowhere
in [the] . . . statute is there any requirement that to be patentable
an invention must produce a new result."[18] The Court agreed,
concluding "that neither Circuit applied the correct test."[19]

By rejecting the "result test" of invention, the Court brought
to an end a standard of patentability that has created confusion for
far too many years. Even more important is the implication that
in the future § 103 can be used to eliminate other historic tests of
invention that have no rational relationship to the non-obviousness
inquiry required by § 103. It is thus that the approach adopted by
the Court in *Deere* may make it an important turning point in the
history of American patent law. But to understand this possibility
it is necessary first to understand the history.

The generally received history seems to be that the non-obviousness test of § 103 was articulated in the very first patentability case
before the Supreme Court, *Hotchkiss v. Greenwood*,[20] and has
remained the test of invention ever since, with the possible exception of certain "hostile" Supreme Court decisions after 1930.[21] Thus,
the Supreme Court concluded in *Deere* that § 103 "was intended
to codify judicial precedents embracing the principle long ago an-

---

[16] 333 F.2d at 534.

[17] 219 F.2d at 519.   [19] 383 U.S. at 4.

[18] *Supra* note 15, at 26.   [20] 11 How. 248 (1851).

[21] Discussion of this thesis generally centers on Great Atl. & Pac. Tea Co. v.
Supermarket Equip. Corp., 340 U.S. 147 (1950), and Cuno Eng'r Corp. v. Automatic
Devices Corp., 314 U.S. 84 (1941), as the most hostile. But under the non-obvious-
ness test, the *Supermarket* case was clearly right on its facts and *Cuno* arguably so.
General Elec. Co. v. Jewel Incandescent Lamp Co., 326 U.S. 242 (1945), discussed
below, appears really to be the most hostile: wrong both on its facts and its law.
But two Terms earlier the Court had held a doubtful patent valid. Goodyear Tire
& Rubber Co. v. Ray-O-Vac Co., 321 U.S. 275 (1944).

nounced by this Court in *Hotchkiss*."[22] And at oral argument all counsel appeared to agree that the test of invention is the same today as it was a century ago.[23]

The idea that the history of a test for invention has so stable a continuity, however, is simply misleading. The history of invention in American patent law only begins to make sense if it is first understood that there have been not one but three different tests which, during the twentieth century, have existed side by side in the decisions of the courts. Section 103 can properly be construed as a selection of one of those three tests and a rejection of the other two. If it is so construed, the law based on the other two tests should now be rejected. Until *Deere*, however, the lower federal courts were not dealing with § 103 in this way. Rather they seemed to assume that since § 103 dealt with invention, all prior law dealing with invention was relevant in applying the section to particular cases. For example, even though Judge Hand recognized that § 103 had changed the prior law, his decision in *Lyon v. Bausch & Lomb Optical Co.*[24] apparently would preserve as relevant all earlier tests of invention no matter what their doctrinal underpinnings.

This incorporative approach is apparent in the history of the *Graham* patent litigation. The Fifth and Eighth Circuits turned to the issue of "result" because they were dealing with a problem of "invention," and the case law on "invention" is full of talk about result. But result is a subject of inquiry related to one of the two tests rejected by § 103. The Supreme Court properly rejected its use as a focus of inquiry. Similar treatment should be afforded other subjects of inquiry based on the tests rejected by *Deere*. For they, too, can no longer be relevant.

I. The Three Tests

The three distinct tests of patentability can be denominated, in the order of their historic development, the "novelty" test, the "genius" test, and the "non-obviousness" test. It is the thesis of this paper that only the last survives the decision in *Deere*.

---

[22] 383 U.S. at 3–4.

[23] 34 U.S.L. WEEK 3125 (1965).

[24] 224 F.2d 530 (2d Cir. 1955).

A. THE NOVELTY TEST

The novelty test focuses inquiry on a simple question: Is the device new? If the device is new, then it is patentable. This was the test of the Statute of Monopolies[25] and of the American patent acts of 1793,[26] 1836,[27] and 1870.[28]

In its simple, natural law form, the rationale can be stated as follows. In the specification of his patent the inventor has given to society something that is, by definition, new, something that society did not have before. Because he has given this to society, it is only natural justice that society should give him the exclusive right to its commercial development.

If one prefers an economic justification to one based on "natural right," an argument can also be made that the test of patentability should be "newness." In this view, the purpose of the patent system is not only to encourage invention but to encourage the production and marketing of new products. A new process or product that would be of marginal entrepreneurial interest when facing free entry might become an attractive investment proposition if the right to commercial development were exclusive. Thus, in 1837 Willard Phillips wrote in his *Law of Patents for Inventions:*[29]

> [W]ithout some encouragement and hope of indemnity for expenses, held out by the law, many inventions, after being made, would not be rendered practically useful. . . . Now without the encouragement of a patent, how is any man to engage in a novel and expensive process, if the moment he succeeds, at the cost of all this outlay, he must be sure that his neighbors, who were cautious enough to shun all chances of loss, will come into competition with him, and make the remuneration of all this outlay impossible?

In 1942, Judge Frank stated this rationale at some length:[30]

> [T]here seems still to be room for some kind of patent monopoly which, through hope of rewards to be gained through such a monopoly, will induce venturesome investors to risk large sums needed to bring to the commercially useful stage those new ideas which require immense expenditures for that pur-

---

25 21 James I c.3 (1623).   27 5 Stat. 117 (1836).

26 1 Stat. 318 (1793).   28 16 Stat. 198 (1870).

29 PHILLIPS, THE LAW OF PATENTS FOR INVENTIONS 12–14 (1837).

30 Picard v. United Aircraft Corp., 128 F.2d 632, 642 (2d Cir. 1942) (concurring).

pose. . . . [I]f we never needed, or do not now need, patents as bait for inventors, we may still need them, in some instances, as a lure to investors.

Judge Frank recognized the argument against this position. "Some persons, to be sure, argue that the too rapid obsolescence of plant and equipment through new developments is socially undesirable."[31] His response was both unanswerable and unresponsive. "[R]etardation of our nation's technology now seems of doubtful value since it weakens preparedness for war with another country which has not similarly, in pre-war days, retarded its technology."[32]

This same reasoning controls important governmental policies at the present time. In 1965, the Administrator of the National Aeronautics and Space Administration informed a committee of the United States Senate, with obvious satisfaction, that patents developed on NASA research contracts at government expense would be available for only two years on a non-exclusive, royalty-free basis. But "after the 2-year period, if the benefits of the invention have not been brought to the public, NASA will grant an exclusive license to exploit the invention."[33]

This is either sloppy or bad economics. It is sloppy because there is no effort to clarify whether the costs of commercial development that investors should be induced to meet are costs that must be borne by any entrant into the field, or whether they are costs of innovation that must be borne by only the first entrant. If they are of the latter kind, the point is reasonably sound. But it can be taken care of either by granting patents for the first innovation—the one to be developed—or by granting patents for the additional innovations that are necessary before commercial exploitation is achieved. An advocate of the non-obviousness test—to jump ahead for a moment—would argue that if commercial development requires only the exercise of the ordinary skill of the art, it hardly requires a patent to call it forth. In addition, it should be noted that the whole issue is in part a false one since the development work that concerned Judge Frank and the director NASA (nylon is commonly given as the great example) will usually involve processes and

---

[31] *Id.* at 645.   [32] *Ibid.*

[33] *Hearings on S. 789, S. 1809 and S. 1899 before the Subcommittee on Patents, Trademarks, and Copyrights of the Senate Committee on the Judiciary,* 89th Cong., 1st Sess., pt. 1, 149, 155 (1965) (statement of James E. Webb).

technical know-how that can probably be kept secret for a sub-stantial period of time.

If the costs that concerned Frank and the director of NASA are of a kind that must be borne by every entrant into the field, costs such as investment in production and marketing facilities, then the argument is bad economics. Neither Frank nor the director of NASA seems to realize that there is no a priori principle dictating that the development of the new is the best use of capital resources. If capital can earn a higher return elsewhere absent the prospect of monopoly for the new product, it may well be because that capital is better applied to the alternative use. But that is a point directly contrary to the very existence of NASA, an existence which can be rationalized only by means of an appeal to national defense or national honor, the same unanswerable and yet unresponsive argu-ment that Frank offered. But again, both NASA and Frank make the same error by assuming that "retardation" of commercial ex-ploitation is the same thing as "retardation" of technology. They are not necessarily the same. An adequate military or space tech-nology potential is not assured by incentives for commercial inno-vation. And, conversely, the costs of developing and maintaining this technological potential are not reduced by the grant of monop-oly incentives to include "spinoff" in the civilian economy.

B. THE GENIUS TEST

The genius test is an extension of the natural law argument for the novelty test. But it is based on a negative economic premise about patents. A patent monopoly is costly to the consumer and should not be granted without good reason. It is a reward that should be given only for worthy achievements, for the achievements of genius. The history of this test has been the unfolding of an effort to define this achievement, the true inventive act, as a certain kind of mental process.[34] One inevitable result of this approach has been the eco-nomically absurd conclusion that organized, plodding, group re-search does not produce patentable discoveries because a group does not have genius.[35] Section 103 of the 1952 Act provides that "pat-

---

[34] This effort received its fullest exposition in ROBINSON, THE LAW OF PATENTS FOR USEFUL INVENTIONS (1890).

[35] Potts v. Coe, 145 F.2d 27, 28 (D.C. Cir. 1944) (Arnold, J.): "A discovery which is the result of step-by-step experimentation does not rise to the level of invention." Cf. Picard v. United Aircraft Corp., 128 F.2d 632, 636 (2d Cir. 1942) (Hand, J.). Arnold went on to observe that "the research laboratory has gradually raised the

entability shall not be negatived by the manner in which the invention was made,"[36] thereby eliminating the test of "genius" from the
patent law.[37]

C. THE NON-OBVIOUSNESS TEST

The non-obviousness test shares the economic premises of both
the novelty and genius tests. With the novelty test it shares the
premise that innovation should be encouraged. With the genius test
it shares the premise that patent monopolies represent a substantial
cost to the consumer. These two premises are accommodated by the
basic principle on which the non-obviousness test is based: a patent
should not be granted for an innovation unless the innovation would
have been unlikely to have been developed absent the prospect of
a patent. Unlike the novelty test, it does not view the inducement
of investment in production and marketing facilities, after the
innovation has been developed, as an appropriate function of the
patent system. These are costs that must be borne by everyone who
wishes to market the innovation and if, in the face of competition,
investors do not find the innovation an attractive prospect, that is
because there are better uses for their capital elsewhere, not because
the competitive situation should be altered. The non-obviousness
test makes an effort, necessarily an awkward one, to sort out those
innovations that would not be developed absent a patent system.
Through the years the test has been variously phrased, but the focus
has always been on the question whether the innovation could have
been achieved by one of ordinary skill in the art, or whether its
achievement is of a greater degree of difficulty.

If an innovator must bear costs that need not be borne equally
by his competitors (because they will have the advantage of his
work) and that he cannot recoup, he will not make the expenditures
to innovate. But in a competitive system some non-recurring costs

---

level of industrial art until discoveries by ordinary skilled men, which would have
seemed miraculous in the last century, are definitely predictable if money is available for organized research." 145 F.2d at 30. But why will the money be expended
if it cannot be recovered by means of a patent monopoly?

[36] 35 U.S.C. § 103 (1964).

[37] In response to the suggestion of the amicus curiae brief of the State Bar of
Texas, the Court expressly noted the demise of the "flash of genius" test in *Deere*.
383 U.S. at 15.

can be recouped because the innovator has the advantage of the lead time inherent in his position. Even in the case of products that can be easily imitated the innovator has the advantage of the good will and additional experience inherent in the position of being first in the field. The argument that the innovator can reasonably expect to recoup his costs simply by being first has been seriously offered as an argument against any patent system at all.[38] The difficulty is that as a matter of empirical fact it is not known to what extent the position of innovator gives one an advantage in a competitive situation, nor is it possible to determine the magnitude of a particular innovator's costs to determine whether he can recoup them without an exclusive grant. But what the economic argument does under-line is that much innovation will occur in a competitive system with no patent rights. Only the costlier kinds of innovation will be retarded by the absence of patents. That these innovations will probably be the socially and economically more important only underlines the importance of the patent system. But the central point is that not every innovation needs the patent system to induce its appearance. In fact in many cases, the desire to obtain a superior competitive position by being known as "advanced" and first on the market will induce the appearance of the new product or process. An innovation obvious to one of ordinary skill in the art may indeed be new, in the sense that it did not exist before, and the costs may indeed be substantial if it takes a long time to perfect. But it is the implied judgment of the test that the cost of innovation of this order of difficulty can probably be recouped in a competitive situation while the costs of innovation of a greater difficulty cannot.

The argument has to be made somewhat differently in relation to processes that can be commercially exploited in secrecy. Inno-vations in this area would occur absent the patent system so long as there was reasonable assurance that the techniques involved could be kept secret. Here the function of the patent system is to induce disclosure of innovations that would otherwise be kept secret. This is desirable, not only because at the expiration of the patent the innovation becomes freely available, but also because during the period of the patent the nature of the innovation is dis-

---

[38] Plant, *The Economic Theory concerning Patents for Inventions*, ECONOMICA No. 1, 30, 43–44 (1934).

closed on the public record, and this knowledge may make it possible for others to make further innovations in the same or related fields. But since the patent grant is not to be given lightly, it should be given only to obtain the disclosure of innovations that would otherwise be unlikely to become known. If one of ordinary skill in the art could develop the innovation, it is likely to become known with reasonable ease. Only the non-obvious innovation has any prospect of remaining secret for long and therefore justifies the award of a patent to induce its disclosure.

II. THE HISTORY

These three tests, then, are the components of the history of the idea of invention in the patent law. But for the first eighty-five years there was one basic test, the test of novelty. The Act of 1793 provided that a patent should issue for the invention of any "machine, manufacture, or composition of matter" which was "new and useful."[39] (The earlier Act of 1790 had provided that a patent should issue if the invention was "sufficiently useful and important."[40] It has no significance in the history of the requirement of patentability.) The text of the Act of 1793 makes it clear that new as used in the Act means new and no more. But the drafters felt constrained to add that "simply changing the form or the proportions of any machine, or composition of matter, in any degree, shall not be deemed a discovery."[41]

For the next eighty-two years American patent law followed the process of working out rules designed to prevent trivial advances from falling within the concept of patentable novelty. The problem was to distinguish between changes that were merely changes of form and changes that were changes of substance. "The sufficiency of the invention," Phillips wrote in 1837, "depends not upon the labor, skill, study, or expense applied or bestowed upon it, but upon its being diverse and distinguishable from what

---

[39] 1 Stat. 318–19 (1793).

[40] 1 Stat. 110 (1790). Section 7 of the 1836 Act, 5 Stat. 119–20 (1836), provided that "if the Commissioner shall deem it to be sufficiently useful and important, it shall be his duty to issue a patent therefor," but the courts never treated this language as legally significant. This provision was continued in § 31 of the 1870 Act, 16 Stat. 202 (1870), but it has no counterpart in the present law.

[41] 1 Stat. at 321.

is familiar and well known, and also substantially and materially, not slightly and trivially so. This requisite of an invention is sometimes expressed to be a difference in principle."[42] These distinctions have the ring of metaphysical debate and indeed the efforts of the courts to distinguish between the new and the really new were to lead them to distinctions that sound metaphysical and were meaningless. To quote Justice Story, "The doctrine of patents may truly be said to constitute the metaphysics of law."[43]

The pressures that led to this line of development are not difficult to identify. On the one hand, the courts were bound by the conceptual framework of a statute whose only requirement was that the invention be "new." On the other hand, they were confronted by a quickening pace of technological advance, particularly after the Civil War, that threatened to bring every commodity within a private patent grant. This pressure was revealed and its consequences described in an 1826 opinion:[44]

> The most frivolous and useless alterations in articles in common use are denominated improvements, and made pretexts for increasing their prices, while all complaint and remonstrance are effectually resisted by an exhibition of the great seal. Implements and utensils, as old as the civilization of man, are daily, by means of some ingenious artifice, converted into subjects for patents. If they have usually been made straight, some man of genius will have them made crooked, and, in the phraseology of the privileged order, will swear out a patent. If, from time immemorial, their form has been circular, some distinguished artisan will make them triangular, and he will swear out a patent, relying upon combinations among themselves, and that love of novelty which pervades the human race, and is the besetting sin of our own people, to exclude the old and introduce the new article into use, with an enhanced price for the pretended improvement. . . . More than three thousand patents have been granted since the year 1790. The number obtained for the same or similar objects is well worthy of observation. Eighty are for improvements on the steam engine and on steam boats; more than a hundred for different modes of manufacturing nails; from sixty to seventy for washing machines; from forty to fifty for threshing machines; sixty for pumps; fifty for churns; and a still greater number for stoves. The demand for

---

[42] PHILLIPS, op. cit. supra note 29, at 127.

[43] Barrett v. Hall, 2 Fed. Cas. 914, 923 (No. 1,047) (C.C. D. Mass. 1818).

[44] Thompson v. Haight, 23 Fed. Cas. 1040, 41 (No. 13,957) (C.C. S.D. N.Y. 1826).

this article has called forth much ingenuity and competition. There are now not less than sixty patents for stoves, pretended to be constructed upon different principles. Some are patented, as it is called, because they have ten plates; some, because they have eleven; some because the smoke is permitted to escape at one side, and some because it is let out at the other. Some indefatigable projectors have contrived them with a door on each side, and others, still more acute and profound, make them with a door on one side. . . . The contribution levied upon the community, in the sale of these articles, is enormous, and would be sufficient to satisfy the most inordinate avarice, if it were not distributed among so many men of merit.

The point thus made by Judge Van Ness is that as the pace of obsolescence in a society quickens, the standard of invention must be raised lest every common product be the subject of a patent monopoly. Thus it was logical for Judge Van Ness to raise the specter of no "barriers against the growth and introduction of all the evils that distinguished the ancient system of monopolies," when "all trade and commerce, whether foreign or domestic, was appropriated by monopolists."[45] Much of Judge Van Ness's complaint was directed to the absence of an examination system under the statute of 1793, a complaint to which Congress finally responded in 1836. But a necessary implication of his remarks is that the substantive law should be more demanding. For at least some of his parade of horribles, such as changes in the chimneys of stoves, were properly patentable under the law of his own day.

The central influence on the development of the law of inventive novelty was nascent American legal scholarship. By the year 1850, American patent law had been the subject of three different treatises: Fessenden,[46] Phillips,[47] and Curtis.[48] No other area received so much special attention, and the tradition of ponderous treatises on patent law extended into the first decade of this century before finally expiring.[49] Reasons readily suggest themselves. First, patent

---

[45] *Id.* at 1042.

[46] FESSENDEN, AN ESSAY ON THE LAW OF PATENTS FOR NEW INVENTIONS (1810) (2d ed. 1822).

[47] PHILLIPS, *op. cit. supra* note 29.

[48] CURTIS, THE LAW OF PATENTS FOR USEFUL INVENTIONS (1849) (2d ed. 1854; 3d ed. 1867; 4th ed. 1873).

[49] The "death bed" efforts seem to be MACOMBER, THE FIXED LAW OF PATENTS (1909), and ROGERS, THE LAW OF PATENTS (1914).

law, designed to induce technological innovation, had great appeal to scholars of a young country that prided itself on modernity and progress. Second, systematic English concern with the problem was relatively recent,[50] and thus the Americans were less likely to be overawed in this area. Third, American patent law was a creature of statute and English cases could be dismissed as irrelevant.[51] Fessenden, Phillips, and Curtis—together with the omniscient and omnipresent Story on circuit—laid the foundations.

Viewing the complexities of patent law from the perspective of the 1960's, it is difficult to return to the spirit of the law of the first half of the nineteenth century. The pace of technological innovation was slower and the pressure of commercial activity less constant. The first relevant reported decision indicates the difference. The case is *Park v. Little*,[52] decided by Justice Bushrod Washington on circuit in 1813. The plaintiff complained of an infringement of his patent. The plaintiff, Park, a member of a company of volunteer firemen in Philadelphia, was an enterprising fellow who undertook to improve the efficiency of his comrades. Many of the fires that were the objects of the regular ministrations of this company occurred at night. The custom was that when the cry of fire was raised, the engine would proceed directly to the scene. It was the duty of the members of the company to leave their homes and join the engine there. But this could be the occasion of delay, for the members of the company might become confused and, hearing the sound of another engine, join up with the wrong company. Park undertook to remedy this situation by placing a bell on the engine. But it was not an ordinary bell. He mounted the bell on the end of a horizonal arm attached to the top of a flexible upright. On top of the upright was a ball weighing four or five pounds. As the horses pulled the engine through the streets, this arrangement would become agitated and the bell would ring. The device was a great success until the defendants, members of another company, copied the idea—they varied the details—and

---

[50] The first systematic English treatment of patent law appears to be RANKIN, AN ANALYSIS OF THE LAW OF PATENTS (1824).

[51] But see FESSENDEN, *op. cit. supra* note 46, at 41–42. That English decisions under the Statute of Monopolies would be consulted was established in Pennock v. Dialogue, 2 Pet. 1 (1829).

[52] 18 Fed. Cas. 1107 (No. 10,715) (C.C. D. Pa. 1813).

set a similar bell upon their engine. This caused no end of confusion to the members of the complainant's company, who could never be sure that they were pursuing the sound of their own bell rather than that of the interlopers. Park brought his patent to court to eliminate this difficulty. "Whether this is a new and a useful invention, you must decide," Justice Washington instructed the jury. "But the question is not, whether bells to give alarm or notice are new, but whether the use and application of them to fire engines, to be rung, not by manual action, but by the motion of the carriage, for the purpose of alarm or notice, is a new invention, or improvement of an old one? The power of steam is not new, and yet its application for propelling boats would be considered as such."[53] The jury, displaying more wisdom than fidelity to these instructions, found for the defendant.

The principles were equally clear for Justice Story. In *Earle v. Sawyer*[54] the jury had found against the defendant for infringement and awarded $300 damages. The defendant moved for a new trial, contending that the plaintiff's patent was invalid. The patent related to a device known as a shingle mill, apparently an apparatus for cutting lumber into shingles. The particular patent, issued in 1822, was an improvement on an earlier patent issued to the plaintiff in 1813. The improvement of the first machine over the second was "to admit the use and application in said machine of the circular saw, instead of the perpendicular saw heretofore used, and the substitution of such other parts as are rendered necessary by these alterations."[55] The defendant's counsel argued in prescient terms that the patent was invalid:[56]

> It is not sufficient, that a thing is new and useful, to entitle the author of it to a patent. He must do more. He must find out by mental labor and intellectual creation. If the result of accident, it must be what would not occur to all persons skilled in the art, who wished to produce the same result. There must be some addition to the common stock of knowledge, and not merely the first use of what was known before. The patent act gives a reward for the communication of that, which might be otherwise withholden. An invention is the finding out by some effort of the understanding. The mere putting of two things together, although never done before, is no invention.

---

[53] *Id.* at 1108.

[54] 8 Fed. Cas. 254 (No. 4,247) (C.C. D. Mass. 1825).

[55] *Id.* at 254.

[56] *Id.* at 255.

Story's answer was unequivocal. "It . . . does not appear to me now, that this mode of reasoning upon the metaphysical nature, or the abstract definition of an invention, can justly be applied to cases under the patent act."[57] And he added, "It is of no consequence, whether the thing be simple or complicated; whether it be by accident, or by long, laborious thought, or by an instantaneous flash of mind, that it is first done. The law looks to the fact, and not to the process by which it is accomplished."[58] It must be new, and it must be useful, and that is all.

But *Earle v. Sawyer* is not evidence that the judges were not capable of using the test of inventive novelty to strike down patents. *Earle v. Sawyer* was an unusual case on its facts. The patent claimed exactly what was concededly new, and no more. But if the patent claimed more than the inventor's exact contribution, which was usually the case, the patentee faced a more exacting standard. Thus, in the case of *Woodcock v. Parker*,[59] involving a patent on a machine for splitting leather, Justice Story instructed the jury that:[60]

> [I]f the machine, for which the plaintiff obtained a patent, substantially existed before, and the plaintiff made an improvement only therein, he is entitled to a patent for such improvement only, and not for the whole machine; and under such circumstances, as this present patent is admitted to comprehend the whole machine, it is too broad, and therefore void. . . . If he claim a patent for a whole machine, it must in substance be a new machine; that is, it must be a new mode, method or application of mechanism, to produce some new effect, or to produce an old effect in a new way.

Justice Story groped for words and the test of invention was born. "A new mode, method or application of mechanism, to produce some new effect, or to produce an old effect in a new way." In 1818, the judges began to speak of changes in principle, as opposed to changes in form.[61] "The question for your determination,"

---

[57] *Ibid.*

[58] *Id.* at 256.

[59] 30 Fed. Cas. 491 (No. 17,971) (C.C. D. Mass. 1813).

[60] *Id.* at 492.

[61] Barrett v. Hall, 2 Fed. Cas. 914 (No. 1,047) (C.C. D. Mass. 1818) (Story, J.); Pettibone v. Derringer, 19 Fed. Cas. 387 (No. 11,043) (C.C. D. Pa. 1818) (Washington, J.). In so doing, they adopted the language of the English decisions. See Boulton v. Bull, 2 H. Bl. 463, 126 Eng. Rep. 651 (C.P. 1795). This change may have resulted from the language of the Supreme Court in Evans v. Eaton, 3 Wheat. 454 (1818), and the extensive note on the English patent case to be found *id.* at Appendix, p. 13.

Washington explained, is "whether it is an improvement on the principle [of the prior art] . . . or whether it is merely a change in the form, or proportions."[62] But although the concept of a "principle" was later to be the subject of learned exposition, the courts first used it as a shorthand way of stating Justice Story's earlier instruction. The issue of novelty, said Story, "in the present improved state of mechanics, . . . is often a point of intrinsic difficulty."[63]

This remained the law of invention until 1875, so far as the Supreme Court Justices were concerned. *Hotchkiss v. Greenwood*,[64] decided in the 1850 Term, can be understood only against this background. For an examination of that opinion reveals that despite all the significance that has been attributed to it, it merely re-affirmed the law as it then existed, adding only a minor wrinkle that in context liberalized the standard of invention still further. This addition, the non-obviousness test, was understood as a specialized doctrine applicable in a narrow situation, and it was only later that the case became a "leading" case.

The patent in the *Hotchkiss* case was for an improved method of making knobs for "locks, doors, cabinet furniture, and for all other purposes for which wood and metal or other material knobs are used."[65] "This improvement consists," explained the specifications of the patent, "in making said knobs of potter's clay, such as is used in any species of pottery; also of porcelain."[66] The key passage in the specifications stated:[67]

> [T]he modes of fitting them for their application to doors, locks, furniture, and other uses will be as various as the uses to which they may be applied, but chiefly predicated on one principle, that of having the cavity in which the screw or shank is inserted, by which they are fastened, largest at the bottom of its depth, in form of a dovetail, and a screw formed therein by pouring in metal in a fused state.

The evidence at trial developed two important facts. First, the defendant was unable to adduce any evidence that knobs of clay had ever been made before. Second, it had been common to fasten

---

[62] 19 Fed. Cas. at 390.

[63] Lowell v. Lewis, 15 Fed. Cas. 1018, 1019 (No. 8,568) (C.C. D. Mass. 1817).

[64] 11 How. 248 (1850).   [66] *Ibid.*

[65] *Id.* at 249.   [67] *Ibid.*

knobs made of other materials to their spindles by means of the dovetail fastening described in the plaintiff's specifications. The significance of these uncontroverted facts was the legal issue of the case.

The plaintiff had requested an instruction that the patent was valid "if such shank and spindle had never before been attached in this mode to a knob of potter's clay, and it required skill and invention to attach the same to a knob of this description, so that they would be firmly united, and make a strong and substantial article, and which, when thus made, would become an article much better and cheaper than the knobs made of metal or other materials."[68] This was in substance a request for a directed verdict for the plaintiff, for as the trial court correctly observed, "it requires skill and thought to attach a spindle to any kind of knob."[69] Indeed, it requires skill and thought to do any kind of mechanical work. The trial court rejected the instruction because it failed to take account of the requirement that the knob, to be patentable, must embody a new principle. And, insisted the trial court, improved quality and economy did not mean that the article embodied a new principle. (This was an issue that was still agitating the courts of appeals in the *Deere* case and that provoked a dissent from Justice Woodbury in *Hotchkiss*.) The trial court took the position that if the material was old and the mode of fastening the material to the spindle was old, there was no new principle in the operation of the knob and gave the jury an instruction that amounted to a directed verdict for the defendant. The patent was therefore void, added the court, because the material was in common use, and no other ingenuity or skill was necessary to construct the knob than that of an ordinary mechanic acquainted with the business.[70] This implied that a patent might still be valid even if it did not embody a new principle if it required more than mechanical skill for its development. But what is more important, it took the issue away from the jury and held that the knobs had not required more than mechanical skill for their construction. The jury had no choice but to find for the defendant.

In his argument before the Supreme Court, this was the point the defendant raised. The lower court had taken "upon themselves

---

[68] *Id.* at 263–64.

[69] 12 Fed. Cas. 551, 552 (No. 6,718) (C.C. D. Ohio 1848).   [70] *Id.* at 553.

to determine in the negative the question whether 'it required skill and thought and invention to attach the knob of clay to the metal shank and spindle, so that they would unite firmly, and make a solid, substantial article of manufacture,' instead of submitting it to the jury. It was a question of fact . . . depending upon evidence, and ought to have been submitted to the jury."[71] The argument fell on unsympathetic ears, for in his opinion Justice Nelson misunderstood the instruction as having put to the jury the issue whether the construction of the device had required more than mechanical skill, and the dissent accepted this interpretation. It is important to note, however, that in his argument plaintiff continued to insist on the language of his requested instruction. "Skill, thought and invention," under the principle of *ejusdem generis*, seems to mean that invention is simply the exercise of skill and thought. One possible interpretation of Justice Nelson's opinion is that he understood the objection to the instructions to be that a requirement of "more than mechanical skill" was too severe and he simply rejected that ground. For it could have been argued under the law prior to *Hotchkiss v. Greenwood* that if an innovation did not incorporate a new principle it was not patentable, even if the innovation required more than mechanical skill, because it would still not be new.

The invasion of the competence of the jury was not, however, the principal argument of the plaintiff. He quoted Curtis: "The mere substitution of one metal for another in a particular manufacture might be the subject of a patent, if the new article were better, more useful, or cheaper than the old."[72] Clay and porcelain knobs, he argued, were better than the earlier knobs of wood and metal:[73]

> It is indeed an invention of much more than common importance and merit. It is the combination of two materials, metal and earth, never before united in this manner, so as to give to the new manufacture the strength of iron with the durability and beauty of the clay or porcelain; its exemption from the corrosive action of acids and other chemical agents, and its consequent freedom from tarnish.

---

[71] 11 How. at 253.

[72] *Id.* at 255, quoting CURTIS, *op. cit. supra* note 48, at 27.

[73] *Id.* at 257.

The defendant based his argument on two alternative construc-
tions of the patent. "Does the patent . . . confine its claim to a mere
right to use clay or porcelain for the purpose of making . . . knobs,
or does it claim to cover the manufacturing [of] knobs of clay and
porcelain in the manner . . . set forth in the specification?"[74] He
argued for the latter construction. He favored this construction
because if the patent covered knobs of clay attached to spindles
by means of the dovetail fastening, then the patent covered both
old and new matter. He, too, relied on Curtis: "[I]f it turns out that
any thing claimed is not new, the patent is void, however small
or unimportant such asserted invention may be."[75] This had the
ironic result of making the narrower construction of the claim the
invalid one. If the patent covered all clay knobs, it might be valid;
if it covered only clay knobs of this type, it might be invalid. The
argument, however, was a literal application of the controlling law.

The case was more difficult for the defendant if the patent was
construed as simply claiming knobs of clay and porcelain. His
argument on this contingency required a creative analogy. A
number of earlier circuit court decisions had decided that a new
use for an old machine did not entitle one to a patent for the machine, since the machine, after all, was not new.[76] Clay and porcelain, the defendant pointed out, were old materials and the patent
was simply for a new use of an old material.[77] Therefore it was
not new, and not patentable.

Writing for the Court, Justice Nelson first answered the plaintiff's contention that the knobs were patentable because they were
better. That they are better "is doubtless true," he said, "but the
peculiar effect . . . is not distinguishable from that which would
exist in the case of the wood knob, or one of bone or ivory, or
of other materials that might be mentioned."[78] Justice Woodbury,
citing *Earle v. Sawyer*, dissented on this point.[79] For an article that
is better, he reasoned, must surely be new.

Nelson went on in his opinion to admit of an exception. The
knob might be patentable, even though there was no new principle
or effect, if "more ingenuity and skill in applying the old method

---

[74] *Ibid.*   [75] *Id.* at 259, quoting Curtis, *op. cit. supra* note 48, at 133.

[76] Bean v. Smallwood, 2 Fed. Cas. 1142 (No. 1,173) (C.C. D. Mass. 1843); Howe
v. Abbott, 12 Fed. Cas. 656 (No. 6,766) (C.C. D. Mass. 1842).

[77] 11 How. at 261.   [78] *Id.* at 266.   [79] *Id.* at 266–71.

of fastening the shank and the knob were required in the application of it to the clay or porcelain knob than were possessed by an ordinary mechanic acquainted with the business."[80] But since in this case the jury had found that no such skill was exercised, a conclusion Nelson reached because of his misunderstanding of the instruction, "there was an absence of that degree of skill and ingenuity which constitute essential elements of every invention."[81] It was this phrase that presaged wider application of the test. For its time, the rule of *Hotchkiss v. Greenwood* was that a change of materials is not of itself patentable even if it results in an improvement, unless the application of the material to the use requires more than mechanical skill. In his 1854 edition Curtis added a special section on *Hotchkiss*. He could accommodate it without difficulty:[82]

> [T]he end, effect, or result attained must be new; and . . . if the same end, effect, or result has been attained before, it is not new, and there has been no invention. . . . So, too the substitution of one material for another, in a particular manufacture, if the inventive faculty has not been at work, has been held by the Supreme Court of the United States not to be sufficient to support a patent. . . . But on the other hand, if the end, effect, or result is new, although the same means may previously have been used to produce a different effect, and for a different purpose, there may be a patent for the application of the materials to produce the new effect or result.

In 1850 Curtis' was the leading treatise on patent law. The first edition of *Treatise on the Law of Patents for Useful Inventions* had appeared the year before and, as the summary of the arguments of counsel in *Hotchkiss* makes clear, it was already regarded as authoritative. It was shortly completely to supersede an older and better work: Phillips' *Treatise* of 1837.[83] Phillips' was a fine and careful book. Fessenden's, which preceded it, was largely a collection of cases followed by a sketchy and badly organized "synthetical view of the Law of Patents for New Inventions, together with such rules as may appear best calculated to prevent, as far as possible, future disputes on the subject."[84] Phillips was

---

[80] *Id.* at 266.   [81] *Ibid.*

[82] CURTIS, *op. cit. supra* note 48, at 45–49 (2d ed.).

[83] PHILLIPS, *op. cit. supra* note 29.

[84] FESSENDEN, *op cit. supra* note 46, at 186–89 (1st ed.); 362–89 (2d ed.).

the first to pursue the implications of the general approach adopted by the courts. The general problem was: when is a patent covering a change that is not entirely new valid? Since every innovation will build on existing technology, this is a question that must be answered in relation to every patent. The general answer preferred was that the innovation is patentable if it is an application of a new principle or if it produces a new effect or result. Phillips began to divide this general problem into subcategories. These were: improvement; new use; combination; and change of form, proportions, or materials. By dealing separately with the different classes of innovation, Phillips hoped to add precision to the application of the ambiguous generality of the controlling rule. But he was aware that the categories were treacherous:[85]

> [W]e are without the usual help to satisfactory speculation, that is, clear language, intelligible to every one, which proves, in this, as in other cases, a double hindrance, first to clear and discriminate thinking, and second, to the ready and perspicuous communication of thought. As the different expressions used in describing patentable subjects are very analogous to each other in signification, and are mutually blended and implicated together in their meaning, and in the application made of them in the cases, the most convenient mode of treating of them, at least the most concise, will be to enumerate them all, and examine them successively.

If later writers had remained as sensitive to these difficulties, perhaps these categories would not have been raised to the dogmas they have become. But Phillips had one basic limitation. He saw himself as expositor of the law, not as commentator on it. The categories were useful, not for analytic purposes, but in order to set out the law with greater precision.

Of the four categories, improvement was the most general. On this Phillips said that either a new effect or a new method of obtaining an old effect was patentable.[86] But what of an improvement which applies known apparatus to achieve a new effect? Not patentable said Phillips: "There is no instance in which it has been held that a mere new effect of the use of a machine already known, without any new combination, machinery, or process, is the subject of a valid patent."[87] But what of the problem of combinations?

---

[85] PHILLIPS, op. cit. supra note 29, at 77.

[86] Id. at 122–23.   [87] Id. at 109.

"It is sufficient . . . that the combination is new, though the separate things combined may have been before in use and well known."[88] But then is a change of materials patentable? For a change of materials, after all, is a combination of an old device with a different material. "The substitution of one material for another is not, at least ordinarily, an invention for which a patent can be claimed."[89] The upshot of these inconsistencies was that it made a great deal of difference under which category an innovation was subsumed. The argument in *Hotchkiss v. Greenwood* was an argument for competing categories. "Our invention," argued the plaintiff, "is a combination of dissimilar materials."[90] "[W]e maintain," responded the defendant, "that they cannot obtain a patent for a new use, or double use, of the article of clay."[91]

In 1849, Curtis did not give these categories the same prominence. He re-emphasized the general rule that the "line of demarkation between invention and a mere application to a new use" is "that the end, effect, or result attained must be new"[92] and, unlike Phillips, he seemed to assume that this rule applied to combinations as much as to any other kind of innovation.[93] But after Phillips the important thing is that the conceptual structure he created began to dominate the cases.

Cases before the Supreme Court raising issues of patentable novelty after *Hotchkiss* were infrequent. The small number, a characteristic of the entire period from 1793 to 1870, certainly cannot be explained by the ease with which the controlling rules could be applied. The concept of change of "principle" was ambiguous and the text writers' categories were inconsistent. The simplest explanation lies in the small number of patents issued each year prior to the Civil War.[94] But even when computed as a percentage of the patent cases litigated, there appears to have been a marked rise in the incidence of the patentability issue after 1870. The rules as applied resulted in the validation of most patents and, except in the unusual case, the issue of patentability did not represent a fruitful avenue of attack for defendants. So long as

---

88 *Id*. at 115.

89 *Id*. at 133.

90 11 How. at 256.

91 *Id*. at 261.

92 CURTIS, *op. cit. supra* note 48, at 45.

93 *Id*. at 41–44.

94 1840: 458; 1850: 883; 1860: 4,357. U.S. DEPT. OF COMMERCE, THE STORY OF THE U.S. PATENT OFFICE 34 (1965).

the controlling approach was that anything new was patentable, only the most trivial innovations would pose a serious problem. After 1836 many of these were screened out by the Patent Office examining procedure with which the Court seems to have been satisfied. "It is evident," the Court said in 1854, "that a patent . . . issued, after an inquisition of examination made by skillful and sworn public officers, appointed for the purpose of protecting the public against false claims or useless inventions, is entitled to much more respect, as evidence of novelty and utility, than those formerly issued without any such investigation."[95] The few cases decided by the Court on the issue address themselves to the problem of working out the categories suggested by the early circuit decisions and organized by Phillips. There are so few of them that they can be catalogued.

The first case after *Hotchkiss* was *Winans v. Denmead*,[96] a change-of-form case. The plaintiff had patented an improvement of cars for transporting coal. The Court without difficulty concluded that the car was patentable: "[B]y means of this change of form, the patentee has introduced a mode of operation not before employed in burden cars."[97] *Phillips v. Page*,[98] was both a new-use and change-of-size case. The patent was on a saw mill. The plaintiff's saw was larger than the earlier saws in use and was meant to be used on full-sized saw logs instead of small blocks. The Court said the enlargement of the machine was no ground for a patent. Using the language of the non-obviousness test, the Court observed that enlarging a machine is "done every day by the ordinary mechanic in making a working machine from the patent model." But it then concluded that novelty rather than non-obviousness was the appropriate standard by adding that "in order to reach invention," the patentee "must contrive the means of adapting the enlarged old organization to the new use."[99] Neither a change of size nor a new use made the saw a patentable device.

The pace accelerated in 1870. *Stimpson v. Woodman*[100] was an improvement case. The patent was for a machine for ornamenting leather by means of a figured roller. Previously a figured roller had been applied by hand for the same purpose, but the same

---

[95] Corning v. Burden, 15 How. 252, 270 (1854).

[96] 15 How. 329 (1854).

[97] *Id.* at 338.

[98] 24 How. 164 (1861).

[99] *Id.* at 167.

[100] 10 Wall. 117 (1870).

machine had existed using a smooth roller. The Court reversed the trial court for refusing to give a requested instruction that "if they should find that the form of the surface of the rollers in the plaintiff's machine is not material to the mechanical action of the roller in combination with the other devices and their arrangements, by which the roller is moved, the leather supported, and the pressure made,"[101] the patent is invalid. The Court added that the improvement "required no invention; the change with the existing knowledge in the art involved simply mechanical skill, which is not patentable."[102] Although the approved instruction said nothing about mechanical skill, this sentence was apparently thought to justify the instruction, not to constitute an independent test of invention. *Seymour v. Osborne*,[103] was also an improvement case and was explicit in ruling that non-obviousness did not constitute an independent ground of invalidity. "Improvements for which a patent may be granted," explained the Court, "must be new and useful, within the meaning of the patent law, or the patent will be void, but the requirement of the patent act in that respect is satisfied if the combination is new and the machine is capable of being beneficially used for the purpose for which it was designed."[104] *Tucker v. Spalding*,[105] held that a new use of an old device was not patentable, leaving to the jury the question whether the patented device was identical to an earlier device or not. *Hicks v. Kelsey*,[106] held a change of materials unpatentable, and represented the first time in twenty-three years that *Hotchkiss* was cited in an opinion of the Court.[107]

Hailes v. Van Wormer[108] was a combination case in which Justice Strong pompously gave forth the doctrine of aggregation. The doctrine managed to combine the appearance of complex significance with the substance, if not the grace, of a nonsense rhyme:[109]

> [T]he results must be a product of the combination, and not a mere aggregate of several results each the complete product of

---

[101] *Id.* at 119.

[102] *Id.* at 121.

[103] 11 Wall. 516 (1871).

[104] *Id.* at 548–49.

[105] 13 Wall. 453 (1872).

[106] 18 Wall. 670 (1874).

[107] *Hotchkiss* had been cited by Justice Campbell, dissenting, in *Winans v. Denmead*, arguing that a patent on a change of form should be held invalid as equivalent to a patent on a change of material. 15 How. at 344.

[108] 20 Wall. 353 (1874).

[109] *Id.* at 368.

one of the combined elements. Combined results are not necessarily a novel result, nor are they an old result obtained in a
new and improved manner. Merely bringing old devices into
juxtaposition, and there allowing each to work out its own effect without the production of something novel, is not invention. No one by bringing together several old devices without
producing a new and useful result, the joint product of the elements of the combination and something more than an aggre-
gate of old results, can acquire a right to prevent others from
using the same devices, either singly or in other combinations.

Rubber Tip Pencil Co. v. Howard,[110] held invalid a patent for placing an eraser on the end of a pencil. It was a good idea, the Court
conceded, but the device itself incorporated nothing new.

The 1874 Term brought a change. It was a silent change, unac-
knowledged by the Court. It first appeared in *Smith v. Nichols,*[111] involving a patent for an improved fabric. The Court held the patent
invalid, although it conceded that the cloth was better, because
the improvements were only improvements in degree. "Doing substantially the same thing in the same way by substantially the same
means with better results, is not such invention as will sustain a
patent."[112] This holding suggests that novelty alone is not enough
but was not very different from *Hotchkiss v. Greenwood.* The Court
added a phrase, however, suggestive of a new approach. "A patentable invention is a mental result."[113] For the first time the Court
did not speak of an invention, a thing, which must be new and useful. Now it spoke of invention, an act, something that must be
done, and implied that this too was a requirement of patentability.

Less than two months after *Nichols,* the Court decided *Collar
Company v. Van Dusen.*[114] The patent was for a shirt "collar
made of long-fibre paper."[115] The contribution of the patentee
was to find a quality of paper suitable for making paper collars
which, prior to his innovation, had always been found unsatisfactory. Collars already existed. The paper already existed. The Court
might easily have disposed of the case as a change of materials
case. But it did not:[116]

---

110 20 Wall. 498 (1874).

111 21 Wall. 112 (1875).   114 23 Wall. 530 (1875).

112 *Id.* at 119.   115 *Id.* at 542.

113 *Id.* at 118.   116 *Id.* at 563.

Articles of manufacture may be new in the commercial sense when they are not new in the sense of patent law. New articles of commerce are not patentable as new manufactures, unless it appears in the given case that the production of the new article involved the exercise of invention or discovery beyond what was necessary to construct the apparatus for its manufacture or production.

For the first time *Hotchkiss v. Greenwood* was cited as a case of general application, standing for the proposition that "nothing short of invention or discovery will support a patent."[117] Invention became a third requirement for patentability.

This was a change of ultimate significance but of little immediate effect. The Court had recognized a new requirement, invention, but it still had no idea what it was. The Court simply fell back on older patent cases and their tests of novelty. At first, the cases experimented with language about genius and what it means to invent;[118] only slowly does the non-obviousness test come to the forefront.[119] Indeed, the change may have been at the time imperceptible to both the Court and its bar.[120] Not until 1885, in *Thompson v. Boisselier*, did the Court take pains to point out that "it is not enough that a thing shall be new, in the sense that in the shape or form in which it is produced it shall not have been before known, and that it shall be useful, but it must, under the Constitution and the statute, amount to an invention or discovery."[121]

---

[117] *Ibid.*

[118] See, *e.g.*, Densmore v. Scofield, 102 U.S. 375, 378 (1880): "It does not appear . . . that there was a 'flash of thought' by which such a result . . . was reached, or that there was any exercise of the inventive faculty, more or less thoughtful, whereby anything entitled to the protection of a patent was produced."

[119] The non-obviousness test predominated after 1880. But it never became the exclusive test.

[120] The lower federal courts never recognized the *Paper Collar* case as a turning point. *Hotchkiss*, which eventually came to be cited as the leading case establishing the requirement of invention, was not even cited by the lower federal courts of general jurisdiction until 1882. Scott v. Evans, 11 Fed. 726, 727 (C.C. W.D. Pa. 1882). It was there cited as a change of material case. (It was cited in review of a Patent Office decision in *In re* Maynard, MacArthur's Patent Cases 536, 537–38 (C.C. Dist. Col. 1857).) It was first cited for the general proposition that "not every trifling device, nor any obvious improvement in the material already possessed is intended to be rewarded" by the patent laws, in Leonard v. Lovell, 29 Fed. 310, 314 (C.C. W.D. Mich. 1886).

[121] 114 U.S. 1, 11 (1885).

Perhaps the reference to the Constitution was felt necessary to validate the pronounced change. But, in spite of this strong position, the Court was confronted the next Term with the argument that "the statute makes novelty and utility the only tests of patentability."[122] "It is sufficient answer to these suggestions," Justice Blatchford wrote, "to say that the questions presented are not open ones in this court."[123]

It was fortuitous that the Court's change of position took place when it did. The 1836 statute had always been susceptible of two different readings. The statute provided that "any person or persons [who] discovered or invented any new and useful" device was eligible for a patent.[124] The problem was how to read "discovered or invented." Was it the equivalent of "found," if what is found is "new and useful?" Or did "discovered or invented" connote some additional requirement? The original interpretation posited two requirements for patentability: novelty and utility. The new reading posited three: novelty, utility, and invention. As early as 1856, a district judge had read the statute in the second way, instructing a jury that "it is required that there should be an invention, that the invention should be new, and that it should be useful. In other words, before a patent can be issued, the thing patented must appear to be of such a character, as to involve or require 'invention' for its production—require the exercise of the genius of an inventor as contradistinguished from the ordinary skill of a mechanic in construction."[125]

A satisfactory explanation of the Court's shift can only be found in non-legal forces at work in the country after the Civil War. First and foremost is the sharp rise in the number of patents issued immediately after the cessation of hostilities. In 1860, 4,357 original patents were issued on inventions.[126] After a decline during the war, the number jumped to 8,863 in 1866. In 1867 the number jumped again to 12,277. The number of patents issued annually

---

122 Gardner v. Herz, 118 U.S. 180, 191 (1886).   123 Ibid.

124 § 6, 5 Stat. 117, 119 (1836). The 1793 Act had provided simply that the person must have "invented." § 1, 1 Stat. 318 (1793). The 1870 statute said "any person who has invented or discovered. . . ." § 24, 16 Stat. 198, 201 (1870).

125 Ransom v. New York, 20 Fed. Cas. 286, 288 (No. 11,573) (C.C. S.D. N.Y.) 1856.

126 U.S. DEPT. OF COMMERCE, op. cit. supra note 94, at 34.

remained at about this level until 1880, when it rose to an annual level of about 20,000. This is in striking contrast to the 883 patents issued the year *Hotchkiss* was decided. This increase was reflected in a rapidly expanding volume of patent litigation before the courts. At the same time, the patent abolition controversy in England and on the Continent[127] exacerbated worry about the threat of the patent system to a competitive economy. During the debate on the codification of 1870, one senator put the question "whether our whole patent system is not founded in an error" and quoted from an abolitionist a statement "that patents are injurious alike to the inventor, the public, and the manufacturer."[128] Although the patent abolition position never gained substantial support in the United States, it gave impetus to the drive to limit patents. "The time is not yet ripe for the propagation of this idea [of the abolition of patents] in the United States," explained an editorial writer in the *New York Times* in 1870, but "another phase of it, which will in due time lead up to the great issue, is the tendency . . . [in official American circles] not, indeed to repress the introduction of inventions, but to confine the period and chances of their reward to narrower limits."[129]

By the 1870's the Patent Office had lost the prestige it had once enjoyed. During the Civil War charges of misappropriation of funds had been made against the commissioner. An investigating committee of the House found no evidence of misappropriation, but ample evidence of mismanagement.[130] During the debate on the codification of 1870 some of the speakers suggested corruption in the Patent Office,[131] and a new provision was put in the patent laws to prevent employees of the office from taking a personal interest in patents issued.[132]

The quickening pace of innovation also made patents seem less necessary. In 1872, an engineer and inventor suggested that the art

---

[127] Assorted documents related to this controversy may be found in RECENT DISCUSSIONS ON THE ABOLITION OF PATENTS FOR INVENTIONS (1869) and 2 COPYRIGHT AND PATENTS FOR INVENTIONS (Macfie ed. 1883).

[128] CONG. GLOBE, 41st Cong., 2d Sess. 4827 (1870).

[129] N.Y. Times, March 20, 1870, p. 4, col. 4.

[130] H.R. REP. No. 48, 37th Cong., 3d Sess. (1863).

[131] CONG. GLOBE, 41st Cong., 2d Sess. 2874, 4825 (1870).

[132] 16 Stat. 200 (1870), 35 U.S.C. § 4 (1964).

of inventing had advanced to the point where "bribes for discovery" were no longer necessary:[133]

> We no longer need the incentive of personal right in invention or demonstration to develop our arts, and the writer, from his own observation, both in England and America, finds that the better class of engineers and mechanics have come already to look with disfavor upon patents, a question of fact which will be confirmed by as many as have noticed the matter, and one that can be determined by searching the records of the patent office for the names of our best engineers.

Only once, however, did the Court take notice of all this in its opinions. In 1882 the Court observed:[134]

> It was never the object of . . . [the patent] laws to grant a monopoly for every trifling device, every shadow of a shade of an idea, which would naturally and spontaneously occur to any skilled mechanic or operator in the ordinary progress of manufactures. Such an indiscriminate creation of exclusive privileges tends rather to obstruct than to stimulate invention. It creates a class of speculative schemers who make it their business to watch the advancing wave of improvement, and gather its foam in the form of patented monopolies, which enable them to lay a heavy tax upon the industry of the country, without contributing anything to the real advancement of the arts. It embarrasses the honest pursuit of business with fears and apprehensions of concealed liens and unknown liabilities to lawsuits and vexatious accountings for profits made in good faith.

The story of the Court's efforts after 1874 to delimit the boundaries of the concept of invention is the story of failure. The non-obvious test predominated; yet in 1892 the Court upheld the barbed-wire patent without a mention of non-obviousness, observing tersely that "in the law of patents it is the last step that wins."[135] In the preceding Term the Court had apparently despaired of ever defining invention:[136]

> The truth is the word cannot be defined in such manner as to afford any substantial aid in determining whether a particular device involves an exercise of the inventive faculty or not. In a

---

133 Richards, *Patent Invention*, 63 J. FRANKLIN INST. 17, 21 (1872).

134 Atlantic Works v. Brady, 107 U.S. 192, 200 (1883).

135 The Barbed Wire Patent, 143 U.S. 275, 283 (1892).

136 McClain v. Ortmayer, 141 U.S. 419, 427 (1891).

given case we may be able to say that there is present invention of a very high order. In another we can see that there is lacking that impalpable something which distinguishes invention from simple mechanical skill.

Novelty, genius, and non-obviousness are all part of the requirement. In the infamous *Cuno* case of 1941,[137] Mr. Justice Douglas referred to all three in almost the same breath:[138]

> [T]he new device, however useful it may be, must reveal the flash of creative genius not merely the skill of the calling. . . . Tested by that principle Mead's device was not patentable. We cannot conclude that his skill in making this contribution reached the level of inventive genius. . . . A new application of an old device may not be patented if the "result claimed as new is the same in character as the original result. . . ."

The reason for the Court's inability to settle on the non-obviousness test as the controlling one may be due to the fact that it was never acknowledged to be a new test, but rather a continuation of an old one always required by the statute. This myth, largely the myth of *Hotchkiss v. Greenwood,* meant that the Court continued to treat the earlier cases as good law, and forced the concept of non-obviousness into an unhappy marriage with a concept of novelty and its doctrines of "new principle," "new result," or "new function." In one case, the Court attempted to accommodate these quite different notions by propounding a rule of evidence. "It may be laid down as a general rule, though perhaps not an invariable one, that if a new combination and arrangement of known elements produce a new and beneficial result, never attained before, it is evidence of invention."[139] But the irrelevance of "new result" to "non-obviousness" made this a hopeless solution. The inherent instability was only increased by the additional test of genius, and the Court's actions became erratic and unpredictable. Ironically, in the 1940's the inventive novelty tests, originally favorable to patents, were used by the Court to invalidate patents on substantial technical advances.[140]

The analytic dilemma was clearly revealed in the secondary lit-

---

[137] Cuno Eng'r Corp. v. Automatic Devices Corp., 314 U.S. 84 (1941).

[138] *Id.* at 91.

[139] Loom Co. v. Higgins, 105 U.S. 580, 591 (1882).

[140] See General Elec. Co. v. Jewel Incandescent Lamp Co., 326 U.S. 242 (1945); Cuno Eng'r Corp. v. Automatic Devices Corp., 314 U.S. 84 (1941).

erature of the last quarter of the nineteenth century. In 1883, Henry
Merwin attempted to resolve the problem by creating two categories.[141] Turning to the language of the statute, he made the original observation that it did not say "invented," but "invented or
discovered." For Merwin this perception put everything in place.
A patent was valid if it was either invented or discovered. Some
cases dealt with one category, some cases with the other. In his
introductory essay he wrote that "Most patents are granted for
inventions strictly."[142] But there is another class, where "the patentee has discovered a new principle, and if he makes some practical application thereof . . . he may obtain a valid patent."[143] Merwin
went on to explain that in the case of a discovery "no inquiry need
be made into the mental process by which a knowledge of the
principle was attained. It is sufficient that the principle upon which
the patent is based should be new, *i.e.*, that it should not have been
known till the patentee revealed it."[144] This division made it possible for Merwin to accommodate the old novelty (discovery) cases
with the new invention cases. Merwin lavished his warmest attention on the description of invention: "Invention is imagination;
it is the very opposite of reasoning or inference; it is a single act
of the mind; rather an instantaneous operation than a process. It
has no stages; the essence of it is that it dispenses with them."[145]
But the discussion was a failure. And with a sigh of resignation, he
admitted that his was "a distinction which has not, in terms, been
taken by the courts."[146]

A far more comprehensive work than Merwin's, a three-volume
work by William C. Robinson of the Yale law faculty, appeared in
1890.[147] Robinson did not look for an easy way out. For Robinson, it
was the nature of the inventive act that would furnish "a correct
and definite apprehension of the attributes which must be found
in every true invention."[148] Each inventive act consists of two ele-

---

141 MERWIN, THE PATENTABILITY OF INVENTIONS (1883).

142 *Id.* at 3.   144 *Ibid.*

143 *Ibid.*   145 *Id.* at 22.   146 *Id.* at 557.

147 ROBINSON, THE LAW OF PATENTS FOR USEFUL INVENTIONS (1890). It was described in Davis, *Proposed Modifications in the Patent System*, 12 LAW & CONTEMP.
PROB. 796, 806 (1947), as "perhaps the most profound study of our patent system
ever made."

148 ROBINSON, *op. cit. supra* note 147, at 115.

ments: "(1) An idea conceived by the inventor; (2) An application of that idea to the production of a practical result."[140] This second element incorporated the traditional idea that there must be a reduction to practice. Most interesting was Robinson's definition of the necessary mental element: "an exercise of the creative faculties, generating an idea which is clearly recognized and comprehended by the inventor, and is both complete in itself and capable of application to a practical result."[150] Thus he was able to transform the old novelty doctrine into a test of the inventive act and thereby harmonize the old cases with the new. His solution has three fundamental defects. First, it involves tests that have little relation to reality, or to the extent they are based on reality, that reality is exclusively one of mechanical improvements. Second, the tests are derived inductively from a given concept of invention without any reference to the economic functions a patent system might or should perform. And, third, it is discriminatory because it suggests that of two people who discover the same thing, only one might have invented it. Only the person who understands the "idea" is worthy of a patent. Robinson extended the metaphysics of invention begun in Story's early opinions. He was the last scholar to attempt to move directly from "invention" to a test of patentability on the basis of inductive logic. It is as if the thoroughness of his attempt proved once and for all the futility of the approach.

Walker's *Text-Book of the Patent Laws*, published in 1883, is much different from the works of both Merwin and Robinson. Merwin and Robinson conceived of themselves as walking among the inventors of genius they so laboriously describe. Walker, on the other hand, plods through the cases. This is both the weakness of his analysis and the source of the book's endurance for more than eighty years. Walker does not solve the analytic dilemma, he encapsulates it. And fossilized in Walker, the dilemma has been treated as the law down to the *Deere* decision. Walker is quick to acknowledge that "invention" is not defined. "There is no affirmative rule by which to determine the presence or absence of invention in every case."[151] But Walker does have something to offer: "negative rules of invention" derived from the cases in which patents have been held invalid. For the most part these are the old novelty

---

[149] *Id.* at 116.   [150] *Id.* at 132.

[151] WALKER, TEXT-BOOK OF THE PATENT LAWS 18 (1883).

tests put into the negative. For instance, Walker announces that "aggregation is not invention."[152] The negative novelty tests are supplemented by a negative non-obviousness test: "It is not invention to produce a device or process which any skillful mechanic or chemist would produce whenever required."[153] Commercial success is used to resolve borderline cases: "When the other facts in a case leave the question of invention in doubt, the fact that the device has gone into general use, and has displaced other devices which had previously been employed for analogous uses, is sufficient to turn the scale in favor of the existence of invention."[154]

The use of the negative form was a rhetorical device that eased the tension between the old novelty tests and the new requirement of invention. When the Court said that a new result is evidence of invention, that left the basic problem what is invention if its presence can be proved by a new result. But if one says that aggregation is not invention, there is no such problem because the rule in form does not claim to say anything about what invention is. Thus Walker's contribution was to give the new requirement of invention and the old tests of novelty a framework in which they could coexist in an uneasy but apparently permanent peace. The 1937 edition,[155] the sixth version of the book to appear, contains these same tests, illustrated in greater detail by cases that relied on earlier editions. And if the structure of the 1964 edition is substantially affected by the 1952 statute, the negative novelty tests are still given a prominent role,[156] in spite of the fact that they find no basis in § 103.

Walker captured the inconsistencies of the law of his day as well as anyone could. But having structured the analytic dilemma, he

---

[152] *Id.* at 24.   [154] *Id.* at 30.

[153] *Id.* at 18.   [155] DELLER, WALKER ON PATENTS (1937).

[156] DELLER, WALKER ON PATENTS (3d ed. 1964). The negative tests were summarized as follows: "(1) mere exercise of skill expected of a person having ordinary skill in the art; (2) substitution of materials or elements; (3) change of location, size, degree and form; (4) reversal of parts; (5) unification or multiplication of parts; (6) making old devices adjustable, durable, portable or moveable; (7) change of proportion; (8) duplication of parts; (9) omission of parts with a corresponding omission of function; (10) substitution of equivalents; (11) new use for a new and analogous purpose; (12) conversion of manual to a mechanical operation; (13) superior or excellent workmanship; and (14) aggregation." 2 *id.* at 75. This framework treats non-obviousness as one of many tests rather than as the controlling test of invention.

made it harder for the Court to move away from it. In 1962 Congress explicitly legislated that non-obviousness was the controlling test of invention and thus eliminated any basis for the old novelty tests. In *Deere*, the Court applied the non-obviousness test and rejected new result as a relevant subject for inquiry. Now that new result has fallen, all tests of invention, whether negative or affirmative, based on a test of novelty should quickly follow. Patent law has too long suffered under the confusing concepts of "combination," "aggregation," "new effect," and "new use." These tests only complicate the inquiry into non-obviousness that is required by § 103.

III. Novelty and Inventive Novelty: Adams

This conclusion may bury tests based on inventive novelty before their demise. Their past durability suggests that they will not fall simply on the basis of the Court's action in the *Deere* case. Section 101 provides that "whoever invents or discovers any new and useful process, machine, manufacture, or composition of matter, or any new and useful improvement thereof, may obtain a patent therefor, subject to the conditions and requirements of this title."[157] This is the language of § 24 of the 1870 codification, the very language on which Walker based his negative tests. Some courts consider the inventive novelty tests to derive from § 101 rather than § 103.[158]

The answer to this position must be that in a statute that contains § 103, "new" in § 101 should be interpreted as it was in *Earle v. Sawyer*.[159] The whole metaphysical apparatus that developed to distinguish the new from the trivially new would never have been necessary in a statute that contained a non-obviousness test. Now that the statute does contain such a test, the apparatus can be dispensed with and new can once again be interpreted as meaning new. The only good reason for inserting § 103 in the statute was to choose one of the three competing tests of invention. If tests implicitly rejected by § 103 are to reappear in § 101, these statutory changes will prove fruitless. Several of the nineteenth-century cases clearly imply that the Court then thought that a finding of non-

---

[157] 35 U.S.C. § 101 (1964).

[158] See, *e.g.*, Gould-Nat'l Batteries, Inc. v. Gulton Indus. Inc., 150 U.S. P.Q. 77 (3d Cir. 1966), applying the doctrine of aggregation under § 101 rather than § 103.

[159] See text *supra*, at notes 54–58.

obviousness would override a finding of lack of inventive novelty.[160] This was the case in *Hotchkiss* itself where Justice Nelson went on to discuss the non-obviousness issue after he had already found no new effect.

The decision of the Court in *United States v. Adams*[161] can be read, if with some difficulty, as confronting this issue. The record in *Adams* made the non-obviousness issue a simple one. In 1939 Adams had found, after considerable experimentation, that a battery with unusual properties could be made from a positive electrode of magnesium, a negative electrode of cuprous chloride, and an electrolyte of water with a carbon catalyst. The battery was light in weight relative to its output. It could be activated in the field with impure water, even salt water. It produced a constant voltage and current throughout the period of its life. Once activated, the battery produced heat, which meant that it would continue to operate in extremely low temperatures. That a battery with these characteristics could be constructed was not suggested by anything previously known to the art. In fact, the scientists of the Army Signal Corps whom Adams tried to interest in his discovery at first thought it was not workable. Adams' battery was clearly non-obvious.

The Government, defendant in the infringement action in the Court of Claims, nevertheless argued for the invalidity of the patent. Not because anything in the prior art suggested that a battery with these characteristics could be built. But because the prior art suggested that a battery made of these materials was not new. The Government's brief spelled this out:[162]

> [I]f, as we submit, the combination of magnesium and cuprous chloride in the Adams battery was not patentable because it represented either no change or an insignificant change as compared to prior battery designs, the fact that, wholly unexpectedly, the battery showed certain valuable operating advantages over other batteries would certainly not justify a patent on the essentially old formula.

---

[160] *E.g.*, Ansonia Brass & Copper Co. v. Electrical Supply Co., 144 U.S. 11, 18 (1892); "[I]f an old device or process be put to a new use which is not analogous to the old one, and the adaption of such process to the new use is of such a character as to require the exercise of inventive skill to produce it, such new use will not be denied the merit of patentability."

[161] 383 U.S. 39 (1966).   [162] Brief for the United States, pp. 21–22.

Although the Government did not cite it,[163] the strongest case in support of the Government position was *General Electric Co. v. Jewel Incandescent Lamp Co.*[164] The Court in that case held a patent for an inside-frosted light bulb invalid. Earlier frosted light bulbs had either been frosted on the outside so that dirt collected in the crevices or on the inside which made them weak and easily broken. The patent in issue taught that if a bulb was frosted on the inside twice, the second etching treatment would increase the strength of the bulb because the angular crevices formed by the first frosting would be smoothed into saucer-shaped pits. Before this discovery, it was not known that a second treatment would strengthen the bulb, and the Court practically conceded that this characteristic was non-obvious. But the Court held the patent invalid on grounds of lack of novelty even though theretofore "electric bulbs had [not] been frosted on the interior with rounded rather than sharp angular crevices or pits."[165] The Court's reason was that the prior art revealed both the inside-frosted bulb and that double etching would affect the surface of the glass, although for decorative and light-diffusing purposes, not for strengthening purposes. A patent is invalid when "the prior art discloses the method of making an article having the characteristics of the patented product, though all the advantageous properties of the product had not been fully appreciated."[166]

The facts in the *Adams* case could easily have brought the patent within this rule. Not only would an elementary table of electrochemical characteristics have suggested a battery of magnesium and cuprous chloride, but a British patent of 1880 showed a battery with magnesium and cuprous chloride electrodes in a liquid electrolyte. The chief difference between the two batteries seems to be that the British patent showed the carbon in the cuprous chloride

---

[163] The Government placed its chief reliance on Sinclair & Carroll Corp. v. Interchemical Co., 325 U.S. 327 (1945). That case held a patent on a printing ink invalid. The ink was developed through the use of solvents whose relevant characteristics could be obtained from the manufacturer's catalogue. Thus, unlike the battery in *Adams*, the properties of the ink were obvious to one skilled in the art. The Court distinguished the case on this ground. But it also said that "here [unlike *Sinclair*] . . . the Adams battery is shown to embrace elements having an interdependent functional relationship." 383 U.S. at 50. This language suggests that the Court was using the doctrine of aggregation to distinguish the cases, although one would have thought that the solvents in *Sinclair* also had such a relationship with the ink.

[164] 326 U.S. 242 (1945).   [165] *Id.* at 248.   [166] *Ibid.*

electrode rather than in the electrolyte. It was perfectly possible for the Court again to hold that lack of inventive novelty made the patent invalid even in the face of non-obviousness.

The Court did not do so. It found the patent valid. But not on the ground that simple novelty was enough. The Court dismissed the British patent on the ground that it had been shown to be inoperable, although there was no explanation of why the British patent was inoperable and the Adams patent highly useful. And it dismissed the contention that the Adams discovery simply involved the substitution of known electrochemical equivalents, and therefore was not new, on the ground that its characteristics were wholly unexpected. This seems to be the Court's way of saying that simple novelty is enough where non-obviousness is present. The *Adams* decision can and should be read as overruling the *General Electric Co.* case and holding that simple novelty is enough under § 101. If it is so read, the inventive novelty tests have no place under either § 101 or § 103.

IV. COMMERCIAL SUCCESS: THE COOK CASES

The elimination of the inventive novelty tests cannot be effected by a simple declaration. Tests based on inventive novelty so permeate the patent cases that it is necessary to analyze each test in terms of its relation to non-obviousness. That much work remains to be done was revealed in the *Cook Chemical Co.*[167] cases, which turned on the role to be assigned to commercial success and long-felt need in a determination of non-obviousness. The patent was for a hold-down cap on the pump-type sprayers so familiar to every American housewife. Before the development of the patented cap, it had been necessary to distribute the fluids in bottles with regular caps and the sprayer separately attached to the package. After purchase, the customer had to remove the cap and put the sprayer on the bottle. The sprayer, thus exposed, was subject to loss and breakage. The patented cap holds the pump in retracted position and provides a seal effective against even low viscosity insecticides, making it possible to ship the fluids with the sprayer on the bottle forming a compact, break-resistant unit. The cap is, as the description should indicate, a simple device. The district

---

[167] Decided together with Graham v. John Deere Co., 383 U.S. 1 (1966).

court found it patentable on the basis of evidence that for at least five years the industry had been aware of the need for a sprayer that could be shipped on the bottle and that once the patented device was developed, it was a commercial success. Citing the *Barbed Wire Patent* case, the court concluded that "the last step is the one that wins and he who takes it when others could not, is entitled to patent protection."[168] The Court of Appeals affirmed, observing that "instantaneous industry, as well as public acceptance of the device in issue, confirms our belief invention was produced."[169]

The Supreme Court held the patent invalid, answering that in this case factors such as commercial success and long-felt need did not "tip the scales of patentability."[170] The Court added, however, that "such inquiries may lend a helping hand to the judiciary which, as Mr. Justice Frankfurter observed, is most ill-fitted to discharge the technological duties cast upon it by patent legislation. . . . They may also serve to 'guard against slipping into hindsight,' . . . and to resist the temptation to read into the prior art the teachings of the invention in issue."[171] The effect of this language is to leave commercial success the role it has traditionally enjoyed. Even when rejecting commercial success in a particular case, the Court has almost always conceded that "commercial success may be decisive where invention is in doubt."[172]

But how is commercial success relevant to non-obviousness? The argument for commercial success is set out in a law review comment cited with apparent approval by the Court in *Cook:*[173]

> The possibility of market success attendant upon the solution of an existing problem may induce innovators to attempt a solution. If in fact a product attains a high degree of commercial success, there is a basis for inferring that such attempts have been made and have failed. Thus the rationale is similar to that

---

[168] 220 F. Supp. 414, 421 (W.D. Mo. 1963).

[169] 336 F.2d 110, 114 (8th Cir. 1964). [170] 383 U.S. at 36.

[171] *Ibid.*, citing Marconi Wireless Co. v. United States, 320 U.S. 1, 60 (1943), and Monroe Auto Equip. Co. v. Heckethorn Mfg. & Supply Co., 332 F.2d 406, 412 (6th Cir. 1964).

[172] Textile Mach. Works v. Louis Hirsch Textile Mach., Inc., 302 U.S. 490, 498 (1938).

[173] *Subtests of "Nonobviousness": A Nontechnical Approach to Patent Validity,* 112 U. Pa. L. Rev. 1169, 1175 (1964).

of longfelt demand and is for the same reasons a legitimate test
of invention.

This argument involves four inferences. First, that the commercial
success is due to the innovation. Second, that if an improvement
has in fact become commercially successful, it is likely that this
potential commercial success was perceived before its development.
Third, the potential commercial success having been perceived, it
is likely that efforts were made to develop the improvement. Fourth,
the efforts having been made by men of skill in the art, they failed
because the patentee was the first to reduce his development to
practice. Since men of skill in the art tried but failed, the improvement is clearly non-obvious.

Each inference is weak. The commercial success might not be
due to the innovation but rather, as the petitioners in *Cook* argued,
to "sales promotion ability, manufacturing technique, ready access
to markets, consumer appeal design factors, and advertising budg-
et."[174] But given the commercial success of the innovation, why
is it likely that the commercial potential was perceived in advance?
And why is it likely that because the commercial potential was
perceived, men of skill began to work on the problems of that
innovation as opposed to other potential improvements? And if men
of skill start to work on the improvement, why does the fact that
the patentee was first to perfect the improvement mean the others
failed? Perhaps they were only a little slower. This seems a fragile
thread on which to hang a conclusion of non-obviousness, particularly in a case where the patentee shows only commercial success
but does not show that the commercial potential was perceived or
that attempts actually were made that failed. How, then, does commercial success constitute a helping hand? The Court said that
"these legal inferences or subtests do focus attention on economic
and motivational rather than technical issues and are, therefore,
more susceptible of judicial treatment than are the highly technical
facts often present in patent litigation."[175] Perhaps commercial success is a familiar distraction for judges confused by the facts.

It is not difficult to see why lawyers for patent owners are eager
to introduce evidence of commercial success. By introducing evidence of commercial success the lawyer is telling the judge that his
client's patent is very valuable and that if the judge holds the patent

---

[174] Brief for Petitioner Calmar, p. 30.   [175] 383 U.S. at 35–36.

invalid he is destroying expectations of great value. This is not an argument without persuasiveness. The Supreme Court itself was once led to recognize an exclusive right simply because the plaintiff's right was valuable and he had created it.[176] When Walker suggested to the courts that they should resolve borderline cases on the basis of commercial success, he was really saying, "Decide all of the borderline cases where the patent is worth something in favor of the patentee, decide all the other borderline cases against the patentee." Since it is unlikely that patents that are not commercially successful will be brought to litigation, this amounts to a suggestion that borderline cases be decided in favor of patentees. In fact, if one is willing to infer from the litigation itself that the patent is valuable because it is worth litigating, and that since it is valuable it must be commercially successful, one ends up with the rule that all patents that are litigated should be held valid.[177]

If commercial success is a relevant "economic issue," then one can argue that it should be a factor weighing against patentability in borderline cases. Commercially successful patents are the ones that truly impose a monopoly tax on the market, and therefore courts should be even more cautious in holding them valid. Furthermore, it is in the area of innovations that quickly meet consumer acceptance that the innovator has the best chance of recovering his special costs without a patent monopoly. The chances of doing this in any particular case depend, of course, on the good-will advantages of being first and the speed with which potential competitors can enter. But the more quickly a substantial market can be developed and its profit returns enjoyed, the greater (as a general rule) would seem to be the advantages accruing to the innovator who enters the market first. He will not need extensive market development that will alert potential competitors before the profits begin. Thus, in the area of the commercially successful improvement quickly recognized by the market, a patent is less likely to

---

[176] See International News Service v. Associated Press, 248 U.S. 215 (1918). Use of commercial success as a basis for validity in patent cases reached its peak in Temco Elec. Motor Co. v. Apco Mfg. Co., 275 U.S. 319, 328 (1928), where the Court reversed a holding of invalidity because the patent's "usefulness was demonstrated by ten years' use in such large numbers and by such profitable business."

[177] Cf. Diamond Rubber Co. v. Consolidated Rubber Tire Co., 220 U.S. 428, 441 (1911): ". . . the utility of a device may be attested by the litigation over it, as litigation 'shows and measures the existence of the public demand for its use.' " See also Eames v. Andrews, 122 U.S. 40, 47 (1887).

be necessary to evoke the improvement. The argument assumes, of course, that the commercial potential is perceived in advance by the innovator so that it can affect his decision to develop the innovation. This is not necessarily so, but the same assumption is made by the traditional argument for commercial success as a factor favoring a finding of invention. At the very least, these two arguments should cancel each other and leave commercial success with no role to play in a non-obviousness inquiry.

Commercial success entered the picture because it was relevant to the issue of inventive novelty.[178] If an innovation is received by the commercial community as a substantial improvement, it is hardly for the courts to hold that it is only a trivial advance. "[I]f there be anything material and new," said an often quoted English judge in 1785, "which is an improvement of the trade, that will be sufficient to support a patent."[179] In 1849, a federal district judge explained to a jury that the higher the degree of utility, the stronger the evidence that "some new principle, or mechanical power, or mode of operation, producing a new kind of result, has been introduced."[180] "It is said," reported Curtis, "that whenever utility is proved to exist in a very great degree a sufficiency of invention to support a patent must be presumed."[181] The Supreme Court, citing the same authority as Curtis—an essay by an English writer[182] —recognized the doctrine in 1877.

In *Smith v. Goodyear Dental Vulcanite Co.*[183] the defendants contended that the plaintiff's patent for denture plates of hard rubber was invalid because it simply involved a change of materials. Justice Strong rejected this contention, writing of the merits of the plaintiff's teeth as if he himself had acquired a pair: "It was capable of being perfectly fitted to the roof and alveolar processes of the mouth. It was easy for the wearer, and favorable for perfect

---

178 This relationship was spelled out in Strobridge v. Lindsay, Sterritt & Co., 2 Fed. 692 (C.C. W.D. Pa. 1880). The case was decided at a time when the federal trial courts were still applying the test of inventive novelty alone.

179 Rex v. Arkwright, 1 Webs. Pat. Cas. 64, 71 (K.B. 1785) (Buller, J.).

180 Many v. Sizer, 16 Fed. Cas. 684, 688 (No. 9,056) (C.C. D. Mass. 1849).

181 CURTIS, *op. cit. supra* note 48, at 37.

182 Webster, *On the Subject Matter of Letters-Patent for Inventions,* reprinted as an appendix to CURTIS, *op. cit. supra* note 48, at 521 (2d ed.).

183 93 U.S. 486 (1877).

articulation. It was light and elastic, yet sufficiently strong and firm for purposes of mastication."[184] Observing that many thousands of "operators" were using the new improvement in preference to older devices, he concluded that "all this is sufficient . . . to justify the inference that what Cummings [the inventor] accomplished was more than substitution of one material for another; more than the exercise of mechanical judgment and taste [sic];—that it was, in truth, invention."[185]

Fifteen years later, the Court reversed its position and rejected commercial success: "If the generality of sales were made the test of patentability, it would result that a person by securing a patent upon some trifling variation from previously known methods might, by energy in pushing sales or by superiority in finishing or decorating his goods, drive competitors out of the market and secure a practical monopoly, without in fact having made the slightest contribution of value to the useful arts."[186] But when the Court upheld the barbed wire patent, it laid heavy emphasis on the widespread use of the improvement covered by the patent.[187] Although commercial success has often been rejected in particular cases, its general relevance has never again been questioned.

Like new result, commercial success passed into the potpourri of the law of invention without any attempt to relate it to non-obviousness. If the Court is going to follow the logical implications of its approach in *Deere*, it will be necessary to reject commercial success as a standard, not only in particular cases but generally. It only distracts judges from the issue of validity and draws their attention to the value of the patent. Unlike actual proof of long-felt need or efforts that failed, it is not a relevant "motivational or economic" issue.

V. Problems for the Future: The Prior Art

Should the Court be willing to pursue the implications of *Deere* and focus the issue of invention on an inquiry into non-obviousness, subsidiary tests of invention unrelated to non-obviousness must be rejected. Tests so old and so familiar will not disappear

---

184 *Id*. at 494.   185 *Id*. at 495.

186 McClain v. Ortmayer, 141 U.S. 419, 428 (1891).

187 The Barbed Wire Patent, 143 U.S. 275, 282–84 (1892).

unless the Court subjects each one to the inquiry: what does this test have to do with non-obviousness?

Given the present state of the law on invention, this will constitute a substantial departure. But it is, in fact, only a beginning not an end. It should help the courts to concentrate on the resolution of the factual issues instead of relying on inherited, irrelevant doctrinal crutches. But the test of non-obviousness is not without its own difficulties. The Court said in *Deere:* "Under § 103, the scope and content of the prior art are to be determined; differences between the prior art and the claims at issue are to be ascertained; and the level of ordinary skill in the pertinent art resolved."[188] Although the resolution of these factual issues is often difficult, the issues themselves are reasonably clear. But underlying each of the three steps there is one central problem that has never really been faced: the meaning of the "pertinent art." This is a crucial issue because it plays a double role: it determines both the relevant prior subject matter and relevant level of skill. Nevertheless, it has barely been touched on in the cases or the secondary literature.

There are, at least, two possible approaches. One is to define the "pertinent art" as the art of the industry for which the innovation is designed. This can be called the "product-function" approach. The second is to define the "pertinent art" as the art of dealing with the kind of problem which the innovation is designed to solve. This is the "problem-solving" approach.

To illustrate. In *Cook* the basic, unarticulated premise of the patentee-respondent was that the relevant art was the "shipper-sprayer" industry. Since Calmar, an important member of this industry, had worked unsuccessfully for ten years to produce an integrated breakage-resistant sprayer, it was beyond argument, the patentee contended, that the development of such a successful device was non-obvious. "Either the technicians employed by Calmar to solve the problem did not possess ordinary skill in the art or the subject matter of the Scoggin patent was not obvious at the time the invention was made to persons possessing such skill."[189] The patentee dismissed the first possibility facetiously, citing the testimony of the president that the company had " 'for a good many years a number of good, clever people' engaged in research

---

[188] 383 U.S. at 17.

[189] Brief for Respondent, pp. 33–34.

efforts."[190] Indeed, this conception of the pertinent art was so narrow that he argued that a patent for a seal on a cover for a pouring spout "had nothing to do with a sprayer."[191]

Colgate argued for a somewhat broader art, but gave the same kind of definition: "the art of making dispensers for liquids in containers for household use."[192] Rejecting the contention that a patent relating to a pouring spout was not pertinent art, the Court offered a definition of the pertinent art different from that advanced by either side. "The problems confronting Scoggin and the insecticide industry were not insecticide problems; they were mechanical closure problems."[193] The Court defined the pertinent art, not in terms of the industry or the type of product, but in terms of the kind of problem that the patent was designed to solve.

The product-function approach to the prior art is compatible with the inventive novelty test. If the issue is whether the device is new, the sensible place to look for anticipation is in the industry where it is used. It is also the implicit concept of the art that lies behind the commercial success test. If the innovation was commercially successful in the industry it must be new to the industry, and since the industry is the relevant "art" it is patentable. It is the concept of the art that lies behind the Patent Office classification system: "[T]he characteristic selected as the basis of classification is that of essential function or effect. Arts or instruments having like functions, producing like products, or achieving like effects are brought together."[194]

There is a basic difficulty with the product-function approach to the definition of the art when it is used in conjunction with the non-obviousness test. It can be called the problem of the dumb art. The respondent in *Cook* raised this problem when he facetiously suggested that Calmar's technicians might not have possessed ordinary skill in the art. The respondent could flippantly dismiss this possibility because Calmar was such an important part of the consumer pump-sprayer industry. But suppose Calmar's technicians were in fact incompetent to develop a satisfactory breakage-resistant sprayer? Should the innovation be patentable because the industry is staffed by unskilled men? The product-function ap-

---

[190] *Id.* at 34.

[191] *Id.* at 25.

[192] Brief for Petitioner Colgate, p. 4.

[193] 383 U.S. at 35.

[194] U.S. PATENT OFFICE, MANUAL OF CLASSIFICATION 1 (1964).

proach would suggest that it should be. But if patents are viewed in relation to their economic function this is an unsettling result. In terms of economic purpose, the idea behind the non-obviousness test is to evaluate the magnitude of the costs involved in a given innovation. What are the costs of a development that is non-obvious only to the dumb industry? They are the costs of hiring the personnel with the skill to deal with the problems in need of solution. If the solution to the problems is indeed obvious to the person with skill in the art concerned with solving them, these costs should not be very great. A patent hardly seems necessary in order to enable the innovator to recover his costs.

A recent example of a case where the traditional approach to the definition of the pertinent art was carried to its logical extreme is *Abington Textile Machinery Works v. Carding Specialists Ltd.*[195] The patent in suit was for an improvement in cotton-carding machinery. The improvement consisted of an addition to the machine of a pair of rollers that would crush impurities in the cotton, causing the impurities to fall out at later stages in the processing. A professor in the School of Textiles at North Carolina State College testified for the parties attacking the patent that at the time the invention was made it would have been obvious to him. The district court dismissed this testimony on the grounds the professor was a man of extraordinary skill in the art. The question, said the district court, was whether the improvement would "have been obvious in 1957 to a person having ordinary skill in the art, namely, a typical card operator in a fine cotton processing mill."[196] Clearly, there is a great deal of difference between the "art" of the men who actually operate the machines and the "art" of the men who concern themselves with the design and effective operation of textile-processing machinery. If the "pertinent art" is the first, then the Court was clearly right in dismissing the professor's testimony. But if the art is the art of solving problems in textile processing, then perhaps the professor really was a man of ordinary skill in that art. The crucial issue in the case was whether similar crushing rollers used in different processing systems—woolen, worsted, and cotton-condenser systems—made the use of the rollers

---

[195] 249 F. Supp. 823 (D. D.C. 1965). An older example is *In re* Peddrick, 48 F.2d 415 (C. C. P. A. 1931).

[196] 249 F. Supp. at 829.

in a fine cotton-processing system obvious. The chief difference between the other uses of crushing rollers and the use in the patent in suit was that the earlier uses put the crushing rollers in place before further carding operations. The parties attacking the validity of the patent argued that "since the conventional single cylinder cotton carding machine used in fine cotton mills provides a web at only one location,"[197] and since the crushing rollers had to be applied to a web, it was obvious to locate them where the innovation in issue did. The court dismissed this on the grounds that it was obvious only after one had decided to use crushing rollers in such a machine. The court assumed that the innovation must be obvious, not to one trying to improve cotton processing, but to the day-to-day operator of the machinery.

Defining the art in terms of the problem to be solved also has its difficulties. If the relevant art is the art of inventing, all inventions become obvious because the improvement was obvious to its inventor. This definitional quandary clearly appears in the design-patent cases. Design patents are an archaic survival of the nineteenth-century view that copyright did not provide a basis for design protection. They do, however, provide some examples of the problems of the non-obviousness test. So long as the only requirement was that the design be new, the concept of an inventive design patent was not inherently absurd.[198] But it is impossible to apply the non-obviousness test. In desperation the courts have fallen back on distinguishing between the designs of genius and designs not of genius,[199] which reduces to an attempt to discriminate between good art and bad art. The application of the test requires that there be a craft with norms of problem solving whose skills are reasonably widely known and which are directed to the solution of the type of problems the innovation in question is designed to solve. To advance a tentative definition of the "pertinent art," it is the art to which one can reasonably be expected to look for a solution to the problem which the patented device attempts to solve.

---

[197] Id. at 834.

[198] See, e.g., Untermeyer v. Freund, 37 Fed. 342 (C.C. S.D. N.Y. 1889); Smith v. Stewart, 55 Fed. 481 (C.C. E.D. Pa. 1893).

[199] General Time Instruments Corp. v. United States Time Corp., 165 F.2d 853, 854 (2d Cir. 1948); "In short, the test is whether the design involved a step beyond the prior art requiring what is termed 'inventive genius.'"

This is the definition of the pertinent art that the Supreme Court adopted in *Cook*.

This definition raises two issues. First, what of the device that solves no problem? Is it non-obvious? Second, what of the innovation where the solution was obvious but the existence of the problem was not?

The first difficulty is only of theoretical curiosity. And there is no need to confront this rhetorically plausible problem. The device is not patentable for lack of utility. The Court only recently reaffirmed the requirement that utility is necessary for patentability,[200] so that every patentable device must respond, with some degree of success, to some need.

The second difficulty is an important one. The case that provides the most useful example of the problem is *Great Atlantic & Pacific Tea Co. v. Supermarket Equipment Corp.*[201] That case turned on the validity of a patent for a counter extension and frame used to pull groceries along a checkout counter. The frame was simplicity itself, made of three pieces of wood fastened together and a handle to enable the cash register operator to pull it forward along the counter. The evidence in the record showed that the patentee, a district supervisor for a supermarket chain, had developed it in a short period of time after being confronted with the need to be able to handle more customers in one of his stores that lacked adequate space to install an additional checkout counter.[202] The Court chose to speak in terms of inventive novelty and found the device lacked invention on the grounds that it was an aggregation that performed no new function. This conclusion was contrary to the facts. But the conclusion of the Court that the device lacked invention is nonetheless proper. Surely the device was an obvious solution to the problem of speeding up the flow of customers through the checkout lane. But the evidence also suggested that what had not been obvious to the industry was

---

200 Brenner v. Manson, 383 U.S. 519 (1966).

201 340 U.S. 147 (1950), *reversing* 179 F.2d 636 (6th Cir. 1950).

202 The Court did not note this fact. The Court of Appeals described the patentee as an employee "who was assigned the task of solving the problem" of speeding up the flow of customers in the checkout lane. 179 F.2d at 636. This gives the impression that the development was the result of a concerted effort to solve a perceived problem. In fact, the patentee-employee was assigned to solve the "problem" of an unhappy store manager, if necessary by the installation of an additional counter. Record, p. 55.

the problem about the rate of flow through checkout lanes, or that it might be possible to improve it. The contribution of the patentee was the recognition of the need to improve the flow and a willingness to investigate the problem. The problem was surely non-obvious to an industry that had ignored it for years. And if the problem was non-obvious, why was its solution not also non-obvious, since there can be no solution without a problem? A traditional verbal answer to this contention in patent law has been that the patent is on the solution, not the problem, and therefore the solution must contain the "invention" or the non-obvious element.[203] But there is a serious economic argument for this position as well. The patent law is designed to induce innovations that would not otherwise appear in a competitive system. The prospect of a patent gives the innovator the assurance that if he is successful he will make profits, and this prospect of profits makes the expenditures on experimentation, whether they be expenditures of time or money or both, a reasonable investment. But before the prospect of a patent can begin to operate in this fashion, the person must have been confronted with the decision whether to innovate or not. If he has no knowledge that there is a problem to be solved, he is hardly in a position to decide whether or not to try solving it. Once he has a perception that there is a problem, no matter how general that perception may be, he is then in a position to decide whether to expend time and money to solve it. And only if he is confronted with such a decision, can the prospect of a patent have any role to play. So when an innovation results merely from the perception of a problem, rather than the working-out of a non-obvious solution, no patent should issue. That seems a sensible way to state the holding of the *Supermarket Equipment Corp.* case. And if that is so, the situation creates no difficulty for the tendered definition of the "pertinent art," because every patentable innovation must be responsive to a problem.

VI. The Court's Responsibility

Deere, Adams, and *Cook* are hopeful signs that the courts will begin to work out the implications of the non-obviousness test that have been ignored. If the courts begin to face and solve

---

[203] Robinson stated that the idea generated by the mental part of the inventive act must be "an idea of means as distinguished from an idea of end." Robinson, *op. cit. supra* note 34, at 155.

these analytic issues, the administration of § 103 should be made easier. But the Supreme Court did not think the problem of § 103 was one for the courts at all. "[I]t must be remembered," said the Court, "that the primary responsibility for sifting out unpatentable material lies in the Patent Office. To wait litigation is—for all practical purposes—to debilitate the patent system. We have observed a notorious difference between the standards applied by the Patent Office and by the courts."[204] Although gentler in language, this criticism of the Patent Office is in the tradition of the attack on the office made by Mr. Justice Douglas in his concurring opinion in the *Supermarket Equipment Corp.* case.[205] This attack accuses the Patent Office of ruining the patent system because of its failure to apply the invention requirement with sufficient rigor. The problem with this statement is not that it is untrue but that it is unwise. The Court should be more sensitive to the roots of its power even in so small a matter. Can the Court seriously expect men who have dedicated themselves to the operation of the Patent Office and the patent system to respond warmly to the charge that they have debilitated the patent system? Yet the co-operation of these men is essential if there is going to be any change in Patent Office practice.

The usual complaint is that the Patent Office issues many patents that are invalid under § 103. This appears to be true, but how does it debilitate the system? The explanation offered is that each of the invalid patents issued is a "license to litigate" which can be used as a "threat" to "coerce" weaker competitiors into submission. The problem is presently receiving serious attention from the Antitrust Division, which has filed a suit against the Minnesota Mining and Manufacturing Company charging abuse of patents in this manner.[206] But if the patents are invalid, how are they such an effective threat? The answer is that the defense of an infringement suit, even if the patent is held invalid, is expensive and that the patentee can always offer a settlement cheaper than the litigation costs. A leading patent lawyer has estimated the costs for

[204] 383 U.S. at 18.   [205] 340 U.S. at 154.

[206] United States v. Minnesota Mining & Mfg. Co., Civ. No. 66C627 (N.D. Ill. April 7, 1966). "According to the suit, the company has attempted to control the industries by systematic coercion of competitors, through suits or threatened suits for patent infringement, to accept illegal patent license agreements." 5 TRADE REG. REP. ¶ 45,066 (1966).

each side in a patent infringement suit at a minimum of $50,000.[207] Invalid patents, in the hands of unscrupulous and powerful men, are worth money. This debilitates the patent system because it makes patents the vehicles for suppression of competition rather than the reward for invention.

But why is it so expensive to defend a patent suit? The answer is twofold. First, there are endless procedural devices in the hands of a patent holder willing to use them. And, second, the factual issues in patent cases are made unnecessarily complex by the doctrinal difficulties of the invention requirement. These are not the fault of the Patent Office. If fault is the appropriate word, surely Congress and the Supreme Court must share the blame.

A determined patent holder is in a position to keep relitigating the validity of his patent against the infringing manufacturer and his customers. These suits can be brought in every part of the country.[208] Motions under § 1404(a) for transfer and consolidation can be made, ruled on, and taken to the courts of appeals.[209] The factual issues are "complicated" and summary judgment is seldom available. Discovery procedures can be used to increase the costs that a patent-infringement action inflicts on the defendant. The Supreme Court must bear some responsibility for failing to keep these abuses in check.

For fifteen years the Supreme Court failed to take cases raising the issue of non-obviousness. Differences have arisen among the circuits, encouraging litigants to engage in complex maneuvering to get in the "right" court. It is traditionally said that the facts in patent cases are extremely complicated. This is not true. The facts in patent cases, as in any other class of cases, are sometimes com-

[207] Statement of Tom Arnold, Chairman, Section on Patent, Trademark, and Copyright Law, The American Bar Association, *Hearings before the Subcommittee on Patents, Trademarks, and Copyrights of the Senate Committee on the Judiciary on S.789, S.1809 and S.1899*, 89th Cong., 1st Sess., pt. 1, 268, 271 (1965): "Patent infringement suits cost at a minimum on the order of $50,000, and they go up from there. They go away up from there."

[208] 28 U.S.C. § 1400 provides for venue where "the defendant has committed acts of infringement and has a regular and established place of business." In the case of an infringing product sold throughout the country, the provision permits suit to be brought almost anywhere.

[209] I have discussed these problems elsewhere. Kitch, *Section 1404(a) of the Judicial Code: In the Interest of Justice or Injustice*, 40 IND. L.J. 99 (1965). They are particularly troublesome in patent cases.

plicated and sometimes simple. *Deere, Adams,* and *Cook* are examples of cases in which the facts themselves are simple and easily understood. But even simple facts become complicated if there are no controlling legal principles around which they can be organized. In a case as simple as *Deere* two circuits differed on the validity of the patent, not because they differed on the facts, but because they differed regarding the law. These failures of the Court are perhaps minor when one considers the heavy responsibilities that it has in other more important areas. But it ill becomes the Court, whose own performance in the area has suffered from lack of interest, to castigate the Patent Office for "debilitating" the patent system.

The Patent Office has remained insensitive to the requirement that invention must be shown for patentability because it applies the "inventive novelty" law that was in force prior to 1875. The basic question for a Patent Office examination is whether the device is new. The primary effort of the examiner is to have the claims narrowed so that they only read on what is new in the development. There seem to be two important reasons for this apparent disregard of the invention requirement. The first lies in the history of the Patent Office and the law. The Patent Office as presently organized has been an on-going institution since 1836. During the first thirty-nine years of its life, it quite appropriately applied the controlling law of inventive novelty. Since that time its internal traditions have perpetuated the approach. This tendency has been condoned by the Supreme Court, which never, until *Deere,* suggested that the inventive novelty approach was inconsistent with non-obviousness. The second reason is the organization of the Patent Office itself. Because of the heavy backlog of applications there is pressure on examiners to dispose of them. If an examiner approves the application, the matter is closed. If he denies it, the applicant has a right of appeal up through the Patent Office to the Court of Customs and Patent Appeals and now to the Supreme Court.[210] Such an appeal places additional burdens on the office. At the very least, it is considered undesirable for an examiner to be reversed once an appeal is taken.[211] In this situation even a

---

[210] Brenner v. Manson, 383 U.S. 519 (1966), established the existence of certiorari jurisdiction over the Court of Customs and Patent Appeals.

[211] See Stedman, *The U.S. Patent System and Its Current Problems,* 42 TEXAS L. REV. 450, 463–64 (1964).

conscientious examiner is unlikely to reject an application unless he is sure of his ground. A rejection for lack of novelty is relatively stable ground. If something is not new, it is hard for the applicant to argue that it is. But a rejection on grounds of non-obviousness is shakier because it may involve differences in judgment between the examiner and the review board.

It is even possible to argue that it is not the duty of the Patent Office to screen out non-obvious patents. Why should not the Patent Office concentrate on weeding out those applications that do not involve new developments? When a patent is granted on an innovation, it assures that information about it is placed on the public record. At the Patent Office stage in the proceedings it is difficult to predict whether the patent will ever be important or the subject of controversy. The *ex parte* proceeding of the Patent Office is not the best forum in which fully to ventilate the validity issue.[212] If the validity issue is determined negatively, the information about the innovation is never placed on the public record. Why should the resources necessary to make the non-obviousness determination be expended unless the validity of the patent actually matters? Once it matters, the courts can provide a forum in which the validity issue can be litigated. Although this is not the system contemplated by the statute, it has long been the *de facto* system in American patent law.[213] And it would work, if the courts provided a reasonably efficient and conclusive forum

---

[212] In Walker Process Equip., Inc. v. Food Mach. & Chem. Co., 382 U.S. 172 (1965), the Court held that the enforcement of a patent obtained by fraud on the Patent Office is actionable under the Sherman Act. If "fraud" is interpreted to include negligent failures to cite prior art, the decision should have an impact on the amount of prior art brought to the examiner's attention. But it may not be wise to reform Patent Office procedure by using the threat of a punitive statute to force the applicant to be his own adversary.

[213] The Court of Customs and Patent Appeals and the Patent Office recognize this in the "rule of doubt." This rule is that in cases of doubt concerning patentability, the doubt should be resolved in favor of the applicant. "There are very sound policy reasons underlying the rule applied in this court, and supposedly in the Patent Office, that doubts are to be resolved in favor of applicants. Several of the factors properly taken into account in determining patentability, especially unobviousness and utility, are often not known at the time when the application is being prosecuted in the Patent Office but are developed later, perhaps even after the patent is issued. It therefore is proper that doubt should be resolved in favor of applicants so that they shall not be denied patents which later events may show them entitled to." *In re* Hofstetter, 150 U.S.P.Q. 105, 109 (C. C. P. A. 1966).

for the adjudication of validity. The present statutory framework makes this difficult for the courts, but they have not done their best to maximize their effectiveness even within this framework.

Deere points in the direction of removing complicating doctrinal irrelevancies and returning patent law to the relative simplicity of the statute. It is a significant step toward the improvement of the patent system if the courts are willing to insist that the inquiry be focused on the statutory test of non-obviousness. It is perfectly possible for the tradition-minded reader to interpret the opinions in *Deere, Adams,* and *Cook* as simply continuing past doctrine.[214] The myth of *Hotchkiss v. Greenwood* seems to be part of an even larger myth in patent law—the myth that invention decisions differ only on the "facts" or the "attitude" of the court, but that they all embody the same law. The courts ought not permit this myth to overtake *Deere.*

---

[214] See Brumbaugh, *The Standard of Patentability Now,* 21 RECORD 291 (1966). Brumbaugh reads *Adams* as continuing the inventive novelty tests under § 101 and views § 103 as simply an additional negative test. This is, of course, the scheme of the Walker treatise.

WILLIAM E. LEUCHTENBURG

THE ORIGINS OF FRANKLIN D. ROOSEVELT'S "COURT-PACKING" PLAN

No event of twentieth-century American constitutional history is better remembered than Franklin D. Roosevelt's ill-fated "Court-packing" scheme of 1937; yet the origins of the plan remain obscure and often misstated. The proposal has been variously attributed to Felix Frankfurter, who abhorred it; to Benjamin Cohen and Thomas Corcoran, who favored a different remedy and had no hand in shaping this one; and to Samuel I. Rosenman, who played only a minor role after the decision had already been made.[1] Among those who have been said to have helped frame the plan were James M. Landis, who had heard only rumors of it before it was announced, and Robert H. Jackson, who first learned of the President's plan when he read about it in a Philadelphia newspaper.[2]

William E. Leuchtenburg is Professor of History, Columbia University.

[1] Mallon, *Purely Confidential*, Detroit News, Feb. 8, Apr. 2, May 21, 1937; MASON, BRANDEIS: A FREE MAN'S LIFE 625 (1946); MOLEY, AFTER SEVEN YEARS 357-59 (1939) (hereinafter MOLEY); Raymond Clapper MS Diary, Feb. 8, 1937, Clapper MSS, Library of Congress (hereinafter LC); 7 Frances Perkins, Columbia Oral History Collection 128 (hereinafter COHC); Washington Post, Feb. 13, 1937. Of Frankfurter, James M. Landis recalled that he "caught hell from him" for supporting the plan. Landis, COHC 49, 302. See, too, Clapper MS Diary, Sept. 28, 1938; Frank Buxton to William Allen White, June 2, 1937, White MSS, LC, Box 189.

[2] Mallon, *Purely Confidential*, Detroit News, Apr. 2, 1937; Landis, COHC 44-45; MICHELSON, THE GHOST TALKS 169-70 (1944); GERHART, AMERICA'S ADVOCATE: ROBERT H. JACKSON 105 (1958).

The project has been described either as an impulsive act born of the *hubris* created by FDR's landslide victory in 1936 or as a calculated plot hatched many months before in angry resentment at the *Schechter* verdict. Roosevelt himself never did anything to clear up the confusion. Three weeks after the President launched the proposal, Senator Hiram Johnson of California wrote a friend: "He has been beaten from pillar to post upon when he conceived the brilliant idea, and how he conceived it."[3]

I. PROLOGUE

The constitutional crisis of 1937 had been brewing for a long time. Franklin Roosevelt began his political career at the time that his distant cousin Theodore was assaulting the sanctity of the courts and the air was loud with cries for the recall of judges and judicial decisions. In the 1920's there was mounting progressive animus toward the Taft Court manifested in such forms as the La Follette platform of 1924, which called for empowering Congress to override the Supreme Court. In the Hoover years, progressives had waged fierce contests against the confirmations of John J. Parker and Charles Evans Hughes. Increasingly, liberal critics of the Court believed that a majority of the Justices spoke for the interests of the rich and well-born.[4]

Even before Roosevelt took office, he had aroused speculation over whether his presidency would result in a confrontation with the Supreme Court. In a campaign speech in Baltimore on October 5, 1932, Roosevelt blurted out: "After March 4, 1929, the Republican party was in complete control of all branches of the government—the Legislature, with the Senate and Congress; and the executive departments; and I may add, for full measure, to make it complete, the United States Supreme Court as well."[5] This statement had been interpolated in the original text of the address, but the next day, Roosevelt told Senator James F. Byrnes: "What I said last night about the judiciary is true, and whatever is in a man's

[3] Johnson to John Francis Neylan, Feb. 26, 1937, Johnson MSS, Bancroft Library, University of California, Berkeley.

[4] St. Louis Star, June 23, 1930, clipping, Pierce Butler MSS, Minnesota Historical Society, St. Paul; 2 PUSEY, CHARLES EVANS HUGHES 655–62 (1951).

[5] 1 FRANKLIN D. ROOSEVELT, PUBLIC PAPERS AND ADDRESSES 837 (1938) (hereinafter PUBLIC PAPERS).

heart is apt to come to his tongue—I shall not make any explanations or apology for it!"[6] Republicans hopped on Roosevelt's statement as a warning that, if elected President, he might, in Herbert Hoover's words, "reduce the tribunal to an instrument of party policy."[7]

Roosevelt, who was right in thinking that the composition of the federal courts was heavily Republican,[8] found an even greater source of concern in the doctrines pronounced by the Court in such recent decisions as that in the *Oklahoma Ice* case.[9] The New Dealers recognized that much that they proposed to do would be invalidated by the Court if it followed the line of reasoning adopted by the Taft Court, but they hoped that the Court would recognize the depression to be an emergency justifying unprecedented government action. In his inaugural address on March 4, 1933, the new president stated: "Our Constitution is so simple and practical that it is possible always to meet extraordinary needs by changes in emphasis and arrangement without loss of essential form."[10]

Yet Roosevelt was wary of relying on the tolerance of the Court for New Deal experiments. The Administration deliberately postponed tests of the constitutionality of the legislation of the Hundred Days as long as possible; the Supreme Court did not have the opportunity to rule on a New Deal statute until 1935. Meanwhile, the New Dealers were heartened by two 1934 opinions which appeared to recognize that the emergency might be the occasion for governmental restrictions on property rights.[11] Especially encouraging was Justice Roberts' statement in the *Nebbia* case: "[T]his court from the early days affirmed that the power to promote the general welfare is inherent in government."[12]

---

[6] BYRNES, ALL IN ONE LIFETIME 65 (1958).

[7] N.Y. Times, Feb. 11, 1937.

[8] In the autumn of 1933, Roosevelt's Attorney General sent him a memorandum noting that of the 266 judges in the federal courts, only 28 per cent were Democrats. Homer Cummings to FDR, Nov. 8, 1933, Franklin D. Roosevelt Library, Hyde Park, N.Y. (henceforth cited as FDRL) OF 41, Box 114.

[9] New State Ice Co. v. Liebmann, 285 U.S. 262 (1932).

[10] 2 PUBLIC PAPERS 14–15.

[11] Home Building & Loan Ass'n v. Blaisdell, 290 U.S. 398 (1934); Nebbia v. New York, 291 U.S. 502 (1934).

[12] 291 U.S. at 524.

Such pronouncements served, for the moment, to dispel the conviction that a collision between Roosevelt and the Supreme Court was inevitable and that steps should be taken to reconstitute the Court, ideas that emerged remarkably early in the Roosevelt administration. Almost two years before the Court had invalidated the first New Deal law, an Illinois man wrote the President: "Sometimes I get thinking about the many millions who are unemployed, and I wonder if we really can get them back to work, and retain our social order. . . . If the Supreme Court's membership could be increased to twelve, without too much trouble, perhaps the Constitution would be found to be quite elastic."[13]

As early as January, 1934, the *Literary Digest* reported: "In the intimate Presidential circle the idea of reconstituting the Supreme Court has been considered. . . . In the conversation within the Roosevelt circle, a court of fifteen, instead of the present nine, has been mentioned."[14] The *Digest* added that the *Blaisdell* opinion, which appeared to indicate a liberal majority on the Court, had caused such talk among the New Dealers to subside. Yet conservatives remained uneasy. The following month, Henry Prather Fletcher, soon to be chosen Republican national chairman, wrote the columnist Mark Sullivan: "You seem to rely on the Courts for relief in the last analysis. Let us hope the Supreme Court will not bend before the storm—but even if it does not, it is the weakest of the three coordinate branches of the Government and an administration as fully in control as this one is can pack it as easily as an English Government can pack the House of Lords."[15]

II. Gold Clauses and Railroad Pensions

Early in 1935 the period of nervous calm was abruptly shattered. On January 7, 1935, in its first ruling on a New Deal law, the Court invalidated the "hot oil" provisions of the National Industrial Recovery Act.[16] The Republican New York *Herald-Tribune* commented:[17]

---

[13] John P. Byrne to FDR, Apr. 18, 1933, FDRL OF 41-A.

[14] *News and Comment from the National Capital,* 117 LITERARY DIGEST 10 (Jan. 20, 1934).

[15] Fletcher to Sullivan, Feb. 28, 1934, Fletcher MSS, LC, Box 16.

[16] Panama Refining Co. v. Ryan, 293 U.S. 388 (1935); Charles Fahy, COHC 148.

[17] *New Deal Meets Tests in Supreme Court,* 119 LITERARY DIGEST 5-6 (Jan. 19, 1935).

In the skylarking days of 1933–34, the happy administrators of the New Deal brushed aside the Supreme Court as they brushed aside Congress and the Constitution. . . . The President paid perfunctory lip-service to the nation's charter of liberty. Behind the scene the whispers were loud enough to be beyond misunderstanding. Let the Supreme Court try to halt the march of the new order, according to F. D. R., an Act of Congress would be passed adding to its membership and packing it with enough Tugwellian jurists to overturn any conservative decision overnight.

Now, the *Tribune* exulted, the 8-to-1 decision had thrown "this revolutionary nonsense into the Potomac where it belongs."

In fact, the New Dealers took the "hot oil" decision in stride. Since the Court's objections had rested on procedural defects that could easily be corrected, the Administration was not greatly concerned by the judgment. Much more alarming were the series of tests of the constitutionality of gold legislation that were making their way relentlessly toward the Supreme Court. A ruling by the Court for the plaintiffs would deny Congress the right to regulate the currency at a time of national economic disaster and threatened financial chaos by increasing the country's debt by nearly $70 billion.[18] Washington officials, observed Arthur Krock, were more absorbed with the question of how the Court would decide than by any subject since the bank holiday of March, 1933. In contemplation of that opinion, cold shivers "chase up and down their spines when they waken in the night."[19]

At a cabinet meeting on January 11, 1935, Attorney General Homer Cummings reported on the gold clause cases, which he had just finished arguing. Secretary of the Interior Harold L. Ickes noted in his diary:[20]

> The Attorney General said that if the Court should decide against the Government in the gold certificate and Liberty Bond cases, the situation could be saved by Congress hurrying through a statute taking away from the citizens the right to sue the Government for the damages that they might claim by reason of having accepted payment in currency on bonds that, by their terms, were stated to be payable in gold. . . .
> The Attorney General went so far as to say that if the Court

---

[18] SCHLESINGER, THE POLITICS OF UPHEAVAL 255–56 (1960) (hereinafter SCHLE-SINGER).

[19] N.Y. Times, Jan. 15, 1935.

[20] 1 SECRET DIARY OF HAROLD L. ICKES 273–74 (1953) (hereinafter ICKES).

went against the Government, the number of justices should be increased at once so as to give a favorable majority. As a matter of fact, the President suggested this possibility to me during our interview on Thursday, and I told him that that is precisely what ought to be done. It wouldn't be the first time that the Supreme Court had been increased in size to meet a temporary emergency and it certainly would be justified in this case.

Many in the Administration had an almost apocalyptic sense of inevitable conflict. After the cabinet meeting on January 11, Ickes reported:[21]

I told the President yesterday that only a few years ago I had predicted that sooner or later the Supreme Court would become a political issue as the result of its continued blocking of the popular will through declaring acts of Congress unconstitutional. During the discussion today the Vice President said that he had read a pamphlet which had been written about a hundred years ago in which the author advanced the theory that sooner or later, through the aggrandizement of power by the Supreme Court, a political crisis of major magnitude would be precipitated in this country.

Close observers anticipated that the President would not permit the Court to disrupt his attempts to achieve recovery, even if this led to a constitutional crisis. In his Kings Feature Syndicate column, Arthur Brisbane created a stir when he questioned whether there was any constitutional authority for the practice of judicial review. Brisbane wrote:[22]

As a matter of constitutional law, as actually written by the constitutional convention, if the Supreme Court should say to the President of the United States "We find unconstitutional, and ask you to revoke, your law abolishing the gold clause," the President might reasonably reply, "I have your message and respectfully request that you show me what part of the Constitution authorizes you to nullify a law passed by the Congress of the United States and signed by the President."

If he sent that message, the Supreme Court would be puzzled, for it could show nothing in the Constitution.

Roosevelt was, in fact, ready to act much as Brisbane suggested. A month earlier, in response to an inquiry from the President, Robert Jackson, general counsel of the Bureau of Internal Revenue,

---

[21] *Id.* at 274.

[22] Brisbane to FDR, Feb. 11, 1935, FDRL OF 41-A, Box 116.

had suggested that the government might withdraw its consent to be sued.[23] Accordingly, a message to Congress was drafted recommending the withdrawal of the right to sue the United States for more than the face value of government bonds and other obligations. In the event of an adverse decision, Roosevelt was ready with a proclamation of national emergency to regulate currency transactions; for ninety days, no payment on any contract would be permitted save at the rate of $35 for an ounce of gold, the rate fixed by the President on January 31, 1934, under authority of the Gold Reserve Act.[24]

If the Supreme Court ruled against the government, Roosevelt was prepared to deliver a defiant radio address in which he would declare that the decisions, if enforced, would result in "unconscionable" profit to investors, bankruptcy for almost every railroad and for many corporations, default by state and local governments, and wholesale mortgage foreclosures on farms and in cities. It would not only increase the national debt by a staggering sum but would catapult the nation "into an infinitely more serious economic plight than we have yet experienced."[25] He did not seek a quarrel with the Supreme Court, but he did think it appropriate to quote a sentence from Lincoln's First Inaugural Address: "At the same time, the candid citizen must confess that if the policy of the government, upon vital questions affecting the whole people, is to be irrevocably fixed by decisions of the Supreme Court, the instant they are made, in ordinary litigation between parties in personal actions, the people will have ceased to be their own rulers, having to that extent practically resigned their government into the hands of that eminent tribunal."

Neither the President nor Congress, Roosevelt planned to say, could "stand idly by and . . . permit the decision of the Supreme Court to be carried through to its logical, inescapable conclusion," because this would "imperil the economic and political security of this nation." He sought only to carry out the principle that "For value received the same value should be repaid," a doctrine "in accordance with the Golden Rule, with the precepts of the Scrip-

---

[23] Robert Jackson, COHC.

[24] 1 BLUM, FROM THE MORGENTHAU DIARIES 126–27 (1959) (hereinafter MORGENTHAU).

[25] Draft of message, FDRL PSF Supreme Court.

tures, and the dictates of common sense." "In order to attain this reasonable end," the President intended to announce, "I shall immediately take such steps as may be necessary, by proclamation and by message to the Congress of the United States."

On February 18, as word reached the White House that the Court had assembled, Roosevelt took his place at the cabinet table to await word. Minutes later, the tension broke, as it became clear that in each of a series of cases, the government had won.[26] On the following day, the President sent a saucy note to Joseph P. Kennedy, chairman of the SEC:[27]

> With you I think Monday, February eighteenth, was an historic day. As a lawyer it seems to me that the Supreme Court has at last definitely put human values ahead of the "pound of flesh" called for by a contract.
> The Chairman of the Securities Exchange Commission turns out to be far more accurate than the Associated Press in that he reported the decisions accurately. How fortunate it is that his Exchanges will never know how close they came to being closed up by a stroke of the pen of one "J.P.K."
> Likewise, the Nation will never know what a great treat it missed in not hearing the marvelous radio address the "Pres" had prepared for delivery to the Nation Monday night if the cases had gone the other way.

Roosevelt could not have been pleased by the scolding he received from Chief Justice Hughes in the majority opinion, and he was aware that he had had a close call. "In spite of our rejoicing," he wrote, "I shudder at the closeness of five to four decisions in these important matters!"[28] Congressmen began to talk more seriously about the need to find some way to restrain the Court. Senator George Norris of Nebraska protested: "These five to four Supreme Court decisions on the constitutionality of congressional acts it seems to me are illogical and should not occur in a country like ours."[29] Yet, since the government had been upheld, most of the expressions of dissatisfaction came not from New Deal supporters but from the outraged conservatives, many of whom echoed

---

[26] Norman v. B. & O. R.R., 294 U.S. 240 (1935), and related cases; 1 MORGENTHAU 130.

[27] FDR to Kennedy, Feb. 19, 1935, 1 F.D.R.: HIS PERSONAL LETTERS 455 (1950) (hereinafter LETTERS).

[28] FDR to Angus MacLean, Feb. 21, 1935, FDRL OF 10-F.

[29] Norris to Layton Spicher, Mar. 29, 1935, Norris MSS, LC, Tray 27, Box 4.

Justice McReynolds' irate dissent: "Shame and humiliation are upon us now."[30]

Three months later, it was the liberals' turn to be discomforted by the Court. In another 5-to-4 decision, with Justice Roberts joining the majority, the Court invalidated the Railway Pension Act.[31] For the first time since Roosevelt took office, the Court had delivered an opinion that antagonized an important interest group who could demand restrictions on the Court's powers.[32] The president of one Railroad Brotherhood called the decision, which affected a million railroad workers, a "bitter disappointment."[33] From Wichita Falls, Texas, one man wrote Roosevelt: "I Had an idea they would turn Down that Railroad Pension. I told you the Rich Men always Run to the Supreme Court to Beat Our Laws. . . . The Supreme Court is a Public Nuisance."[34]

The implications of the rail pension decision were not limited to its effects on railroad workers. Many believed that if Justice Roberts disposed of other cases as he had this one, the pending social security legislation would also be invalidated. "Congratulations to rail carriers over pension decision yesterday," the general attorney for the Cudahy Packing Company wired a spokesman for the railroads: "That monumental decision so parallels our necessities in connection with Social Security legislation that we owe you a debt for fight now vindicating constitutional interpretation upon which all American business stands for future welfare all citizens."[35] The opinion, wrote *Business Week*, indicated that the

---

[30] There is a copy of McReynolds' extemporaneous dissent, with corrections in his handwriting, in McReynolds MSS, Alderman Library, University of Virginia, Charlottesville, Va., Folder H-2. For conservative dismay, see L. E. Armstrong to Willis Van Devanter, Feb. 26, 1935, Van Devanter MSS, LC; James Beck to J. C. McReynolds, Apr. 13, 1934, Beck MSS, Princeton University Library, Carton 2; Alfred James McClure to Homer Cummings, Feb. 19, 1935, NA Dept. of Justice 105-42-11; letters in Charles Evans Hughes MSS, LC, Box 157.

[31] Retirement Board v. Alton R. Co., 295 U.S. 330 (1935).

[32] The Court had, of course, angered groups like bondholders by its decisions in the gold cases, but since these elements viewed the Court as a bulwark against social change, they were unlikely to support any movement to limit the Court's powers.

[33] D. B. Robertson to FDR, Jan. 22, 1936, NA Dept. of Justice 235460.

[34] P. J. Hasey to FDR, May 6, 1935, NA Dept. of Justice 235460.

[35] Thomas Creigh to Paul Shoup, May 7, 1935, Shoup MSS, Stanford University Library, Stanford, California, Box 1.

Court "would smash any social security legislation that may be passed by Congress."[36]

Prodded by the rail pension decision, which raised the alarming likelihood that Justice Roberts had joined the conservatives to create a permanent 5-to-4 majority against the New Deal, Cummings began to explore possibilities of counter actions. Before the week was out, Cummings sent a memorandum to Assistant Attorney General Angus MacLean:[37]

> Has any study been made in this office of the question of the right of the Congress, by legislation, to limit the terms and conditions upon which the Supreme Court can pass on constitutional questions? I have seen several memoranda from time to time spelling out a theory by which this result could be achieved without a constitutional amendment. My recollection is that our files will somewhere disclose briefs on the theory that the Supreme Court has no right to pass on constitutional questions at all. Of course, quite a learned document could be prepared dealing with the historical aspects of this matter and the way in which it has developed.
>
> I think it would be well to have this pretty thoroughly covered, but in addition to this it would be well to cover the subject I first above mentioned; namely, the question of legislation which would not cut off the right of the Supreme Court to pass on constitutional questions, but which would limit it somewhere with a view to avoid 5 to 4 decisions.

III. BLACK MONDAY, 1935 VERSION

On "Black Monday," May 27, 1935, in three 9-to-0 decisions, the Court invalidated the National Industrial Recovery Act and the Frazier-Lemke Act and ruled, in the *Humphrey* case, that the President could not remove members of independent regulatory commissions save as Congress provided.[38] Roosevelt was incensed by the overturning of the NRA, the keystone of his industrial recovery program.[39] The Court's language in denouncing the dele-

---

[36] *5 to 4 Against*, Business Week 7–8 (May 11, 1935).

[37] Cummings to MacLean, May 11, 1935, NA Dept. of Justice 235773.

[38] Schechter Corp. v. United States, 295 U.S. 495 (1935); Louisville Bank v. Radford, 295 U.S. 555 (1935); Humphrey's Executor v. United States, 295 U.S. 602 (1935).

[39] It is often said that Roosevelt was relieved by the *Schechter* decision, because the NRA had become an intolerable burden. In fact, he believed strongly in the NRA approach, and persisted in later years in trying to revive it. On Roosevelt's

gation of powers and its narrow construction of the Commerce Clause appeared to place other New Deal laws in jeopardy and to bar the way to new legislation.[40] He was even more outraged by the *Humphrey* decision, which, in view of the history of the *Myers* opinion,[41] seemed a deliberate assault by the Court on his own prerogatives.[42] The unanimity of the Court in all three cases was bewildering. "Well, where was Ben Cardozo?" he asked. "And what about old Isaiah?"[43]

For four days, while the country speculated about what he would do, the President said nothing. On May 31, reporters were summoned to the White House. As they filed in, they saw on the President's desk a copy of the *Schechter* opinion and a sheaf of telegrams. Eleanor Roosevelt, seated next to her friend Mrs. Felix Frankfurter, busied herself knitting on a blue sock. For the next hour and a half, while reporters listened intently, Roosevelt, in an unusually somber mood, discoursed on the implications of the Court's opinion. Thumbing the copy of the *Schechter* decision as he spoke, the President argued that the Court's ruling had stripped the national government of its power to cope with critical national problems. "We are facing a very, very great national non-partisan issue," he said. "We have got to decide one way or the other . . . whether in some way we are going to . . . restore to the Federal Government the powers which exist in the national Governments of every other Nation in the world."[44] Of all the words the President spoke at the extraordinary conference, newspapermen singled out one sentence which headline writers emblazoned on late afternoon newspapers: "We have been relegated to the horse-and-buggy definition of interstate commerce."[45]

---

indignation at the *Schechter* opinion, see Raymond Clapper MS Diary, Feb. 24, 1937.

[40] Roosevelt wrote: "It is the 'dictum' in the Schechter case opinion that is disturbing because . . . if the 'dictum' is followed in the future the Court would probably find only ten per cent of actual transactions to be directly in interstate commerce." FDR to Henry L. Stimson, June 10, 1935, 1 LETTERS 484.

[41] Myers v. United States, 272 U.S. 52 (1926).

[42] Landis, COHC 39–41; GERHART, *op. cit. supra* note 2, at 99.

[43] GERHART, *op. cit. supra* note 2, at 99. "Isaiah" was a familiar term for Justice Brandeis.

[44] 4 PUBLIC PAPERS 200–22; Washington Post, June 1, 1935.

[45] SCHLESINGER 284–87.

The President's "horse-and-buggy" conference created a furor. The next day, Raymond Clapper wrote in his Scripps-Howard column:[46]

> Within an hour after President Roosevelt held his press conference yesterday, you could almost feel the electric excitement about Washington.
> Gossip travels with lightning speed through the National Capital. . . . Long before the first newspapers reached the street corners . . . , the whole city knew that something of unusual importance had occurred.

Most commentators upbraided the President severely. The Washington *Post* typified much of the newspaper response with an editorial bluntly titled, "A President Leaves His Party." Henry Stimson wrote Roosevelt a long letter in which he protested that the "horse-and-buggy" observation "was a wrong statement, an unfair statement and, if it had not been so extreme as to be recognizable as hyperbole, a rather dangerous and inflammatory statement."[47] Senator Arthur Vandenberg, Michigan Republican, declared: "I don't think the President has any thought of emulating Mussolini, Hitler or Stalin, but his utterance as I have heard it is exactly what these men would say."[48]

Nor were all liberals pleased with Roosevelt's remarks. The Tennessee editor George Fort Milton wrote the President that his target should be not the Court but the Constitution. After all, Milton pointed out, men like Cardozo, Stone, Hughes, and the Brandeis of the *Oklahoma Ice* dissent had joined in the *Schechter* judgment; given our Constitution, they had had no other choice. Milton counseled:[49]

> Take the lead in a great program of constitutional reform. That is what we need to have done. Let the Constitution be amended so that the Congress will be given power to control indirect as well as direct effects of Interstate Commerce. Let the Constitution be amended to provide for an intelligent measure of delegation. I believe that you will get a very important and effective support from progressives all over the coun-

---

[46] Washington Post, June 1, 1935.

[47] Stimson to FDR, June 10, 1935, FDRL PPF 20.

[48] Washington Post, June 1, 1935; cf. Ralph Hayes to Newton Baker, June 8, 1935, Baker MSS, LC, Box 117.

[49] Milton to FDR, June 4, 1935, Milton MSS, LC, Box 18.

try on a program such as this. But I do not believe that there would be nearly so much support and strength for a program bottomed on a criticism of the Court itself.

Despite his lengthy press conference, Roosevelt never stated directly what he proposed to do. When reporters asked him in what manner the question might be resolved, he replied: "We haven't got to that yet." Nor did he suggest immediate action: "I don't mean this summer or winter or next fall, but over a period, perhaps of five or ten years."[50]

From both within and outside the Administration, Roosevelt was urged to act immediately. In the confusion after the horse-and-buggy conference, Raymond Moley, one of the original members of the Brain Trust, called Vice President John N. Garner and Senators Byrnes and Robert M. La Follette, Jr., together and found that they, like he, favored a constitutional amendment. Encouraged by the meeting, Moley wrote an editorial for *Today* advocating this course, and Byrnes spoke in support of the idea in Charleston, South Carolina. In Congress, the demand for action produced a freshet of new proposals. Some wanted to make constitutional grants of power to Congress more explicit; others, like Senator Norris, wished to require at least a 7-to-2 vote by the Supreme Court to invalidate legislation.[51]

In the nation there was growing anti-Court sentiment, which those who wished to act right away might tap. To the forces arrayed against the Court by the rail pension opinion, the *Schechter* decision had added both those groups which had benefited from the NRA and people who resented any setback to Roosevelt and the New Deal. A Memphis man advised the President to balk the Court by declaring martial law,[52] and a Kentucky attorney wrote: "I should think that you and Congress were as tired of the Supreme Court stunts as the people are."[53]

But Roosevelt decided against immediate action. For a moment, Moley recalls, the President showed a "flicker of enthusiasm," but

---

[50] 4 PUBLIC PAPERS 222.

[51] MOLEY 307; SCHLESINGER 288; H.R. No. 7997, Robert Ramsay MSS, University of West Virginia, Morgantown, W.Va.; Washington Post, May 29–June 1, 1935.

[52] Edward J. Brown to FDR, June 7, 1935, FDRL OF 41-A, Box 116.

[53] H. M. Stanley to FDR, July 2, 1935, FDRL OF 41-A, Box 116.

this soon dwindled.[54] Roosevelt sensed that the time was not yet ripe. The NRA had its supporters, but its detractors were more numerous; he could not go to the country with that kind of an appeal. The clamor raised by the horse-and-buggy conference indicated that the Court would have to antagonize a much larger portion of the nation before it would be politically safe to challenge it.[55] The difficulties in the way of winning approval for a constitutional amendment were inhibiting. Norris conceded: "It looks now as though it would be an absolute impossibility to pass it through the Senate or the House by the necessary two-thirds majority in order to submit it to the states."[56] Nor had the explorations in the Department of Justice proceeded far enough so that Roosevelt was ready with a specific proposal.

For the next year Roosevelt bided his time. He made no public reference to the Supreme Court even when additional adverse decisions appeared to require some sort of response. He left the impression that he was accepting the Court's verdicts without complaint and that, after having had his knuckles rapped for his horse-and-buggy remarks, he proposed neither to say nor to do anything further. In fact, as Tugwell has written, "If open battle was not at once joined, a kind of twilight war did begin."[57]

In June, 1935, the American ambassador to Italy, Breckinridge Long, returned for a brief visit to the United States; he found "one thing . . . uppermost on the minds of political America": the *Schechter* decision. At lunch alone with Long on the White House porch, Roosevelt spoke freely about the course he planned to pursue. He would move other cases up to the Supreme Court to give it an opportunity to modify its interpretation of the Commerce Clause. If the Court did not do so, then it might be necessary to

---

[54] MOLEY 307.

[55] TUGWELL, THE DEMOCRATIC ROOSEVELT 385 (1957).

[56] George W. Norris to William A. Ahern, July 10, 1935, Norris MSS, Tray 27, Box 4.

[57] TUGWELL, *op. cit. supra* note 55, at 385. For Roosevelt's continued concern, see FDR to Armstead Brown, July 6, 1935, FDRL PPF 2669. In a letter marked "Personal," he told the judge of the Supreme Court of Florida: "I am not worrying in any way about 1936, but I am, of course, concerned about future Supreme Court decisions. After all, we do not want to take away State's rights but, at the same time, there are a good many problems which, under modern conditions, can be solved only by Federal action."

propose an amendment. Long noted in his diary: "The amendments are not yet in specific or concrete form but might be broached under three headings: first, to define Inter-State Commerce with authority to Congress to legislate on the subject; second, to define certain phases of Inter-State Commerce; and third, taking a page from Lloyd George, to give authority to the Congress to pass over the veto of the Supreme Court legislation which the Court held unconstitutional."[58]

If and when the time came to act, the amendment route seemed the most promising path, although not everyone agreed about this. Some thought that the problem lay not in the Constitution but the Court; hence, they reasoned either that the composition of the Court must be altered or that the Court must, and perhaps could, be persuaded to change its views. The Felix Frankfurter cadre, which had always disliked the NRA anyway, opposed the amendment approach. From a different standpoint, Homer Cummings, angered by the *Schechter* decision, fumed: "I tell you, Mr. President, they mean to destroy us. . . . We will have to find a way to get rid of the present membership of the Supreme Court."[59] Yet the unanimity of the Court made it seem unlikely that the New Deal could win a majority, and it argued against solving the problem by appointing a few additional judges. After the *Schechter* opinion was handed down, Raymond Clapper wrote: "Talk of blackjacking the court by enlarging its membership collapsed when all nine justices joined in the decision. That subterfuge of packing the court, a weak and uncertain one at best, becomes ridiculous to think of now."[60]

Both Roosevelt and Cummings agreed that the Justice Department should continue to seek out solutions for the impasse. A week after the horse-and-buggy conference, Alexander Holtzoff, who was to be a central figure in the search for a plan, sent Cummings a memorandum responding to the suggestion that the Court might be stripped of most or all of its appellate jurisdiction. When Holtzoff explained that such a proposal would encounter too much

---

[58] Breckinridge Long MS Diary, LC, June 12, June 17, 1935. That same month, the President's son James Roosevelt, in a speech in Missouri, called for "an earlier determination of the constitutionality of the acts of the Legislature." Carlisle Bargeron, *Along the Potomac*, Washington Post, June 13, 1935, clipping in John Taber MSS, Cornell University Collection of Regional History, Ithaca, N.Y., Box 62.

[59] SCHLESINGER, 282, 288–89.   [60] Washington Post, May 29, 1935.

opposition and still would not eliminate all the problems confronting the Administration, Cummings was unsatisfied and told him to develop his point "a little more fully." On June 22 Holtzoff sent another five-page memorandum on the question, but the matter did not end there. On August 15, W. W. Gardner prepared a fourteen-page study for the Solicitor General in which he, too, looked into whether "the power of the Supreme Court to pass upon the constitutional validity of congressional legislation might be abolished or restricted by an Act of Congress." But he also found objections to the proposal, and the search for a satisfactory plan continued.[61]

The President displayed a lively interest in these inquiries. In July, for example, he sent Cummings a memorandum calling to his attention "two extremely interesting articles by Harold Laski" in the Manchester *Guardian*.[62] Roosevelt also corresponded with critics of the Court outside the government. In August, 1935, Charlton Ogburn, counsel for the American Federation of Labor, informed the President that he had submitted a proposed constitutional amendment to the executive council of the Federation for approval.[63] That same month, Roosevelt told Charles E. Wyzanski, Jr., solicitor of the Department of Labor: "Of course, if the Supreme Court should knock out the AAA, then the constitutional amendment would be the real issue. It probably will be anyway, and there will be less difficulty in phrasing it than many people think."[64]

Finding a satisfactory plan was only one part of Roosevelt's strategy; another part was building popular support for such a move. The horse-and-buggy conference had been one move toward that end. In August the President took another step when he met at the White House with George Creel. In collaboration with Creel, a veteran of reform wars, Roosevelt sometimes used the pages of *Collier's* to launch trial balloons. For an article entitled "Looking Ahead with Roosevelt," the President now dictated to Creel:[65]

---

61 Holtzoff, Memorandum for the Attorney General, June 6, 1935; Cummings, Memorandum for Mr. Holtzoff, June 13, 1935; Holtzoff, Memorandum for the Attorney General, June 22, 1935; W. W. Gardner, Memorandum for the Solicitor General, Aug. 15, 1935, NA Dept. of Justice 235773.

62 FDR to Cummings, July 5, 1935, FDRL OF 142.

63 Charlton Ogburn to FDR, Aug. 7, 20, 1935, FDRL OF 142.

64 3 SCHLESINGER 453. See, too, Rev. Francis Haas to FDR, Oct. 25, 1935, Haas MSS, Catholic University of America, Washington, D.C.

65 CREEL, REBEL AT LARGE 291–92 (1935).

In the next few months, the Supreme Court will hand down fresh pronouncements with respect to New Deal laws, and it is possible the President will get another "licking." If so, much will depend on the language of the licking. In event that unconstitutionality is found, perhaps the decisions will point the way to statutory amendments. If, however, the Constitution is construed technically; if it is held that one hundred and fifty years have no bearing on the case, and that the present generation is powerless to meet social and economic problems that were not within the knowledge of the founding fathers, and therefore not made the subject of their specific consideration, then the President will have no other alternative than to go to the country with a Constitutional amendment that will lift the Dead Hand, giving the people of today the right to deal with today's vital issues.

He told Creel grimly: "Fire that as an opening gun."[66]

Contrary to Roosevelt's expectation, the trial balloon attracted almost no notice. Most of the nation in 1935 was still either indifferent to the Court question or outrightly opposed to tethering the Court. To the query: "As a general principle, would you favor limiting the power of the Supreme Court to declare acts of Congress unconstitutional?" the Gallup Poll in the autumn of 1935 received the following replies: yes, 31 per cent; no, 53 per cent; no opinion, 16 per cent. The most articulate anti-Court feeling came from those who felt they had been hurt by specific decisions. A Virginian objected: "The Supreme Court turned down my railroad pension." But many more thought the Justices wise, the system of checks and balances sacred, and Congress mercurial, even if their conception of these institutions was sometimes primitive. Asked his view of the Court, an Illinois man replied: "It's permanent. Congress is just the whims and fancies of the people." An Ohio reliefer said: "If they didn't know more than the other courts, they wouldn't be called the Supreme Court."[67]

Despite this discouraging response, the President pushed ahead quietly with his plans. At a long lunch at the White House on November 12, 1935, Ickes and Roosevelt fell to talking about the Court. The President remarked that he did not think that any Justices would retire and permit him to make new appointments. "Then," Ickes noted, "he said that while the matter could not be talked about now, he believed that the way to mend the situation was to adopt a constitutional amendment which would give

---

[66] *Id*. at 292.   [67] N.Y. Herald-Tribune, Nov. 3, 1935.

the Attorney General the right, if he has any doubt of the constitutionality of a legislative act, to apply to the Supreme Court for a ruling, that ruling to state specifically in which respects the act is unconstitutional. Then, if the next succeeding Congress, with this opinion of the Supreme Court before it, should re-enact that statute, it would, by that fact, be purged of its unconstitutionality and become the law of the land."[68]

During their conversation, the President made use of an analogy that was to crop up frequently in succeeding months in discussions of the judiciary crisis. Ickes wrote in his diary:[69]

> The President's mind went back to the difficulty in England, where the House of Lords repeatedly refused to adopt legislation sent up from the House of Commons. He recalled that when Lloyd George came into power some years ago under Edward VII, he went to the King and asked his consent to announce that if the Lords refused again to accept the bill for Irish autonomy, which had been pressed upon them several times since the days of Gladstone, he would create several hundred new peers, enough to outvote the existing House of Lords. With this threat confronting them, the bill passed the Lords.

Roosevelt's recollection was faulty—the episode actually concerned Asquith and the attempt to reform the House of Lords—but the British analogy was clearly important for him, because he recurred to it once more on December 27 at a cabinet meeting at which the Supreme Court question was again reviewed at length.[70] This time he referred not only to the Irish Home Rule Bill, but to Lloyd George's success in pushing through a social security act by the threat to create three hundred new peers.[71]

After the cabinet meeting, Ickes made a new entry in his diary:[72]

> Clearly, it is running in the President's mind that substantially all of the New Deal bills will be declared unconstitutional by the Supreme Court. This will mean that everything that this Administration has done of any moment will be nullified. The President pointed out that there were three ways of meeting such a situation: (1) by packing the Supreme Court, which

---

[68] 1 Ickes 467–68.   [69] *Ibid.*

[70] *Id.* at 494–95. The Asquith precedent was to be mentioned often during the Court fight. See, for example, Martin J. Lide to Kenneth McKellar, Feb. 16, 1937, McKellar MSS, Memphis Public Library, Memphis, Tenn., Box 229.

[71] 1 Ickes 495.   [72] *Ibid.*

was a distasteful idea; (2) by trying to put through a number of amendments to the Constitution to meet the various situations; and (3) by a method that he asked us to consider very carefully.

The third method is, in substance, this: an amendment to the Constitution conferring explicit power on the Supreme Court to declare acts of Congress unconstitutional, a power which is not given anywhere in the Constitution as it stands. The amendment would also give the Supreme Court original jurisdiction on constitutional questions affecting statutes. If the Supreme Court should declare an act of Congress to be unconstitutional, then—a congressional election having intervened—if Congress should repass the law so declared to be unconstitutional, the taint of unconstitutionality would be removed and the law would be a valid one. By this method there would be in effect a referendum to the country, although an indirect one. At the intervening congressional election the question of the constitutionality or unconstitutionality of the law would undoubtedly be an issue.

In essence, the President's strategy was to leave the power of decision to the Supreme Court. If the Court upheld New Deal legislation, the issue would fade away. But if all the legislation were thrown out, Roosevelt warned, there would be "marching farmers and marching miners and marching workingmen throughout the land." For almost half a year, while the Court was recessed, the conflict between the President and the Court had simmered on a low flame. But during those months, as Roosevelt was keenly aware, such significant questions as the AAA processing tax had been making their way through the lower courts; the Supreme Court could be expected to render decisions on such matters early in 1936. "If the Court does send the AAA flying like the NRA," the President had told Wyzanski, "there might even be a revolution."[73]

IV. The Court Nullifies the New Deal

On January 6, 1936, the Supreme Court handed down its long-awaited decision on the AAA processing tax.[74] Divided 6 to 3, the Court ruled the tax unconstitutional, thus overturning the second of the two most important New Deal recovery programs. In an opinion that earned him scorching comments from the law journals, Justice Roberts held the levy to be an illegitimate use of the

---

[73] 3 Schlesinger 453.   [74] United States v. Butler, 297 U.S. 1 (1936),

taxing power, "the expropriation of money from one group for the benefit of another."[75]

The *Butler* decision aroused acrimonious criticism of the Court. Coming on top of the 1935 opinions, the *Butler* verdict appeared to indicate a determination by the Court to wipe out all of the New Deal. "Is Poe's Raven who croaked 'Never More' their model?" asked one man. An Oklahoman penciled a letter to the Attorney General stating that he wanted to impeach every judge who had declared the AAA invalid, and another man wrote the President: "I'm in favor of doing away with the Constitution if it's going to interfere with the general welfare of the people." The head of a Chicago advertising agency asked: "Are you aware that the people at large are getting damned tired of the United States Supreme Court, and that, if left to a popular vote, it would be kicked out?"[76]

A nation of tinkerers, the country flooded Washington with home-made inventions to improve the government machinery. Many of the contrivances stressed either the age of the Justices or the device of packing the Court, or both. A South Carolina attorney wrote: "We are hoping and believing that you and the Congress of the United States will not allow six old men to destroy this Country." A Minnesota lawyer urged compulsory retirement at 65 or 70, "whichever would retire the majority of the present members of the Court." A Los Angeles man questioned the fitness of "that body of nine old hasbeens, half-deaf, half-blind, full-of-palsy men. . . . That they are behind the times is very plain—all you have to do is to look at Charles Hughes' whiskers."[77]

---

[75] *Id.* at 61.

[76] Maurice Daley to Homer Cummings, Jan. 13, 1936, NA Dept. of Justice 5-36-346; George Thomason to Cummings, NA Dept. of Justice 235773; John W. White to FDR, Jan. 7, 1936, NA Dept. of Justice 5-36-346; W. K. Cochrane to Stephen Early, Jan. 25, 1936, FDRL OF 41-A, Box 120. Governor George Earle of Pennsylvania denounced the Court as "a political body" with "six members committed to the politics of the Liberty League." Address of George H. Earle, Jan. 18, 1935, Earle MSS, Bryn Mawr, Pa., privately held, Speech and News File No. 73. Some of the indignation was aroused by the "windfall" millers anticipated as a consequence of the decision. Clifford Hope to Chester Stevens, Apr. 21, 1936, Hope MSS, Kansas State Historical Society, Topeka, Kans., Tax (Legis.) folder, Legislative Correspondence, 1935–36.

[77] Joe P. Lane to FDR, Jan. 7, 1936, FDRL OF 274, Box 3; S. C. Odenborg to FDR, Feb. 3, 1936, NA Dept. of Justice 235241; John B. Muller to FDR, Jan. 9, 1936, FDRL OF 1-K, Misc. 1936.

From different parts of the nation came calls for additional Justices "with younger minds." Some wanted four more Justices, like the Memphis businessman who pointed out: "Business does not accept an applicant with twelve gray hairs on his head." Others thought six new Justices would have to be added to "reverse this infamy." An Arizona attorney recommended: "In order to avoid the impending seizure of this government by the special interests it is incumbent on you to increase the membership of the Supreme Court to fifteen; and appoint the new membership from the Frankfurters, Olsons, and other men who place human rights above the rights of predatory wealth." From Richmond, Virginia, came a demand for a Court of "at least twenty or more members. Nine OLD MEN, whose total age amounts to about 650 years, should have additional help." A member of the Kansas House of Representatives had an even more radical suggestion: add sixteen new members, "the new members to be not over thirty-five years of age, and retired at forty. This would put men on the court that are in step with TO-DAY."[78]

A number of correspondents seemed to believe that Roosevelt was unaware of the Court's infamy or that he needed to be stiffened to oppose the Court. A Seattle woman wrote:[79]

> I have just this minute heard the decision of the U.S. Supreme Court on the A.A.A.
> Mr. Roosevelt, are you going to sit back and let these few men, controlled by the selfish elements of our country, control the destinies of intelligent, thinking and country-loving people, who really make this great country of ours?

A Kansan asserted: "One who is really a man will resist to the end being governed by men who lived one hundred and fifty years ago." A Miami attorney assured the President: "If you, as the Executive, and Congress will make the Supreme Court an issue in this country it will not fail. Jackson did not fail, Grant did not fail, and the Dred-Scott decision was treated with contempt."[80]

---

[78] W. J. Young to FDR, Jan. 7, 1936, NA Dept. of Justice 5-36-346; W. B. Mills to FDR, Jan. 13, 1936; Thomas Duncan to FDR, Jan. 7, 1936; Elmer Graham to FDR, Jan. 7, 1936, NA Dept. of Justice 235773; W. F. Betts to FDR, Jan. 6, 1936, FDRL OF 1-K Misc. 1936; W. H. (Bill) Reed to FDR, Jan. 21, 1936, NA Dept. of Justice 235868.

[79] Auzias de Turenne to FDR, Jan. 6, 1936, FDRL OF 1-K Misc. 1936.

[80] R. W. Sholders to FDR, Jan. 6, 1936, NA Dept. of Justice 5-36-246; Rudolph Isom to FDR, Jan. 13, 1936, FDRL OF 41-A, Box 120.

A Mississippi editor wired Roosevelt:[81]

> On behalf of farmers and workers urge that you set aside
> Supreme Court decision and destroy their assumed right to de-
> clare laws of Congress unconstitutional. . . . President Andrew
> Jackson, our greatest Democrat, defied Supreme Court on this
> very point. Hope you will do the same. Sincerely believe that
> future of Democratic government hinges on whether you will
> take the bull by the horns. Drastic action is imperative. Amer-
> ica is depending on you. Perhaps civilization and its perpetuity
> is involved in your acts. God grant that you have the courage
> to do right.

Roosevelt's strategy of "watchful waiting" seemed to be paying
off. The Court, which had antagonized groups like railway employees in 1935, had now angered farmers who would be denied
more than two billion dollars in AAA benefit checks in the next
year. Edward A. O'Neal, president of the American Farm Bureau
Federation, warned: "Those who believe the American farmer
will stand idly by and watch his program for economic justice fall
without a fight are badly mistaken. The fight is on—and this time
it will be with the gloves off."[82] O'Neal planned to meet with the
A. F. of L.'s general counsel, Charlton Ogburn, to lay plans for a
farmer-labor alliance to achieve common objectives.

Yet none of this agitation moved Roosevelt to act. Despite constant prodding, he refused even to comment on the *Butler* decision.
He believed that the time had not yet come. An election year was
not the propitious moment to give the opposition, which was bereft
of issues, an opportunity to stand by the flag. Nor had the coali-
tion against the Court yet reached full strength. If O'Neal denounced the *Butler* opinion, other farm leaders approved it, and a
Gallup Poll, which appeared the day before the decision was rendered, showed a majority of the country opposed to the AAA.[83]
Nor had opponents of the Court yet reached agreement on a
proposal. Ogburn, for one, thought that nothing should be done
at present save to make the amending process easier.[84]

Moreover, the Administration was not yet ready for a fight on
the Court issue, because it had not yet come up with a satisfactory

---

81 H. B. Sanders to FDR, Jan. 7, 1936, NA Dept. of Justice 5-36-346.

82 Washington Post, Jan. 7, 1936.   83 Washington Post, Jan. 8, 1936.

84 Charlton Ogburn to FDR, Jan. 9, 1936, FDRL OF 274.

plan. Shortly after the *Butler* verdict was rendered, Assistant Attorney General John Dickinson wrote:[85]

> The way in which the high command has apparently decided to treat the AAA decision has been to smother its effect as much as possible. I am not at all sure that this is a wise strategy, but apparently the feeling is that there is a widespread readiness, throughout the country, to blaze up against the Supreme Court and that this state of mind must be wet-blanketed, for fear that otherwise it would drive the Administration into the position of either attacking the Court, or calling for an amendment, which they are not yet prepared to do.

While maintaining public silence, Roosevelt indicated privately that he was preparing for a showdown with the Court. At the cabinet meeting on January 24, 1936, Ickes recorded:[86]

> The President said that word is coming to him from widely separated parts of the country that people are beginning to show a great deal of interest in the constitutional questions that have been raised by recent Supreme Court decisions. . . . The President made the point, based upon some statement by Harold J. Laski, that the Supreme Court, in its decisions on New Deal legislation, was dictating what it believed should be the social philosophy of the nation, without reference to the law or the Constitution. . . . It is plain to see, from what the President said today and has said on other occasions, that he is not at all averse to the Supreme Court declaring one New Deal statute after another unconstitutional. I think he believes that the Court will find itself pretty far out on a limb before it is through with it and that a real issue will be joined on which we can go to the country.
>
> For my part, I hope so. Here is an issue that must be faced by the country sooner or later, unless we are prepared to submit to the arbitrary and final dictates of a group of men who are not elected by the people and who are not responsible to the people: in short, a judicial tyranny imposed by men appointed for life and who cannot be reached except by the slow and cumbersome process of impeachment.

That same day, Roosevelt prepared a memorandum for the files, with a copy to Moley, stating:[87]

> It has been well said by a prominent historian that fifty years from now the Supreme Court's AAA decision will, in all probability, be described somewhat as follows:

---

[85] Dickinson to George Fort Milton, Jan. 13, 1936, Milton MSS, Box 19.

[86] 1 Ickes 524.   [87] Memorandum, Jan. 24, 1936, FDRL OF 1-K.

(1) The decision virtually prohibits the President and Congress from the right, under modern conditions, to intervene reasonably in the regulation of nation-wide commerce and nation-wide agriculture.

(2) The Supreme Court arrived at this result by selecting from several possible techniques of constitutional interpretation a special technique. The objective of the Court's purpose was to make reasonableness in passing legislation a matter to be settled not by the views of the elected Senate and House of Representatives and not by the views of an elected President but rather by the private, social philosophy of a majority of nine appointed members of the Supreme Court itself.

Roosevelt continued to move ahead on the study of plans to curb the Court. A week after the *Butler* decision, he wrote Cummings: "What was the McArdle case . . .? I am told that the Congress withdrew some act from the jurisdiction of the Supreme Court."[88] The Attorney General replied: "The case of ex parte McCardle . . . to which you refer . . . is one of the classic cases to which we refer when considering the possibility of limiting the jurisdiction of Federal Courts. This whole matter has been the subject of considerable study in this Department, and, in view of recent developments, is apt to be increasingly important."

The exchange between the President and the Attorney General suggests the crucial development in the early weeks of 1936: loss of faith in the amendment solution and rising belief that the Court could be curbed by an act of Congress. Perhaps the most important influence on this change of plans was the division of the Court in the *Butler* case and Justice Harlan Stone's ringing dissent, less because the minority voted to sustain the processing tax than because of Stone's vigorous assault on judicial usurpation. Cummings wrote Stone:[89]

Your dissenting opinion is on a high plane—sound, constructive and human.

It may not be the law *now*—but it will be the law later, un-

---

[88] FDR to Cummings, Jan. 14, 1936; Cummings to FDR, Jan. 16, 1936, FDRL PSF Supreme Court.

[89] Cummings to Stone, Jan. 8, 1936, FDRL PSF Justice. Stone responded: "Thank you for your generous note. When one finds himself outvoted two to one he should be humble and perhaps skeptical of his own judgment. But I have a sincere faith that history and long time perspective will see the function of our court in a different light from that in which it is viewed at the moment." For Stone's views, see Mason, Harlan Fiske Stone 417 (1956).

less governmental functions are to be permanently frozen in an unescapable mold.

You spoke at a great moment and in a great way. Congratulations.

The split in the Court confirmed those who had been arguing that the problem lay not in the Constitution but in the composition of this particular Court, and Justice Stone's dissent made it easier to argue that Congress must act to regain powers which the Court had usurped. The amendment route was not abandoned, but the search for a suitable amendment now concentrated for the first time on compelling the retirement of Justices at 70, thus altering the makeup of the Court. In addition, increasing attention was given to finding a way to meet the difficulty by statute.[90]

On January 29, 1936, after talking over the Court issue at lunch with Senator Norris, the President continued the same discussion with Ickes. He told Ickes that he had reached the conclusion that he could achieve Court reform without resort to an amendment; he had also confided this to Norris. Roosevelt favored an act of Congress which would strip the lower courts of the power to pass upon the constitutionality of statutes and would confer this power on the Supreme Court as a matter of original jurisdiction. The Supreme Court would be required to give an advisory opinion on the constitutionality of a bill before it was enacted. Congress could then alter the bill to conform with the advice of the Court or it could pass it once more in its original form, and it would then become the law of the land. Ickes noted:[91]

> I made the obvious remark that the Supreme Court would declare unconstitutional such an act as the President had in mind and he said that of course it would. To meet that situation his plan would be somewhat as follows: Congress would pass a law, the Supreme Court would declare it unconstitutional, the President would then go to Congress and ask it to instruct him whether he was to follow the mandate of Congress or the mandate of the Court. If the Congress should declare

---

[90] 3 SCHLESINGER 493–94; FDR Memorandum to Homer Cummings, Feb. 24, 1936; FDR Memorandum for Chairman Hatton Sumners, FDRL OF 41, Box 114. During the 1936 campaign, one correspondent wrote the President: "Why not make a campaign on the opinions of Justice Stone? By taking the words of a member of the court itself there can be no justifiable charge of usurpation." Paul Webb to FDR, June 4, 1936, FDRL OF 41-A, Box 116.

[91] 1 ICKES 529–30.

that its own mandate was to be followed, the President would carry out the will of Congress through the offices of the United States Marshals and ignore the Court.

After their talk, Ickes reflected:[92]

> There isn't any doubt at all that the President is really hoping that the Supreme Court will continue to make a clean sweep of all New Deal legislation, throwing out the TVA Act, the Securities Act, the Railroad Retirement Act, the Social Security Act, the Guffey Coal Act, and others. He thinks the country is beginning to sense this issue but that enough people have not yet been affected by adverse decisions so as to make a sufficient feeling on a Supreme Court issue.
>
> I told the President that I hoped this would be the issue in the next campaign. I believe it will have to be fought out sooner or later, and I remarked to him that the President who faced this issue and drastically curbed the usurped power of the Supreme Court would go down through all the ages of history as one of the great Presidents.

Two days later, at a cabinet meeting, Cummings raised the question whether the government should appeal a lower court decision denying the federal government the right to condemn property for a low-cost housing project. Tom Corcoran and Ben Cohen were but two of the President's advisers who thought the government should drop the case, in part because they feared an adverse opinion from the Supreme Court that might wipe out the Public Works Administration. Ickes noted:[93]

> The President was firmly of the opinion that we ought to go ahead with the case. He scouted the idea that anyone could draw an act which would pass the scrutiny of the Supreme Court in its present outlook on New Deal legislation. He thought that if all PWA projects should be suspended as the result of an adverse decision by the Supreme Court, it would be all to the good. . . . There doesn't seem to me to be any doubt that he is entirely willing to have the Supreme Court knock out every New Deal law. It is clear that he is willing to go to the country on this issue but he wants the issue to be as strong and clear as possible, which means that he hopes the

---

[92] *Id.* at 530.

[93] *Id.* at 531–32. Ickes added: "It happens that I am fully in accord with the President's view on this matter. I believe that this issue will have to be fought out sooner or later and no more important issue has arisen since the Civil War. Naturally, I would like to be in this fight and be a member of the Administration that is carrying it on."

Supreme Court will declare unconstitutional every New Deal case that comes before it.

Yet, while blithely accepting this prospect of a constitutional Armageddon, the President continued to say nothing publicly. Early in February, George Fort Milton confided:[94]

> I thought a month ago that the Court and the Constitution were very definitely going to be in this year's presidential debate. But everything in Washington is of the hush, hush attitude. . . . What I am feeling is that maybe he is depending too much on his resourcefulness and that he could do some thinking on what would be the usefulness of being re-elected if he was going to have to go into a second term denied the essential powers of nationality. Wouldn't he be all dressed up and have nowhere to go?

Roosevelt's silence, which some interpreted as acquiescence in the Court's decisions, left the initiative for public action to Congress. In the 1936 session, congressmen introduced more than a hundred proposals to restrict the federal courts. Some measures, such as the "Human Rights Amendment," aimed to expand the powers of Congress to enact social legislation. Others, like the Cross bill, sought to strip the courts of the prerogative of judicial review. Still others resorted to enlarging the bench. In January, 1936, Representative Ernest Lundeen of Minnesota filed a bill to increase the Supreme Court by two Justices so that the Court could handle more work and because "new blood will mean a more liberal outlook on constitutional questions." Lundeen pointed out that when his bill had been adopted, and when Justice Willis Van Devanter carried out his purported plan to retire, the President would be able to name three new Justices and thus assure a liberal majority. A week earlier, Representative James L. Quinn had gone even further; he had introduced a measure to expand the Court to fifteen Justices.[95]

On February 12, 1936, George Norris delivered a major address on the floor of the Senate. He denounced the Supreme Court as a "continuous constitutional convention." To the contention that the processing tax was invalid because agricultural production was not mentioned in the Constitution, Norris retorted: "Nowhere in

---

[94] Milton to George Foster Peabody, Feb. 10, 1936, Milton MSS, Box 19.

[95] Thomas R. Amlie to W. Jett Lauck, Mar. 6, 1937, Amlie MSS, State Historical Society of Wisconsin, Madison, Wisc., Box 6; O. H. Cross to Stanley Reed, Jan. 17, 1936, NA Dept. of Justice 235868.

that great document is there a syllable, a word, or a sentence giving to any court the right to declare an act of Congress unconstitutional." Norris expostulated: "The members of the Supreme Court are not elected by anybody. They are responsible to nobody. Yet they hold dominion over everybody."[96] Rejecting the amendment procedure he had once favored as "impracticable," Norris asked Congress to have the "courage" to enact legislation requiring a unanimous decision to invalidate an act of Congress.

The columnist Robert S. Allen wrote Norris:[97]

> I have been wondering for weeks what the hell this session was for. Your matchless speech on the Supreme Court this afternoon cleared up the mystery. The session was solely so you could deliver this superb exposition—so it could go into the Record for all history to read—so you could say what everybody was thinking, but no other leader had the guts to say out loud.
>
> It was a grand and unequaled job, Senator. And what was no less significant was the tremendous response it is being accorded. It is really amazing the extraordinary press coverage it has received. Even the filthy Hearst jackals carried almost a column of your remarks. It was also amazing to me how deeply moved the press gallery was. Reactionary old bastards who haven't had an intelligent idea in decades spoke respectfully of your views.

Norris' concern over the Court question was long-standing, but it was heightened during these weeks by anxiety over the fate of the Tennessee Valley Authority, of which he was acknowledged to be the "father." In January, Norris had written: "Up to the time this decision was rendered in the AAA case, I had no doubt whatsoever that the Supreme Court would sustain the TVA Act. . . . Since the AAA decision, however, I would not be surprised if the Court would hold the TVA Act unconstitutional."[98] On February 17, the Court, by a surprising 8-to-1 vote, diminished these

---

[96] "Legislation by the Judiciary," Copy in the George Norris MSS. See, too, Norris to Francis Heney, Apr. 25, 1936, Heney MSS, Bancroft Library, University of California, Berkeley, Calif. The Norris idea was a familiar one. In January, a Tacoma assessor had written the President: "The extreme penalty is not exacted from the vilest culprit, save on a unanimous verdict. Why should the will of the people be crucified for less?" Fred A. Smith to FDR, Jan. 9, 1936, NA Dept. of Justice 235773.

[97] Allen to George W. Norris, Feb. 12, 1936, Norris MSS, Tray 27, Box 4.

[98] George W. Norris to Irving Brant, Jan. 11, 1936, Norris MSS, Tray 27, Box 5.

anxieties by upholding the power of the TVA to dispose of power generated at Wilson Dam.[99]

Although some critics pointed out that the Court still had not rendered a decisive judgment on the constitutionality of the TVA, friends of public power were delighted by the opinion. "I had completely resigned myself to a bad decision, only holding out hope that we would have some crumb of comfort in that unlike AAA and NRA we would not be swept completely out to sea, bag and baggage," wrote David Lilienthal.[100] "The decision, clearing away so many of the clouds hanging over us, makes me feel very humble. We are given an almost incredible grant of power."[101] The opinion served, for the moment, to quiet demands for reform of the judiciary.[102] By showing the fairness of the Court, the decision, observed the Washington *Post*, "should do more than anything else to end the campaign for limitation of the Court's authority."[103] From Chattanooga, George Fort Milton wrote gleefully:[104]

> Well, after TVA, I think we ought to start talking about "one old man and the eight young men." . . .
> I suspect that some of the members of the Court set themselves forward deliberately to show that they could render other than a Tory decision. Would you call this modernizing Mr. Dooley, so that the Supreme Court precedes the election returns?

The respite provided by the TVA decision proved short-lived. Six weeks later, the Court rebuked the Securities and Exchange Commission,[105] and on May 18, 1936, it went out of its way in the *Carter* case[106] to strike down the Guffey Coal Act in an opinion that appeared to doom not only the Wagner Labor Relations Act

---

[99] Ashwander v. T.V.A., 297 U.S. 288 (1936).

[100] 1 JOURNALS OF DAVID E. LILIENTHAL 59 (1964).

[101] Lilienthal to Felix Frankfurter, Feb. 17, 1936, Lilienthal MSS, Princeton University Library.

[102] Knoxville News-Sentinel, Feb. 18–20, 1936, clippings, David Lilienthal Scrapbooks, Lilienthal MSS, Princeton University Library.

[103] Knoxville News-Sentinel, Feb. 18, 1936.

[104] George Fort Milton to Francis Coker, Feb. 18, 1936, Milton MSS, Box 19. *Cf.* Newton Baker to James M. Beck, Mar. 19, 1936, Beck MSS.

[105] Jones v. S.E.C., 298 U.S. 1 (1936).

[106] Carter v. Carter Coal Co., 298 U.S. 238 (1936).

but any attempt by act of Congress to control wages and hours. The *Carter* decision started a new wave of condemnations of the Court and demands for restrictions. Once more, the age of the Justices and the possibilities offered by "packing" were pointed out. "We permit old men 90, probably as childish as boys of 9, to sit on the Supreme Court bench and in case of a 5 to 4 vote one old man controls the affairs of the nation," one critic wrote the President. "In reviewing the Constitution of the United States," noted a Pennsylvania man, "it comes to my attention the fact that there is no limit to the Personell of the Supreme Court." A Los Angeles man urged the President to name four more Justices. He added helpfully: "For these four positions I nominate Senator Hiram Johnson of California and Senator Geo. W. Norris of Nebraska. Now you name two." Yet Roosevelt not only would not heed such advice but when newsmen pressed him for a statement on the *Carter* decision he brusquely closed off that line of questioning.[107]

The *Carter* decision turned out to be only the first in a series of rapid-fire blows the Court delivered at the New Deal. On successive Mondays in the spring of 1936, the Court handed down the *Carter* opinion, overturned the Municipal Bankruptcy Act,[108] and, in the most momentous ruling of all, invalidated the New York state minimum-wage law in the *Tipaldo* case.[109] Each decision came from a divided court.

For critics of the Court, the *Tipaldo* opinion was the last straw. Before that decision, even some New Dealers hoped to avoid a direct confrontation with the Court. After it, Tugwell has written, liberals agreed that "something must be done."[110] Not since the *Dred Scott* disaster had the Court inflicted on itself so deep a wound. As Alpheus T. Mason has observed: "At any time up to June 1, 1936, the Court might have retreated and thus avoided a showdown. The New York Minimum Wage opinion, handed down

107 Wendell Berge to E. L. Woodcos, May 20, 1936, Berge MSS, LC, Box 10; L. C. Weiss to FDR, May 20, 1936; H. C. Holland to FDR, May 23, 1936; Jan Byrd to FDR, May 20, 1936, NA Dept. of Justice 235773; Washington Post, May 20, 1936; John D. Miller to the New York Times, May 19, 1936, Miller MSS, Cornell University Collection of Regional History.

108 St. Joseph Stockyards Co. v. United States, 298 U.S. 38 (1936).

109 Morehead v. New York *ex rel.* Tipaldo, 298 U.S. 587 (1936).

110 TUGWELL, *op. cit. supra* note 55, at 391.

that day, convinced even the most reverent that five stubborn old men had planted themselves squarely in the path of progress.[111]

The *Tipaldo* decision produced a national outcry against the Court. Ickes noted angrily: "The sacred right of liberty of contract again—the right of an immature child or a helpless woman to drive a bargain with a great corporation. If this decision does not outrage the moral sense of the country, then nothing will."[112] But it was not only New Dealers who objected to the opinion. The Court had embarrassed Administration critics who had argued that protection of the rights of labor should be left to state action. "Hereafter," wrote Franklyn Waltman in the Washington *Post*, "whenever New Dealers are taunted with trying to break down the rights of the States to manage their own affairs, the taunters will have this decision tossed in their faces."[113] The *Post* labeled the opinion "An Unfortunate Decision," and Herbert Hoover called for an amendment to restore to the states "the power they thought they already had."[114]

Once more, Roosevelt was pressed to act. From California, the head of the Stockton Democratic Club wrote the President: "By another 4 to 5 decision on the part of JUDOCRACY, *one man* has been able . . . to nullify the progress of half a century along humanitarian lines, exposing the Motherhood of America to further exploitation on the part of unscrupulous employers. If this be Democracy—may God save the mark!" A telegram from Brooklyn urged: "Increase number of justices in Supreme Court with men in their fifties." The head of a New York printing firm warned the President that it would be "useless" for him to pursue his program unless he pushed through an amendment. "You can't side-step the issue," he scolded. "The people who will re-elect you will expect you to have something to say about this matter."[115]

At a press conference on June 2, 1936, Roosevelt broke his silence. For the first time since the "horse-and-buggy" meeting,

---

[111] MASON, *op. cit. supra* note 89, at 438.

[112] 1 ICKES 614.

[113] Washington Post, June 2, 1936.

[114] N.Y. Times, June 7, 1936.

[115] James A. Metcalf to FDR, June 3, 1936, NA Dept. of Justice 224196; E. Larkin to FDR, June 4, 1936, FDRL OF 41-A, Box 116; Earl Salley to FDR, June 5, 1936, FDRL OF 274, Box 3.

he commented on a decision of the Court. Of the *Tipaldo* opinion, he said:[116]

> It seems to be fairly clear, as a result of this decision and former decisions, using this question of minimum wage as an example, that the "no-man's-land" where no Government— State or Federal—can function is being more clearly defined. A State cannot do it, and the Federal Government cannot do it.

But when a reporter asked, "How can you meet that situation?" the President replied, "I think that is about all there is to say on it."

Roosevelt was no less circumspect about drafting the 1936 Democratic platform. Both the President and Senator Robert Wagner of New York, chairman of the Resolutions Committee, were urged to incorporate in the platform commitments to specific proposals, such as requiring a 7-to-2 majority to invalidate a law, or amending the Constitution to empower Congress and the states to enact minimum-wage laws.[117] But the Administration was determined to keep the platform ambiguous, not only because it wanted to remove the Court issue from the campaign, but because it had not yet decided on any particular plan.

In drafting their platform, the Democrats had to cope with the fact that the Republicans had already committed themselves to an amendment to overcome the *Tipaldo* decision. As Cummings warned the President, if the Democrats sought to outbid the Republicans they ran the risk of going so far as to shift the whole emphasis of the campaign to the constitutional question. Cummings hoped to avoid any specific plank, but if one were necessary he favored one so vaguely worded that it should leave the door open "to the thought that perhaps, after all, an amendment may not be necessary." Four days earlier, Donald Richberg, who had been a prominent labor attorney and chairman of the National Industrial Recovery Board, had also submitted a draft which was adroitly phrased to escape any definite commitment.[118]

On the Sunday before the 1936 Democratic convention, Roosevelt, Wagner, and several others met after dinner in the White

[116] 5 Public Papers 191–92.

[117] Louis Boehm to Robert Wagner, June 6, 1936; Clarence V. Tiers to Stephen Early, June 24, 1936, FDRL OF 1871-A.

[118] Detroit News, June 25, 1936, clipping, Blair Moody Scrapbooks, Moody MSS, Michigan Historical Collections of the University of Michigan, Ann Arbor, Mich.; Cummings to FDR, June 20, 1936, FDRL PSF Justice; Richberg to FDR, June 16, 1936, FDRL PSF Supreme Court.

House to draft the platform. When they encountered difficulties, it was decided to ask two of the participants, Samuel I. Rosenman, another member of the original Brain Trust, and Stanley High, a skillful phrase-maker, to try their hands after the meeting broke up. They worked all night at a typewriter, and by morning the President had their draft on his breakfast tray. Certain parts, including a Supreme Court plank, were still missing. After breakfast, Rosenman and High went into the President's bedroom, where they found Donald Richberg.

Recognizing that more aid might be required, the President had summoned Richberg to the White House. Richberg, who guessed why he had been called, turned up shortly after breakfast with a carbon of his proposed plank in his pocket. When Roosevelt told him that Wagner needed help, Richberg handed him the draft to read. After going over it, the President whistled softly and said, "I think this is it." The others gathered in the President's bedroom agreed, and, with minor changes, Richberg's plank was incorporated in the platform. Purposely vague, it proposed an attempt to achieve a "clarifying amendment" only "if these problems cannot be effectively solved by legislation."[119]

In the 1936 campaign, Roosevelt maintained a studied silence on the Court question despite counsel from different sides that he urge action to alter the Court or that he assure the country that he would not pack the Court. The President wanted the campaign to center not on the Constitution but on the concrete achievements of the New Deal and the past iniquities of Herbert Hoover. Within the Roosevelt circle, Felix Frankfurter and Frances Perkins opposed making an issue of the Court's rulings, and even Ickes conceded that the groundwork for it had not been laid.[120] One correspondent urged the President to leave the Court matter "till after the campaign, so as not to supply ammunition to the 'constitution cryers.' When the campaign is over, Congress could proceed in a calm mood and adopt certain changes. . . . Congress could suggest to the President to add to the present Tribunal two, four or six justices to make the number 11, 13, or 15."[121]

Nonetheless, the constitutional issue surfaced in different parts

---

[119] RICHBERG, MY HERO 204–05 (1954); ROSENMAN, WORKING WITH ROOSEVELT 100–03 (1953); MOLEY 346–47.

[120] 1 ICKES 524, 531, 602.

[121] Jacob Hayman to FDR, Feb. 24, 1936, FDRL OF 41-A, Box 116.

of the country where conservatives warned that a Roosevelt victory would menace the Court. They were unpersuaded by New Deal avowals of reverence for the Constitution. Rexford Tugwell's theology was acceptable, noted one writer, but his actions were unorthodox, "like a Renaissance cardinal with children." Conceivably, a few votes may have been swung by the Court question. One man wrote: "In my opinion any man who sneered at the United States Supreme Court like he did in May 1935, when they ruled against N.R.A., is not worthy of my vote though I have been voting the Democratic Ticket since 1884." Yet Roosevelt's studied silence made it possible for Stephen Duggan, director of the Institute of International Education, to write a long letter, which the *New York Times* published, urging support of the President, who "has given no evidence that he wants to 'pack' the court," and for a conservative senator like Josiah Bailey of North Carolina to defend Roosevelt on the Court question. Enlarging the Supreme Court, wrote Frederick Lewis Allen shortly before the election, "need hardly be regarded as a serious possibility in the immediate future: it would be too obviously a cowardly move."[122]

V. ELECTION LANDSLIDE

In November, 1936, Franklin Roosevelt rolled up the greatest landslide victory in the history of two-party competition by capturing the electoral votes of all but two of the forty-eight states. His political opponents routed, his policies vindicated, he could now give full attention to the challenge posed by the Supreme Court. Time was short. In just two more months the Court would reconvene; awaiting it were tests of the validity of the Social Security Act, the Wagner Labor Relations Act, the Railway Labor

---

122 STERNSHER, REXFORD TUGWELL AND THE NEW DEAL 349 (1964); Raymond Clapper MS Diary, Aug. 24, 1937; S. H. Boddinghouse to Daniel Roper, Nov. 6, 1936, FDRL OF 41-A, Box 116; Henry Teigan to C. Schoening, Feb. 16, 1937, Teigan MSS, Minnesota Historical Society, Box 14; Chicago Tribune, July 24, 1936, clipping, Frank Murphy Collection, University of Michigan Law School; Frank Gannett to Alexander Falck, Mar. 7, 1936, Gannett MSS, Cornell University Collection of Regional History, Box 16; James H. Winston to FDR, Aug. 1, 1936, FDRL PPF 1786; J. A. Mulhern to Newton Baker, Oct. 22, 1936, Baker MSS, Box 52; Stephen Duggan to FDR, Nov. 13, 1936, FDRL OF 274; John Robert Moore, "Josiah William Bailey: A Political Biography," unpublished Ph.D. dissertation, Duke University, 1965; James Hamilton Lewis to Arthur Vandenberg, Sept. 18, 1936, Lewis MSS, LC; Allen, *Behind the Campaign*, 173 HARPER'S 476 (Oct., 1936).

Act, the Commodity Exchange Act, state minimum-wage and un-employment compensation laws, and of the powers of the PWA, the SEC, and the Federal Communications Commission. Even the gold clause resolution faced another contest.

In view of this prospect, what was Roosevelt to do? He might just wait for vacancies to develop. The laws of nature were on his side, for never in our history had a Court been composed of so elderly a group. Moreover, Justices Van Devanter and Sutherland had talked of retiring. Yet Roosevelt had seen nearly four years go by without one opportunity to make an appointment, an ex-perience that had occurred in no other full presidential term save for the special instance of Andrew Johnson's tenure. Anyone fa-miliar with the conversation of Justices knew enough to place a high discount on talk of retiring, and these particular Justices seemed determined to stay on the bench so long as Roosevelt was in the White House. At the first cabinet meeting after the election, the President, in a spirit of gallows humor, said that Justice Mc-Reynolds would still be on the tribunal when he was 105.[123]

Still, Roosevelt might wait to see whether the Court would fol-low the election returns. The switch of even one Justice could be decisive. It might be anticipated that the emphatic outcome of the election would surprise some Justices who had believed that they were speaking for a nation outraged by the New Deal. (It is clear from Van Devanter's correspondence that he thought the election would be close.)[124] Nor, it has been argued, was Justice Roberts as set against the New Deal as he appeared to be.

Yet there were risks in waiting. The Court had behaved so ar-rogantly in the spring of 1936 that the prospects for a change of views seemed slim. Not only did the Court's line of reasoning in its last Term leave little reason to suppose that the Court would

---

[123] John H. Clarke to Newton Baker, Apr. 6, 1934, Jan. 3, 1936, Baker MSS, Box 60; Detroit News, June 2, 1937; Willis Van Devanter to Mrs. John Lacey, Jan. 11, 1933, Van Devanter MSS, Vol. 46; 1 Ickes 705.

It is not clear why the Administration did not move more forcefully to expedite the Sumners bill to make retirement more attractive. On the early history of this bill, see James M. Landis to Donald R. Richberg, Richberg MSS, LC, Box 1; Alex-ander Holtzoff to the Attorney General, Mar. 5, 1935, NA Dept. of Justice 235241. For post-election response, see Cummings to FDR, Dec. 29, 1936, FDRL PSF Supreme Court.

[124] Van Devanter to Dennis Flynn, Oct. 19, 1936; Van Devanter to Mrs. John W. Lacey, Nov. 2, 1936, Van Devanter MSS, Vol. 52.

not strike down such landmarks as the Wagner Act and the Social Security law, but it barred the way to new legislation. Returned to office with a tremendous grant of power, Roosevelt might be denied by the Court the opportunity to use that power. If he waited to see what the Court did, he might find himself with his past achievements obliterated and the momentum for future change lost.

Roosevelt had a strong sense of his own place in history. He would not countenance being written off in the history books as a man who had been frustrated in his attempts to lead the country out of the depression and to create a more humane social order. "When I retire to private life on January 20, 1941," he remarked, "I do not want to leave the country in the condition Buchanan left it to Lincoln."[125] Nor did he wish to be known as a President who had permitted judicial usurpers to impair the office of the Executive. Finally, it should be noted, the Court, by such decisions as that in the *Humphrey* case, had wounded his self-esteem, and, by other acts, had convinced Roosevelt that it was personally hostile to him.[126] He now sought a way not merely to liberalize the Court but to chastise the Justices for their past behavior.

Six days after the election, Roosevelt returned to Washington from Hyde Park; on his very first night in the capital, he summoned Cummings to the White House to report to him on what progress had been made at the Justice Department. Cummings told him that, over the summer, work had intensified as men like Edward S. Corwin, professor of jurisprudence at Princeton University, and William Draper Lewis of the American Law Institute had been asked for advice. Within the department, under the direction of Cummings and Solicitor General Stanley Reed, arguments were being assembled for and against specific proposals.

Both Roosevelt and Cummings had a tacit understanding that at some point action would have to be taken, and they now agreed that the Court was unlikely to be changed in its ways by the election returns. Yet the President still did not indicate that the time to act had come. He treated the meeting as yet another occasion on which the Attorney General had been asked for a progress

---

125 29 TIME 13 (Mar. 8, 1937).

126 For Roosevelt's belief that he had been snubbed by the Justices in 1936, see the penciled memorandum, "Court story," Harry Hopkins MSS, FDRL, Box 325. The account in SHERWOOD, ROOSEVELT AND HOPKINS 94 (1948) is slightly inaccurate.

report, and told him to come back as soon as he had something new to recommend. Meanwhile he was to maintain the closest secrecy on his research.[127]

Cummings, who may have sensed that Roosevelt was more disposed to act than he indicated, sped back to the Justice Department to order his research aides to devote full time, and overtime, to preparing reports and digests of reports for the President. Speed was important, because Roosevelt was to leave on a South American cruise on November 18. For the next nine days, messengers carried memorandums from the Justice Department to the White House and the President's comments back in the other direction. Almost every day, the Attorney General, arriving secretly through a private entrance, conferred at the White House with the President.[128]

Day after day they went over the great variety of recommendations that had come to them in the past two years. The uninvited counsel the President had received in the aftermath of the election indicated that opinion was still unsettled and that no one solution had emerged as the inevitable answer. Some urged pressing for an amendment. A Philadelphia attorney wrote, "We hope . . . you will recommend an amendment clearly adequate in scope, not only for today but for tomorrow also, when even broader needs will arise but may be met by stronger reactionary barriers." Similarly, a group of five Utah labor organizations wanted their legislature to memorialize Congress for an amendment to give Congress the power to regulate the hours of labor.[129] But other letters recommended packing the Court and emphasized the old-age theme. A Baltimore lawyer wanted "a law to be enacted at once that the personnel of the Supreme Court be increased to not less than two more judges," and a Memphis man wrote: "I think you the grandest President we have ever had, and I think God will give you a hand. . . . Mr. President, the labor people want you and Congress

---

[127] ALSOP & CATLEDGE, THE 168 DAYS 20, 23–24 (1938) (hereinafter ALSOP); N.Y. Times, Feb. 12, 1937; Raymond Clapper MS Diary, Feb. 8, 1937.

[128] ALSOP 27.

[129] L. Stauffer Oliver to FDR, Nov. 12, 1936; George C. Christiansen *et al.* to C. W. Spence, Dec. 12, 1936, FDRL OF 274, Box 4. See, too, Virgil V. Johnson to FDR, Nov. 13, 1936, FDRL PPF 200, Reelect Cong–J.

to curb the Supreme Court. You all know just 9 old men should not rule this grand country."[130]

Roosevelt dismissed the amendment route as unacceptable for a number of reasons. In the first place, he thought an amendment would be difficult to frame. Two years of study in the Justice Department had not yet yielded a satisfactory draft, and liberals outside the government were far from a consensus. When the National Consumers' League, which had spearheaded the drive for minimum-wage legislation, polled national legal experts after the *Tipaldo* decision on whether a campaign for an amendment should be launched, the results were discouraging. Half of those polled—including Felix Frankfurter—opposed agitation for an amendment, and the other half were so far apart on what kind of an amendment should be sought that the League decided against any action at all.[131]

Even if an amendment could be framed, and approved by two-thirds of each house of Congress, it would have to run the gantlet of ratification by three-fourths of the states. If ratification was by state legislatures, as seemed most likely, it would require an adverse vote by only one house in thirteen legislatures to defeat an amendment, and the state legislatures were known to overrepresent conservative interests. Nor did Roosevelt have much faith in the probity of these assemblies. As he wrote a prominent New York lawyer three months later: "If you were not as scrupulous and ethical as you happen to be, you could make five million dollars as easy as rolling off a log by undertaking a campaign to prevent the ratification by one house of the Legislature, or even the summoning of a constitutional convention in thirteen states for the next four years. Easy money."[132] In a conversation with Ickes, Tom Corcoran had no trouble in ticking off the thirteen states "that would naturally be against a broadening amendment or in which money could be used to defeat it."[133]

---

[130] John B. McGraw to Stephen Early, Dec. 8, 1936, FDRL OF 274, Box 4; L. L. Wilson to FDR, Dec. 3, 1936, NA Dept. of Justice 235773. See, too, B. F. Welty to FDR, Dec. 29, 1936, FDRL OF 41, Box 114.

[131] Report of the Committee of Inquiry to the Board, Nov. 5, 1936, Mary Dewson MSS, FDRL, Box 6. The Dewson Papers also contain the original replies.

[132] FDR to Charles C. Burlingham, Feb. 23, 1937, 1 LETTERS 662.

[133] 2 ICKES 33–34.

At best, ratification would take a long time, and time was invaluable. Conscious of the brief span allotted to reform movements, Roosevelt wanted to exploit his landslide victory to drive through legislation such as a wages and hours bill while Congress still felt the full force of his popular indorsement. To be sure, the Norris lame-duck amendment had been adopted quickly, but that, he thought, was because it had not been opposed by any strongly entrenched interest. A constitutional amendment affecting the courts would not only be rejected by business interests but would encounter state legislatures largely composed of lawyers, who would be likely to be more disapproving of tinkering with the courts than would other groups.[134]

Roosevelt was especially influenced by the long, unsuccessful experience with attempting to win ratification for the child-labor amendment, a struggle then in its thirteenth year. As LaRue Brown, formerly Assistant Attorney General under Wilson, told the National Consumers' League:[135]

> My personal experience with the Child Labor Amendment leads me to view with great dubiety the prospect of ratification of an amendment increasing federal power. Our side is at so tremendous a disadvantage as to resources and so many truly liberal folk are so questioning as to the ultimate intendments of increasing the federal authority that I fear we should simply wear our hearts out in another hopeless fight.

Subsequently, Stephen Early, Roosevelt's press secretary, summed up the objections for Raymond Clapper. Clapper set down in his diary:[136]

> Steve said that the president had given him sidelight this morning on court proposal that he thought he would pass on to me to use or not as I saw fit. It was this—that people who talked about an amendment either didn't realize difficulties in that method or else did realize them and for that reason advocated this course. Steve said that to seek an amendment meant

---

134 Mallon, *Purely Confidential*, Detroit News, Feb. 13, 1937; N.Y. Times, Feb. 12, 1937.

135 Brown to Lucy R. Mason, Sept. 9, 1936, Mary Dewson MSS, Box 6. See, too, Donald Richberg to Raymond Clapper, Feb. 26, 1937, Richberg MSS, Box 2. Advocates of amendments pointed out that the child-labor amendment had been improperly drafted, and that the ratification process could involve conventions rather than legislatures.

136 Raymond Clapper MS Diary, Feb. 8, 1937.

getting two-thirds of both houses and then submitting it to states where ¾ needed. He said suppose 13 governors refused to submit amendment. It dead then. He said all of us who ever been around legislatures know how easy be for moneyed interests to buy up enough legislatures to prevent action. Said this not like prohibition—here are vast and powerful groups determined to prevent action. Said another reason would be that to follow amendment course would make this an issue in 1938 campaign and might lose a number of "our congressmen." Might cost them their seats.

Even if all these objections were overcome and an amendment went through, any legislation enacted under authorization of such an amendment would still be subject to review in the courts, unless such an amendment was purely procedural. "In view of what Mr. Justice Roberts did to a clause as broad and sweeping as 'the general welfare,'" wrote Charles A. Beard, "I can see other justices of his mental outlook macerating almost any clarifying amendment less generous in its terms. If there is any phrase wider than providing for the general welfare, I am unable to conjure it up in my mind."[137] Besides, if the President should sponsor an amendment enlarging federal powers, it might seem tantamount to conceding that he had been wrong and the Supreme Court right in their dispute over the constitutionality of New Deal measures, and this Roosevelt, especially after his bracing election triumph, was less willing than ever to do.[138]

After eliminating amendment proposals, Roosevelt and Cummings next looked into various suggestions that would require only an act of Congress. First, they considered a bill stipulating more than a majority of Justices to invalidate a law; they dismissed this, because they feared that the Court would void such a statute. As Richberg later explained: "A mere statute to this effect would either be disregarded by the court, or have the result that Justices anxious to preserve the prestige of the court would join unwillingly with the majority so as to make a decision of the court effective." Moreover, such a law would limit the Court's role as a protector of civil liberties. They then examined a bill to withdraw appellate

---

[137] Beard, *Rendezvous with the Supreme Court*, 88 NEW REPUBLIC 93 (Sept. 2, 1936); Beard to Nicholas Kelley, Aug. 8, 1936, Mary Dewson MSS, Box 6.

[138] Washington Herald, Mar. 14, 1937, clipping, Frank Murphy Collection, University of Michigan Law School.

jurisdiction, but they were troubled by the recognition that the Court would still have original jurisdiction, especially in cases involving conflicts among states, and that the lower courts would retain their powers. By the end of the nine days, both men were leaning toward court-packing as the only feasible solution, but they were not yet committed to it, nor had they decided on the form it should take.[139]

Just before departing for South America, Roosevelt met once more with Cummings in the President's office. This time the President told an elated Cummings that he had made his decision; he would present a Court bill to Congress as soon as one was ready. Cummings gave him two stout volumes of proposed amendments and bills to take aboard ship to study, and they agreed that if any new ideas were developed they would be dispatched to the President at his ports of call. Roosevelt also took with him two lengthy memorandums from Donald Richberg, which stated that he "should not simply *defend* reasonable exercises of legislative power, but should aggressively *attack* the unconstitutional exercise of judicial power." On November 18, the President set sail for southern waters, after charging Cummings to have a plan ready for him on his return.[140]

VI. McReynolds' Petard

During the four weeks the President was touring South America, Cummings and his aides worked prodigiously at canvassing the possibilities for judicial reform. But when Roosevelt returned on December 15, they still had not found a solution. The main result of their labors was an exhaustive 65-page report which W. W. Gardner submitted to Reed, and the Solicitor General forwarded to Cummings. ("This matter has been handled confidentially," Reed assured him, "and I have my copy of the memorandum under lock.") Scholarly, shrewd, carefully written, the report was more valuable for warning of the pitfalls in various proposals than in pointing out what should be done.[141]

---

[139] Alsop 28–30; N.Y. Times, Feb. 12, 1937; Washington Post, Feb. 13, 1937; Richberg to Clapper, Feb. 26, 1937, Richberg MSS, Box 2.

[140] Alsop 30–31; Richberg to FDR, Nov. 16, 1936, FDRL PPF 2418.

[141] Raymond Clapper MS Diary, Feb. 8, 1937; Reed, Memorandum for the Attorney General from the Solicitor General, Dec. 19, 1936, NA Dept. of Justice 235773.

Meanwhile, a much more fruitful exchange was being carried on between Cummings and Professor Corwin. The author of numerous articles and books excoriating the infringement by the Court on the prerogatives of other branches of government, Corwin had developed a close relationship with the Justice Department. Like other constitutional authorities, he had oscillated between different answers to the conflict between the President and the Court—from believing the Court should correct its own errors to favoring amendments, especially one to require more than a simple majority to invalidate laws.[142] His thinking may have been turned in a new direction by a letter he received early in September from Charles E. Clark, dean of the Yale Law School: "I do think that the possibility of increasing the size of the Court ought to be more considered in Congress than apparently it has."[143]

After the election, Corwin wrote a series of newspaper articles on the Court question. On December 3, Cummings wrote the President, who was still in South America:[144]

> Professor Corwin, of Princeton, has prepared a series of articles dealing with some of our Constitutional difficulties. These articles will shortly be published in the Philadelphia Record. They are especially pertinent to the last discussion I had with you on this subject. I have just received from Doctor Corwin the proof sheets of the articles, which I enclose herewith. I am very sure that you will find them well worth reading.

Corwin's series was a curious performance. With corrosive wit, he derided the record of the Court during the New Deal. In exposing the inadequacies of the panaceas that had been offered, he wrote brilliantly. But his own remedies were murky and even contradictory. After showing with devastating clarity why the Administration should not resort to amendments, he stated that some amendments might be needed. He called for the Court to reform itself, yet conceded that this particular Court could not be expected to do so. But one sentence in the final article emerged boldly: "No reform could be better adopted than the requirement, to be laid

---

[142] Corwin had helped prepare the Government's brief in the *Carter* case. CORWIN, THE COMMERCE POWER VS. STATES RIGHTS 263–67 (1936); Corwin to Lucy R. Mason, Sept. 24, 1936, Mary Dewson MSS, Box 6; John Dickinson to Corwin, June 15, 1936.

[143] Clark to Corwin, Sept. 3, 1936, Corwin MSS, Princeton University Library.

[144] Cummings to FDR, Dec. 3, 1936, FDRL OF 41-A, Box 116; Cummings to Corwin, Dec. 3, 1936, Corwin MSS.

down by an act of Congress, or, if necessary, by constitutional amendment, that no Judge may hold office under the United States beyond his seventieth birthday."[145]

In the series, Corwin appeared to be trimming some of his beliefs in order to avoid exciting unnecessary quarrels. In particular, his deference to the amendment approach seemed less than heartfelt. On December 16, he wrote Cummings:[146]

> It is probably utopian to hope that the Court will supply the needed remedy for a situation which it has itself created. Hence we must turn either to constitutional amendment or Congressional action.
>
> As to the latter, I did not care to go on record as favoring a *tour de force;* yet it is essential to face the fact that Congressional action may be necessary.

Nor, he added, had his articles exhausted the possibilities of action. Corwin continued:

> A friend of mine has made this ingenious suggestion: that the President be authorized, whenever a majority of the Justices, or half of the Justices, are seventy or more years old, to nominate enough new Justices of less than that age to make a majority. This, too, would require only an act of Congress, and something of a legislative precedent for such a measure is furnished by § 375 of title 28, of the U.S. Code.
>
> Mr. Reed appears to think that I put too much emphasis on my age-limit proposal, but I'm not so sure. A 70-year age-limit would secure more rapid replacement of justices. Furthermore, it might serve to draw the attention of the appointing power more frequently to the faculties of our great Law-schools where superior talent emerges at an earlier age than in practice at the Bar.

---

145 The proofs are in FDRL OF 41-A, Box 116. Clark argued that Corwin had underestimated the possibilities of the amendment process. Clark to Corwin, Dec. 11, 1936, and Corwin's reply, Dec. 16, 1936. See, too, Clark to Corwin, Aug. 18, 1936, Corwin MSS.

146 The penciled draft of this letter in the Corwin Papers is undated. The letter could have been sent at any time between December 4 and 16, but December 16 seems highly probable. That same day, Corwin wrote Reed: "I was glad to get your comments on those articles—I believe that my age limit proposal, if adopted, may have considerable effect. It might not get more liberal judges, but it would assure a more rapid replacement of the Bench. Today Jefferson's complaint is well justified: 'Few die and none resign.'—indeed the statement might be made stronger. . . . I believe it could be validly accomplished by an act of Congress." Corwin to Reed, Dec. 16, 1936, NA Dept. of Justice 235868. Reed appears to have been unenthusiastic about the plan both at this point and when it finally emerged.

Since Corwin had pointed out in his series the folly of enlarging the Court, this suggestion marked an important new departure. For the first time, compulsory retirement at 70 was linked to the appointment of new Justices. On the very next day, Cummings replied to Corwin:[147]

> Of course, I realize that there is a good deal of prejudice against "packing the Court." I have been wondering to what extent we have been frightened by the phrase.
>
> Quite apart from immediate consideration, and as a mere matter of general policy, I have often thought that much was to be said for a constitutional amendment requiring retirements when the age of 70 is reached. I am wondering if there would be much opposition to such an amendment if it were so framed as not to affect the present judiciary by making it apply to future appointments only.

Corwin's contribution reached Cummings at a propitious moment. Both the Attorney General and the President had been attracted to "court-packing" for some weeks, but they recognized that the proposition violated taboos and that some principle would have to be found to justify it. Corwin offered such a formula by relating new appointments to the ages of Justices. If Corwin's suggestion (or that of Corwin's "friend") was adopted, Cummings could exploit growing popular resentment at the age of the bench.

By now, it had become commonplace to refer to the Justices as the "nine old men." A. A. Berle had used the term in passing in 1933,[148] and a column in a Kentucky newspaper reflected a popular notion when it referred to the Court as "nine old back-number owls (appointed by by-gone Presidents) who sit on the leafless, fruitless limb of an old dead tree." But it was the publication on October 26, 1936 of *The Nine Old Men* by Drew Pearson and Robert S. Allen which made the phrase a household word. The book quickly climbed onto the best-seller lists, and it was serialized in newspapers across the country. Even critics of the Justices were disturbed by the book's tone and by its inaccuracies, but this exposé helped concentrate popular attention on both the age and the viewpoint of the Court as a more sober account might not have done. Representative Thomas Amlie of Wisconsin, while regretting the book's innuendos, thought "that Pearson and Allen have done a particu-

---

[147] Cummings to Corwin, Dec. 17, 1936, Corwin MSS.

[148] Berle, *Law and the Social Revolution*, 22 SURVEY GRAPHIC 594 (Dec., 1933).

larly good job on the Constitutional law angle," and Senator Joseph Guffey of Pennsylvania called for a Senate investigation of the allegations made in the book. Guffey called the volume "the most disturbing—I would say shocking book on public officials I have ever read. Its purported disclosures are sensational."[149]

After receiving Corwin's letter, Cummings was close to the end of the trail. Yet Corwin still had not shown him the precise route the Attorney General was seeking, and Cummings' reply suggests that he was still thinking that an amendment might be required, and that the present Justices might be exempted. However, once Corwin had blazed the path this far, it did not take Cummings long to discover the rest of the way.

At some point in the next five days, Cummings found his answer. While carrying on his other duties, the Attorney General had also been writing a history of his department, in collaboration with his aide, Carl McFarland. One passage in *Federal Justice*, which was about to be published, now stood out from the pages as it had not before, a recommendation that Justice McReynolds, when serving as Wilson's Attorney General, had made in 1913.

McReynolds' recommendation stated:[150]

> Judges of the United States Courts, at the age of 70, after having served 10 years, may retire upon full pay. In the past, many judges have availed themselves of this privilege. Some, however, have remained upon the bench long beyond the time that they are able to adequately discharge their duties, and in consequence the administration of justice has suffered. ... I suggest an act providing that when any judge of a Federal court below the Supreme Court fails to avail himself of the privilege of retiring now granted by law, that the President be required, with the advice and consent of the Senate, to appoint another judge, who would preside over the affairs of the court and have precedence over the older one. This will insure at all times the presence of a judge sufficiently active to discharge promptly and adequately the duties of the court.

---

[149] Charles N. Crewdson to Louis Howe, Jan. 7, 1936, FDRL OF 41-A, Box 116; Thomas Reed Powell to William O. Douglas, n.d., Douglas MSS, LC, Box 20; Herbert Hoover to Charles Evans Hughes, Feb. 19, 1937, Hughes MSS, Box 6; James A. Stone to William T. Evjue, Mar. 17, 1937, Stone MSS, Minnesota Historical Society, Box 28; Thomas R. Amlie to Donald A. Butchart, Mar. 6, 1937, Amlie MSS, Box 36; N.Y. Times, Jan. 27, 1937.

[150] REPORT OF THE ATTORNEY GENERAL FOR THE FISCAL YEAR ENDING JUNE 30, 1913 5, CUMMINGS & McFARLAND, FEDERAL JUSTICE (1937).

Cummings now reasoned that McReynolds' prescription, which had been limited to the lower courts, might also be applied to the Supreme Court. Once the principle of retirement was adopted, any age might be stipulated, but 70 seemed especially compelling. It had been the age that, on different occasions, McReynolds, Cummings, and Corwin had all hit upon, and it had the not inconsiderable advantage of having biblical sanction. That summer, an Oklahoma newspaper had proposed to retire Supreme Court Justices at seventy, "as set out in Holy Writ as the reasonable span of human life."[151] With the retirement age fixed at 70, Roosevelt would be able to name six new Justices, thus practically assuring a bench that would approve New Deal legislation.

Before presenting the plan to Roosevelt, Cummings directed his assistants in the Justice Department to prepare a series of reports. He deliberately parceled out work so that the scheme would be kept a secret even from his own aides. Except for Cummings and Reed, no one in the department save for Holtzoff and McFarland appears to have known the full scope of the proposal until it was announced. When his assistants reported back to Cummings, each gave a favorable reply. One report approved the plan's constitutionality. Another turned up historical precedent in an 1869 bill that had passed the House of Representatives. A third pulled together statistics to show that the formula would also supply enough new judges for the lower courts.[152]

Cummings' search had ended. On December 22, he sent a penciled note to the President: "I am 'bursting' with ideas anent our constitutional problems; and have a plan (of substance & approach) I would like to talk over with you when you have the time."[153] By this point, Roosevelt was already determined to "pack" the Court, but he did not yet know how, and he still thought of the idea as a birch rod to be taken out of the closet only if the Court did not mend its ways in the new Term.

He now summoned George Creel to the White House once more to prepare an article, this one to be called "Roosevelt's Plans and Purposes." During the afternoon and evening they worked to-

---

[151] *The Federal Constitution*, Shawnee (Okla.) County Democrat, Aug. 7, 1936, clipping, FDRL OF 274, Box 4.

[152] Alsop 34; Raymond Clapper MS Diary, June 12, 1938.

[153] Cummings to FDR, Dec. 22, 1936, FDRL PSF Supreme Court.

gether, Creel was struck by the fact that the President, understandably, viewed the election as a purely personal victory. He told Creel that the social objectives he cherished would all have to run the gantlet of the Supreme Court. But his face brightened as he said: "I've thought of a better way than a constitutional amendment stripping the Court of its power to nullify acts of Congress. The time element makes that method useless. Granted that Congress could agree on such an amendment for submission to the several states, it would be two, three, or four years before the legislatures could or would act. What do you think of this?"[154] From a drawer in his desk, he extracted a heavily marked copy of the Constitution and riffled the pages as he read off passages and commented on the powers of Congress to act for the general welfare.

After reading Article III, § 1, he asked: "Where is there anything in that which gives the Supreme Court the right to override the legislative branch?" As the President talked, Creel wrote afterward, "I was amazed by his reading on the subject and by the grip of his mind on what he conceived to be essential facts. For example, he quoted at length from Madison's *Journal* and Elliot's *Debates,* citing them as his authority for the statement that the framers of the Constitution had voted on four separate occasions against giving judges the power to pass upon the constitutionality of acts of Congress."[155]

If Congress was to reclaim the powers that had been usurped from it, Roosevelt reasoned, it should add a rider to each bill at the next session charging the Supreme Court to remember that the Constitution vested all legislative power in Congress and authorized it to provide for the general welfare. Suppose this proved ineffective? Creel related: " 'Then,' said the President, his face like a fist, 'Congress can *enlarge* the Supreme Court, increasing the number of justices so as to permit the appointment of men in tune with the spirit of the age.' " When *Collier's* published this article on December 26, with three columns discussing the Supreme Court, Creel expected an explosion in Congress and the press. Yet, once again, the President's explicit words were ignored.[156]

On the same day that Creel's article appeared, Cummings went

---

[154] CREEL, *op. cit. supra* note 65, at 292–94; Richberg to FDR, Nov. 16, 1936, FDRL PPF 2418.

[155] CREEL, *op. cit. supra* note 65, at 293–94.   [156] *Ibid.*

to the White House to report to Roosevelt. According to one account, not altogether probable, the Attorney General handed the President a packet of plans with the new scheme on the bottom. He then watched agitatedly while Roosevelt turned over each in turn until he came to Cummings' favorite; to the Attorney General's immense pleasure, Roosevelt was delighted. However it happened, it is clear that the President gave his approval that day. He was gratified that the proposal was unquestionably constitutional, and he took a mischievous pleasure in the fact that it could be attributed to McReynolds.[157]

Buoyed by the President's approval, Cummings now turned his hand to sketching the remaining details of the plan. He wanted not only to liberalize the Court but to reform the entire judiciary. By presenting "court-packing" in the guise of judicial reform, he would make the plan more palatable. Yet Cummings' interest in reform was not just expedient. He had long cherished the aim of overhauling the structure of the courts, and Roosevelt shared some of his ardor. Once they launched what they knew would be a historic fight, they wanted it to be remembered for improving the judicial system as well as for overcoming the intransigence of the Supreme Court.

For two years, William Denman, Judge of the Ninth Circuit Court of Appeals, had been bombarding Roosevelt with pleas for more lower-court judges in order to relieve congestion in the courts and prevent miscarriages of justice. Denman also argued that the lower-court system was illogically organized, and, he proposed, among other suggestions, the appointment of a proctor of the Supreme Court to supervise lower courts and the creation of "roving judges" to clear up congestion. The Judicial Conference had also, more than once, pointed out the need for additional district judges. Cummings now decided to tie all these ideas together into a single package, but to relate the call for more lower-court judges to the principle of age.[158]

---

157 ALSOP 34–35; Raymond Clapper MS Diary, June 12, 1938. Rexford Tugwell has written: "Of all the ways open to him Franklin does seem to have chosen the one most upsetting to judicial dignity." TUGWELL, *op. cit. supra* note 55, at 392.

158 Raymond Clapper MS Diary, Feb. 8, 1937; Denman to Cummings, Mar. 19, 1936; Denman to FDR, Mar. 20, 1936, FDRL OF 209-I; Memorandum for the Attorney General, Apr. 29, 1936; Denman to M. H. McIntyre, Mar. 17, 1936, FDRL PPF 336; Denman to FDR, Sept. 5, 1936, FDRL OF 41, Box 114; Charles Evans Hughes

By the end of the year, the Justice Department had prepared the first draft of the bill. In all, it went through twelve full drafts and numerous minor revisions. The measure embraced four proposals: (1) that when a judge of a federal court who had served ten years did not resign or retire within six months after his seventieth birthday, the President might name another judge as co-adjutor; (2) that the Supreme Court should not have more than six added Justices, nor any lower-court bench more than two, nor the total federal judiciary more than fifty; (3) that lower-court judges might be assigned to exceptionally busy courts; and (4) that the lower courts should be supervised by the Supreme Court through a proctor.[159]

Roosevelt and Cummings decided it would be helpful to accompany the bill with both a message from the President and a letter from the Attorney General. Instead of concentrating on the desirability of a more liberal court, both documents would stress the incapacity of aged judges and the need for additional appointments to get the Court abreast of its work. By emphasizing the theme of greater efficiency, they hoped the whole plan would be accepted as a project for judicial reform rather than a stratagem to pack the Court. Once again, Cummings parceled out assignments within the department so that men were called on to supply statistics on denial of certiorari or the ages of judges without ever being told why this information was wanted or being given enough to do to be able to piece together what was happening.

When all three documents were taken to the White House, the President offered little comment on the bill, but he gave the letter, to which Holtzoff had made important contributions, a thorough going-over, and Cummings had to revise it before Roosevelt would give his approval. Even more care was lavished on the President's message, which Roosevelt recognized would be an important state paper. In the third week in January, Donald Richberg was called in to polish the draft, and on the night of January 30, when Judge Rosenman arrived at the White House for the President's birthday party, he was asked to contribute his talents. It was the first he had

---

to FDR, May 30, 1934, FDRL OF 41-A; Mallon, *Purely Confidential,* Detroit News, Apr. 2, 1937; ALSOP 31–35.

[159] By January 5, the bill had reached a fifth draft. "Draft No. 5, January 5, 1937," FDRL PSF Supreme Court.

heard of the plan, even though he had helped write both the State-of-the-Union message and the Inaugural Address that month. When Rosenman told Corcoran, who had also been kept in the dark, what was happening, the President agreed that Corcoran, too, should be asked to go over the final draft of the message. But he instructed Rosenman not to let Cummings know that Corcoran was involved.[160]

The President's insistence on secrecy combined fear of premature disclosure that might promote bickering with his love of the dramatic. Save for Cummings, no one in the cabinet, not even the ubiquitous Ickes, knew of the plan. Indeed, Roosevelt, at one cabinet meeting in January, deliberately misrepresented what was going on. Nor was any member of Congress told. Some of the men who would soon bear the burden of defending it were busy drafting quite different proposals, and Henry Fountain Ashurst, who would shortly be called on to move the President's proposal through the Senate Judiciary Committee, was publicly denouncing court-packing as "the prelude to tyranny."[161]

Through all of this, the President gave almost no indication of the surprise he was about to spring. As Moley later wrote: "Roosevelt's pronouncements in the course of his good-will trip to South America would not have frightened the birds of St. Francis."[162] Despite some shafts aimed at the Supreme Court, Roosevelt's State-of-the-Union message was praised for its good-tempered restraint, and he made no mention at all of the Court in his Inaugural Address. Informed observers predicted that the President would wait to see

---

[160] ALSOP 43–47; RICHBERG, op. cit. supra note 119, at 221–22; Raymond Clapper MS Diary, Jan. 14, 1938; ROSENMAN, op. cit. supra note 119, at 145–50. Two drafts of the message have been retained in the Samuel I. Rosenman MSS, FDRL, "Message to Congress on the Judiciary" folder.

[161] Washington Post, Feb. 13, 1937; 2 ICKES 31; Henry Morgenthau, Jr., MS Diary, FDRL, Feb. 6, 1937; Raymond Clapper MS Diary, Feb. 5, 1937; Edward Rees to William Allen White, n.d., White MSS, Box 186; CONG. REC., 75th Cong., 1st Sess., 562. After the plan was announced, Clapper reported on an interview with the President's press secretary, Stephen Early: "Steve says that only five people were told of plan by President. He said president wouldn't want him to reveal names but he thought I knew them. Said none was in Congress. . . . Steve said reason Rvt didn't talk it over with more people was that he was afraid of a leak which would tip off opposition and enable them to start hostile build up before he got his plan out." Clapper MS Diary, Feb. 8, 1937.

[162] MOLEY 356.

how the Court disposed of the Wagner cases before taking any action. On January 24, Dean Dinwoodey, editor of *United States Law Week*, wrote that "last week it was made plain that he does not at the present time have in mind any legislation directed at the Court."[163]

VII. Roosevelt Entertains the Court

By the beginning of February, the bill, the letter, and the message had all been drafted, except for a few final details. All that remained was to decide when to launch the plan. It is conceivable that Roosevelt might have waited until the Wagner cases had been decided, although this seems unlikely, but if he had any such intention, he felt compelled to abandon it. The situation in Congress, where more and more members were committing themselves publicly to divergent proposals, was getting out of hand. Outside the government, progressives had called a national conference to reach agreement on an amendment. Most important, word of Roosevelt's own plan had begun to leak out, and speculation about what the President intended was getting closer and closer to the mark.[164]

Not everyone had thought that Roosevelt's State-of-the-Union address signaled inaction. Breckinridge Long noted in his diary:[165]

> After I heard the speech I went home and read the printed speech twice. It is rather mysterious in that it is enshrouded somewhat in mystery in that he makes no intimation of his specific plan, but it is very plain that he has something definitely in mind. I say it is very plain, but I mean that it is very plain to those who read with a discriminating eye the words of his message and use as a background his whole history in connection with the Supreme Court.

The conservative Republican congressman from Minnesota, Harold Knutson, also found the address unsettling. He wrote: "I rather

---

[163] 29 Time 13–14 (Jan. 18, 1937); N.Y. Times, Jan. 5, 7, 10, 24, 1937.

[164] Mallon, *Purely Confidential*, Detroit News, Feb. 13, 1937; Mary Dewson to Stanley Reed, Dec. 10, 1936; Dewson to Mrs. Armstrong, n.d.; Elmer F. Andrews to Members of the New York State Minimum Wage Conference, Jan. 26, 1937; Mrs. J. C. Pryer to Mary Dewson, Jan. 11, 1937, Dewson MSS; Alfred M. Bingham to Thomas R. Amlie, Jan. 5, 1937, Amlie MSS, Box 35. Subsequently, Clapper summed up what Cummings had told him: "Didn't know until last minute whether Rvt would go through with it or not." Clapper MS Diary, Feb. 8, 1937.

[165] Breckinridge Long MS Diary, Jan. 6, 1937.

thought the President's message contained one or two disquieting features and the question that is bothering me is, will he attempt to 'pack' the Supreme Court. There is no limit on the number of judges that may be appointed to the Supreme Court and by adding two or three he could easily secure control of the judiciary. Will he go that far?"[166]

In divining the President's intentions, Long had an advantage. On the same day that Roosevelt gave his address, Long had lunched with Cummings. Afterward, he set down in his diary:[167]

> Homer has devised a means and has a specific draft to carry out the provisions intimated. It contemplates a large treatment for the whole judicial system and is not confined to the Supreme Court alone. He thinks the President has the matter definitely in mind. Procedure along that line would permit the drafting of a bill to disqualify members of the judiciary over the age of 70 years, if they have not retired voluntarily within six months after they have passed that age, and the appointment of a successor. More than that, it makes various changes in the structure of the judiciary and mobilizes the framework of the system. Whether anything will come of it is to be determined only in the future, but in the light of the President's Annual Message to the Congress it seems to my mind clearly that he has some definite proposal in mind, and after my conversation today I am of the opinion that it is this proposal.

Roosevelt's speech-writers were no more discreet than his Attorney General. Over cocktails on January 20, Donald Richberg let slip what was going on. Ray Clapper noted in his diary:[168]

> Richberg says Rvt has a number of bombshells ready to shoot which will astound country—says Rvt is in audacious mood and is even thinking of proposing to pack Supreme Court by enlarging it. R seems favor instead compulsory retirement. He says Rvt is determined to curb the court and put it in its place, and will go ahead even if many people think it unwise.

Before the month was out, the Senate began to sense what was happening. On January 24, Irving Brant, who as editor of the editorial page of the St. Louis *Star-Times* had often written on constitutional subjects, wrote the President: "Several senators have

---

166 Knutson to Elmer E. Adams, Jan. 11, 1937, Adams MSS, Minnesota Historical Society, Box 42. See, too, Ray Lyman Wilbur to Dr. Arthur H. Daniels, Jan. 8, 1937, Wilbur MSS, Stanford University Library.

167 Breckinridge Long MS Diary, Jan. 6, 1937.

168 Raymond Clapper MS Diary, Jan. 20, 1937.

told me that you expect to make a statement about the Supreme Court within a few days."[169] On February 2, in a speech that seemed to imply more than it said, Senator William Borah of Idaho deprecated the "purloining" of state powers by the federal government and lauded the Supreme Court as the shield of individual liberties.[170] Alert Washington columnists knew that something was in the wind, but they had not yet discovered what it was. "Strange things are being said in Congress," Paul Mallon noted in his column of February 4. First there had been a speech by Ashurst, then one by Congressman Samuel Pettengill, now Borah. But what were they aiming at? Borah, he pointed out, "left the definite impression he was attacking something Mr. Roosevelt was going to propose, but he did not say what."[171]

Roosevelt could wait no longer. Since the Court was scheduled to begin hearings on the constitutionality of the Wagner Act on Monday, February 8, he wanted to submit the message before then so that it would not be interpreted as a threat to the Court. On February 2, he was scheduled to entertain the judiciary at dinner at the White House; so he could not very well present the plan before then.[172] Richberg later recalled that the President had said impishly that "his choice should be whether to take only one cocktail before dinner and have it a very amiable affair, or to have a mimeographed copy of the program laid beside the plate of each justice and then take three cocktails to fortify himself against their reactions."[173] The President was thus limited to the interval between February 3 and February 6. On February 3, the Senate recessed until February 5; so Friday, February 5, became the day the President chose to act.

The real ending of the odyssey of the search for the Court plan came not on February 5 but three days earlier when the guests assembled in the East Room of the White House for the judiciary dinner. It was a gala evening. Among the ninety guests were most of the Supreme Court Justices, Mrs. Woodrow Wilson, Senator Borah, and the Gene Tunneys. In the room sat men like Reed, whom the Justices did not suspect might soon be their colleague,

---

[169] Brant to FDR, Jan. 24, 1937, FDRL PPF 2293; Washington Post, Feb. 13, 1937.

[170] N.Y. Times, Feb. 2, 1937; Detroit News, Feb. 2, 1937.

[171] Mallon, *Purely Confidential*, Detroit News, Feb. 4, 1937.

[172] Washington Post, Feb. 13, 1937; Raymond Clapper MS Diary, Feb. 8, 1937.

[173] RICHBERG, *op. cit. supra* note 119, at 222.

and Cummings, who was told by Rosenman that he had the lean and hungry look proper to a conspirator.[174] Two of those present, Senator Ashurst and Representative Hatton Sumners, chairmen of the Senate and House Judiciary Committees, would in three more days be handed a bill to curb the power of the honored guests of the evening. As the guests filed out of the dining room, Roosevelt, in high spirits, remained seated talking to Justices Hughes and Van Devanter. Borah, seeing them together, remarked: "That reminds me of the Roman Emperor who looked around his dinner table and began to laugh when he thought how many of those heads would be rolling on the morrow."[175]

VIII. The Reality and the Myth

To put together the complete puzzle of the origins of the Court plan, one still needs a few pieces. The opening of the Homer Cummings papers, now privately held, and of the Stanley Reed memoir in the Columbia Oral History Collection, now closed, should be instructive. But most of the pieces are now available. It is clear that many of the men alleged to have been authors of the plan either knew nothing of it or played quite minor roles. The main operation, from beginning to end, involved a very few men, all of them concentrated in the Justice Department. Of those who exerted influence from outside the department, Corwin, a department consultant, was more important than such putative architects as Corcoran.

Of the plan itself, few have found much good to say. Much of this criticism is surely justified. Yet the presentation of the plan was not a capricious act but the result of a long period of gestation. During this time, other alternatives were carefully examined, favored for a while, and then discarded on not unreasonable grounds. Throughout this same period, Roosevelt was called on repeatedly to take action, and it appeared, in particular, that he would have a sizable following for a recommendation which would justify the appointment of additional Justices by stressing the infirmity of the Hughes Court. That Roosevelt misjudged the state of opinion seems probable in retrospect, but, at the time, the plan seemed to have an inherent logic and even inevitability.

---

174 Rosenman, *op. cit. supra* note 119, at 153–54.

175 Richberg, *op. cit. supra* note 119, at 222; 29 Time 15 (Feb. 15, 1937); *id.* at 13 (Mar. 1, 1937).